OLD TESTAMENT

JOURNEYS OF FAITH

Old Testament

Journeys of Faith

Their lives…*and* our lives

Norman Grubb

ISBN: 1512267279
ISBN 13: 9781512267273

This book is dedicated to
Laurie Hills
for her diligent pursuit in encouraging Norman Grubb
to do this series of
Old Testament lives and also for recording them.

ACKNOWLEDGEMENTS

There are hardly adequate words to thank all who have made this book a reality. There have been transcribers, proof readers, artists, advisors and encouragers. My deepest gratitude and thanks go out to Laurie Hills for these recordings…Fred Pruitt for his Foreword…Marian Sandbek, Millie Baldwin, Betty Brooks, Nancy Thompson, Vijayan Paramsothy, Vivien Chan, Nancy Thompson, Ray Sandbek, Morgan Cox, Rhonda Oldland, Sara Tinetti, David Heisler, Tom Difloure, Linda Bunting, Harriet Wearren, John Bunting, John Collings, Judy Dunn, Linda Rose, Sue Stewart and Tony Maden for various contributions in all of the above…and especially to Norman Grubb who heard the voice of the Holy Spirit and left these recordings for future generations!

"Not God and...but God <u>only!</u>"

Norman Grubb

TABLE OF CONTENTS

FOREWORD

When I was nine, my parents gave me a copy of Egermeier's Bible Story Book. Two summers before my mother had enrolled me in the local library's summer reading program. Ever since then I had been a voracious reader of anything I could get my hands on, so when that book appeared, I think as a birthday present, I just ate it up.

Since we were only intermittent church attenders in my preteen years, the result was that I didn't attend enough Sunday School classes to learn anything consistent about the stories. I remember making "Bible-days houses" as crafts, but that's about it. The only consistent thing I do remember is that every different Sunday School class or church we attended or visited had the maps of Paul's three missionary journeys on the wall!

However, when Egermeier's came on the scene, I believe the Spirit began His "training" of me, teaching me through the Old and New Testaments stories the simple things of God, through the lives of the simple people of God. Of course, at nine years old, I was not aware of the Greater Plan God was cooking up. I just loved the stories. Even though we didn't go regularly to church, I had always believed in God. So in my childlike way, I didn't question the miracles described in some of the stories, but instead believed and remembered them. Even though I was not actually reading scripture, the stories themselves had

LIFE in them and I was getting some good child-size doses of it! That is why they have survived some 5,000 years!

I loved it all, from the sad story of Adam and Eve, on to Noah and the Ark and from there to the Tower of Babel! When Abraham appeared on the scene the story of everyone on earth changed into the story of one man, his wife, his heir, and their descendants since. First there was Abraham's journey from Haran and his adventures in Canaan. Then for famine's sake Abraham takes his family into Egypt and returns, signifying both the story of the children of Israel returning to Canaan from Egypt, as well as the return of the child Jesus from Egypt into Galilee, after the death of Herod the Great. (Hos 11:1).

I read of the plagues on Egypt and the miraculous story of the children of Israel in the wilderness. It was just as good and exciting reading as the children's science fiction I was also reading at the time! There was the story of Joshua and the taking of the Land of Promise, then the period of the Judges and the exploits of Gideon, Samson and others. One of my favorites was the story of little Samuel and the old priest Eli at the Tabernacle, and how God talked to Samuel in the middle of the night, but Samuel thought it must have been Eli. I can still see the picture in my mind of little Samuel coming into Eli's chamber.

That is how it was for me as a child. But children do grow up, and one thing that is part of growing up, is that we put childhood behind us. It is as Paul wrote, *"When I was a child, I spake as a child, I understood as a child, I thought as a child: but when I became a man, I put away childish things."* (1 Cor 13:11)

Part of those "childish things" for me in late adolescence, was my childhood "belief" in God and the significance of all those stories. I disavowed it all and declared myself an agnostic. I know some people might think, "The devil got him and pulled him away from knowing Christ." In one sense, I know that is absolutely true. However, in another, truer and eternal sense, I was **never** outside the plan and favor of the One Who separated me from my mother's womb, Who one day would reveal The Son in <u>me</u>! But I didn't know any of that then. I just threw it all out.

When in a few years the Lord revealed Himself in His grace, first "to" me, with regard to Christian doctrine, I had become a clean slate. That is what all that throwing out the baby with the bathwater had done – it had emptied me of everything, until late one night nothing was left but God Himself.

The Spirit started me over, as an adult, at that point. I started reading the stories again, and lo and behold, the Light was still there, and shining even brighter than it ever had before. But also, in those early days, I was just trying to "suck in" all the Bible "knowledge" I could cram in, with little regard for deeper understanding. Little tidbits began to come out of my Old Testament readings, but they were very misty at first. But I knew, again, that I was on to something. But it seemed for a while to be so very long in coming.

A few years into that, the Spirit put me in the path of Norman Grubb. A roughly one-hour afternoon visit with him changed Janis' and my life forever. A total paradigm shift began that day inside me that took me from an almost total outward outlook and outward "judger of situations," into being an inner person, beginning to grasp "inner" consciousness, where we "know" God in our spirits. It is not an empirical knowing, like knowing facts, but a "knowing" in which we <u>are</u> what we know. Like a person who knows and makes his living doing plumbing, we call a plumber!)

Before we met Norman, in most Christian circles the Old Testament stories were often presented as moral tales – "Don't do what he did, or you'll get punished!" In that environment, people use the stories as examples of family and human dysfunctions, with an eye on "fixing" people so that they become better Christians and/or husbands, wives, sons, daughters, etc.

But I knew there was more to them than that, and I first began to hear that when I listened to Norman's tape series on Abraham, which is included in this book. A whole new glory opened up for me! My goodness!

I understand now the soldier's exclamation after failing to arrest Jesus in John 7:46, *"No man ever spoke like this man!"* I have never heard anyone tell these stories like Norman did, and in going over them all these years later after I was exposed to them, my testimony of 4+ decades in Christ, is that there are no deeper or plainer writings on coming to full mature fatherhood in Christ, than the stories presented here as told orally and extemporaneously by Norman Grubb, on the face of the earth.

Now, I've been greatly blessed by the Spirit revealing various "types" in these stories, and that has been my major thrust with them. But Norman does not get into the "types and shadows." Not a bit. That is what makes these outpourings of the Spirit so tremendous, because they are so wonderfully and completely fully HUMAN! And at the same time, they are so wonderfully and completely fully DIVINE! They add the inner fabric in our consciousness of grasping our oneness, that WE are HE living in the world.

These Old Testament character talks, now finally published in writing for everyone, to me are the ultimate of Norman Grubb's legacy. To me, they go further and past all his books, all his pamphlets, etc., and without any holding back continually in every instance of everything, firmly declare and affirm God is All in all. For some, this may be a challenging read. Some of it rattled my chains, and I have been at this a long time.

We always had a joke about Norman and his frequent declarations that something was, "the final word." Someone would give a great message at a conference and Norman would say, "Yes, it's the final word!" Praise God, there were a lot of "final words!"

Well, dear, dear readers. The contents of this book contain a more priceless treasure than one can imagine, because He is, as Paul wrote,

"Him that is able to do exceeding abundantly above all that we ask or think." Because of Who He Is, He Himself can only be the true "Final Word." But as far as human "final words," this is a BIG ONE! It transported me to heaven! And back!

Fred Pruitt

INTRODUCTION

Precious in the sight of the Lord is the death of His godly ones. Oh Lord, surely I am Thy servant, I am Thy servant the son of Thy handmaid, Thou hast loosed my bonds. To Thee I shall offer a sacrifice of thanksgiving, and call upon the name of the Lord."

Psalm 116: 15-17

This is the seventh book of Norman Grubb's works that I have had published. I thought there could be none more exciting than the first...*Knight of Faith, Volume I*...the first of three books of Norman's letters which also included *Knight of Faith, Volume II* and *My Dear C.U.M.B.*...that consumed eleven years of my life, and covered the entire world in the lives Norman touched by his pen and his insights over a seventy-eight year span. Each book that followed has held its own special thrill, but this collection of Old Testament lives has found a hallowed place in my heart.

Abraham...Isaac & Jacob...Moses...Joseph...David...Esther...Job......

We have heard these stories told in our churches, Sunday school classes, Bible studies, Hollywood movies and in our own personal reading
throughout the years as we sought to understand more of God, His
people and His ways. I have read and heard and studied them countless times, but as I edited these transcriptions I found myself pros-
trate in thankfulness with a heart lifted in praise for many precious
discoveries and fresh perspectives awakening in me. I was uncovering
simply amazing gems and pearls! Norman makes these all too familiar
stories new, and they come alive *because he also had walked the same tests
of faith* given to these men and women by God. Little did I realize that
much of my *previous* thinking, understanding and teaching about the
people and events in Biblical history would cause me to 'collide' with
Norman's sweeping insight and his *always* upward reconciling view of
life, of God and of His ways. If you have ever questioned God, and His
actions in the Old Testament, this book offers a different perspective.
You are certain to find new answers and meaning of the One who "is
upholding *all* things".

I found *myself* in *their* lives...over and over and over...and I suspect
you, too, will recognize yourself and *your* journey, while discovering
many deeper truths hidden in these well-known 'friends' from our
family history!

As Norman talks about those who lived so long ago we see how
each life expresses a similar pattern...the *process* of faith...as God
trains them to live and walk, not by human efforts, but by trusting
in Someone they could only know by faith. In every single man and
woman he points out how they first tried to accomplish, in their human strength and by 'very *reasonable*' ways through *their* efforts, what
God had spoken to them...always resulting in failure. Each one experienced a 'death' as to how they *envisioned* God in Who He was, and in
how to *fulfill* the vision He had given them. They discovered that God

never *intended* them to bring about His plans. That was *only* His to do! Their answer to God's call was *only* and *always* **faith**.

One example is in the life of Abraham. God spoke to Abraham saying that his descendants would be as the multitudes of stars in the sky. When Sarah could not produce a child Abraham had one in what seemed like a 'reasonable' way with Sarah's maid, Hagar. Then God spoke to him a second time when he was ninety-nine and Sarah was far past her child-bearing years. This time God added that He would make him the father of *many* nations. Out of Abraham's 'death' to *his* efforts to fulfill God's word, which produced Ishmael, *faith* rose in him and *God* brought forth Isaac, the Son of Promise…beginning the lineage of Jesus Christ!

In Moses' life we find God taking His people into a *further* level of His *plan for humanity.* Moses is most often remembered for the Ten Commandments. That was the first step of His preparation to reveal to them their sin. But God's greatest accomplishment through Moses was the building of the Tabernacle, the *outer* representation of the **true** tabernacle – people – who are "temples of the living God!" Through God's interaction with him Moses became settled in knowing he spoke and acted *as God* to the people, and ultimately that he was an *intercessor* for them. Moses' intercession made the way for the Israelites to enter the Promised Land. What a picture of the coming Christ – The Intercessor for us! God *prepares* us through the law, which exposes our sin, in order to move into a *new* relationship with Him – one of grace and mercy – knowing "I live; yet not I, but Christ liveth in me" – a *living* tabernacle containing the living God!

It is interesting to see the similarities in *our* world in all that threatened to destroy Israel and her people. Today the quest to destroy Christianity, as well as Israel, is evidenced in synagogue and church bombings, beheadings, rampages through Christian cities and villages slaughtering all in sight, and even through the media and political bias towards anything Christian or Jew. There is a concerted effort to destroy Christian holy sites around the world eliminating the *outward* expression of God in history, but no one and no event can destroy a "temple not made with hands" – the inner living Christ in His body – each believer. Today, as in Biblical times, the answer is the same...**faith and trust** *in* the One Who is All in all.

This excerpt from Esther and Mordecai is still applicable...

"......*all* of history had shown that God *did* come through when there were those, even one man, who dared to believe Him! One man to say, 'God, *You've* got the power.' Moses did it. Joshua did it. David put the enemies out and started the temple. Where these men showed that *they were in union with God* in His world and purposes, they could, **by faith**, affirm the *resources* of God, and God would come through for them. It is remarkable as we follow the wars of Israel how *little* they fought when they trusted in God!"

And..."That is why we are saying, these Old Testament lives are *full of vital meaning to our ordinary lives.* Because no life is ordinary! It is only ordinary in itself. It is *extraordinary* in this **cooperation** with God!"

When Fred Pruitt sent me his Foreword for *Journeys of Faith* he also included a personal note with a few comments about the impact Norman's words had on him, which I thought were significant and would provide insight to this book...

None of the words or concepts were new. It was his *emphasis* that so struck me. I understand somewhat, because of both writing and speaking, that when one writes for publication, it has a greater sense of permanence than giving a talk in a living room, and because of that, one might take a more conservative path in a book or magazine article, which exists in print for all time to come. However, when one is sitting in a living room just giving the stuff as it is coming out, there is no editing facility. Or not much of one, anyway. One might always stop and say, "I didn't express that correctly. Let me explain." But that is not the case in a writing "graven in stone" as a book is, etc. It is there forever for everyone to read. That's why these "unbridled," and none of them "self-edited" as he might have done if he had fully prepared them for publication; raw outpourings are just PURE SPIRIT!!! Praise GOD we have them!! Whoever encouraged him to do them, bless them!

He pulls no punches! He says the whole truth and nothing but the truth.

Norman's motto was **"Not God *and*...but God only!"** It was with these words of truth that he signed most of his books when asked for a personal autograph. He only saw a life of unity...oneness...union...the same 'seeing' you will find throughout this book. His new 'eyes' came as a young missionary in the Congo when God brought him to a *screeching* halt. He writes in *The Key to Everything*, and also in *Once Caught, No Escape*, his auto-biography, that shortly after arriving in the Congo to join C.T. Studd's mission he found himself an *utter failure* when it came to loving the Africans – the people for whom *God* had called him to serve and to bring Jesus Christ. He also had the *crushing* question as to whether he was just giving the Africans another code of ethics... rules...laws...by which to live.

In his despair the Holy Spirit brought Norman two Scriptures which *redirected* the rest of his life. In I John 4:8 the Spirit illuminated "God **IS** love"...not God *has* love that He would give Norman to use, but that He IS love and He would be that *in Norman*. Norman then saw that love is a Person, not an attribute! Secondly, there was Galatians 2:20, "I am crucified with Christ: nevertheless I live; yet not I, but Christ liveth in me: and the life I now live in the flesh I live by the faith *of* the Son of God, who loved me, and gave Himself for me." Norman saw it wasn't *his* love; it wasn't *his* life; it wasn't *his* faith! It was earthshaking to him to 'see' that Christianity was not a set of rules, but was a Life – the living, resurrected, ascended Christ who had returned in the Person of His Holy Spirit and was living *as* Norman Grubb...as well as *every* believer!

Journeys of Faith begins with Job since Job is considered to be the first book written in the Bible. It also sets the stage for the other books as God took Job from seeing life and God from a consciousness of separation to seeing with a single eye...from law to grace. The others stories are in chronological order. Norman edited Job and added a Foreword and an Afterword, as well as Scripture references throughout.

Each of these characters held unique truths all their own, but in editing Gideon I tumbled across a sentence that I had *never once heard* Norman say – "God *clothes* Himself with us." Just *think* of that! God, Who was before all things and Who created all things, *puts us on* to be made manifest...to be seen, and known, and experienced in *this* world! "The Spirit of the Lord *came upon* Gideon." (Judges 6:34 KJV) The *exact* Hebrew translation – "He *clothed* Himself with Gideon." Christ by His Holy Spirit comes again *clothed* as Sara, as John, as Sue, as Greg...as every single believer! This is one of the gems I 'mined' in these Old Testament characters. I will let you discover yours!

In each of the previous six books I have included a favorite quote of Norman's. It is from Brother A. Vida Schudder in *The Gold Cord* and I remember the first time that I heard him recite it, I was stunned. It said to me that others throughout the centuries had known the same truth of our unity, our oneness with God, which Jesus prayed for *all* those to come in His final prayer before going to His Cross.

"There is an element in the gospel of Christ so disturbing that the world will forever reject it, but never forget it; and the Church will forever waiver between patronage and persecution. Yours is the present, for the world will ridicule or crucify us; but I think the future is ours."

I think this quote typifies the lives in this book. In every life there is the option to go with the status quo, or the *radical* life that Jesus Christ lived by the power of Another – the Father – as did these men and women of faith. They trusted in One they could not see...could only know *inside* themselves, but Who was more real than all else! Is that not true of our lives today?

———— ✿ ————

These talks were recorded in the 1970's at the encouragement of Laurie Hills and enjoyed by many of those who knew Norman... and now on the Internet by countless folks who only know him by reputation. In the foreword Norman added to Job he says he "unwillingly agreed to because I was not certain that I could get it out on tape, and folks would find my English diction difficult; but it was evident that God did bring light by them. Although I think this booklet on Job does bring out the secret of the Spirit in Job's life, I remind you that since it was given quite conversationally on tape, that approach will be visible as we go through the book together."

The audio version can be heard at www.normangrubb.com/audio.

In all of Norman's transcribed talks I have used 'creative' punctuation in order to separate his *impossibly* long sentences and thoughts, as he excitedly shared these living truths that tumble over and interrupt each other, in order to put them in readable and understandable form without altering the text.

Each book cover has *truly* been an *adventure*! As I told friends, Dale Cole and Debbie Yarborough, about the book cover and how it came about I observed their thrill, and I decided the story needed to be included. As I got closer to finishing my attention began to turn toward what the cover would be. While thinking about the sub-title, *Their Lives...and Our Lives*, I began to picture shadowy people on the Israel terrain depicting folks from thousands of years ago, as well as from today. Then one day on FaceBook Ole Henrik Skjelstad posted a beautiful photo of a spectacular Norwegian night sky he had taken. That sky stopped me in my tracks! I had used another of his beautiful photographs on the cover of *Think on These Things*.

The very next day I received an email from a woman in South Carolina, whom I had only met by email, and had not heard from in a couple of years, Rhonda Oldland. She wrote that she had begun painting and wanted me to see her work. I was really busy with editing and let it sit in my Inbox several days before opening it. When I finally did *there* in her paintings were my shadowy people! I quickly wrote to her telling her what I had envisioned and her paintings impact on me. She excitedly agreed to paint Ole Henrik's starry sky with her people on an Israeli terrain. I praise God for Rhonda's glorious painting and patience in so willingly interpreting my vision! She wrote that it was an honor for her to be able to give back to Norman Grubb in a small way for all she had gotten from him.

Sara Tinetti, a talented graphic artist by profession who has designed the last two book covers for me, then worked her magic for this beautiful presentation! I find that the unveiling of this book cover is but a small example of *all of life already being in* the Father's mind...and all we have to do is take the next step towards its completion!

My dear friend, Sheila Mayo, wrote to me after reading an excerpt from Samson on the daily Notes from Norman – "This suddenly made some questions no longer questions!"

May Norman Grubb's rare and exceptional insights into these familiar stories permeate your heart, mind and understanding as you discover new truth, as well as *your* similar journey in this life of faith!

DeeDee Winter

JOB

FOREWORD

There are many different ways by which thirsty seekers can drink from the rivers of the Spirit in the Scriptures and have their thirst quenched. My way has been to seek to catch in a wider sense what the Spirit is saying to us in a whole book of the Bible or life of one of God's servants for our practical application, without following through every detail of the record, though we know that actually every sentence of that inspired book is filled with light. By this means I have sought to catch a wholeness of understanding of that particular revelation, as Paul said to the Ephesians, "The eyes of their understanding being enlightened" (Eph. 1:18). And, since he wrote to those who already had much light, there is always more! They would move on to "Christ dwelling in their heart by faith" (Eph. 3:17) and thus to experiencing that "height, length, breadth and depth" of "knowing the love of Christ which passes knowledge and being filled with all the fullness of God" (Eph. 3:18-19).

I did this with many of the men of the Bible and with some of Paul's, James', and John's letters and was then pressed by my friend Laurie Hills to give them in tape form. This I unwillingly agreed to because I was not certain that I could get it out on tape, and folks would find my English diction difficult; but it was evident that God did bring light by them. Then other friends rose up, led by God to spend the many hours in putting them into type-script. The first was

Betty Brooks, doing this one on Job and then taking on the distribution of others to people who kindly asked for them. Although I think this booklet on Job does bring out the secret of the Spirit in Job's life, I remind you that since it was given quite conversationally on tape, that approach will be visible as we go through the book together.

I. JOB'S TEMPTATION (CHAPTERS 1-3:29-31)

We will now look at these 41 chapters and pick out the message from the record and the varied conversations...with their discussion... points of view...and counter points of view.

The three friends each spoke about three times...Job eight or ten times, then Elihu, and finally God Himself. There is a great deal of interchange going on...*whole streams* of different comments, questions, remarks...many of them startling ones! I have selected statements that give a *general presentation* of what each is saying, thus bringing out the *mainstream* of what is being revealed to us.

Now we understand that the basis of this book is God's *necessary and purposed* action in *every* life. It is a *prototype* because, as far as we know, it is the first book of the Bible. Job stands out by himself as if he were a very lonely figure. The *point* is this isn't a man's book; it's a GOD book. It's God's *determined and necessary* way of producing a perfect relationship...of bringing a man into the union and communion by which he knows God, himself, and their interrelationship...and lives in the confidence and liberty of what has become real to him...a reality he can now transmit so that it becomes real to other people. That's what the book is – a transmission to us of what became real to him! So it is a God-book, with as its base, God's *determined purpose* of transmitting **perfect love** to **perfect man**!

A man is **only** *perfect* when he is in perfect harmony, union, communion and understanding with Him Who is the All in all in the universe...and *man* is the form of the All in all, and is to function as such! So that is our background. In other words, it's a book of perfect love by the perfect Lover, which to a *natural man* seems to take strange forms. It seems to center on the meaning of perfection.

The next remarkable fact is that it is about God's ways with a man in Whose eyes he is *already* the most perfect on earth! It's God's ways of *completing* His revelation to the man who is already the top man, in God's sight, of human history of *that* era. That's what God said of him…"There is none like him in the earth, a perfect and upright man, one that fears God and eschews evil." (1:8)

We must understand the *only* perfection that can be perfection before God is the perfection which is in **grace** – the perfection that is imparted from God, not claimed by man. So when he called Job the perfect upright man, he was not saying that Job was upright by his *own* self-righteousness, but because he was in a *grace relationship* with the living God, as interpreted in those days. We know that because he had great concern to be sure that his sons were in a grace relationship by way of sacrifice, which was *their* way of understanding the *necessary* atonement which would make a relationship to God possible. He was concerned that his sons' lives should be built on the reality of the atonement by which *they* could be justified people in the sight of God. He was a justified man – he knew God, was accepted by God as a son, and was not a lost sinner.

When we are in the *accepted relationship* with God that means the Spirit has begun *His* operation in us and is beginning to manifest Himself by us. So a justified man is bearing the fruits of the justification in his Spirit-renewed life…as is borne out by chapters 29 and 31…which come bursting out of Job's own heart in the course of his agonizing inquiries…an exposure of the kind of man he was! That doesn't mean a man boasting that he was that by himself, but it was the consequence of this relationship he had with the living God that was the Spirit *causing* him to live in a certain way. Those chapters give a startling account of the quality of a life of a man in conditions which we would say were heathen. It's just about as beautiful a presentation as you can get of a fruit-bearing Christian life!

He started by saying that he was in a very prosperous condition: "I washed my steps with butter and the rock poured out for me rivers of oil." (29:6) Evidently, he was a *universally* respected man in the city in which he lived. If he didn't tell us that, you would think, by the first chapter that he was more like a Texas farmer with his 100,000 acres of land, cattle and sheep. However, he was not only a leading man in the city, but was universally respected! It says in 29:7, "I went out to the gate through the city; I prepared my seat in the street," which was the way, in those days, of describing the importance of a man, like being a city counselor. In that position both young and old respected him. "Young men saw me and hid themselves"; "the princes refrained from talking and laid their hand over their mouths"; "when the ear heard me then it blessed me; and when the eye saw me, it gave witness to me." (29:8)

So his *whole* life gave evidence of his being the finest type of man there could be in their city. The way his life underlined those facts is remarkable! He was always concerned with the poor. He "delivered the poor." (29:12) When poor fathers were in need, he was the man to come along to solve their problems. (29:12) With the maimed and disabled, the same thing; he was "eyes for the blind and feet to the lame." (29:15-16) He named several other things...one was he didn't compromise with sin! He openly confronted and exposed it. In 29:17, "I break the jaw of the wicked, I pluck the spoil out of their teeth." He didn't let the wicked get away with it! He was not just a soft, easy man who let other people do what they liked. He wasn't going to sit, as far as he was able, alongside men who were misusing people.

Then he said a *remarkable* thing about himself! He affirmed his *moral* purity. Of course, sex is a prevalent fact in our humanity. But *he* stuck to moral purity. Now this was a great man! Obviously, illicit relationships could have come very easily to his hand, but he made these very interesting remarks, "I made a covenant with mine eyes; why then should I look upon a maid?" (31:1) "My heart didn't walk after my eyes." (31:7) That *perfectly* fits Jesus' comment that the adulterer is a person who gazes upon a woman and *desires* to seduce her. The adultery is not in the eyes but *in* the heart. "Whosoever looketh on a woman to lust after her hath committed adultery with her already in his heart." (Matt. 5:28)

The **heart** is where you make a *choice.* Your eyes lead to your heart. In other words, my eyes can see all sorts of things! OK, that's temptation. *That* isn't sin. If my heart walks after my eyes, if I *purpose* to do something I shouldn't do, that's sin. Job went on, "If my heart has been deceived by a woman, or if I have laid wait at my neighbor's door, then let my wife grind unto another and let others bow down upon her." (31:9) He was continually saying how he lived free from these moral snares.

He said other *remarkable* things which are equally up to date! For instance, he had employees but did not "despise the cause of my man-servant or my maidservant." (31:13) So he was concerned for the rights of his employees – that's very modern! He didn't just *use* his employees...he was concerned for their rights and their needs and their comforts, and that's wonderful. We'd call that very "Christian" today. He wanted his house to be a social center. He loved company. He had not "eaten my morsel alone" (31:17), or been a person who wanted to be solitary and didn't want to express love in his home. Of course, being a godly man, his friendship would be on a godly *basis.* Godly people can also have fun! Another little touch...he helped folks in need, "If I have seen any perish for want of clothing, or any poor without covering; if his loins have not blessed me, and if he were not warmed with the fleece of my sheep...then let my arm fall from its shoulder blade..." (31:19-22)

He didn't live for his wealth. This is the Spirit of God in a man! "If I've made my gold my hope or said to my god, thou are my confidence, if I rejoice because my wealth was great because my hand has gotten much, I should have denied the God that is above." (31:24, 28) So he said...I wasn't a man who made my gold or my wealth my confidence. They were just a means to an end. *That's* the fruit of the Spirit! Neither had he rejoiced at the destruction of his enemies. (31:29) In 1 Cor. 13:6 we are told that love "rejoiceth not in iniquity, but rejoiceth in the truth." Finally, his doors were open to the people he didn't know – strangers. He not only welcomed those that he did know to this center of hospitality, his home, but he welcomed those people he didn't know who came across his path. So in Job 31:32, "The stranger did not lodge in the street, but I opened my doors to the traveler." This was the perfect man – perfect because he was perfect in the grace of God through the sacrifices which he made, which for him was equivalent to the sacrifice of Christ. When your faith is in God's grace and you are in communion with God, the Spirit operates in you and you produce the fruits of God's grace...you lead the gracious life.

Now this was the man upon whom the thunder roared and the lightning flashed from the throne of God – on the perfect man. Why? *Because* of perfection. Perfection is total, but it's *His* total perfection – where there is only God and you are self-absorbed *in* God. What happens to you isn't the point because it is a part of what *God* is doing. *Self has become absorbed in God.* In other words, you move beyond the *separated* self in which you are only an agent of God and *apart from* God.

The *removal of this barrier of separation* is the **purpose** of this book. Job was still in the relationship of separation...not unification. It was still he **and** God in a relationship...not *just* God! As a consequence... self wasn't *so God-absorbed* that all that happened to self was just a form of *God* in action. That was all he needed! Job was still concerned with self-preservation and self-security. For example, Job said, "For the thing which I greatly feared has come upon me." (3:25) But fear is negative faith, whereas faith is substance. So watch out! What you fear...you are *believing in*! You fear it because the fear means you are believing it. It's *real* to you. You don't like it, but you are believing in it. Your believing is the *real* thing. *Fear is believing in the reality of the evil thing, and what you believe, you get, because* faith is substance. You experience what you believe. So you had better watch out, because the *whole* of life is in our inner attitudes and the inner attitudes produce the outer substance. Job greatly feared that there were situations he wouldn't want to be in, and he got them. So beware. He said, "The things my soul refused to touch are my sorrowful meat." (6:7) It is dangerous to say of anything in life, "I couldn't have *that*." Beware! You are believing in a "that" which isn't good...when you're *meant* to find good in everything! (Rom. 8:28)

You've got to find the Cross *good* because of what comes out of it. You may say, "I couldn't stand it," but then you say, "Of course it's OK. God will give grace if it comes." But Job meant, "I won't have that; God save me from that." Be careful. Back in 29:18, Job said, "I shall die in my nest." A nice comfy nest with oil poured on me from out of the rock and my steps washed in butter. Must have been a bit slippery! Beware, that's selfish. That means you want just what *you* want. The glory is to be what other people *need*! Self-interest and gratification turn out to be hell in the end. That was why God *wouldn't* leave him there. We are part of a God Who is a self-giver...and that alone is heaven. If I am not moving in with the God of self-giving where my life is laid out for others, I am in hell, not heaven, because that's the *only* heaven there is! That's why the world can *never* get a heaven out of their self-gratifications, only hell, because self-centeredness is *against* the law of the universe.

But deep down this wasn't Job's true self. His *true* self was the God-self. There was just an element which had a little hold on him. Don't mistake him...he was a God man...he wasn't a flesh man. For him, *God's* way was his perfection. *God* was his exceeding joy. Basically... what God had for him, that's what he wanted! But there was a certain element which made him a *divided* self. He hadn't had that *final* crucifixion and resurrection which unites you to God...where you move into the total dimension of *God's* being...which is for other people... where you are settled...where you are fixed and that other has been cleared out. So "Watch," "Beware," lest you are caught up with these same fears, which are a *negative believing in evil* and bring their consequences on you!

You may say, "Yes, but I do have such fears. I can't help myself. I can't get rid of them. So what do I do?" The answer we find is in this book of Job and in Job's experience by the *end* of it. When, like Job, I finally know who I am, I enter into that inner knowledge of the real "I" being He in me, *as me*, to whom I am joined by faith *and* fact. These same fears may often assault me on the outer soul level of my emotions and reasons...but I now know they have been replaced at my center, my spirit level...where "Christ is my life" is the "real me" (Gal. 2:20). *Then* I know how to replace my fears. I don't fight them but accept them *by my inner knowing* of Him in me, as me. I live by such faith-recognition as Paul did in his 2 Cor. 12:7-10 experience, and in Heb. 2:14,15, and have the same "treasure" as Paul in that last word of his in 2 Cor. 12:10.

So we see that doesn't mean such fear can't recur to you in a sudden *temptation*...but it means not something that is hanging around *inside*, but an *outside* pull of "I wouldn't like that, I wouldn't want that." It isn't a part of you really, it's just something that assaults you from without, and you put it off again. *That's* different. That's what all the redeemed are after... because no man can be a perfected man until he and God are one, and his *real being* is God fulfilling His perfect love-life *through* him. *We* are *expressions of God* in His lover-life! Self is just the *agency*. The lover-life is the self-*giving* life, and of course that's heaven! *This* Job hadn't got. In other words, in our New Testament phraseology, he was moving into the school of faith. He *had* moved into the birth of faith; he was a born-again man. He was a man of the Spirit and he was now moving into the *school of faith*...by which he could then move on into the *life of faith* where he could be a father. (1 John 2:12-14) The school of faith is where *you* may be perfectly adjusted. When *you're* perfectly adjusted, *then* you can be a father. That's the background.

Now comes the next startling revelation, the *heart of the revelation of the book* which is mistaken by so many, including Bible teachers, because the *natural* man can't take it. That is that Satan is in a *permanent* relationship with God. That has to be described in human terms because you can't put spirit things in spirit terms, just as Paul says in Rom. 6:10 and other places, because we are not yet *total* spirit people. We are spirit people of course...*but* in outer-flesh life. So things have to be put in flesh forms. Phrases have to be used...which are the best that can describe what we can't quite describe as a spirit relationship.

Chapters 1 and 2 describe how Satan regularly pays visits to God among His sons, because, of course, Satan **is** a distorted son. He is a son gone wrong. It is presented in this outer picture as the sons of God coming to present themselves before the Lord...a continuous relationship. This isn't a sudden thing that happened in B.C. and doesn't happen in A.D. It always **is** happening, because there is no past, present or future with God. It is all one; all the present is a NOW relationship between God and this perverted son of His who came into His presence about Job. The *remarkable* revelation is, the Father, God, setting about *using* the adversary to perfect His people! It *isn't* the adversary doing things, and God sitting by and permitting those things. *No*...**God** is the main agent, actually setting the adversary on to certain actions which are used to perfect His people...so that when they have become perfected, they can perfect other people...because perfection is union, making all the difference! If our outlook on life is, "Well, the devil is about and does things, and I must sit by and suppose that God permits it," we are in trouble! But no, God **means** it! God *sets* him on you. It isn't God sitting by and the devil doing things and we saying, "God, come rescue me." No. God is saying, "This is the way *I* am perfecting you, by having you beaten up by the devil." That's why God *appears* a little nasty sometimes, until you *see* the right way around. That's really the *most important* **basic fact** of the book.

In the first chapter the sons of God came to present themselves before the Lord and Satan came among them. *Then*, "the Lord said to Satan" (1:7). Satan did *not* speak first. It was the Lord *directing* Satan to certain ends. The Lord did the directing! So you have to see at *all times* that God is directing certain situations to come into our lives – our difficulties and distresses, our sicknesses, our diseases, our family disasters.

Now, that's a very wonderful thing! Of course it's a means of your *releasing* your problems, if you know *God* directed them...and that makes all the difference! The *way* God puts His purposes into action is interesting. He doesn't *do* it, because God never does evil, but God has at His disposal one who will do evil things. God doesn't do the evil things, but He causes that person to *fulfill his own will* – his *own* evil things. The evil person does the evil things, but God has directed him because *He* is going to use those evil things for *ultimate fullness of blessing!* So you see evil isn't *done* by God. God gives *freedom. Evil is a misuse of freedom.* Satan is a misuser, a free person misusing his freedom. We *fallen* people are free persons misusing our freedom. So God, having got persons who are real persons misusing their freedom, will in different ways direct those persons to do certain things. The things they do are their *own* devilish things. He doesn't do them...but because people that *do* those things will do them when they get a chance, He directs them to do them – to *use* them for purposes of His fullness of blessing. The fullness of blessing is that you bless *others*, not yourself... but you only pass on what you get and *you've* got to get it first.

All that God said to Satan was this – knowing what Satan would say..."Have you seen my special man? Have you seen Job? Have you considered my servant Job, that there is none like him in the earth? A perfect and upright man, one that fears God and escheweth evil." (1:8) That annoyed Satan – you only *see* what you *are.* Satan only sees everybody's negative. He can't see a person positively...because that person has the Spirit of God, and is living in the positive ways and walk of God. A negative person is a person living his own ways which are satanic ways.

So Satan laughed and said, "Don't You tell me there is somebody who lives Your ways for You and for others. There aren't such people. Give me a chance and I'll prove it to You." (1:9-17)

That was Satan's reaction...the reaction of course that God *meant* to get out of him! Then Satan said to God, "Doth Job fear God for naught?" (1:9) "Don't you kid me," Satan said. He could see *only* the negative, because they operate in different dimensions. Light and darkness don't *know* each other. That's why God doesn't know darkness, because He doesn't know *sin*. Conversely, darkness doesn't know light and so darkness *can't* see light. That's why unsaved men can't believe we are as we are! They can't see change. They see *something* different in you, but they don't know yet what it is. We know what it is! They can only see its effect.

Satan said, "Hast Thou not made a hedge about him, and about his house, and about all he hath on every side? Thou has blessed the work of his hands, and his substance has increased in the land. But put forth Thine hand now and touch all he hath and he will curse Thee to Thy face." (2:10-11) Satan, mocking God, said that Job would curse God because Job lived only for his *own* benefit. But you see... *God* knew He presented Satan with a born-again man, and a born-again man has *a fixed center*. His *center* is God! His center is the Holy Spirit and you can't move him. *He* is there. *He's* got you. It's not *really* you. The Spirit of God has taken you over within...and you are living by the impartation *into you* of God as your *real* self!

So God said to Satan, "Go to it." But God *always* puts hedges around us. He doesn't allow Satan to do more than *He* means for Satan to do. You get that little touch with the rider on the black horse...in Revelation...who brought famine, "but see thou preserve the wine and the oil.'" (Rev. 6:6) "If you, Satan, give famine, leave something behind, a little touch, don't take it all." So God *preserved* something. He wouldn't allow Satan to take more than would suit the situation, and so He said to him, "Go ahead, all he has is in your power; only don't touch him." (1:2) *That* was the first phase.

So this almost *unimaginable* disaster fell on Job! I suppose the same day, destruction after destruction destroyed all he had. His cattle were raided, and the servants looking after the cattle were killed. (1:13-15)

Then something like lightning struck and burned up the sheep and the shepherds. (1:16) Finally a great tornado hit their home where his sons and daughters were all socializing together and killed the whole lot. So in one week, *everything* he had was swept out.

Job already knew the truth…all he needed was a *confirmation* of it. If you are born again, *you* know the truth because John says twice over (in 1 John 2:27)…you have the anointing of the Holy One and *you know* all things. You need not any man teach you. *All* you need is *confirmation*, not teaching. Inwardly, we know it! If you are in a God relationship, you *know* the truth. So it wasn't really that Job needed to know something; he merely needed a confirmation of what he already knew. It had to be worked out so that it became *operative* in his life. So he made this remarkable statement, far more than most Christians would make today: "Naked I came out of my mother's womb and naked I shall return; the Lord gave and the Lord hath taken away; blessed be the name of the Lord." (1:21)

Mostly we have a double outlook – a two-power outlook. We see good *and* evil. We take good from God, evil from the devil…and we're stymied. But Job *saw through* when he said, "The *Lord* gave and the *Lord* hath taken away; blessed be the name of the Lord."

Yet that wasn't enough to prove the *final* point – that the real Job was, as we say, the Christ *in* Job…and the faith *of* God operated in him. So there came another day with another of these interviews between God and His sons, which are continually going on. Again, God asked Satan where he had been, and again He turned Satan's attention back to Job and said in effect, "You told Me he would curse Me to My face if your evil struck him, but he hasn't. He has preserved his integrity." (2:3) Integrity is faith. Perfection is *only* by faith. Everything which isn't of faith is sin. There is only *one* sin – the sin of unbelief – of not believing God to be as He is. Integrity *isn't* doing good things. Integrity is *believing* that God is God. Nothing else but seeing and believing God in *every* situation! Whenever I am not *seeing God*, it is sin! "Whatsoever is not of faith is sin." (Rom. 4:21) That is the *only* sin. So goodness is *faith*...sin is *unbelief.* Jesus said long ago, "When the Holy Ghost comes, He will convict you of sin because you believe not on Me." (John 16:8) *That* was Job's integrity!

So God said, "Well, you didn't win that round, Satan. He preserved his integrity." "Oh," said Satan, "give me another chance; let me get at his body." "Skin for skin, all a man has he will give for his life." (2:4) All Satan could see was *flesh,* for that's *all* flesh can see! "If I can't shake him up by the loss of his goods and his family, let me have his body." But we are *not* body...we are spirit people, thank God! "Put forth Thine hand and touch his bone and his flesh and he will curse You to Your face." (2:5-6) So the Lord said, "OK, but save his life. There is a hedge; don't take his life." God didn't even do *that* for Jesus! He said, "Take His life", and the devil got the worst of that one...in the resurrection!

He left Job his life because He wanted to perfect things *in* Job for *our* benefit. So Satan went out and brought some kind of horrible disease on him, "sore boils" it is called in 27:7...apparently dreadfully disfiguring, painful, probably extremely irritating, because he had to have a potsherd to scrape himself, maybe scraping the scabs off the sores. That is a horrible picture, this man who had been living in oil and butter, now sat in an ash heap. He was covered with boils and his breath was so bad that his wife couldn't stand the smell of him (17:1 and 19:17) and turned on him.

Now you live by what's *inside* you. The problem of Job, as we see, wasn't what happened to him, it was *how he took* it! That's the whole message. *What is inside you is what holds fast.* Inside, Job knew God is perfect...God is right...God is true...and could *truly* say in his heart, "I am with God in His present purposes and in His future purposes; I am for God!" So he didn't hesitate to side with God against his wife and to denounce her, when she said to him, "Dost thou still retain thine integrity (his faith)? Curse God and die." (2:9) She was the mouthpiece of Satan, telling him the very thing Satan said he would do! But he rounded on her..."Thou speaketh as one of the foolish women speaketh. Shall we receive good at the hand of God and shall we not receive evil?" (2:10)

That man knew the *unified outlook*! Most people don't say that to-day...not even in churches! They think you receive good from God and evil from the devil. But the Bible *doesn't say so*! No, you receive your evil from God...as well as the good. "In all this, Job did not sin with his lips." (2:10) He had a conscious, an intelligent (and more than intelligent, because his *heart* went with it) understanding of our relationship with God, but it needed further exposure and then adjustment for it to become a *settled fact* in life. It evidently wasn't a settled fact because he could be unsettled. If you really *are* settled with God (1 Peter 5:10), you are not unsettled again! You can be momentarily, but you are now settled because you are *fixed* in God.

You *only* know God...and faith is the knowledge of God in His perfection. You don't know evil...it's not there. Evil disappears. With God in Christ Jesus...law is not there...judgment is not there...sin is not there. You don't see it! Nor does God! You are living in that dimension and you are not unsettled. When a little unsettlement comes... like a temptation...you say, "OK, God, You are in it," and go on. You are not unsettled. You don't dive down to unsettlement. You *only* rise above it. If you argue about it, it shows you are not yet settled – that you've caught the truth, but it hasn't quite caught *you* yet.

II. Friendly Advisors (Chapters 4-36)

That's where Job was...he *did* know this truth, but there still was a *mixed attitude* underneath. The settled inner knowing hadn't become a fact. Then three friends came along...good men and his great friends. These weren't critics; these weren't judgmental people. They were *terribly* disturbed to hear about their beloved Job, with whom undoubtedly they had had years of fellowship and talked of the precious things of God together. They didn't know God as Job knew Him. They surely had the *equivalent* of what we call a *new birth experience*, because they did know God forgives and restores; they talked that language. So they did have some concept of the grace of God, but it was greatly mixed with the **old** concept of God with a great frown on His face. He hasn't got any frown on His face! *We* attribute that to Him. That is a projection of the Fall.

We project the frown because we have come within range of the warning, "Don't eat that tree; life in life. If you do eat that tree, I warn you, you are getting something you won't like." (Gen. 2:15-17) We are now on the *warning* side...the only fact if you are not in with God...if you and God are *not* one. *Then* He appears to you the other way round. That curse is not in the law; it is *in you*...the effect of the self-centered life! So God *appears* to you as a frown and that's the best many Christians know – God will punish you a bit. He will judge you. He is frowning on you. It is a *mixture of law and grace.* But there is *no law* in grace! **It is finished.** *That* is why we are free. But *until* you know that, there appears a mixture. So there is a God with a smile *and* a God with a frown...and the frown is to many Christians that God punishes. It is horrible to hear people say, "Of course, God had to punish me." But there is only grace! He takes us through things which will *settle us* more and more in grace...all positive. But many Christians don't see that. Many Christians say, "I got that as a punishment for what I did," instead of seeing it as a stepping stone to the *fullness* of God's *grace*...whatever form it might be.

These friends of Job had a negative outlook. You project what you *are. We see in others what we are ourselves.* The whole world is a reflecting mirror, and if you've got a negative outlook on a person, you'll arouse the negative *in them.* That's all these men could do! They knew a little more because they let a little bit out about God's forgiveness, but the main line was a negative one. "God judges, and if you've got a disease, it is because God has had to judge you. There must be something wrong with you because God judges you like that." So I've got to learn not to look negatively at people...*even* if they are lost souls. See them as sons, not prodigals. God doesn't assess as we do.

The greatest known adulterer in the scriptures is the nearest to God's heart, and that is David. Sex sins aren't the trouble to God; it's the *spirit sins*. Spirit is my seeing negatively when I should see positively. Now that takes some doing, because of course, being human, I see the thing I don't like which may hit *me* in my very home. Now this is great practicing ground for me. I sink plenty into it and come out again, but God doesn't mind kinks...they *aren't* sins! Sins you *mean* to do; kinks you slip into. We, as sons, slip into them...we don't *live* in them. The Precious Blood is there if we walk in the light, and the Blood is *always* cleansing. If we are conscious of a slip as a sin, we confess it and to confess, as in 1 John 1:9, is the Latin word "to say with," to agree with God about it. As we do that, the rest of the verses operate for us, and God says, "It's not there! I don't see slips; I see perfect people in Jesus Christ. It is finished; go on." *We* make such a fuss about being sure we recognize our sins and confess them. But John says, "I write this that you sin not." I don't write to confirm you in sinning, but *if* you do sin, "we have an advocate with the Father" Who is always the propitiation for us. (1 John 2:1-2) I don't write that you hang your thoughts around your sins, but around the fact that you *are* a delivered person...*living as delivered*! That's why the first epistle of John is the great union epistle...union worked out in life.

The trouble with these men was that they were dear men, but they only knew that kind of negative outlook. From their viewpoint, if things happen to you, *you* are wrong somewhere or God would never treat you like that...because God has a frown on His face for those who need it...and *you* had better get out of that frown! *That* was their philosophy. *Of course* that aroused a reaction in Job! They were his precious friends. They came all the way to see him and even when they saw him from a distance, they wept and rent their clothes the way they did in those days to show distress. They sprinkled dust on their heads, sat down with him seven days and seven nights and said nothing, but imparted a good deal by the way they looked. They didn't give joy...well, they *couldn't*! Nor would you if you didn't know better! We aren't very good at giving joy to a person in that condition.

That's why sympathy can be dangerous, but compassion is right. Sympathy means you want people to know you feel as they do, which is really only self. "Oh! The dear person, she is so hurt." That's really comforting *you* – that you are the nice, dear person that feels hurt – so you let her know *you* feel hurt. It may be helping you, but it helps her *remain* poor. Compassion isn't what is best for you, and you may get hurt in saying to another, "Praise the Lord!" "What are you talking about, 'Praise the Lord?'" is the response. So compassion may be *your* getting a knock back, but you are saying the word which hits home... for it is the truth! "Praise the Lord! That's OK." That's for *his* sake you say that...and that's the difference between sympathy and compassion.

These men transmitted a big moan and that brought a cry out of Job. He started his cry, "Oh, I wish I had never been born." (3:1-16) He was a human and he couldn't express what he hadn't *settled into* yet. He hadn't got settled into that glorious phrase, "The Lord gave the evil." (2:10) He got it...then he got off it because you need to be settled. So he said, now, "I wish I wasn't born into this awful life." He pours out, in chapter 3, "Let the day perish in which I was born and the night which said a man child is conceived; let that day be dark." (3:3-4) Judgmentally Eliphaz, Bildad and Zopher each spoke three times. Eliphaz said in his first statement to Job, "Remember, I pray thee, whoever perished being innocent?" He's not helping you very much, is He? No wonder Job had a thing or two to say! "Is not thy wickedness and thy iniquities infinite?" (22:5) These men emphasized getting right but not receiving God's grace, so in the same chapter Eliphaz said, "Job, acquaint thyself with Him and be at peace with God". "If you return to the Almighty, you will be built up." (22:23) You are not innocent or you wouldn't be on the way to perishing, as it looks as if you are. "Where were the righteous cut off?" You aren't righteous or you wouldn't be treated like this. (4:7)

Then in 8:3, 20, Bildad asked accusingly, "Does God pervert justice?" In other words, you are getting what you *should* get. God doesn't pervert judgment. God doesn't twist His justice around. "Behold, God will not cast away a perfect man." In other words, "You aren't the perfect man, Job that God said you were." "God will not cast out a perfect man (so you obviously are not the perfect one) and he won't help evildoers." (8:20) He's not helping you very much, is He? No wonder Job had a thing or two to say! "Is not thy wickedness and thy iniquities infinite?" (22:5) These men emphasized getting right but not receiving God's grace, so in the same chapter Eliphaz said, "Job, acquaint thyself with Him and be at peace with God". "If you return to the Almighty, you will be built up." (22:23) So he preached *that kind* of a gospel – *if* you get better, God will accept you. *If* you get rid of your sins, God looks at you. So these men did not know the God of forgiveness, grace, and acceptance...to a point.

Now Job became confused...because *the way of clarification is through confusion.* The confusion took this path: he would not take what they said because they meant by sins – theft, murder, adultery, blasphemy... that kind of thing. Job had not done those things. (29) But the difference *between* sins and sin was not clarified to Job...even in terms by which the Holy Spirit could make plain in those days before Christ. *Sins* are the products; *sin* is the producer, the root cause. Sin is that spirit of error that captured Adam and Eve and infected them with the virus of self-centered self. S*in is the deluded self, believing in itself instead of believing in God.* Sin is therefore the inner belief of Satan – the *primary* unbeliever expressed by us – when, as Jesus said to the Pharisees, "Your father is the devil; the lusts of your father ye will do." (John 8:44) Those are the sins, the *products* of the satanic producer.

Job, not understanding the *difference*, was responding to the accusation of sins and said, "I have not done those things; I'm not going to dive in." He was quite right. They implied he had sinned when he hadn't. So he took some time in justifying himself on a certain level, "My righteousness I hold fast, and will not let it go..." (27:6) That was not self-justification as though building his own righteousness. He was justifying himself because he hadn't done the things they said he had done. He would not take it, because he wasn't that kind of a sinner. God was not judging him, because he had *been* that kind of a person. In that sense, he was right. He says to God, "Thou knowest that I am not wicked." (10:7) Sometimes the Psalmist says things like that too. "Thou knowest I am not wicked," because he was not wicked in those outer terms. He didn't understand and he went on to say, "'Thy hands have made and fashioned me, and Thou dost destroy me" (10:8)...but not on the basis of his wickedness. *That* was his point. Again, "My face is foul with weeping, and on my eyelids is a shadow of death; not for any injustice in my hands: also my prayer is pure." (16:16-17) On that level, his suffering has nothing to do with "injustice in my hands or hypocrisy in my praying." (16:17)

The confusion of Job was that, in another sense, he wasn't right before God. Bildad said, "God will not cast away a perfect man." (8:20) Job retorted, "I know it is so in truth, but how should man be just with God? If I justify myself, mine own mouth shall condemn me." (9:2-3) Confused, he justified himself and then said...I can't justify myself! He cried to God, "I have sinned, what shall I do unto thee, Oh thou preserver of men?" (7:20) He had just said he didn't sin and *then* admitted he had sinned. *There* is a mixture! I've sinned, what shall I do about it? "Why dost thou set thee me as a mark against me?"

He was so *exasperated* with the negativeness of his friends that he lashed out at them. It shows how negativeness tears you up. We do that so much by condemning people; we leave them torn up...because we don't see the fact that *God* is doing His work of grace in them *all* the time. We don't lift them *that* way. So Job felt intensely how these men tore him up. "My brethren have dealt deceitfully as a brook..." (6:15) "...Ye are nothing; ye see my casting down, and are afraid." (6:21) He hit out at them in one very famous phrase, "No doubt ye are the people and wisdom will die with you." (12:1) "But ye are forgers of lies and you are physicians of no value." (13:4) That's what negative people are – they are telling lies; they aren't telling the truth about you. For, **even** if you are a lost person, the *truth* is God is there working on you and you **are** an image of God and reconciled to Him…and don't know it! (2 Cor. 5:19)

So he accused them of pointing out what they *thought* was wrong, but giving no *remedy.* "Even what you point out as wrong is not the real wrong." Then in the same chapter he said, "I wish you would shut up." "Hold your peace; let me alone, that I may speak…" (13:13) "You are a bunch of miserable comforters." (16:2) "Miserable comforters" is a bit of a paradox! It's not much of a comfort to project misery, is it? "As for you all, do you return now; go away, for I cannot find one wise man among you." (17:10) As Jacob was deceived by Laban ten times, so Job exclaimed, "These ten times have you reproached me." (19:3) "Have pity upon me, oh ye my friends." (21:19)

But his *real* cry was to God. "I'm not taking what these brothers say yet I do admit I can't say I am right. What does it all mean?" You can't *know* God if you know *only* law! You only know God if you know *grace.* So, Job poured out his complaints to God because he was a God man. He felt he was being hedged in somewhere. When you are in perfect union with God, you are not hedged in. What *appear* to be hedges are only God's open door! There are no hedges. If you don't *see* God's open way, there is the hedge. There are no prisoners except yourself. The only prison is *yourself!* There isn't a prison on earth unless you *see* it as a prison. If you see that *God* has put you there because God has some light to shine through the situation, you are in the *wide open* door of what only *appears* to be a prison. So you live by your own attitude. It's how *you* see things. *Reason* can't find God, because fallen reason can find nothing but aspects of the Fall. Only by faith…which takes God on His terms…can you find God, because then *He* finds you! Faith has knowledge. Faith is the evidence. Faith in the unseen is the *evidence* of the unseen. (Heb. 11:1) When you take Him by faith, you *have* Him. You have found Him because He has found you from the beginning!

Job cried out, "Wherefore hidest Thou thy face, and holdest me for thine enemy?" (13:34) If you see God as law, you haven't seen His face. Many folks go to Sunday morning church services who have *never seen God* because they only see law. They are told not to do this or that, and they go out with a false concept of God. You don't find God by hearing something *about* God. You find God by knowing Him within. So "Why do you hide your face?" Job cried out. Many of us have cried out with Job, "Oh that I might know where I might find Him, that I might come even to His seat." (23:3) That's the *real heart cry* of the whole world, because all are lost while they are away from Him. "Oh, that I might know where to find Him, that I might come even to His seat." *But it's faith that finds; the searcher cannot find.* "Behold, I go forward, but He is not there; and backward, but I can't perceive Him. On the left hand where He doth work, but I cannot behold Him: He hideth Himself on the right hand, that I cannot see Him." (23:8-9)

We all go through that 'apartness' from God in order to come to the moment of *faith*. "Oh, that I might know where I might find Him."

"Where shall this wisdom be found? And where is the place of understanding? Man knoweth not the price thereof; neither is it found in the land of the living. The depth saith...It is not in me; and the sea saith...It is not in me. It cannot be gotten for gold; neither shall silver be weighed for the price thereof. It cannot be valued with the gold of Ophir...for the price of wisdom is above rubies." (28:12—18)

Can't we find it here or there? Where is it? It's there all the time, but only by the freedom of the *way of faith* – not by finding...but *accepting* and *recognizing*!

Beyond all these confused statements, these outstretchings of Job, he knew the truth and it flashes out like a beacon, because he *knew* it! There is no sign that these other men had this light. They may have had some 'believing relationship' with God, but Job had a *knowledge* relationship – a faith one – and sometimes it just burst out of him! "He knoweth the way that I take: when He had tried me, I shall come forth as gold." (23:10) *That's* faith!

Then, in 13:15, he made the most famous statement in this book...
with an element of the negative in it. "Though he slay me, yet will I
trust Him." In other words – it is with gritted teeth I hold on! Now,
reality is *not* holding on. It's being *held onto* and enjoying it. But it was
the word of faith and faith gives substance and evidence of things not
seen. (Heb. 11:1) Then Job added a self-effort word, "But I will maintain my own ways before Him." There is a negative there...well, I *may*
be slain. I suppose millions have stood their ground on this precious
statement.

"Oh, that my words were now written! Oh, that they were printed
in a book! That they were graven with an iron pen and lead in the
rock forever! For I know that my Redeemer liveth..." He is here now
and is going to return. This is the *first direct* statement of the Second
Coming in the Bible! "And that He shall stand at the latter day upon
the earth." Then he went farther and said he is going to have a resurrection body. "Though after my skin the worms destroy this body, yet
in my flesh shall I see God." (Obviously...renewed flesh.) "Whom I
shall see for myself" (person to person), "and mine eyes shall behold
and not another." Out of all this paradox, this man had the *true* inner life and light. "Even though this body is corrupted, yet in my
flesh shall I see Him." I shan't see Him in some *vague* way, I shall see
Him fact to face. "Mine eye shall behold Him." (19:23-27) He said
to his brothers, "Ye should say, "Why persecute we him, seeing the
root of the matter is found in me?" (19:28) "I have my God, I have my
Redeemer; I am in this redeemed relationship. Somewhere, somehow,
it is going to come to pass. I will be delivered. I throw out this word of
glory in the middle of all this confusion."

What was his problem? *Why* did God afflict him like this? In New
Testament terms it was precisely the "indwelling sin" problem Paul
(and we all) came up against in Romans 7. Not his past sins' problem...for they had *totally disappeared* in the justifying grace of God
through the atoning sacrifice of the shed blood of Christ, as Paul had
described in chapter 3. Now, for Paul, the ultimate sin...not *sins*...was

that of his self-reacting self. The great divide for him was the revelation in chapter 7 into chapter 8… that self-reacting self in *all* its forms is in fact Satan's self-reacting self, expressed in Paul's form. Not I, but "sin that dwelleth in me." (Romans 7:25) The glory of his *deliverance* was the *faith recognition* that *in* Christ's body-death (2 Cor. 5:10-21 and Rom. 6:6-11) *he* had "died to sin," to the indwelling sin-spirit of Satan *and* that spirit of error…which had captured him at the Fall… had been *totally replaced* by Christ's own Spirit of Truth in His body-resurrection. Into this Paul had gloriously entered, as he said in Rom. 8:2 and also in Gal. 2:20.

Paul had to discover that Satan's great *deceit* at the Fall was duping Adam and Eve, and thus us all, into thinking we are independent selves with our own independent-self nature. In fact it was Satan, that spirit of error, that had entered them (when you eat a fruit it goes within you and becomes you) and it was Satan's own independent self – that very root of sin, which *he* was expressing by us. Just as Jesus said to the Pharisees, "You are of your father the devil, and the lusts of your father you will do"…not your lusts, but *Satan's lusts* expressed by our human selves. (John 8:44) That independent self *of* Satan, which he deceived us into thinking was our own human independent selves, was *cast out in* the body-death of Christ and *replaced by* His Spirit of truth!

Job had no understanding of that (as Paul did) nor, of course, his friends. But he gloriously showed that (in New Testament terms – the spirit of error had been replaced in him by the Spirit of truth) when his first response to all those disasters was, "The Lord giveth, the Lord taketh away; blessed be the name of the Lord." (1:21) Satan's spirit of independent self would never have revealed that to Job! But Job had no glimmer of *understanding* yet. He had no idea that sin is Satan's independent self…expressed by our human selves. Those outward sins are merely outer products of **the** sin. Job knew nothing in our terms of the great deceit Satan had played on man, nor of our deliverance in Christ. He did not know what was happening to him when, while he protested against his brethren's unjust accusations, he *knew* he was not somehow in the clear with God!

He did not know what we now know...the difference between *soul and spirit* in Hebrews 4:12. At his spirit-center, God's Spirit *now indwelt* him, and Satan's spirit of error was *out*; yet in his outer soul-self of emotions and reasons, Satan could and did reach him – thus his self-vindication to his friends and self-reactions towards God...almost to the point of blaming and hating God. Job did not know that this very emotional soul-reaction was really Satan getting his independent-self hands on Job's *soul*...not spirit...and causing him to make these complaints and have these questionings...not yet knowing that was not his *inner spirit-center* where the Spirit of God was in union with his spirit. But, because he could not yet *divide between* soul and spirit, these very negative self-responses were Satan reinserting his negative self through Job's soul. But Job *did* come to know that *all-important difference* by the glorious ending of this testimony!

Now that was the end of the interchange that took place between Job and his three friends about the justice of God. But God had not yet answered Job's questions. Job had moved into a legal controversy into which he wouldn't have moved if he were *sure* of the way, because then he wouldn't have seen *law*. The fact that he *responded* to law means he hadn't got truth into focus yet. He saw things on the law level which is the self level – "I *should* be this, I *should* be that...and God punishes." So he had to be lifted onto a permanent level where this law stuff has *disappeared*. So it was *necessary* for him to go through this controversy, attempt justification of himself and question himself...trying to find God, and receiving flashes of revelation.

III. THE FOURTH MAN (CHAPTERS 32-37)

We have, then, the intervention of Elihu before the direct word came from God to Job. We know nothing about Elihu except he was a young man and had something very strongly on his heart to say to Job and his three friends...and it forms a little bit of a preparation for what the *final word* was to be – direct from God! He was a modest young fellow because he said that he had sat with them, and had been quite stirred by the give and take on the part of both the friends and Job. He had waited to speak until the others had spoken because they were older than he. But finally they had been silenced by Job's impressive description of his life in chapter 29.

Elihu didn't make himself out better than other people, but he did say he had a strong urge to speak. He was a man who knew his own spirit *center*, because he said, "Man is a spirit man" and "the inspiration of the Almighty gives understanding." (32:8) He felt he had some further understanding to give and added, "Great men are not always wise: neither do the aged understand their judgment." (32:9) Now he quite modestly asked them to listen to what he had to say, and I think was acceptable to them because he had this *modest* approach. He spoke of himself as being full of matter, the Spirit constraining him. (32:18)

What he did say was really a *rebuke* both to the friends and to Job. He spoke quite plainly to the friends, saying he was disturbed about them because *they* had found no answer, and *yet* condemned Job! *That's* what is upsetting when we pull other people down. They didn't replace what they said by an adequate, satisfactory *alternative*. Of course, thank God, we do move in with the alternative. The emphasis in all our talk, even if we do touch upon the negative, is the alternative – the *replacement* of the negative by the positive.

Concerning Job, Elihu said straight out that he wanted to speak to him because Job was righteous in his *own* eyes. But the real righteousness of Job was not his defense of his own righteousness. It was a *product* of his relationship to God through grace and the Spirit bearing witness to him. It was *that* which Satan couldn't touch! Job had a *fixed inner consciousness* that he was God's man and **all** that came was God's will. But he had got diverted from that by these discussions. However, it appeared to Elihu that he was righteous in his own eyes, and there was *some* truth in it. He repeated what Job had spoken in his hearing, "I'm clean without transgression, I'm innocent; now there is no iniquity in me." (33:8-9) That was true referring to outward sins... but on the other hand he did say he was a sinner before God, and that no man could say he was justified before God. Elihu seemed to pass that over because he felt the other was the major defense Job was raising – that he was OK, righteous.

Then Job was complaining against God, so Elihu cautioned him... "'Job is saying, 'Behold, He findeth occasions against me, He counteth me for his enemy, He putteth my feet in the stocks, He marketh all my paths.'" (33:10-11) He quoted that as being the general attitude of Job...questioning, even moaning against God...as well as defending himself against his friends.

Then Elihu said, "Behold, in this thou art not just: I'll answer that God is greater than man." (33:12) That's about it. Elihu had a clear word there. *God* is greater than man, so what are you doing raising questions, as if you knew better than God? *Then* he came nearer the truth – not saying that God condemns Job or casts him out, or punishes him because he is a sinner...but that God has ways in which He chastens us and says things to us by an inner vision or by outer circumstances *to keep us* from going the wrong way! A man is also "chastened with pain upon his bed" and "the multitude of his bones with strong pain." (33:19) He didn't antagonize Job in the way that his friends had done. He made a few other statements about God which were pertinent as a *preparation*. "If now thou has understanding, hear this: harken to the voice of my words. Shall he that hateth right govern?" (34:17) *That* is a pertinent remark! If you are a governor, you *can't* be governor on the basis of hating right and loving wrong. Therefore, if God is God, He *can't* have built a world in which He hates the right and furthers the wrong. *That* is chaos! We must take it that if God is the governor of the universe, He governs to make the best universe He can! "Is it fit to say to a king, thou art wicked, and to princes, you are ungodly?" (34:18) Well, sometimes it does not work out like that, as we know, but ideally the king is governing in the best way for his people.

Again, God "will not lay upon man more than right; that he should enter into judgment with God." (34:23) What *God* lays upon man is *right* for that man! He was gradually saying some of the things to Job which should counter his *almost* violent questioning of all he had been taken through. So then, "It is meet to be said unto God, 'I have borne chastisement, I will not offend any more...'" (34:31) He took the chastisement line *rather* than the punishment line, which is nearer the truth. But chastisement is not negative restraint from sin. It is *perfection*. It was God's way of leading Job out of the negative attitudes, which *blur* his outlook, to the positive attitudes. Call it chastisement if you like, but it was a part of the *process of perfection*. Perfection is union...*stabilized* union! "That which I see not, teach thou me: if I have done iniquity, I will do no more." (34:32) This was the major part of what Elihu said and it added a *right* corrective to what the brothers had said.

He also claimed to be what Job said he missed – someone between him and his friends who would put his hands on both their shoulders, and *explain* things between him and God. Elihu spoke as the one who understood that this is what *he* was to do. "Behold, I am according to thy wish in God's stead." (33:6) "An interpreter, one among a thousand, to show unto man his righteousness." "A man in a thousand." It's a phrase we use of a special person. (33:23) Here's some touch of a *mediator*...some touch of an *intercessor*. Elihu was one of a thousand who would step in and call on God to deliver Job from destruction, and, in a sense, provide a ransom!

He did speak strongly in the end and rightly struck at Job. "What man is like Job who drinketh up scorning like water?" (34:7) "Job has spoken without knowledge, and his words were without wisdom. My desire is that Job may be tried unto the end....for he adds rebellion to his sin...." (34:35-37) He wanted Job to *have* all the trial he should have – to perfect him for deliverance. That's true! We *wish* that for each other. Let *God* take us all the way down in *preparation* for all the way up! Again, he made a bold statement, a statement which fits the *facts*.

His final word to Job, again, was good. "Harken to this, Oh Job: stand still and consider the wondrous works of God." (37:14) He touched on God's manifestation of Himself in the wonders of nature, which God Himself picks up in full force. Again, he was *preparing* Job for what God is going to say to him.

GOD'S REPLY TO JOB (CHAPTERS 38-41)

Now...there remains what **God** said. Faith is always a leap beyond the *appearance*. A thing may be available...a thing may be desirable...but you cannot prove it is reliable. A thing is *only* proved reliable when we have attached ourselves to it. Faith is also always a leap beyond *reason*. So, when God now spoke to Job, He made no attempt to *reason* with Job. He spoke to him out of a whirlwind and said, "Now you listen to this, Job. You listen to who I am, that's all; *then* you answer." You "darken counsel by words without knowledge." (38:2) He *darkened* it by being caught up in all those inadequate questionings which moved him off a simple *faith*. All God said to Job was, "Listen to what I am saying to you as a revelation of Myself. I'm going to tell you who *I* am." These were the *early* days; a revelation had not yet come in the love of God expressed to us, as it is in Christ. So there is no revelation of *that* type in this presentation of Himself to Job. This was to open Job's eyes to the kind of person God *is*...evidenced by what He does. "Can you do likewise? If you can't, why do you question Me when this and that is being done perfectly around you in the harmonies of creation?" That was the *basis* of His challenge. It comes out in a marvelous and often poetic declaration of God in His creation.

There is great beauty in the statements, besides constant challenge! God kept asking Job, "Could you do this, could you do that?" (Chapters 38-41) He began with the Creation when He said, "Where wast thou when I laid the foundations of the earth? Declare it if thou hast understanding" (38:4) *Then* God indicated the touch of joy there is in the Creation, and the goodness of the Creation which is going to come out in all its glory again one day when the corruption of the Fall is *removed*…"When the morning stars sang together and all the sons of God shouted for joy." Look at the sea…could you have "shut up the sea with doors," and set bounds to the proud waves, and said, "Hitherto shall thou come but no further?" (38:8-11) "Could you produce the wonderful dawn called in its freshness dayspring?" (38:12) This was brought up years after by Zechariah, who rapturously spoke of Jesus as "the dayspring from on high." Can you "open the gates of death?" 38:17 "Can you handle death and its meaning? Do you know where light comes from?" That is a great question of *today* – What is light? *Everything* is light, as modern scientists from Einstein onwards tell us! "Which was where is it…to where the light dwelleth?" (38:19).

He continued to ask things which would take man *totally* out of his depth, and after 5,000 years we are *still* out of our depth in trying to explain them! We are still *feebly* investigating through the most advanced telescopes trying to find the tiniest particle right up to the multimillion galaxies, and discover what they all mean and how they are interrelated. Then on to the marvels of the earth – have you entered the treasures in the snow? Can you produce this beautiful thing that sparkles in the sun? What about the rain that brings freshness where there is drought and famine. Can you do that? Can you cause it to rain? For "I cause the rain in the wilderness where no man is…… to satisfy the desolate ground." "Hath the rain a father?" The ice… out of whose womb did the ice come? "The hoary frost of heaven, who hath gendered it?" (38:26-29) We all know the beauty of the frost when the ice freezes on the trees and every little branch sparkles. Can *you* do that?

Then God turned away from things on earth to the things of heaven. He said…Can you keep together that little group of stars called "the sweet influence of Pleiades?" "Or, could you loosen up that which holds Orion together?" (38:31) Orion is that great constellation like a man with a belt on his waist and one of its great central stars is about a thousand times as big as the sun! As you travel in the tropics, it's a thrill to see the night sky with the Southern Cross shining and Orion among the constellations. Night after night, in the 1920's, when I was going down the Nile to its source, on a little paddle steamer on which I sailed about five times on my tours of the Congo, I used to sit out in a mosquito cabin at night, and there I could see the beautiful tropical sky. Every star seemed to have an extra shine about it. "Can you handle the zodiac?" (38:32) A Mazzaroth is a zodiac. A great deal is talked about the zodiac in astrology. We are supposed to be in the aquatic age today. *All through* history there has been something about the zodiac. It seems to have been some *silent outline of the gospel message.* It may be those wise men from the East saw something in the star which guided them to Bethlehem. I'm not saying there isn't something in the zodiac, for it *is possible* to trace out the process of the gospel through the different signs of the zodiac. Here He mentions it to Job! "Can you bring froth the zodiac?"

Then God turned Job's attention to the marvels and varieties of animals and birds. "Could you satisfy the appetites of the young lions who find their necessary meat?" (38:39) Could you show the raven where to get the food for her young ones, "for which they cry out to God?" (38:41) See Jesus' word that no sparrow falls to the ground "without your Father." (Matt. 10:29) He mentioned some of the freer, wilder types of animals, the breeding of the wild goats. "Can you number the months of their pregnancy?" Can you handle the wild ass who is a very independent gentleman, as donkeys usually are? Could you handle this independent fellow "whose house I have made wilderness......he scorns the multitude of the city and neither regardeth he the crying of the driver?" (39:1-7) He takes no notice of anybody! "The range of the mountains is his pasture; he searches for every green thing" (39:8). The wild ox, the same called unicorn here, will he harrow the valley after you? The birds: could you produce "the goodly wings of the peacock?" Could you produce those lovely colors? Then, at the very opposite end, could you produce a careless, funny bird called the ostrich who goes and lays its eggs in sand where the foot may crush them and leaves the sand to warm them and forgets them? It is God that "deprived her of wisdom." God made her silly, anyhow. Yet God gave her those powerful wings; she "lifts herself upon high and scorns the horse and his rider." The great ostriches with their heads up, caring for nobody...could Job have made them run? (39:9-18)

Then that clean-cut animal with those great limbs and wonderful muscles, a special favorite for sculpture: "Hast thou given the horse strength? Hast thou clothed his neck with thunder? Canst thou make him afraid as a grasshopper? The glory of his nostrils is terrible. He paweth in the valley, and rejoiceth in his strength; he goeth on to meet the armed men. He mocketh at fear, and is not frightened; neither turneth he back from the sword....He swalloweth the ground with fierceness and rage." (39:19-24) You see him thundering in the charge. How helpless you are under the feet of a horse! "He saith among the trumpets, Ha, ha; and he smelleth the battle afar off, the thunder of the captains, and the shouting." (39:25) "Can Job give the horse his strength? Can you provide the hawk with that clear-sighted eye which from way up can see a little creature on the ground? Can you command the magnificent eagle, to mount up and make its nest on the rocks, Job?" (39:26-30)

That was *enough* for Job! God stopped short there and *challenged* Job. "Shall he that contendeth with the Almighty instruct Him?" You *contend* with Me...can *you* instruct Me? Can *you* teach Me how to do this and that? Having seen the immeasurable wisdom and knowledge of God in contrast to the ignorance of man (40:3-5), Job answered, "Behold, I am vile; what shall I answer Thee? I will lay my hand upon my mouth. Once I have spoken....yea, twice, but I will proceed no further." (40:4-5) He had his first *glimpse* of the ignorance of man. Not quite yet his *helplessness*...but his *ignorance* – his know-nothingness. Why are you questioning how God does things? You know nothing! Can you do any of these things? If you could, then "I will confess unto thee that thine own right hand can save thee." (40:14)

Then God added one *final* blow to our human capacities...man's *physical* powerlessness...not to Job's spirit-center, where he had a Holy Spirit relationship with the living God, but to his soul-body humanity and human reasoning. "Take the physical power of two animals, and see if you can match that." He named the elephant which He called "Behemoth," and the crocodile, which He called "Leviathan" – the one noted for its immense strength, the other for its dangerous fierceness. The bones of the elephant are like "pieces of brass, like bars of iron" and its sinews "like stones wrapped together." (40:15-24) The crocodile God likened to the mythical dragon with fire coming from its mouth. "Who can open the doors of his face? His teeth are terrible round about." God said teasingly to Job, "Can you play with him like a bird or have him as a pet for your daughter, or put a hook in his nose or bore his jaws through with a thorn?" (41:1-5)

That finished Job off! Whether it came in some form of a vision or was spoken verbally we don't know, but it was a marvelous presentation. Something happened! Job had seen **he** hadn't got what it took. Now he has seen the *answer* isn't in his knowledge *or* his strength. He has at last *seen the helplessness and nothingness of self in its independent reactions and rationalizings!* This had come home to him now, and he made his final answers to the Lord: "I knoweth that Thou canst do everything, no thought can be withheld from Thee. Hear now, I beseech Thee, and I will speak." (42:1) *Now* he has really heard! Silently the dawn has risen, the dawn of the Spirit, and Job said, "I have heard of Thee by the hearing of the ear, but now mine eye seeth Thee." (42:5) *That's it!* He had the *inner* sight which meant *inner consciousness* by which those illumined men of God "saw" the Lord and lived their transformed God-pleasing, God-used lives...Abraham, Moses, David and the rest who "walked with God" and of whom it was said the Spirit of Christ which was in them "gave them revelations of Himself long before He was on earth". (1 Peter 1:11)

Job now saw God as his **All in all**...whether in "good" or "evil" conditions. What he said in faith at the beginning, "The Lord gave and the Lord hath taken away; blessed be the name of the Lord," now *settled* as a *permanency* in his *inner knowing* – the Spirit joined to spirit of 1 Cor. 6:17 – though not then known by Job in our New Testament terms. The *evidence* was his change from absorption in *his* body concerns, *his* sufferings, *his* attempts at self-justification – **to** a peace, a glorious outburst of a wholly satisfied "seeing" of God, which could only have been *inner* in His total perfection! "Blessed are the pure in heart for they shall see God." (Matt. 5:8) Thus he saw himself **in** a wholly loved and accepted relationship.

Now he saw the difference between the confusion and reactions of an apparently *separated* self – fearing this, questioning that, blaming God – and a self which is now in such *conscious inner union* with God that *all* that happens to him is in perfect love! Already declared righteous before God in the imputed sense as far as being a sinner was concerned...as was Abraham, Gen. 15:6...Job *now knew* he was no longer a tempest-tossed, separated, lonely self, assaulted by devil and man, and fighting *desperately* to maintain the *validity* of that selfhood. **No**...*now* his very *human* selfhood was *aligned* with God in a union-relationship – the nearest equivalent to what we would speak of as the independent self "crucified with Christ". (Gal. 2:20) *Now*...not Job lived, but Christ lived in him, for he cried out, "I abhor myself and repent in dust and ashes." (42:6) He abhorred a self which through Satan's false delusions had seen itself *as* independently self-reacting and self-operating. He repented from, not gross sins, but that independent-self as the *final deepest form of sin*!

Although Job *wasn't* a separated self but united to God by faith, he *had not known* wholly who he was...but the book of Job confirmed that! "The Lord gave and the Lord hath taken away; blessed be the name of the Lord." If the Lord sends what is good, why can't He also send evil? Now Job *saw*! "I am no longer a separated person living a life under my own plans or stresses, ambitions or gains. I am now able to manifest to people the love, beauty, power and presence of God and the availability of God's love and grace to *all* men."

Now he was lifted – resurrected – into this *freedom* from questioning, self-pity, self-condemnation. So he said, "My mind is changed." (Paul's "renewed in the Spirit of your mind" of Rom. 12:2.) "I abhor myself; I repent"...and repentance is a change of mind. "I have dropped this business of I, Job, *need* something or must have something. I'm fully Yours now, Lord...fully Your man, Your agent. I will show to the world what You want me to show to the world." Of course, liberty and joy attract...where self-pity alienates and disturbs...and the self-pity element in Job was *exchanged* in his liberated self for freedom and praise!

A barrier had come between Job and his friends. (42:7-9) But after the Lord spoke to Job and Job had responded (42:10) the likelihood is that his friends heard *something* had happened! "Is Job thanking God, looking at the wonders of the Lord and praising that he is allowed to be the Lord's servant? This is a *different* Job! What has happened?" When the Lord spoke to the friends, they *caught* a new outlook from the Lord. Probably the friends were still there, but because they had just been having this controversy, they had separated themselves as you do separate when there is a little trouble between you. The Voice came to the friends. The friends could now hear God's voice, too, instead of their own opinionating. When the Lord spoke to the friends, to Eliphaz and the others, they had an inner conviction, "Well, yes, we see, *we've* not got that free spirit of Job. We've been wrong somewhere. We've been saying things we shouldn't say."

Whether it came as some direct word from the Lord *inwardly* to the friends, *or* whether it came through the change in Job we are not told. Anyhow, the result was that they must have what Job had. "Ye have not spoken of Me the thing that is right as my servant Job has" (42:7) the Lord said unto them. But Job hadn't been speaking the right things for some time, so, in other words, the Lord was saying, "Job's got it now. *You'd* better get what Job's got. Come on now, go back to Job and he will pray for you, because I accept Job." Job was now busy praying for them to have what *he* had found. Acceptance is freedom!

Acceptance is, "Oh, it's OK with God...I understand now." His prayer for the brethren was the prayer of faith which said, "Come on now... let's be together in this thing." If you have got *free* from wrong attitudes yourself, you are not busy looking at the wrong attitudes of the other person. You'll be busy telling them *you* are free, and come on, let's have the freedom based on atoning sacrifice...and thus *God's* acceptance.

So he prayed for his brothers the prayer of love and fellowship. And then "the Lord turned the captivity of Job, when he prayed for his friends." (42:10) Job was *never* attracted to anything outward. He was never attracted to his body; he was attracted to the things of the *Spirit*. The captivity of Job was an *inner* captivity – that of his *own attitude*. Questioning and doubting – raising barriers between God and his friends of legalism and self-justification was his *captivity*. Long after, Paul said if you confess with your mouth the Lord Jesus, you have salvation. If you believe in your heart, you have justification. Justification is God saying, "In My sight you are right."

You *do* it in the heart. You say, "God, I trusted Jesus." Then God counts *you* righteous! That's in my *heart*. Confession is man's salvation because confession *objectifies* something. Whatever you *objectify* comes back to you as real. You don't get the liberation of salvation just because you believe inwardly. I think there are many in our churches like that...who have had the gospel and inwardly believe and participate in Holy Communion, etc...but *without* this joy and liberty of open confession with their mouth, which also liberates them to transmit to others. That is not their confession of sins to God, as in 1 John 1:9, but confessing with their mouths the Lord Jesus to other people! As *he* affirmed his freedom to the brothers and with the brothers they together got the freedom...*his captivity* was gone! So it was an inward captivity because that is the *only* kind of captivity there is!

Now the *household* was changed. The lonely man became a happy family man because the *spirit* of the household was changed! I reckon that he was getting healed...because when your spirit gets healed your body gets something too. All the family began to gather. (42:11) His brothers and sisters came, I suppose from some distances, and ate bread with him. It's rather difficult to eat bread with a man covered with boils. Likely, he had less boils by then…with fellowship, freedom, fun, joy. This was something new!

What drew the family wasn't a *poor self-pitying* Job on an ash heap. It was Job *exchanging* his ash heap for a treasure heap! He was sitting on a rich treasure now – the treasure of God – in His love, His beauty, His power and His goodness! *This* was what drew them. Job now *praised* the Lord through what he had been and maybe still was suffering, and thus moved their hearts to comfort him (42:11) and pour their gifts on him…in other words, share their *love* with him. I think perhaps Job was comforting them more than they him.

A *family* came into being again. It doesn't always outwardly happen that way, but he had a renewal, a vast increase of his prosperity. Back he got the camels and horses and a large family. He had seven sons more and three daughters! So his wife – I presume he had only one – who already had had those seven grown sons, didn't do badly. She had seven more to bless her and three daughters! And they were beautiful girls (42:15). No women were found so fair as the household of Job. Job lived 140 years…died old and full of days.

Afterword

What are *we* to learn from Job? That by one means or another God takes us all *that* way. By the impact of evil, the opposite, we come into a unified outlook which forces us into saying, "It isn't only the good from God; it is *all* from God." The unified outlook becomes the *unified permanent condition*; this is the union.

We are settled into it through pain and travail (1 Pet. 5:10) in our New Testament reality…as we have experienced through faith our identification with Christ in His death on our behalf, which delivered us from our fallen inner union with the spirit of error, Satan, the god of the separated self. By our identification with Him in His resurrection we make our open confession with Paul: "I am crucified with Christ, nevertheless I live; yet not I, but Christ liveth in me" (Gal. 2:20), the Spirit of truth *replacing* the spirit of error in us. Then we are settled into a unified condition. This is a permanency. This is *God dwelling in us.* We no longer go running around ourselves. We've got a self now that is *God's* agent...which produces comfort and joy and blessing and fulfillment. It is still a *tempted* self because we are here in a tempted world...and we may meet with the world in any situation that happens through temptations. We don't live fussing about temptation. We live *free* people, in God's freedom and God's joy! The new realization is this – All is perfect God! He's the real person and now He's *transmitting Himself through us* to others. I'm occupied with other people getting what I've got.

One final obvious fact – none could have told this story of himself but Job...though put in the third person. So the *liberated* Job could give this vital message of his life to all subsequent generations, because he no longer had his own self-defending or self-explaining to do. He had only to show the wonder of a human self, finding its faith and love relationship with the *living God*, and thus be revealing the light of this the only satisfying Spirit-union open to *all* men through grace. James (5:11) writes that we have all "heard how Job stood firm, and have seen how the Lord treated him in the end, for the Lord is full of pity and compassion."

ABRAHAM

It's the most important life-story presented to us in the Bible, outside, of course, of the Savior Himself, and we just can see how far we can go with it – that's Abraham – because the Bible speaks of him as the father of us all. He's the father of the faith...so we can obviously learn from 'Dad'! And the *processes* of his relationship with his walk with God are given us in some very illuminating details to which we can relate. He came from a family who knew the Lord, and which concerning whom the Lord had told their forefather, Shem...told Noah about Shem and his specifically blessing Shem in his coming family. And the family of Abraham trace back to Shem. So there was a godly background and obviously, therefore, knowledge of the ways of God and the revelations of God which has come up so far through Adam and Abel and Noah and so on. There had been a declension somewhere...whether in the whole family or whether there remained among them individuals who hadn't turned away, we don't know...but Joshua speaks of Abraham's family as serving other gods in his 24th chapter speaking of Abraham, "Your fathers dwelt on the other side of the flood (Terah the father of Abraham) and they served other gods." So they'd declined into some kind of idolatrous faith at Urin...place of the living faith relationship with the Living God. That's what we know.

Whether Abraham was a disturbed person behind the scenes, we don't know, because there *usually* is a disturbance before the flash of revelation comes...but it came to Abraham. Probably there had been disturbances going on because it says the Lord "had said to

Abraham." So the Lord had been talking on different occasions, disturbing Abraham's inner consciousness, and had said to Abraham to get out. Then it says, by one of these comments that you get in the New Testament which so often reveal details about these men of old, Stephen said "the God of glory appeared unto" Abraham, as in Acts 7, that's Stephen's speech. That's very significant because glory is when you *really see* something. Glory is when you see a top thing, "Oh, my, that's it, that's glory!" Some of it catches you. That's worth everything!

So this revelation here came to Abraham. It meant that Abraham had an *inner* revelation to himself of the Living God and what God was saying to him…because ordinarily always we live by inner consciousness. We're inner consciousness…it's all we are! It isn't some outer thing. Occasionally it's recorded that God appeared in outer form, but that's a detail of less importance because we don't deal with outer forms…we deal with inner consciousness because we're inner persons. You know what you know *inside*, not what you know outside. Therefore, when it says that "the God of glory appeared to Abraham," it doesn't mean He appeared as an outer figure. It meant *inside* Abraham, he came to an understanding that this was God Who had come to him, and was speaking to him, and saying something of total importance *to him*! That fixed him then for life, because you're *fixed* by what comes to you – consciousness is total importance! This *fixes* you! What fixed Abraham was that *he* was to be God's human agent for world blessing.

Now it's a wonderful opening right from the earliest chapters of the Bible of the kind of Person God is – that God's Being is to fulfill everybody…to bless everybody…to complete everybody. God's whole Being is *for* His universe…not for Himself. It's how He can **be** the means by which His universe can be perfectly fulfilled, perfect people, perfectly satisfied, perfectly happy, perfectly what they were meant to be through eternity. That's God's perfection! God's perfection is our perfection! So the marvel of this revelation was that He said to Abraham, "Yes, I'll bless you Abraham and I'll make your name great, and I'll curse those that curse you (which is significant in our relationships with people to

Israel today), I'll bless those that bless you." But then He added...this was it, "In thee shall all families of the earth be blessed." That's the glory! "By *you* I'm going to bless all the families of the earth." Because that's where *God* lives – in the completion of all His predestined families in the universe. When we say "on *our* earth"...because it's the only one we know. So this is what set Abraham going...so totally different from the distorted concepts guilty people have in which they project onto God *their* anger, wrath and punishment as if the God in the Old Testament is the god of anger and wrath and punishment and judgment. He was *always* a God of total blessing and nothing else, because He *can't be* anything else! He can only be Himself; that's all He is. And it's *our sense of guilt* which projects onto God as if there's a frown on His face or a big stick in His hand. It's a lie!

So this was Abraham's fundamental drive, motivation...a consciousness that God had picked him up from idolatrous situations and revealed him as he is to be – God's agent, by which the whole earth family could have their total needs met. That's the *same word* as God says to every one of us, the children of Abraham, when we see it. That's why God's...the first word to us where we have to start...is "If you drink Me you will get a new well which springs up an everlasting life. You'll get an artesian well of total fullness. It's always there – the living waters spring up in you into everlasting life. When you've got that, if you continue to recognize, by faith, that I put you in this relationship with Me, and Me with you, now out of you, out of your travail is going to flow rivers, because out of you are going to flow rivers of living waters." That's the second promise, that's in John 7:37 that *we* are to be the *channel* by which a hungry people all over the world are going to be blessed. We have the *same* rights as Abraham, the *same* commission that Abraham had because Abraham's *only a pattern* of Universal Grace. He's the father of the family, and all of the sons have the *same* privileges given them as the father! So it's for *us* to enter in, not only to the acceptance of *who* we are by grace...which is He is the living water in us...but for what we're destined by grace – that out of our cooperation which may have involved a death and resurrection (like travail) will flow rivers of living water. What a promise to take! Out of **me**! *I'm destined*, as out will flow rivers, not just a trickle. That's what Abraham had!

So onto this, the power of the motivation (because you live under the power of your inner consciousness…what has become real to you) that's where you will go…along what's real to you. If Jesus is real to you, go along with Jesus. So under the powers of motivation, Abraham moved out. That probably caused a considerable disturbance. We may take it for granted they were a very leading family there in the Chaldees, and Abraham was breaking with the false worships into which they'd entered. He's breaking with their traditions. Undoubtedly you'd be surrounded by threats and warnings. But he had the blessing of a father who went along with him, so Terah *saw* this as well. He hadn't seen all that Abraham saw, but there are grades of cooperation. And Terah saw enough to know that God was talking to Abraham, and he was going with him.

So God very graciously preserved…gave Abraham a 'cover' in his first youthful step. Probably it made it possible for him to move out, because probably Terah was the older and more respected – the father or grandfather – and if Terah was going…well, they couldn't say much about it. So he left the area of the Chaldees, Mesopotamia, to cross northern Arabia (some journey in those days) to end up in Canaan, the Promised Land, under the leadership of father Terah. Terah was already 70 years old by then, so we may take it he carried some weight and respect among his family who obviously thought he was a fanatic, but maybe didn't try to restrain him. So the family moved out with Sarah, Abraham's wife, and Lot, who was Abraham's nephew. Lot's father had died so Abraham and Sarah took him in like a son. And they set out. They got half way moved to Haran, which is half way across the northern desert of Arabia, and lived there until Terah died. At the time that he moved out with Abraham he must have been considerably more than 70; he was 70 years old was when he begat Abraham. He lived until he was 205. So it was many years after that, probably, before they moved out.

Now that gave Abraham that loving protection in taking his *first* step, which is under his life's convictions and life's revelations, but maybe it might have been most difficult for him to have moved out... or even come out with his life if he'd just been himself, and his wife and nephew. We have to be *very careful* I think about our condescending criticism with these great men. We're talking about a very great man, so everything we say about him is with very great *respect*. It's very easy for us...condescending...to pick up what we think are forms of flesh or something in these men, and make something of it. No, God doesn't see it like that! God doesn't see *flesh* in you. *God only sees Spirit in you when you're His*! So I *very much doubt* the usual comment, which was that Abraham was held back by Terah, and couldn't go from the father until Terah died. I believe this is God's *up-building* process to *prepare* Abraham for the final launch-out...having become free of any further calls back and challenges and threats from the family at Ur. He'd moved out now and settled in halfway. Now, having been *freed* when Terah died, he could now move the *final* way, which was into the land of Canaan.

In *that* spot, when he'd arrived there, God again gave an inner assurance. He 'appeared' unto Abraham...gave an *inner* assurance *this* was the land. The land wasn't the point! The land was to be the *background* by which the people could come into being. Through the people, the Person of the Lord Jesus Christ; through the Lord Jesus Christ, the *ultimate* people – which is the *whole redeemed family* of millions sons of God! By some means they convey – God has ways of conveying things. Keep on that, don't keep on the *outside*. If you keep thinking of outer appearances, you'll go, "Oh, I haven't got an outer appearance." I know! Long ago when I first began to hear about the gospel, I said, "Well, if God spoke to me from heaven like He spoke to Paul, I could hear," as if He had to come some outer way which I had to have a voice from heaven speak to me...I had to go blind or something outside...before I could hear. That outer's not **it**; it's the *inner* hearing! Paul's wasn't...*conversion* wasn't the outer voice; it was the inner response by which he related to...*Jesus*!

So keep our minds off any importance in what may or may not be outer appearances. *An outer appearance is only any good if it produces inner consciousness.* Outer appearance can only be of any value...the Bible can only be of any value in so far as it produces *in you* an inner conviction it's true! It has to become Spirit to you. Letter kills. Spirit is you inside being conscious by the Spirit of God that this is so. That's where I'm an 'I' and you're an 'I' – I AM. Somewhere along this line Abraham was conscious, "That's it! This is the place." And he made his first outer form of *relationship*. They were using outer forms like we have outer forms, can be inner form, and "I'll build an altar," an outer recognition of the inner acceptance of this assurance from God this was the place.

Now, before God can operate by us and work by us in ways, which can be revolutionary to others by which the families of the earth can be blessed. He has to operate in us and has to get us into the true focus. Now the *true* focus is Spirit focus...not a matter focus. We have fallen into a 'matter relationship' in life so we interpret life by its outer forms – the material things and material people to whom we're linked. All our life is controlled and governed by the *effects* of people and things on us. That's all we know...that's the Fall. Because the Fall turned us into self-getters instead of self-givers. A self-getter makes outer things real to you because you're getting 'this', so the world becomes something we get – something you relate to and then we gear our life to this getting. We've lost sight of the truth.

When the Spirit of God's in us, it's just self-giving in us and we're seeing through. Everything's just a form of *God's* self-giving of Himself. The forms disappear. The self-giving in its ultimate...in its endless resources...appear to us as the One just expressing Himself in certain temporary resources. The resources, the outer appearances *aren't* what's affecting us...it's the inner Person expressing Himself through. We move into the realm of ultimate resources – total resources instead of little fragmentary possessions. So if we're to be an agent of the God of self-giving love, Who is Spirit...so that we may find ourselves as eternal expressions of the God of self-giving love, which is ultimate Being... we have to be divorced from the material reliances, and their effects on us so that we become a *freed* person in the Spirit...although we're living in matter conditions. We're people of the Spirit living in matter conditions...and the **Spirit's** coming *through us* in those situations!

So, Abraham had to be taken *through* certain stages which would deliver him from a self-related to the effects of time and sense – controlled by the effects of outer things upon us. The *first* form that took was a sudden period of famine in the Land of Promise to which he had come...a shortage of food. Now, in our normal relationship to human nature, if there's a shortage of food we can get some, because we only can see as far as time and sense take us. If I haven't food, I'll get it. If I haven't got it, I'd better go where it is and search it out. I haven't learned anything about "I'm part of the *God of the Universe food.*" As I relate on the level of the Spirit with the God of the Universe, food **will** turn up. I haven't learned *anything* about that. That's quite obviously what Jesus knew because food would turn up for Him...like when He fed the 5000.

So Abraham had to have his first step of education which would deliver him from his inner self being geared to outer conditions...in this case, lack of food, physical sustenance. He went, like any normal person would, to where there was food, and he heard there was food in Egypt. So he moved down from the Promised Land into Egypt, a wealthy country, *without* any consultation with God, of course, because he had to learn. He went just on the motivation of the self-reaction to situations. Therefore he followed forms of common sense, as we call it, and God is with him.

You **don't** make mistakes with God because God *means* you to make mistakes...so He's in the mistakes! So don't fuss about your mistakes, and don't fuss about your sins. Just commit them, *because God's in all things if you're His.* You're not like an old sinner at all; you're a new person. If you slip, God *means* you to slip. *He's* going to do something about it! So Abraham goes down to Egypt. Once again we are tempted, because we so love to be superior and criticize...to criticize Abraham for doing that. *No...*God was **training** him, settling him in the deliverance from reliance on human supplies...the physical need. A pretty good deliverance! Not many of us have that today.

In so doing, he took a common sense step. Sarah was really a very beautiful woman...so beautiful that wherever she went she got a reputation...just a beautiful woman! If Sarah had a husband...rough men know how to deal with a husband they want to get rid of – stick a knife into him and steal the woman. So Abraham operated on the level which was common sense in those days. She also was his relative, so she informed them in Egypt when they got rather a sensation... because even then he had to have, I suppose, had people with him. I don't know how far he'd become, as he became later on, quite a wealthy owner of sheep and cattle. I don't know. Anyhow, all this became news to Pharaoh, and he got his eyes on Sarah. So Abraham said she was his sister, and she agreed. Why? Because, if she was his sister he could bargain with him; if she was his wife, he'd kill him. Very sensible!

So this was a *very sensible* thing to do...not a wrong thing. It wasn't a cowardly thing to do. It was a sensible thing to do...certainly for the protection of Abraham, and maybe for the protection of Sarah, because, as I say, if she was the wife of Abraham and Pharaoh wanted her, he could pretty soon get Abraham out of the way, and then he'd get her...whereas if she was the sister of Abraham, he'd bargain with him. OK. Very sensible, because he'd have a right to give her in marriage, and so on. So, on *that* level they were in Egypt.

Evidently it was known to Pharaoh and his people that this man was a follower of, and a believer in the Living God. Now again, these were the days of Egyptian idolatry and here was a person who said he was a follower of, and a believer in the Living God. So something happened to Pharaoh. He got some plagues because he took her into his house...and harem...I suppose. Didn't make her his wife yet, but took her into the household on the harem system, I suppose, and he got plagues. So the pharaoh of Moses wasn't the first pharaoh to get plagues! Some hundred years before, this pharaoh got some plagues. We're not told what kind of plagues, but he was plagued and he recognized that they were a *consequence* of something wrong in his relationship with Abraham. He recognized the plagues came, in some sense, in some relationship to this man who said he was the agent and the follower of the Living God. And then he made the discovery that to *that* extent Abraham had tricked him, and she wasn't just his relative... his sister. She was his wife, and therefore he was in process of taking Abraham's wife to be his wife, and that God wasn't going to have that. So you see God's always on your side; always God was on Abraham's side, and God used this to cause Pharaoh to know there *is* a Living God!

Now the pharaoh which turned up a few hundred years later on... he resisted Moses, and had to be destroyed for doing it. He wouldn't let the people of Israel go. He got plague after plague, and he got destruction for doing it. *This* pharaoh listened. He was angry...in a sense he had a right to be angry. "You tricked me! But you are God's, and I see if you touch a man of God, something happens. That's a God! That's the Living God. OK, take your wife and go." Well, there's *every* hope we shall find that pharaoh in heaven because he got a touch of *faith*!

So God used this whole thing...that we 'superior' creatures criticize...as part of the way in which He was *loosening* Abraham from having to rely on outer *tradition* with the bodily needs...a very great reliance today to be able to rely on **God** for provision in outer need when you're without a job and haven't got a salary and so on. It's a lesson we could learn over again today, couldn't we? And at the same time He was set to reveal Himself to a pagan king in a pagan nation, and shake that nation with the plagues which they recognize...come to the Living God...and then because, we may say through fear, though anyhow through reaction...he said, "Off you go, Abraham." That's all. Just send him away. So Abraham learned *that* lesson!

Now then, we're returned to the land of Canaan, once again. That was the place where he expressed his fellowship in an *outer form of worship* through the *altar*. Probably a renewal...recognition of what a fool he was...after all, he hadn't got to go to a man for supplies. His physical needs could be met by the God of *all* sustenance. So he had taken some step...one step in becoming delivered from relationship to *rely* on something material, in this sense, in the physical needs. His interest never was that. It was only a temporary diversion by which he could learn, and move into another stage of a practical faith relationship with the Living God – relation to meeting physical needs. His *interest* never was that! His interest was *persons*. That's all there is! You see, Abraham was a true man because God's a Person. All God's interested in is persons. *Things* are mere external *details* for blessing and benefit and value. They're just details! They could pass and change and be replaced when He likes – like spring replaces winter. Persons is *all* there are! And Abraham was interested in persons and he was to be the agent through which persons could find out **who** they all are, sons of God, and live in all the ***eternal liberation*** of being sons of God!

So he began to find, and I suppose with his first twinges of regret, that Lot wasn't following as totally into deliverance from matter concerns, material concerns, as Abraham was. Lot was God's man...but there was a mixture there, which as we shall see, until later years *remain* a mixture because he had never had the revelation that Abraham had – the inner relationship! He had the inner relationship, a fixed relationship, but not the same quality of **inner personal consciousness** which was the *basis of Abraham's life.* And so it was bothering Lot and his growing herdsmen. They were rich, it says, in cattle and silver and gold. Where this became accumulated, I don't know. This was something real to Lot, and he wanted to have the best pasture he could have for his flocks and herds, and there was some sense of rivalry with him – that maybe he ought to have some better areas to develop his farming activities than Abraham had.

Now, the difference between Lot and Abraham was Lot cared about people. Did I say Lot? **Abraham** cared about people; Lot cared about *things*. Not wholly, see, he's God's, but he's a *mixture*. So *now* there came a situation in which Abraham didn't care about whether he had the best country, and the best place for his cattle and sheep. That was not interesting to him. What was interesting to him was the harmony of brotherhood – that they should remain. They were God's people, and there shouldn't be some public quarrel when there was only this little family representing the Living God...and then they get fighting. That's pretty significant today, isn't it? That mustn't be! So something must happen which would stop it from heading up into a public quarrel between Abraham as a servant of the Living God and Lot, his nephew, and fighting about possessions and who had the best pasture and the best wells to water their flocks, and so on. And so Abraham makes this quiet remark to Lot. He saw this heading up.

Now, you see, there is room for common sense when it's related to *God's* sense, when your real concern is – what is the way in which the God of love, which also means the God of brotherly love, would operate? How can we best settle this question in a way which *preserves* the fact that we are God's, and we are God's children and therefore we're brothers, that we retain our brotherhood? So he came to the conclusion the best way was for Lot to move to a new area as a brother... and to prove he was seeing him as a brother, he could take what he liked. Now that proved 'where' Abraham was, because Abraham was the father, Lot was the son...equivalent to the son. Well usually the father would take what he wants, and the son gets a little bit. But in this case..."*You* take what you like. I want you to be happy and settled and get all you want to have, so that all people can see that we are *harmoniously agreeing* that we got very big in many flocks and herds and so on. But we are brothers...we are family together...and so I want you, as part of my family, to have the very best you can have in the country. I'll stick in somewhere too"…because Abraham's *vision* was people loving each other, which is the manifestation of the Spirit of God – brotherhood. That's beautiful isn't it? That's John 17 worked out way in the beginning, "that they may be one."

So it just says, he said, "Lot, I see the day has come when there will be fights between our herdsmen, if we continually have problems of who should do what to the cattle, or who should have this bit of pasture. OK, I can see that." And he'd catch in Lot, of course. Lot was going to get what he wanted. You can see that. So, see, he was meek on what didn't matter, and *firm on what did* matter. That's meekness! Meekness isn't being *nothing*. It's being meek about what doesn't matter…what doesn't matter is how *you're* hurt, but strong on what does matter… how is **God** glorified? That's meekness!

So Abraham was meek. "OK, Lot, you take what you like. Choose. Look around. Choose…out of all this country which God says is ours. Take what you like, go where you like. I'm meek there; you can trample on me there. You can't turn around on this. We've got to remain brothers, Lot. We're part of the family." It says the Canaanite and the Perizzite were in the land. (You can read it there.) They were watching. So the heathen were watching. Now, it says, if they (that's in the 13th chapter) are watching, it's necessary for them to see we are God's family…the *center* of our life is the Living God. That was true of Lot, as we see later on. It was always the center of his life, but there was a certain mixture there, so God couldn't use Lot as He used Abraham, because there was a certain blockage on the material level…but he was God's.

And so it says, 13:8, "Let there be no strife, I pray thee, between me and thee, and between my herdsmen and thy herdsmen; for we be brethren." That's beautiful. That's the heart of Abraham – brotherhood. It's all there is! Material doesn't matter a hoot. So, "I'm as meek as you like, grab what you like, but you aren't going to touch brotherhood. I'll go to the last limit that we retain that we are brothers, and we affirm our brotherhood. I'll prove I'm a brother to you, Lot, by – you'll be blessed now; you take anything you like. So everybody can see there's love because I'm giving you all you want, and you're satisfied because you'll take what you want, then you're satisfied and we remain brothers." That's beautiful! That's beautiful...not fighting over the kinds of little details that tear us up...us as Christians. There may be details. Well, let's settle them. There may be times when we *appear* to be two different parties, but let's be brothers. Maybe you should function in this area, and I should function in that area. OK. You operate on the "function in the area you're called to function"... but we're brothers. We work together; we love each other. Then the world *sees* we love. So there's room for *variety* in love. *That's* the key! It isn't the variety that matters; it's the **love** that matters. *This* was Abraham.

And so they did it. God *means* us to follow what is *motivating* us. Now, Lot had a mixed motive, which, you see, is wrong. His motive was God, always God, but it was a mixed motive, God **and**....some of the advantages in life. I think we have to say many of us may remain there. **This life is not God and....it's God only!** *Oh, oh?* It's **only.** *That's right!* Abraham committed to the Lord, because only God comes through Abraham, nothing else. After Abraham comes the family of God through Jesus Christ. *That's* the eternal product. And we can have the eternal product, *if* there's been the basis of the right inner relationship, where inside us it's become *God only*, **not** God *and*.

So, you see, for Lot it was God *and*......God *and* a nice place for his flocks, and a nice life. **And when you're there you can be tricked.** There's no saying that Lot knew that Sodom and Gomorrah was a filthy city as it turned out to be...no knowing that. They were a prosperous city, and again, when you're after something for yourself, you see, you can be deceived. And so maybe he caught it from Egypt because it says that he chose to go to Sodom and Gomorrah; it was well-watered there, "like the land of Egypt;" verse 10: "Lot lifted up his eyes, and saw that area well-watered area around Sodom and Gomorrah, like the land of Egypt." That's where the Dead Sea is now. So evidently he caught a little of the *prosperity* of Egypt.

You follow your heart's loves. Where your treasure is there will your heart be also. While Lot had a divided heart his *main* heart was God, but there was a certain element of division there, which therefore prevented God coming in the fullness of blessing through Lot...as He would have done if He could. And in that mixture of motivation, to a certain element, Lot followed the flesh and got himself into trouble. He got himself mixed up with a place which was a hell of wickedness, which is known ever since. The word Sodomy is one of the forms of a special kind of perverted sin. It's labeled, among the labels through history, Sodom and Gomorrah. We're not to say Lot saw that when he came here. We get, later on, to see how he did see it...that he got caught up in that and lost his family as a consequence among other things.

Abraham moved on. Incidentally, then, in that clearness of sight, that he was interested in people and brotherhood, and that he was to be the father of the family through whom the world would be blessed. Incidentally, God said, "This is the land; you'll have it." Now, *land* was never foremost with Abraham. People were foremost. "Incidentally... I'll add something to you." So along the line you get little maybe some advantages – like when you serve the Lord you get you a place in which you will serve Him...or something. *Something* comes along. And this was a time when, after Lot had gone and Abraham was remaining where he was, he thanked God and he got the victory, which was there was no disharmony with Lot.

Now God says, "Yes, you can now see a little more clearly because you're by yourself. You *had* to be; *this* had to be...by yourself...that this is the land you're going to have." And so He goes on then to show him in that chapter, the Lord says to him, "Lift up your eyes and see north, south, east, west, this is the area I'll give you." That's incidental. *Never think* that's fundamental. Abraham's faith wasn't for a country, it was for a people! Very interesting, *that*. That's the way with people of the

Spirit. We don't see that. You see, you would think…we know we talk about the Promised Land. **No!** It's the *Promised People* that Abraham was after. Why? Again, you get the New Testament interpretation by the Spirit in the writer to the Hebrews when he said that Abraham wasn't looking for a country at all. He was looking for a city. Isn't that remarkable? Not a country, but a city!

In Hebrews 11 it talks about Abraham's faith and he said he had dwelt "in the land of promise," he dwelt, "as a strange country." He wasn't interested in dwelling in tabernacles. You see how he'd got freed from materialism? He didn't *ever* build himself some great city, or great castle or something; he just had what was convenient for those days, and lived in tents all his life. Abraham and Isaac and Jacob lived in tents, as a symbol that their interest *wasn't* a land. It then says this: He dwelt "in the land of promise," Hebrews 11: 10, "He looked for a city which hath foundation" – a city – "whose builder and maker is God."

Abraham had begun to know when God *gives* a thing, you *know* He'll give it. There's a difference, as we see as we go on, than when self gets after a thing…like when he went to Egypt etc. When God gives a thing you **know** it! It's *different*. When God gives it you know it. A city… and then He said what *kind* of city. Verse 16 speaks about Abraham could have returned to his old life if he'd been mindful, but they (he and his family) desired "a better country, that is, a heavenly; where-fore, God is not ashamed to be called their God; for He hath prepared for them a city."

So you see Abraham always saw a *vast* population in the brother-hood. He saw the eternal family – a city of vast population! A country is isolation; a land is isolation - there's a farm here and a farm there. You don't think of a country in terms of inter-relations. You think of a country and a land more of isolation. A city means we're a great *family* operating here. And that's what he saw! Isn't that beautiful? He saw the *ultimate* – those are millions of people, all in the flow of coop-eration, excitement and interchange like we have here. Not there's…

I'm/we're at a farm and you're 10 miles away from another farm; we meet twice a month or something. Not that. He *saw* it! So it *isn't a land*. It's in a form of **life**, which is an inter-relation life…and so Paul lines it out in the third of Ephesians (I mean the second of Ephesians) when he says we're fellow citizens with the saints of the household of God and a holy temple – *the different, deep new relationship in this great city fellowship*. We're *fellow citizens with the saints*, the head leaders, and it's lined out for us in Hebrews 12. You'll "come unto the heavenly Jerusalem, the city of the living God," and then it gives some little in-sights into that city. It's the city of the *living* God! It's **life** because life is self-giving love. That's God! **Life**!

There are a vast company of ministers to us there. Angels are min-isters; angels aren't sons. They're a different quality. We don't know except they're not people, because people make choices. A choice is – a person becomes a son. It's only a god can make a choice. We are gods you see, so we make choices. That's the privilege of god-hood. Angels don't make choices like that. That's why it says they that wanted to look into this question of redemption. It's an *honor* to look into this question of redeemed people. You're a *redeemed* person, if you're a *lost* person! You're a lost person, because you're a *real* person. You're only lost, if you're a real person. You're a lost person – you're a *son* who's lost their way. You were redeemed back! That's what sonship is – godhood. That's what *we* are. Angels aren't that.

So in some way, angels are going to be the servants, the servants of the people of God, in a new world with the company of angels. And then the…it speaks about the great assembly, "the church of the firstborn." That's where it says in Hebrews 12 about this "heavenly Jerusalem" and with God in the middle as "the Judge of all." See… we're such poor, we remain in such…drag about with us such *old grave clothes of guilt and wrath*, when we talk about God being the "Judge of all," we think of a terrible person who will judge us. No! He judged! All He will do…He will judge the devil. He doesn't judge *us*. He ac-cepts us! God's the Judge of all; that means He judged *all* of the sin

out. He judged the blessing. *His judgment was to settle everything in the death of Jesus Christ and wiped every sin out in the death of Jesus Christ!* There's *nothing* left...but **freedom**!

So God's judgment – He's *put off forever* that which could bind us so that we could be freed people and could do what we like. **That's** God's judgment. But you see we so often have such guilt. We think judgment means God's going to judge *us*. No! God's judged the devil! The judgment of God is pronounced by Jesus in chapter 16 of John, John 16:11, where He says "The Spirit revealed to you, will speak to you of sin, righteousness and judgment because the prince of this world is judged"...not we! The judgment is on the one who diverted us, and he's cast out. He's no more in existence for us. Sin, judgment, wrath, hell aren't in existence for us. That's judgment! *Judgment for us will be total acceptance*, nothing else. We're just free...God's free children. We do exactly what we like. For all we do, God puts us through anyhow!

So this is what Abraham was for. He wasn't interested in a land except incidentally...as a *convenient* way in which the people could come into being with the family, the children of Israel.

When we *become* free in the Spirit and are motivated by Him, which is by love and what's best for other people – that's when we're free; *that's when we love God and do as we like*. When we're like *that*, the Spirit can move us into unusual actions. We're geared to no law except what we understand to be, the expression of the principle of love...loving... what's the best thing for your God and for your brother, and you move into anything.

Now this very unusual (you might say remarkable) interlude came to Abraham's life when he suddenly became an aggressive general of an army, an army of yokels who had...pitchforks were all they had... whatever was the equivalent in those days. Extraordinary! Abraham was a pacific kind of a person, he was a family person, a great family lover – loved his family, loved his Lot, loved his Ishmael, loved his Isaac, loved them all. He was a lover. Yet he could rise up and he could be a ruthless soldier when he was motivated by the Spirit of self-giving love, and this is how love will *express* itself in fantastic boldness and all the sayings which takes place in war...and that was when this political turmoil broke out between the various rival kings in those areas.

It had been going on for some time and for a dozen years they'd been under one of the dominant men, Chedorlaomer (Gen. 14:1), and then some of them rebelled like they do – wars like we have, forays, local wars, including Sodom and Gomorrah, and one or two other kings with them. And so Chedorlaomer gathered together five allied kings, presumably his satellites, you see (only those over whom he had control) and they were going to attack and destroy and capture Sodom and Gomorrah, and the other two lesser kings of Zoar and some other place around that area. So they attacked and captured the cities, took all of the spoils, took all of their possessions, took them as slaves, moved off back towards their own country. This news came up to Abraham in his peaceful, pastoral life with his many flocks. He was wealthy because he had 300 retainers, a pasture, a large cattle and sheep and so on...up in the pastoral land in the land flowing in milk and honey in Canaan. And this news came to him that Lot...his beloved Lot, part of the family of God...had been taken captive by these heathen kings.

Now, I think, this quiet man is motivated..."That's not to be! That man *belongs* to God. He's part of *my* family. He's not going to be captured by those men!" Wow! See that sudden spring of faith coming up into action? Abraham had great lessons to learn later on, which could impart to us some principles of faith. Sometimes you have to move into an action of faith before you really know its holy principle...its *whole* principles.

David did that. He moved into tremendous action with Goliath. Took a good many years to learn the 'principles of the faith' walk, where it's *God operating* in all things...in all ways *through you,* and all the rest of it. It was the same with Abraham. But sometimes, in your youthful days, you can break out...like a young person can decide to become a great blessing as an evangelist or something, and break out.

And Abraham did that. And the only way, in inner motivation of Spirit he saw he must get back Lot.

Well! These are five kings...totally destroyed the enemies of four kings, captured them and captured all the goods and the cattle, and they were of course burdened down with all their spoils. I suppose it was a great lumbering multitude (and doubtless with great drunken multitude, too) moving back slowly through the northern areas to their own countries. And Abraham rounds up his own retainers, who numbered 318. He armed them. That was good. Actually it was with pitchforks and so on, what he armed them with...and pursued them. Now, that's something! You couldn't do that unless you're convinced God was working for you. How *could* you?

This peaceful, prosperous charmer – who wasn't a military man, had no military resources around him, just had his herdsmen and so on...to arm them and go to attack this great victorious army. He did it! Attacked them by night...evidently showed some strategy because he divided himself against them, verse 15. So he showed some strategy like Joshua in due course. There's a strategy there...and made it two companies where we attack from two ends like a general learns to do. So God guided him into active generalship, and all that kind of thing Joshua knew how to do as a trained militarist. And he destroyed them...*destroyed* the kings! Says later on he slayed them, and brought back with him the kings of Sodom...and their people and their cattle and their wealth and all the accumulated wealth.

In those days armies marched with all kinds of treasures with them...like the lepers who got into the Assyrian camp and gathered all kinds of spoils, because they did that...they brought their treasures with them, like the old Crusaders used to do. So it wasn't just like our people who are armed with a gun and a uniform. They had this *huge* spoil. This, of course, would make Abraham by far the most... the richest and most notable and most powerful person in all of those countries... momentarily elevating him to be the top lord – the top conqueror of all those countries, right the way we may say from

Mesopotamia right up to Egypt...that whole area. So that you could say he could get by human possession what God said He'd give him in one day – take over the land. And there they met. And of course Abraham knew that this was, by the rights of war, what he'd get – the spoils!

Now God steps in again...this time by an outer person...by a unique visitation which has *never* been repeated all through the history of God's dealings with the human race, up to the time Jesus Himself came. God *does* put in our lives...people who make a mark on us. Maybe others of you know that. Man like Rees Howells made a mark on me. Somehow I got something through that man which made a mark on me. Other men too, but just from *something* all through life we look back. This man came in, in an unusual way as a messenger of God – expression of God to be made a mark on me. I got something of him which I've never lost!

So this, we will say, 'strange' thing happened that into this great company of rescued people, including Lot and his family and the kings of Sodom and all the wealth, in came this King of Salem. We're told nothing about him except his name was Melchizedek, yet there was something *so unique* about him. He was a priest – he was a priest – a priest of the most high God and he *stood right out* to Abraham...somebody perfectly unique. And *this* man was *as God* to him! In fact, in the New Testament, it says, "like unto the Son of God." So this was the nearest Abraham had ever met in the flesh – a 'someone' who represented the actual, the deity Himself, in the unique sense. *So unique* that we know nothing about him, and certain interpretations are given of him in the book of Hebrews, yet all through the history of God's people he remained with them in spirit underneath, as a marked person.

It just comes out in the *one* statement, in that Psalm of revelation, one of David's great Psalms, Psalm 110, when he said "The Lord said unto my Lord, sit down at my right hand." You see, Jesus talked like that later on. How could David (who was the lord), talk about *his* Lord showing He was *greater* than David? He was using that to the Israelites to show in the Bible where it says there was an *anointed* Person – a *greater* Lord, a Messiah coming! He used that as *evidence* of the Lord's... how *did* David say the Lord's – He's the Lord? How did the Lord say to me – He's Lord, sit down at my right hand? I had never seen this! **He** was king! The Lord was saying to the Lord of David. Who's the Lord of David?

That's what Jesus was asking. This one will sit on my right hand until his enemies are made a footstool. His *enemies* aren't people...His *lovers* are people! His enemies are the "spirit of error" which captures us – the satanic spirit – that's the *only* enemy God has...*and that's out! It's gone; it's gone, not there!* So He's not waiting to make people His footstool...oh, no! He's going to make people His sons. *That's* the difference! However, that's only "by the way."

Now in that *same* Psalm, the Psalmist writes (hundreds of years after this incident) in the middle of history, between Abraham and the letter to the Hebrews in the New Testament...comes this single worded statement in that one Psalm: "Thou art a priest forever after the order of Melchizedek." "The Lord has sworn, and will not repent; Thou art a priest forever after the order of Melchizedek." That's *all* that is said.

Now that's *interpreted* in the letter to the Hebrews in the seventh chapter, that this man was unique. He was a priest. It's really interesting to know God has these people we don't know of! How foolish we are to tie, say, people up with ones we know – who will know the *historic* Jesus. Melchizedek *never* knew the historic Jesus! He knew the *eternal* Jesus. Yet this was an outstanding man. So there will be *far* more ways to 'see' than we know of, tucked away...not under the name of Christian at all...who are *God's* special men. If you would dig where I do, which are strange places, you'll find and strange people. You'll find some wonderful Mohammedans who knew God as *we* know Him...and better! Some strange things you'll find. You will find some wonderful Hindus. God has some *strange* people (so don't be too superior)...and *here's* one!

Abraham was God's *marked* person. "Through you, Abraham, I'm going to fulfill my purposes through human history in bringing out this great family of redeemed sons, through you." Here comes one greater than *you*...and Abraham *knew* **He** was greater!

So, as I say, sometimes in our lives there comes a *greater* person. If you're a **spirit person** you'll recognize him; he'll come in *any* kind of guise. Oh, *this* person's got something I haven't got. That's it! This person's got something I can 'get' from. Don't try and find them... they will just turn up. Probably all our lives...you'll look back as you go. You'll see people pivotal to you, and mark it. And *this* is one!

That's all we know. It says in Hebrews he had "without father, without mother, without descent, without beginning and ending of life." I can't take that sort of physical interpretation that *this* was Jesus. It says "*like unto* the son of God." It doesn't say it "**was** the Son of God." This is silly; we overstate things. Some people try to know if Melchizedek *was* Jesus. What nonsense! The Son only came once on the earth. He doesn't repeat Himself. He **is** the last Adam...came to produce the Adamic race...**His** true Adamic race. *That's* the One! He never came before, as a person, like that. He had a likeness, and *this* was a likeness. And so we interpret it as...with the *quality* of eternity in His priesthood – which is what symbolized the *eternity of the priesthood,* and the eternal of *our* priesthood **in** The Priest. This was "without father, without mother, without descent, without beginning or ending of life; like unto the Son of God" – King of righteousness; King of peace – interpretation of His name. All that's given us in Hebrews 7 and this symbolized the eternal priest.

A priest is a person *for others*, and we're co-priests. *That's* the marvel! The eternal High Priest has related Himself with co-priests. And the High Priest expresses his priesthood – which is ministry for others – laying our lives down for others that *they* may find the sonship we've found in Christ! It's symbolized and presented to Abraham in this way.

So it was a *symbol* to Abraham that he was the anointed. The special title that Melchizedek gave God was "the most high God, possessor of heaven and earth." This was the top! See, this was the days of, you know, many gods (What you call it?) all kinds of gods – polytheism. Here In the middle of it, as it were, a special confirmation to Abraham which he *never* forgot, because this *man* blessed Abraham. In Hebrews it says, "Without contradiction the less is blessed of the better." So Abraham was *less* than this man. This was a man who was greater than Abraham and he knew it! And this man blessed Abraham. He said, Abraham, you are "blessed of the most high God, possessor of heaven and earth." Now Abraham, don't blow that! You're an expression of the Possessor of the whole universe! Heaven and earth! *Recognize* who you are. *You* aren't bound to the material things.

This came at a crisis moment with all these spoils around him. You aren't bound to little bits of material things, as if they can 'do' for you. That's what Satan tried on Jesus' mount of temptation, "Follow me, I'll give you the world." "I'll have the world anyhow, Satan, but not your way. I'll have a world who *loves* to follow Me, not a world that's *got* to follow Me." That's the difference! People who've *got* to follow you rebel against you. People who *love* to follow you, follow you. "I want *that* kind of world," Jesus said. "I'm going to get the world My way, which is God's way – You die for it!" And it was a little bit like that.

And so this is the title Melchizedek used – "the most high God, possessor of heaven and earth." And he ate with him and fellowshipped with him, very much like the Lord's Supper. That's interesting – the "king of Salem brought forth bread and wine." So he had a little private symbol of the Holy Communion, the union, way back there. This was a private...must have been a private interview. We know it's a private interview, because it says Melchizedek blessed Abraham. Well he wouldn't like to do that in public. This is a very special moment. Abraham accepted the blessing and he *recognized* that this is a blessing, because he gave him a tenth of all there was as a symbol of his giving. And he made a vow to him, and he said, "I lift up my hand unto the

Lord (to Melchizedek), unto the Lord, the most high God." He was appreciative you see. He'd got it now, Abraham had got it now. What you *repeat* you've *got!* "I lift up my hand, Lord, the most high God, possessor of heaven and earth. I won't touch a thread to a shoelatchet of your rubbish."

So you see, all the wealth of Ur he called the rubbish, "Because I've got eternal values, eternal wealth," which is the wealth of love. It may involve a few things of this world, but that's a detail and I don't bother about the detail. They're just conveniences. The *wealth* is the riches of being an other-lover of people – a means through which other people can find their inheritance In Christ. So he said, "I've made a vow." Then the king of Sodom said, quite rightly, "Well, give us the people, but you take the goods." It would have headed him up, of course, as the rich, envied leader of the whole area. It wouldn't have been long before they'd been turning on him behind his back, would it, because possessions breed jealousy and greed. And Abraham said, "Oh, no, no. I've got the whole lot." When you've got the whole lot you don't bother about the little, do you? So he called that stuff "threads and shoelatchet's" which is rather insulting for their gold and pearls. "I wouldn't touch even the thread or shoelatchet's" of the stuff you've got. It's only *stuff.* "I lift up my hand unto the Possessor of heaven and earth."

Now, *that* settled Abraham in as a person of the Spirit, not a person geared to matter. That settled it! This was the inward settlement of Abraham as a person of the Spirit, when **God** was his All in all. Now you operate from that then God can express Himself as All in all *by* you...when He's also God All in all *in* you!

Now, for God to be All in all in you He has to take us *through.* He does it in certain areas in which He settles *us* in so we *know* we're settled in. *God* does that! We don't do a thing. He's *got* you. All right, walk with Him. You got free. But, and if it's necessary, He will settle you in to take you through experiences which settle you in...not do a new thing...settle you in on what is *yours* – **I'm** not for this business. **I'm** not geared to property and things and people in an outer way. **I'm**

God in His human expression, which is today a redeeming God that **I** may be...that other people may share the sonship which I've *found* in Christ, and enter into their wealth in Christ. That's **mine**! That's **my** *only* meaning of life. I'm part of what God in His *eternal purpose* is ready to bring into being...His eternal family for eternal destiny...and I'm a *part* of that! You're a Spirit-person, and *you know* you're a Spirit-person!

That settled it for Abraham. Questions of property and possession never arose again with Abraham. He never had been interested in them, but he had to be confirmed, you see...had to settle him into something through a negative experience which He turns into a positive *deliverance*! The negative experience...when he could have possessed all of this stuff. He retained the balance, which you do, and the balance was he gave his tithes to the King of Salem. That was a pretty big tithe! And in rejecting all that was offered him by Sodom and Gomorrah, he said, "I'll make one exception. Give this share to people who've been with me. That's fair." He says, "I will not take from a thread even to a shoe latchet, I will not take any thing that is thine (this he said to the king of Sodom), lest thou should'st say, 'I have made Abraham rich.' I'm rich already. You can't make me richer. I don't want anything which would make people think that yours...that it's you that made me rich. No, I've got my own riches now. The people will find that out." Riches of Christ! "Save only that which the young men have eaten, and the portion of the men which went with me," and then he named them...certain people who went with him. "Let them take their portion."

So you see he didn't throw *his* conviction on other people. This is what God showed *me*; I'm to walk like this. As for other people, they have their perfect right to their share. That's very beautiful, isn't it? See liberty? Let other people have *their* share that they each have what they should have. God knows what each needs. So, to Melchizedek, he should have his tithes, and this was the greatest of all. *This* was a matter of serving Christ! And the others should have their share of the spoils. The rest...off you go with it.

Now we have a turn in Abraham from the inner to the outer. He was now free to be concerned about what *God* would do *by* him...not what God would do *in* him. This was the *move over* from what we call the **school of faith** to the **life of faith**. The school of faith is what I'm *learning* to be a person of faith. A person of faith is, of course, a person who walks by the recollection of the total God expressing Himself through him. *You* are an expression of the total God, that's all. That's the "you have learned; you will graduate; you graduated" and that's so! The life of faith is how it gets out *through you* now...got to fulfill these promises that He made to Abraham in the next stages. There are the larger promises and then there are the specific immediate manifestations...the next stages in the manifestations...the fulfillment of the promises. And it's one thing to move into the faith for the larger promises. It's another thing to *operate* on your faith, the faith on which the immediate manifestation takes place, the next step. *Both* are necessary.

This was the *finalizing of Abraham* in the larger promises. Now he is no longer what – his old relationship was settled. It was what God would do *by* him, but it started off on the larger level. And so this next area (and we've got a lot of time in between each of these things...of course years must have been passing, details not given) and we get to the next crisis moment. Maybe this wasn't so far after because, as I say, Abraham had the Father's Spirit and human father love, and I doubt he mourned over Lot. I think he probably felt Lot would stay with him after God had given such a warning to Lot. He'd become captured by the kings, and if Abraham hadn't rescued him he'd have been done for – be a slave for life. Well, he had a severe enough warning from God, but no, you follow what you *are*. He was the Lord's, but there remained this *mixture*.

And so, I think there was no doubt that Abraham grieved because, probably the best human reason to say that "Lot must be my heir. Sarah is barren...years have passed...no children...and it looks as if Lot's the one to come with me. He's my heir." And it looks as if he *tried* to make him, but each time Lot pulled out. He *wasn't* God's man. And this was the final crisis. Not the final crisis in Abraham's redemptive work for – to surround Lot, to preserve Lot for God…but the final in the sense of him being in a workable relationship with Abraham. And so the implication is that Abraham felt this loneliness…even as a human has a sense of fear. I'm alone. And so it says here that God again spoke by this inner way in which God speaks…only this time by a vision.

All right…visions may be occasional, but they're not half so valuable as the inner life, because the visions come and go. The inner consciousness *never* changes…so I recommend the consciousness rather than the vision. It's safer. But occasionally visions turn up, all right. And He said to Abraham, "Don't fear, Abraham, I am your shield and exceeding great reward." Now this was out from Abraham. This wasn't a question of Abraham's own relations; *that* was settled. Abraham was geared to God in the Spirit, looking for this heavenly city and God's purposes. That was *settled* in Abraham, but the fulfillment…he was moving into the concern of the fulfillment of it now, and this was bothering Abraham. He said, "It isn't a question of my relation to you, God; that's clear. But You have said that it's to proceed by a family…and this is a land in which that this family is to come into being, and through the family is going to come – the whole world is going to be blessed."

How far…even maybe possibly through his communion with Melchizedek he saw more clearly the I AM, because it says later on, "Jesus said….before Abraham was, I AM….And Abraham rejoiced to see My *day*." Interesting. Didn't see Jesus…saw His day. His "day" was a kind of light surrounding Him. Your 'day' is in a light surrounding things. Now Jesus said, "Before Abraham, I was….Abraham rejoiced to see My day." Likely, Melchizedek. Likely as a shining light he saw very clearly there was going to come a person like unto Melchizedek. Melchizedek was like unto the Son of God, and through this Son of God would come the ultimate world redemption – the whole family being redeemed. And probably *that's* where he saw it, and so he began to catch on. May be. Doesn't ever say so, except that one thing, "Abraham rejoiced to see His day." So he *did* see something, which is more than just his family. He saw something of God's own Self coming in *His Son form*. That's all we know about that.

Anyhow, he was concerned because he hadn't got an heir, and if Lot wasn't available, it says, "Is it to be just my housekeeper, my steward, Eliezer, those two? He said, "That's all I have." And so the word came to Abraham. Now whether the vision had continued, or whether now the vision had ceased, or in the vision came the word. Now the word's always ahead of the thing. Remember the *word of God is what you see inwardly*; that's so! It's not what you see outwardly. The Bible's nothing until it becomes inward to you. So it's *not* "the Bible said so and so." Faith comes by hearing. Hearing it isn't in the Bible...**hearing**...*from the word of God!* I'm such a bad quoter that I'm not quoting that exactly as it says. "Faith comes by hearing and hearing by the word of God." That's Romans 10:17.

So you see faith is an *inner recognition* of a fact. It must be inner because you're an inner person. This isn't just hearing. Hearing is outer. All right...you hear the scriptures. Good. Let people have it. Pour the scriptures out. Pour the Word of God out. They're hearing. Now, out of *that* hearing will come the **word** of God! And the word of God's *inner*. Oh, that's it! Now faith merely is the operation on the fact. It's uniting myself to a fact. The fact comes back and *unites* itself to *me*. All faith is that! It's the inner operation in which you unite yourself to a chair, and the chair comes back and unites itself to you. You unite yourself to the food you eat; the food comes back and unites itself to you. That's faith. It's a union which comes out of an inner recognition of the fact which is available to you and desirable, and you hope reliable. You've got to prove that. You move into it...say, "I'll take that chair, that thing. I'll do that thing." It takes you and then it's become a fact to you.

So, now, the word had come inwardly to Abraham that it would be his own son, come from his own bowels, not somebody just in the family. It would be his own generated son who would be his heir, and that from this son would come such a vast family that it would have two forms. Part of it would be an earth family like sand on the seashore;

the other would be a heavenly family like the stars of heaven. So he'll have a vast earth family out of which would come the heavenly family, which expands out as the family on earth...which is like the sands of the seashore...are still there, still making a challenge in the world, the earth, Israel. Out would come the heavenly Israel (the stars) like the stars in multitude, which is *ourselves – the true Israel!*

Now here comes the statement which has been a key to the gospel of grace in the New Testament, one of the great key statements in the Bible, Genesis 15:6, "He believed *in* the Lord"...not "believed the Lord"..."believed *in* the Lord." Believing may be a mental concept. Believing *in* is – I'm related to that! That's what I'm taking. So believing *in* is an act of the inner Spirit, inner heart, inner consciousness. Believe may be just a preliminary act of the mind, the reason. "He believed *in* the Lord; and He counted it to him for righteousness."

And this is what Paul took up, in Romans 4 and so on, as what *saving* faith is... which is all that (if I use that expression) is *ever* required of us humans...our free ability to relate ourselves to something presented to us as available, as a fact to us and we hope reliable...and *faith is our inner relationship* to that thing. It's a movement of the person, the inner person. Now, in its human symbols it is seen in outer form, and with us it comes out in outer form later on, but we interpret faith on a human symbol that I don't appear to sit in the chair with my inner self. I do! I appear to sit in the chair with my outer body. What it really does, because I've moved inward and said, "I'll take that chair." My body just outwardly confirms my inner choice. If I hadn't first said, "I'll sit," my body wouldn't sit. So my outer is merely *fulfilling* the inner action. I'm an inner person...the inner action of my inner self which says, "I'll sit in that chair." Now that's faith, and faith becomes rightness because the chair you take confirms it to you, "Yes, you took a good chair; you're right. I'm holding you up." It's a reliable chair. That's your righteousness...that's the rightness! The rightness of your faith is you have said, "I'll sit in that chair." You move in and sit in this outer form. You do it with your body, and the chair comes back and says, "Yes, that's quite right. You made a good choice. You're sitting in a chair which holds you." That's the righteousness; that's the righteousness – that's the rightness. Now this is the eternal rightness!

Now this is the real meaning of being – that as in my inner being having discovered I'm a wrong person through the hearing of the word of God (the outer hearing) having learned about God's purpose always to wipe out the wrong spirit which caught me...the wrong sins in which the product of that spirit caught me... wiping it out by His own Son's coming and taking my place, and taking all that should come to me in this wrong relationship where the ultimate destiny is hell (which is a place of self-centeredness)...going there Himself because He was the Son of God over whom the spirit of error had no control! Being God's Son, He rose again and therefore left behind the whole system of the spirit of error, and the sins and their products and the guilt...threw out the whole system that was geared to this life of self-centeredness under the motivation of self-centeredness! Destroyed it! Annulled it! So that now I receive Him on the terms on what He explains He is – that's He's the real Adam, the head of the real race!

I've been caught up in the wrong one that I may learn right *through* wrong...that I only can know right *because* I know wrong first. You've got to know the negative before you know the positive. Having learned that, having that wiped out now, the **real Adam** for whom I was always destined to be a son before the foundation of the world – He's the real Adam, the real head of the real race! *This* is only just a physical Adam [pointing to his body] which had value because out of it comes a physical race, and we are products of physical. So it's good that there was a reproductive Adam...or we shouldn't be. So that out of that God's used the physical Adam, used the physical race...which is we. But that's not the *real* race at all. That's the illusory race. That's the non-life race, self-serving...which is non-life...which the Bible calls death. That's the illusory. That's not the real thing at all! And that Jesus Christ wiped that illusion out by being the Real Person who's the Lover-Person, not the self-loving person...the Lover, the other-lover, the God Person... and Himself taking all this, wiping it out, coming up again now.

Now, then, as a person, it's always a lover-person because he's free in his choice. I'll make my choice. Now my choice is – I having heard this word of God. It has to go further than that. It has to *become* something to me, until this is real to me. He is a Savior for me and I *move in*, and I *believe in*...Him. By *that* means, in my heart, I accept Him as what He is. And *by the **law** of faith* – what you accept you are united to. It takes you over. What you move into moves back...takes you over and you become it! It's *united* to you...and then we begin the rightness. The rightness is, "Yes you are in the right relationship. You are now an expression of the Spirit of Love. I draw Myself to you. That old self, the control under the spirit of self-centeredness is gone. You're your **true** self...your **self** I made in My image. That's Mine now, and *I'm in you* now with a new Spirit and this is the rightness, accounted unto you for rightness. The rightness is *you're* a right person now. *All* the past blotted out and technically using terms "in His death," "died in Him," "now dead to sin," "I'm dead to the law," "Satan has no word to say to me," "I don't belong to him," "I'm out of his dominion, out of his control, nothing to do with it," "I'm dead, cut off from that whole dimension of self-centeredness and sin and wrath and all that stuff." And in the resurrection I am now this new person! I'm in the new dimension, the new Spirit, and I've begun to be a person of love! That's rightness! *I'm* now an expression of the Rightness of the Universe! The Rightness of the Universe is the God who **is** love. That's the righteousness...the right ways of God!

So you believe in the Lord and that's reckoned...God reckons that *to you* that therefore you **are** that...you are *this* now! He not only reckons it, but He confirms it. Now this is the chapter of confirmation. A 'step of faith' *must have* a 'confirmation of faith' because the whole meaning of faith is knowledge. It means *you enter into* the experience of what you are related to. My action in which I related early at first...my first step is not even a human action really because it's being motivated by that which motivates me…in this case, the Spirit of God *causes me to know* I'm lost, and *causes me to see* Jesus as available. So it all comes to me really…it's always the *faith of God* operating in me. Now *my* action is I move in. Now faith will not consummate until you get back the thing you moved into. Faith is consummated when you sit in the chair because the chair holds you…not because you sat in it. The faith is…you are now in a faith relationship which is worked out so that that chair's proving itself a confirmed chair for *you* and holding *you*. Now you've got…the product of your faith is sitting in the chair!

So all of life is faith – is the moving in to get something which comes. **Is** becomes *produced* to you…becomes a substance to you. So Spirit faith…faith – by that I mean by which I as an inner person am relating to Jesus Christ in this realm of the Spirit, because He's no longer in the realm of the flesh. Like Abraham. Abraham believed God… believed God! God doesn't *run* down here. God is this one he heard of "most high God, possessor of heaven and earth." That's the one I'm believing in! Now, that's either craziness or wisdom because you're rejecting what this world has, because you've got the whole lot! You needn't have that little bit of that, because you've got the whole lot. Now, by the principle of faith…if that's a reality…back this fact comes to you and confirms it. And with the inner confirmation, "Yes, this is what You're in; this is the relationship. We *are* one person together. I am operating by You." You are dead to the old and alive to the new and so on. "*You're* in me!" There's the confirmation!

And that's what Abraham asked for. See, he'd taken his step now and in God's sight that was a **fact**. God counted it to him for righteousness. He'd believed in the Lord against every, of course, human appearance. He wasn't bothered by those human appearances on that level then…on the general level. He wasn't bothered, he got through that and he believed in the Lord – that **he** was to be out of stars in the sky and sands on the seashore and all this thing…the whole world's going to be blessed…so he believed in the Lord. Now the Lord counted it. He said, "That's OK, that's right. You're on the right path now;

you're with Me, for Me, for the world. *You're* an expression of God Who is love. That's right! You're on the right path." Abraham didn't know that *until* he'd got the confirmation that God counts a thing righteous. You've got to *experience* this righteousness.

That's why there's some division in Romans 10 between believing and confessing. In Romans 10 it says about the word of faith, verse 8, "the word of faith is the word you speak." It's really...it's **God's word** *in you* coming out through you. You were to say, "All right, God, that's settled. You say it is; I say it is. You say You died for me; I believe it. You're my Savior; I accept it. You say those sins are gone; I believe it"... or whatever you like. You're saying it on the basis of what God is saying in you...the word of faith.

Now, it says that word of faith is "That if thou shalt confess with thy mouth the Lord Jesus (verse 9), and shalt believe in thine heart that God has raised Him from the dead, thou shalt be saved." Then the comment, "For with the heart man believes unto righteousness; but with the mouth confession is made unto salvation." Now the heart is... you have inwardly done this...you have believed in God. Righteousness means *God* counts it as righteous. Abraham believed in God and God said, "You're righteous." That's what *God said*, not what Abraham knows. God said that. In God's sight that's fixed, that's fixed..."You're on the right road. You may not quite know it yet, Abraham, but you're on the right road. I'm saying so because you've moved into believing Me and My faithfulness and grace and so on." He didn't know the Person of Jesus as we knew Him. So that means in God's sight you're on the right, in the right relationship. "With the mouth confession is made unto the salvation." Oh, now I know it! Something happened to me! That's salvation...saves me from my sins! *Jesus*...His name is *Jesus*...**saved** me! Not...God says I'm saved...I know I'm saved. That's salvation!

So righteousness is what God says I am eternally and it's a fact! It doesn't do much for me until *I know* it...and with the mouth confession is made unto salvation. In this case that's used in a simple way – I confess. That's the usual way in our simple ways. Now, when Jesus has died things are simple for us. We just confess Jesus. We didn't always confess it. That confession is like a *symbol* to you. Your word echoes back to you and says "OK." It's like a symbol. It's – you say something. When you say it *you* hear it. Not only other people *hear* it, you hear it. It has a kind of an echo back on you and the echo answers, "That's OK."

Now with Abraham this is the first great movement. This took place by an outer sacrifice Abraham was told to make. See, Abraham asked his question. He had now believed God and that, in God's sight, was it! Now he says, in verse 8, "Lord God, whereby shall I know that I have inherited it?" Oh! "I have believed You. I want to know as a fact." See it must come back to Abraham as a consciousness. See? "I have believed You. I've taken You at Your word. You've given me this vision. You have confirmed it to me; this is going to be so. I've doubted before, but this is a kind of crisis confirmation." From the beginning he believed it in a certain extent. Now this is *fixing* it. "I have believed You. You said that although I haven't got a human heir there's going to be a human heir. Somehow it's *going to* come about and it's going to come as You've said. Through me, all the families of the earth will be blessed and so on. All right. How do I know that? Could You do something for me, which makes me know inwardly so I'll never doubt again?" That's the inner confirmation!

In this case it took by an *outer* sacrifice. That can be. Therefore there **is** a place... sometimes it's by the laying on of hands, maybe some outer forms...that's where maybe things like tongues can come in some people...as long as you don't mistake the tongues for the promise. As long as the tongues are an indication to you that God is what He says He is to you, OK. You may have *any* kind of confirmation outer. I've never had that type of confirmations. You haven't *got* to have them. All you've got to be is confirmed. *How* you're confirmed isn't the point. And in this case it was by a certain sacrifice, making a sacrifice of pigeons and so on, and one of those things He told him to do, and I guess slaying a goat and a heifer...and a period of great darkness. Sometimes there's that.

It says a "terror of great darkness fell upon him." Well, that may be part of the process which confirms you for the light. The deeper darkness then deeper light, and so there often does come that. And then He said, "Now, know of a surety." (Vs 13) That's it! "Now know of a surety, Abraham" that this is what's......I give you some further details. He gave him some further details.

There's going to be 400 years in Egypt and then come back and possess the land – to *center* him around all this question of the people. The point was the *people*. "Thy *seed*." It wasn't the land...no, it's "thy seed shall be a stranger in a land which isn't theirs, serve them four hundred years." That's in Egypt. "And I will judge that nation. On that day thy seed will come out with great substance, and you will go to your fathers in peace, but they, your seed, will come here when the land is ready to be taken." God had to prepare the land – iniquity of the Amorites not yet full; God has His timetable. And He said that this is the land that wasn't of great interest to Abraham, but this was to confirm to Abraham this is where the people are going to come up and become a people. So He gave them outlines again of the land there. Now, by that means He confirmed, at least outwardly, that "Know of a surety" means *inwardly* to Abraham.

So you see there is a confirmation that you're not you...but *God operating by you*. Get that? That's a *high unity*! That's *not* the first confirmation you had, "You're a child of God by faith in Jesus Christ." It isn't even the confirmation that Christ dwells in you as much as **you are Christ** in action. This is the confirmation! You see, **God's** *going to operate by Abraham* now; **He's** *going to come out by Abraham*. **He's** going to *manifest Himself in Abraham and Isaac and so on.* Abraham was to be God in manifested, in manifestation...*God* in manifested action! Now this is what He had confirmed to him here. The confirmation of a unity which does not just mean, "Well, I'm relying on Christ and He abides in me and it's all right." It's, "*I* **am Christ** *in action*." That's the moving in for the fatherhood, because with the fatherhood something comes out *through* **you**. This is Abraham moving into the fatherhood.

So I think, as I saw it myself, that many of us may come into some relationship in which it's "not I, but Christ." It was just a *middle* relationship. That's wonderful! It's no longer a self-relying self. I've got that clear. I accept myself and all of that; I know where **I** fit. It's not I, but Christ. But the third area is – "Now it's I again." Paul says in Galatians 2:20, "I am crucified with Christ." That's the old one out; now, that's the regeneration. Now the middle one, the union, is "I live, no I don't live, Christ lives in me." Now the third, the reproductive element, is "now I live by the faith of the Son of God." God's operating by me, "by the faith of the Son of God," *God's operating* His faith purposes *by me.* Now I'm out living again. *I've* come back again and it's Christ in **my form**…not just Christ. So it isn't "I can't, *He* can." It's "*I* can." That's the third one. That's where Abraham was moving in here!

Now we move on to a *very great further stage*, shall we say, in the operation of this faith through Abraham, *and through us* when I begin to differentiate between the impact of *human* reason on me…which pours in on me all the time…and *a God who operates beyond nature, beyond reason*…if we like to call it, the supernatural. This takes a continued action through life. You see, it's not now a question of my *sins* or my *self*…it's a question of how *God* can come through *by me* in His situations. It's not on that baby stuff at all! **I'm** God's *means* in manifestation! How will God come *through* in situations?

Now, all situations start by their impact on my human reason. That's *all* I can see. I got born that way to see things as they *appear*, allowing God to govern things of every kind as they appear. And that restricts me to operate at up to the level of appearances. It's quite evident these men in the Bible didn't. It's quite evident Jesus Christ didn't – wasn't controlled by how a storm 'appeared' because He replaced it by a calm. He didn't operate by what five loaves can do. He operated by *enough* loaves for five thousand. He didn't operate by death…He called it sleep. He said, "They sleep." And, "Lazarus never has died...only appeared. It's only an illusion. He's always been alive, just didn't know it. Here he sleeps. We'll get him out of that sleep now." The sleep is so rough it can corrupt a body, but still it's only sleep. It said he began to stink. That was only a product of *unbelief*, that's all. He was never 'there' if he'd known it.

Now, *here's* another quality of life which *we* call supernatural. It's *only* really operating for us by eternal laws. It's quite obvious that gravity can't be an eternal law when God/Jesus transcended. When Jesus walks on water He contradicts gravity, because gravity makes you sink. So obviously there's *another* whole dimension of law...of the true laws. Now, you see, we're *governed* by appearances, and the new adventure is to begin to learn how, as things confront us, we can *transcend appearances and replace it by Spirit action*. Now this is *reproductive* faith. This isn't unifying faith or justifying faith. It's reproductive faith! It's fatherhood faith! This is the third one into which Abraham is kind of settled by this assurance. But **he** had to operate it now.

We may say that all life falls into two categories in ordinary living. There's what you might call normal living and special confrontations. By normal livings what you do is spontaneous...spontaneous living. You don't ask guidance, "Shall you cook?" You just cook. You don't ask guidance, "Shall you walk in this room or walk out?" You just walk out. That's what you call spontaneous living. You take it for granted you're an expression of God...and you do the next thing. This isn't bothering you. Well, if it doesn't bother you, it's OK. Do it. My friend, Rees Howells, as I told you before, always said, "I live two lives. I live a natural life...and when the Holy Ghost comes upon me." Now natural life didn't mean he was a man of the flesh. It meant he just enjoyed *spontaneously being* what he was, which was Christ in him, enjoying his gardens, enjoying his place, enjoying this place God had given him... full of fun, full of hospitality, full of love...naturally...did not pray for guidance he *just did* the next thing. That's spontaneous living of which there should be lots in our lives and *this* is this *free life*. You *just be yourself* and forget everything else...do what you like!

Now, in the midst of spontaneous living comes **confronted** living, "Oh, what should I do with that?" Now you're that *disturbed* person. You're no longer spontaneously cooking or something. Something's turned up...maybe some small things, maybe big things. "What should I do with that?" This snag has arisen, maybe small, but You always catch me out...as it may be the big things. Now something has happened... which you don't live spontaneously. Something has happened which bothers you, confronts you. Now, that's where I've got to learn a whole new category of living, which I hardly have begun to learn – which is when I make quick enough (of course, in big things it may take a little longer to say now, if I'm in that situation which confronts me...the need...maybe a financial need, maybe a problem about people, maybe anything you'd like to put in, physical)... anything which *confronts* you is something which you can't handle.

Now you're *beyond* the spontaneous. Something caught you. What do I do with that? And all you will see is **reason**...*reasons why* you must stick it out...just do the best you can...stick it out...go through with it. We say, "**No**," we're people of the Spirit. Spirit operates through matter. Matter is only an expression of Spirit and Spirit operates out. Spirit – **this** is Spirit. Spirit is working through people. We are Spirit in bodies! Spirit takes bodily form. He manifests in bodily form...material form. He doesn't just remain up here. He manifests in bodily form. Jesus Christ *came* in bodily form. That's how God is *known*, because Jesus Christ came in bodily form. *We* are bodily forms of God! He operates on the bodily level, on the matter level. He comes through, but matter shouts at you saying you can't do it!

Matter is just what the reason tells you...for the *world* will say you are. That's – that there's *not enough* money for that; there's *that* problem. All of life is solid with things which you can't handle – you've got sickness, whatever you like. Now reason says, "OK." *We* don't say that! Now, *this* is where we begin to...*can* we begin to learn to operate in the Spirit dimension – *God* in the matter dimension, which quite obviously Jesus did and quite obviously men like Moses did. When you move into a rock to get water out of it, and you say manna will turn up every day in the wilderness...enough to feed two million people and all these things...all these, what we call miracles through the Bible when people operated on the level that there's a Person Who is the All Person with all resources, and where need arises where I'm confronted...now it's local.

This is the local...not the general thing come up 'one day'. This is not a question of Abraham 'one day' the father of the whole faithful, which he is. This is local... what's going to happen *now?* And I'm up *against* something which a nature can make you say, "Well, *I* must take it all in, or work it out as best I can or something." My self answers like that. Now, how quick and how often can I begin to learn to say, "No, *this* is the point...*why* God's put me there...because this is where God, Spirit will manifest in some matter form." Spirit will manifest in some way in which He is seen to be something which is *beyond* nature; what we call beyond nature.

Now that fits us *all* the time. It's a question of how you're awakening. Many of you are not even awake to it. It's *way* beyond! You are directed until you've been *messed-up* as self first, and re-made. Until you've been *transferred* from being a matter person to a Spirit person you won't see this, not in *any* extent. That's why these outer things have to happen first.

Now Abraham came up against it. Sarah was a godly woman. She is presented in 2 Peter 3 as the typical, right-type of wife...only you're not the right type of wife when you subject yourself to your husband instead of subjecting yourself to your Lord. I don't believe she subjected herself to the Lord. She did not subject herself to the Lord; she subjected herself to her husband, and kept him working for her. That's not the way to do it. You only call a person Lord as far as the expression of the Lordship of Christ in you, that's all. Well, so she's a godly woman. She had not yet seen what we talk about a differentiation between matter and Spirit, flesh and Spirit. She hadn't seen that.

As I've said...many of us, we all go through that...many of us, many of God's people have not seen the differentiation between flesh and spirit, when you *become* a spirit-person and *know* you're a spirit-person and *operate* as such. When you *are that*, of course you *know*. You can discern between soul and spirit, flesh and spirit, matter and spirit. You can discern; you *know*! If you don't, you don't.

So Sarah didn't know that...and she knew what she knew of God's dealings with Abraham, because he told her of them...that he was to have a son. It was to come out of his bowels; he was to generate the son. And she was barren and had been so for years. And so, her *rational interpretation* was, "Well there, I'm barren." I don't know by that time, I presume by that time she'd had her change of life because it specifically says later on she'd had the change of life. Therefore it's a way out...having my son.

Well then *reason*...reasoned ways *of God* – it has a God-confirmation. That's OK if it has a God-confirmation...then you know it! You don't bother because you're not governed by reason; you're governed by God-confirmation. Now this hadn't got God-confirmation; it was planning. Watch *your* plan! All right, God operates by us *as long as* you've got a God-confirmation...that which is inside you. "Yeah, OK, I see that's what God means for me. OK." But be sure you get *that* or you're in trouble. You're running by 'help yourself' about that, because she hadn't got that. And so she had made, which is a common custom in those days. This isn't a moral question. It isn't a question of Abraham sinning in adultery or something in taking Hagar. It was a common thing in those days, like polygamy was. I've lived in a polygamous country. I know all about those sort of things.

So it wasn't a question of morality. It's a question of the *higher levels* of operating by faith...and unbelief on those levels isn't sin. It's just you've got to learn a little better next time, that's all. So we all do that. You can call it sin if you like...for the highest part wasn't; because God doesn't *see* you sin, because it's operating on the highest level...*learning* how to do it. So it wasn't a question of morality when she said, "Well, take Hagar." It's a normal way they do it in those days. Of course, the problem, obviously, was Abraham. Again…he didn't get God's confirmation. He could have taken that to God, but of course God is there silent…because God gave no confirmation to that. So he did it *without* God's confirmation.

And so Hagar became pregnant, and this child was born. Now if you haven't got God's confirmation on self, self is very worrisome. It's a little hell of its own! And the self which God hasn't **'confirmed'** is *all for itself.* Now God hadn't confirmed this to Sarah so she didn't like being laughed at by her servant, because you see in those days you were blessed if you had a child; if you were barren you weren't blessed. And the whole of that house of hundreds and hundreds of people saw the slave had the child when Sarah couldn't have one. Wow! That was really slapping Sarah in the face. She couldn't take that one. And the maid had a laugh at that one too. She was better now than her mistress. OK, if God tells you, if God says so, Ok, but God *didn't* say so. When God doesn't say so, you live in a little private hell of your own. My *self* is hell without God, that's all.

You get into a private hell…angry, indignant that this servant girl… it says that she despised Sarah, very likely because Sarah projected the contempt…probably the contempt is more in Sarah's annoyance than in poor Hagar. It may have been. But, of course, she would have been proud. She was going to be the mother of the great Abraham's son… of course she'd have been proud! It wasn't moral…it wasn't a question of moral. It was a question of honorable in those days. So you get the operations of self, and then Sarah not acting as a very meek wife says, "It's your fault Abraham, anyhow." It says so here. And Sarah said to Abraham, "My wrong be upon you. I gave my maiden into your bosom, and then when she saw that she had conceived she despised me; the Lord judge between me and you." So she forgot her submission there.

God *did* judge about blessing the woman. Isn't that like God? God turned this into the salvation of Hagar! Isn't that like God? God wasn't bothered by this, God was rather pleased with it...had to learn a thing or two for us all! This was not some judge, senior judge – this is *learning* – what you do all the time; what we do operating in the flesh, operating by reason...not flesh in the sense of wrong kind of service. It wasn't some kind of wicked self-effort. It was trying to do *God's* job...not the self-effort in the wrong way. Sarah was trying to *help* God through, that's all...trying to do God's job when God says Abraham must have a son. Well she...if he couldn't have a son by Sarah he could have one by Hagar. That's all. So it wasn't on that level self-gratification, or self-stuff at all. It was seeking to do the highest.

So God was rather pleased. He likes for people to make a mess of it now and then, and learn a thing or two. We shouldn't learn it unless we did. That's OK...wanting God to turn this into His blessing on Hagar. That's *how* He judged. God doesn't judge or punish; He *judges by giving* the other person a bigger blessing to accomplish it! Without that you can be so...seem to be so brutal, you know...can't we? So that Sarah so mistreated Hagar that in her pregnancy she ran away. Why we all do that kind of thing, and blame other people! Somehow she so turned on her. It says, Abraham, not asking very much of the Lord, says, "Do to her as it pleases you, Sarah...when Sarah dealt hardly with her, she fled."

Hagar fled into the desert, came to a well...and then where the *Lord* met with Hagar. Get that? I tell you the Lord ministers to *all* sorts of people who never *heard* of Jesus Christ...don't forget it! *The Lord ministers to all sorts of people who never heard of Jesus Christ.* We fundamentalists say it's only by Him; it's by His *nature,* not by His presence. It isn't by His physical presence; no one makes it by the *name.* The name is a **nature**! You can give the name of Jesus Christ *never* having known *the Person* of Jesus Christ at all! So moving on being into God's will – that's Jesus' nature – you're with Jesus! So lots of people are saved who never knew Jesus, don't forget that...and here's one of them.

And God spoke to her, talked to her. Isn't that wonderful? An angel came to her...some apparition in this case, came to her...talked to her. And she told him what happened. Hagar told the angel what happened, and he said, "Return to your mistress and submit yourself unto her hands." Ah! A change of *character* in Hagar. She wasn't going back to be nasty; she was going back to submit. That's different. So there was a change; Hagar went back. So God was mighty good. Sarah said, "All right, let the Lord judge between you, Abraham and me." The Lord *judges by blessing* Hagar. Then he sends Hagar back to be a nice one to them...nice and kind and cooperative. That was very nice. So the Lord blesses! So then she was not so tough after all because that was *His* true spirit, and it released a deep blessing, and He said that, to Hagar, "Yes, you will have a child, you're going to call him Ishmael. He'll be another kind of person, what you call a wild man, out there in the deserts," what we now think of, of course, as the Arabs.

Now remember this – the Arabs are just as precious to God as the Jews. Don't be pro-Israel, anti-Arab. Be pro-both! The Arabs are just as precious to Jesus as the Jews. How do I prove that? Isaiah saw it! Isaiah **saw** it. Long years ago he said it, and made a remarkable statement and we pro-Israelites might want to remember it...do well to remember this. "In that day shall Israel be the third with Egypt and Assyria, even a blessing in the midst of the land, whom the Lord shall bless, saying, Blessed be Egypt, My people...and Assyria, the work of My hands... and Israel, mine inheritance." So it levels up Egypt and Arabia with Israel in the blessing. We proud people say we're for Israel, against Arab. No, no, we're for the lot because God loves them all equally. He's got precious purposes for Israel, for Arabs, just as much as He has for Israel. Remember that. Don't side with the flesh, "we're all for Israel against Arab." Be for both of them. Don't hang onto all this prophecy, interpretation. In most cases it's nonsense anyhow, just makes good reading, that's all. All this *Late Great Planet Earth* and nonsense. Burn it! And live with a **present Jesus** instead of a possible coming Jesus. He'll come one day; He'll come in His own way. That's all. And that way there will come blessing for all these people. Get that? Read it again. "In that day shall Israel be the third with Egypt and Assyria," Isaiah

19:24, "Even a blessing in the midst of the land, whom the Lord of hosts shall bless, saying, Blessed by Egypt, my people, and Assyria, the work of my hands, and Israel, mine inheritance." So the Lord's planned the blessing for the Mohammed of the world as for any other world.

So there passed fourteen years in which these godly people lived... and there's the birth and then the growth of his son, Ishmael, who lived with them...and yet they knew God hadn't spoken because He'd spoken to Hagar and sent her back, but He'd made plain to Hagar that her son was *not* the son He was talking about. He said, "You'll have a son and your son will be a wild man outside. He won't be the one we're talking about, not the son of the promise." So they knew that! Now, after fourteen years God is taking His servant through to *perfect* faith. Perfect faith is what's produced in action – faith which is produced in action.

It's called perfect faith because God came to Abraham fourteen years later, when he was ninety-nine years old, and said, "I am the Almighty God; walk before Me, and be thou perfect." This is mature and perfected faith and this is where James' type of faith comes in, which has works attached to it. And that's what the Bible calls perfect faith – faith which is produced, which produces works which are a product of the faith; an operation, which is a spontaneous operation *motivated* by the inner union relationship of faith. And this is what James talks about as "faith made perfect." He talks about it concerning the sacrifice of Isaac, but equally it can be said about the birth of Isaac, which is centered on the circumcision; it was also an outer action. And so he says, "Seest thou then," in James 2:22, "how faith wrought with his works"...Abraham..."and by faith, by works was faith made perfect." So perfect faith comes out in action...motivated action. Faith *is* action. It's manifestation. It's always that. It isn't just some theoretical spiritual relationship. It comes out in *physical and practical* manifestation...and by works is faith made perfect.

And that's where Abraham "was called a friend of God." You're God's friend *when He can begin to operate by you* all the way through, and come through in new manifestations. Then you're His friend, and you're His fellow…and you're going along with Him and He's enjoying you and you're enjoying Him. That's what's said there…that Abraham then "was called the friend of God."

Now, this standard presentation of productive faith in this 17th chapter, which was consummated in the birth of Isaac…is analyzed for us again by Paul giving us the details of how we operate productive faith. This is given to us in the end of Romans 4 where we're told what Abraham went through in this act of *reproductive* faith which ended in the child of the **impossible**…when Abraham was ninety-nine years old and when Sarah was ninety years old, and birth was impossible! At that age he might be impotent, and she *certainly* couldn't have a child. So it wasn't a very natural condition in which this child of promise could be born.

Now it starts by a renewal of God's confirmation to a person… what He's doing; what we know He's doing. So it's *inner* confirmation. That's where it says that God began to talk to Abraham and reveal His face – which is symbolizing cutting out outer things, *rational* appearances – revealed His face that God could talk to him. And God was renewing in *stronger terms* the general covenant He had given him. He'd said, "Now, the moment is come. I have made you the father of many nations." He hadn't said that before! "And I'm making an *everlasting* covenant with you." He deepened it. "I'm going to change your name as a token of that, to Abraham, which means a father of many nations."

You'll notice there…which is so helpful to faith…that God knows no future; He *only* knows a thing accomplished! So He said to Abraham, "I *have* made you a father of many nations." It's only happening now, thousands of years after this. At that time He knew everything of a father of many nations, he became a father of one son!

That's the basis on which we operate – that God *has done* a thing – that it's coming out because there's no future with God. In the third dimension there's no past or future; there's *only present* which includes the past and the future. And God speaks as a thing *done* when it won't come into historic manifestation maybe for several hundred years. That's how we operate by faith. We operate in the third dimension where there is neither past nor future, only present...and the past and future are *included in* the present. "I have made you a father of many nations." So He repeated in some stronger ways an everlasting covenant. Now this is moving you see...Abraham is a Spirit man now. He hadn't got to talk about a land...that was only a detail. I'm talking about an **everlasting** covenant; this is tremendous! That's going to be...it's our eternal purpose in this fatherhood of the family out of which the *whole world* will be blessed...in which the *whole world* will become the sons of God!

Now He said...you are now to take a step which manifests, to confess with your mouth, that this is the beginning of the 'chosen' people. Who are the chosen? We are the chosen people – the *temporary national chosen people* out of which the world of chosen people (which is ourselves) the **Israel of God** will come. So you are to perform the rite of *circumcision* – which is a symbol of cutting yourself off...a cutting process cutting yourself off from flesh relationships – because you're a Spirit person. You may operate *in* the flesh, but you're not operating *for* the flesh. You're operating for the Spirit. So it was to be in this covenant of circumcision...and now it was a very public thing which happened to Abraham at his age and all the family...all the people in the household. And he therefore was publicly announcing that this is the public pronouncement that *God's family is going to start now*...and His family are special people, and they are cut off from the world. And the outer symbol – like we have outer symbols that are in baptism (the old idea of baptism was circumcision) which can mean nothing, of course, unless there's circumcision of the heart – and the Bible took that up.

Moses took it up and said, "I'll circumcise your *heart*." It comes in Deuteronomy twice over. That's wonderful that Moses saw that! Your *real circumcision* is the heart. And then Paul took it up and in Romans 2 he said, "He is a Jew, which is one *inwardly*." So don't *mistake* Israel for Jews. Jews are...*we're* Jews! Don't make too much of this outer nation business. God may have some *temporary* purpose through it. It's only a little temporary purpose. We're not nation-minded and Israel-minded and Palestine-minded. We're **The Israel of God** minded – church coming out – which includes Egyptians and Assyrians, as well as Israel, and the whole lot! *That's* what we're interested in! And Paul hits it hard. No wonder they crucified him as fast as they could! "He is a Jew which is one inwardly; and circumcision is that of the heart; in the spirit and not in the letter; circumcision is that of the heart; in the spirit and not in the letter; which praise is not of men, but of God."

The *true circumcision*, of course, is – we have died in the heart, which is now Spirit to the old fallen image...in the new one. That's circumcision! But there are places in which in the human world...there are certain symbols, outer symbols are given, so we have our symbol of the circumcision, which is replaced for us by the baptism...and if you like, the continuation of the Lord's Supper. For *those* who get value out of them, bless you.

So he fulfilled this outer circumcision, but before he had done that there continued an inner vital transaction...a completion of a transaction with God, which was the critical moment – and that's where God took one step further in what He said to Abraham. "Not only do I make you a father of many nations" and so on, and have the circumcision, but "It's through Sarah your child's going to be born." Oh! That really was something! Right in the middle of all this, "You're to go circumcising." Before he'd *done* that He'd talked about it...before he'd done that!

God said to Abraham, "As for Sarai, thy wife, thou shalt not call" herself Sarai but Sarah, which is a "Princess." She was to be a Princess now. "I will bless her, and give thee a son also of her: yea I will bless her, and she shall be a mother of nations; and kings of people shall be of her." Now Abraham had risen to his feet by now; when he heard, he went bang on his face on that one! A second time over Abraham fell upon his face...and he laughed.

God loves honest laughing. The difference between Sarah's laughing and Abraham's laughing was Abraham *knew* himself and his *freedom*, and said "Of course I'll laugh. What fool could believe that?" Sarah, because she *didn't* know herself, thought she oughtn't to laugh and concealed it. He said, "Of course I'll laugh!" She thought she *ought* to be a self-righteous Sarah. A *self*-righteous people don't laugh at God's promises...and hide it when you *do* laugh. So the difference between Sarah's laugh and Abraham's laugh (she laughed behind the tent door and got exposed by it) was Abraham's was open. "All right! Who's going to believe that stuff? I'll have a good old laugh on that one!"

God *loves* honesty! He loves you to say what you love, because you're being *yourself*. You're not trying to fix things up. If you feel like laughing, you laugh. If you're hurt, you're hurt. If you're worried, you're worried. Don't kick about and say you're not. That's freedom! Sarah, who hadn't yet learned to accept self...her self still *ought* to be a bit better. She wanted to go and *hide* the fact that she laughed at God. "Mustn't laugh *at* God; that's naughty." That's all this 'pious' church stuff! So she hid it. It wasn't the laughing that was wrong; it was the hedging behind the laugh which was wrong. Are you trying to hide your laugh because you think you are on the "ought not" level...you ought not to laugh, **or** you *expose* your laugh because you are on the "do what you like" level and enjoy a laugh? So Abraham laughed!

And that precious Abraham...always a lover...he said, "Oh, Ishmael, remember Ishmael." "Yeah, I remember Ishmael (God blesses.) I remember Ishmael. But that's not the one Abraham. That's not the one. I've heard you," He says. "I have blessed him and made him fruitful." So God blesses Abraham. He *blesses* the Muslims...doesn't curse them.

"My covenant will I establish with Isaac." That's a *new* name. "Thou shalt call his name Isaac," He said, which means laughter, "and I will establish My covenant with Isaac, which Sarah shall bear at this set time next year. According to the normal biological process you will have this son." He got done talking with Abraham, and God went out from Abraham...and Abraham then circumcised the whole family as a demonstration of what He'd done.

Behind that is this whole process of *how you do believe God*...and that is given to us by Paul in Romans 4 as a standard illustration of what believing means...and he says first of all it *starts with* a *word from God*. You get this in Romans 4 when he's talking about "the just live by faith," – that Abraham is the father of faith, and this is how you believe. He says, "See what Abraham did?" He says it starts by a word *from* God. It says Abraham "against hope believed in hope, that he might become the father of many nations, according to that which was *spoken*. So shall thy seed be." Just simple. It starts by being something in which you see to be what *God* will do. So it's got to start *there*. That's, of course, they hadn't got over Hagar. They hadn't got that word from God, so it sent Abraham into confusion. *Now*, God has said it!

Now, you see that means 'attuned' ears doesn't it, and 'opened' eyes? This is where, I think, *we* are moving on in this life. Certainly, I suppose we *would* say many of us who are, don't get within hearing and seeing distance of this. It's absurdity to them! Maybe some of us here, I don't know. You hear with your ears, but you *see*...to see God say, "I'll do something which is impossible"...you're getting somewhere! "I'll do it *by you*. Now, this is the point, Abraham. You are to have a son and it's going to be Sarah's son." That's ridiculous! "I at my age and Sarah at her age?" It's ridiculous! So this is God saying, "*I'll do it* by you."

Now I don't think many of us are *awake* to that, because if you are you'd be sitting up straight. You'd be conscious in your *own* lives. Are you? I was challenged with this years ago. I learned this with Rees Howells. That's why Rees Howells is my Melchizedek...because the time came and God came and said "I'll do it by **you**." Well!

Our founder, who was the only person that was known in our mission, was dead and he'd been *so operating from God* that people threw him out as a hopeless person. So he was fanatic...and we were fanatics with him! Everybody deserted us. We had thirty-five missionaries on the mission field. They had eight dollars each for that month. That *month*! All they had to live by was eight dollars. And my wife and I had come home to carry on this commission to get the word evangelized.

Now then, you see we're for it. That's when the Lord speaks to you. That was *our* commission. **God said.** What did He say? Well, you listen to God. We didn't have a vision; we had an inner recognition. What is it? What? We listened to God because God said, "What did *I tell* your founder *I* was to do?" Our founder was C. T. Studd. When he worked alone in Africa with nothing – no church behind him, supposed to be a dying man, called crazy for going. They warned young university men in those days not to listen to him...because he was too attractive to them... otherwise they'd go and be mad with him, so they mustn't listen to him. So he went alone. Even his wife was an invalid in her own bed, and he left her. And the last thing in England – the people came and said to him, "You aren't even a Christian to leave your wife in that condition."

And he said, "*God's* told me I'd go. If Jesus Christ be God and has died for me, no sacrifice can be too great for me to make for Him." So he had nothing. And in *that condition* God said, "Oh, this trip...it *isn't only* for the heart of Africa; it's for the whole unevangelized world." Well, the *whole unevangelised world* is pretty big!

But, this is a whole unevangelised world that includes India and Indonesia and Thailand and Japan and Africa, and ooh...some size! Now Studd began just in the heart of Africa. That's big enough when you're sitting there, but there's only one little spot...a few hundred miles this way and that...that's all. It's not only that...for the heart of Africa...for the whole unevangelized world! Then he added (he wrote this back to us. I wasn't there then. It was *before* I was there) that *to the human reason it sounds ridiculous*, but *faith laughs at the impossibility and cries it shall be done!* **Faith laughs at the impossibilities and cries it shall be done!** Now that's from the *general* attitude...like Abraham and his *general* promises.

"Wow, they're all right," we said. The *particular* is the problem. When it comes to the particular, it's the problem. Those are the general. Well, that's something to believe the general. Can you believe the *general*...that this was a general fact that happened? The *particular* came about sixteen years later when Studd died. He'd burned himself out, and gone so far from God that people thought he was crazy. And he left this tremendous fruit in the heart of Africa. When he died there, *all he'd done* was the heart of Africa. He hadn't done any of the other countries at all. And here we were handed over the commission, my wife and I, and the 35 people in mid-Africa with their eight dollars each for the month. That's all they had and that was the days of the Depression.

Now, you see, *that's* what I mean by being **confronted**. When you're confronted...*now* what are you going to do? I'm convinced in many ways, God gives this to each of us in our own way if you can see it, but you've got to be in hearing distance; God's got to *get* you within hearing distance. Maybe He's come, and He's going to do some of the earlier practical work in this first to clear us up, so we're Spirit people. When you're a Spirit person you 'hear' in *Spirit ways*, of course...and *these* are Spirit ways.

Well, of course we were cornered! We *had* to walk this life; we were cornered. We were cornered! What can I do? What did I say *God* said to us? What did I say to your father? Who will evangelize this world? How are you going to do it? That's how we were *confronted to find out* **how** you operate faith. But it starts with something specific, when the Spirit says, "That's what I'll do by you." Of course that may repeat through the years...different things, but I don't know. Maybe most of our lives in some *particular* thing...and then other things as well; I don't know.

This was what bothered Abraham. Now the way he went in his believing was he was not *weak* in faith, because he didn't consider his own body...or in some verses that say he did consider...but, if he did start by considering he didn't go on considering it. Now, see weak in faith means you've got plenty of faith, but not in *that* situation! We *are* a people of faith. Everybody's a 'people of faith'. They all say we're a people of faith. OK, so say you're a person of faith…you're weak in faith…not *this* faith, but it's a question of "Have you faith **there**?" You're weak in faith unless you can say, "In *this* situation **God's** going to do what *cannot* be done!"

Now, you look weak in faith when you're facing up to that, because it means you say, "It can't be!" That's your start. Your *self* cannot believe it, "It can't be, but I'm *not* taking that!" That's "considering not your body as good as dead." You start from the negative, "This is ridiculous! It can't happen! But God has said this is to happen, so I'm not considering." This is where you pass out of the *reason*, the thing which caught them over Hagar. *Reason* said, "Find *another means* of getting a baby. If I can't help him, find another moral means in getting one." So reason always finds this one out, and then we live all the time by it. All the time we get caught up in it, because the smallest things you are operating by, "What? Where on earth in that? I'm stuck. I'm stuck." I'm talking here about big things. It can happen in small things. I can say, "See? This, of course, is given to us as a biggie…this." Now, in that weakened faith, when you say, "No, I'm not going to. I'm not going to be controlled by what appears to be and what is…and that's it. I'm not going to be controlled by these *appearances*." If I'm not controlled by the *appearances*, what am I controlled by?

Paul makes the other statement. He says, Abraham "staggered not at the promise of God through unbelief." Staggering is to be shaken by something. Staggering is *something*…a blow is struck you…Oh, for goodness sake! You haven't; you're not…knocked down. You say, "Wait a minute. Who's going to take that?" The next step of Abraham's faith was "I do take that. I do take that; I won't say it can't be." It's ridiculous, but I not only don't become a self which thinks it's ridiculous…I also say, "What God said, He'll do; **He'll do**. I'm not being staggered." Now that's the next stage. You replace your rejection, if you like, for being staggered by the appearance, but don't consider that. And you're equally not staggered by the thing which *God says* He will do; that's what

He'll do! That's how we went through in our own affairs, of course. We took this up, and that's how the work's become what it is today.

Having done that…the third stage given us here in verse 20, "was strong in faith, giving glory to God." "He staggered not at the promise of God through unbelief, but was strong in faith, giving glory to God." Giving glory is outer of course. Glory comes out. Giving glory is not inner. It's not inner at all in how you give it; you give it outer. Giving glory means he *praised*; he came out with it. He said, "It's all right. *God's going to do that.*" Now then, that is being strong in faith. You come out, and you're on the limb and you say, "God said that is going to happen." Other people know it now. Now you come out. You've walked out onto the tightrope.

That's strong in faith, giving glory to God. Now the giving glory to God is this, "Oh, I'm saying God's going to do that; it's a done thing. I am saying so, and I'll let you know that I've said so." That's this faith. That's what we did at that time when we said, "Ok, now God's going to begin to make straight in His ways this year, giving us what is impossible, not only supply our needs, supply new workers and so on." And we declared, "By the end of this year the first ten will come, the next year twenty-five will come, next year fifty will come, next year seventy-five will come," and they came step by step! We moved out every time by giving glory to God by the statements of faith, and of course, lots of other things since then. And in doing that you get the inner witness…"being fully persuaded." By giving glory to God there comes back to you then the reflex action, the fullness of faith…and that's it! God's going to do it. He's able to do what He says He will…and do it! Now that is presented to us as the analysis of what practical believing is.

There comes now a…shall I call it another interlude…in Abraham's life which again relates back unkindly for Lot, and exposes…opens something of the principles of intercession, and also has its most important objective in preparing Sarah to be the mother of Isaac which, as we see, is a total physical impossibility! So there turn up these three men...one who is spoken of "as the Lord" and the other two, who moved on to visit Lot...were angels. I can't make any more differentiation than that, which is all that's told us. They came as men and Abraham offered them very gracious hospitality. I reckon that he sensed *in* them something different, because of the very special welcome he gave them, and the meal he provided for them...even doing it with his own hands, and going and fetching the calf which had been the center of the feast and so on. So he took very special care of them. I think this is the case the Hebrew writer refers to when he says, "You will entertain angels unawares when you entertain people."

Of course, we entertain sons of God unawares...and we aren't so unaware, either, are we? And he started with what was his...certainly his *major* objective...because the great objective was that there should be the birth process through which all His plan of the ages should be fulfilled in the coming of the last Adam and the new race. And so he started off by speaking about Sarah who, according to the customs of those days, didn't eat with them and was behind the tent door...I suppose a canvas tent door, where he spoke right out, of course, because he intended it to reach her...that she would have a son. And that's why it specifically says that she had the change of life anyhow and she must have been...she's ninety! And so she had the obvious reaction – she laughed within herself.

Now, this was one of the many ways in which God exposes to us our *misunderstanding of the self,* as if the self should change. It *shouldn't* do this; it *should* do the other. That's when we live under this law...this law of life...when we condemn ourselves because we're this, and trying to be that and can't be – the Romans 7 life. And Sarah laughed.

Now, of course she hadn't got it clear that true sonship is God living His life through our normal humanity, and using *our normal humanity's reactions* as the *agents that express **His** reactions.* She obviously felt guilty that she had laughed, because she evidently *understood* that this was the Lord. He'd made Himself known by then because it says, "The Lord spoke to Abraham," and said, "Why did Sarah laugh?" And said,

"Is anything too hard for the Lord?" And repeated that He'd come, and in due course that she'd have a son. Now, then because she'd got this *false concept of a self* which *shouldn't* do things, and you're wrong if you respond to your *human* reactions, she denied it. "Oh, I didn't laugh." Because you preserve your own false righteousness...because she had laughed inside herself. That's where she was caught! She'd not laughed outwardly like Abraham had, so she thought she could kid God and kid him by, "No, I didn't laugh," but she'd laughed inside... but God said, "You did laugh." Now, Sarah was an honest woman. She's was God's woman. She'd gone along...so when the chips were down, she'd respond to light and she saw!

Said nothing about it...except this marvelous change in Sarah which is so beautifully picked up by the Hebrew writer, because God's *always busy justifying* people...not condemning them. He loves to justify His people – to be proud of what they do...is responsive of the Spirit in them. So it says what is never said here, verse 11, "Through faith also Sarah herself received strength to conceive seed." **Through faith.** "And was delivered a child when she was past age, because she had judged Him faithful who had promised." Well, she *just* laughed. So, you see the change? She didn't judge Him faithful; she judged Him ridiculous...*until* she suddenly saw! "You did laugh." "Oh, God knows what I am, and it isn't a question of what I am, it's a question, all right, if *God said* it."

And she moved up, and she was able to see the difference between the *human self* which had its *normal reactions*...and *her self as a container of the divine self,* which always had been so...she just hadn't seen it. She had moved into what we call the union relationship. And so she had faith now. *Now* God's going to operate by *His faith* in her. Yes, it's true, and that means she took it, because it says she judged Him faithful...when she'd just judged Him ridiculous. Now she judged Him faithful...so we know this change of the operation, free operation of the Spirit by her had now taken place and it affected her physically. So here's a good evidence that faith does affect you physically because it says, "Through faith she received strength to conceive seed." So it wasn't just a normal bodily condition which made it impossible. Something happened to her bodily condition *through recognizing the life of God* which caused her very organs to alter, to function against nature.

So I think it covers very much the whole question of physical faith – physical health. And when, instead of fussing around my physical condition I say, "OK, I've got a physical condition, temporarily anyhow. What I am is in God's perfect life. I walk in the positive. I see myself in God's perfect life. I'm not seeing this other thing. I'm seeing this." As I do that, at perhaps the same time I say, "Well, Lord I'd like to see You, but it probably means…now I take it *You're* going to fiddle with this thing too, change that thing." Your eyes are not on the change, but on God. Your eyes are not on how do you change. You keep saying, "I'm in *God's life*, and, *because* I'm in God's life I'm expecting that this change will take. Now I'm not looking at the thing I'm expecting. I'm looking at the fact I'm in *God's life*…(I'll not skip there or I'll get back to looking at self again, and when I do that I think that's a way.)…in many times the ways in which the new life operates me physically, you know. There are what we call healing's, certainly took place in her, didn't it, biologically?

Now, before that birth took place there is this final bringing in by the Spirit of Abraham for God's other beloved servant, beloved son Lot…and God loved him, and so God wasn't going to have him torn up by the devil. And, again, one of the most striking things, exposures you get in the New Testament, which runs so contrary to our judgmentalism. We say, "Oh, look at Lot; he's bad," and all this. Not necessarily. The Bible sees him as a just and precious person, which is very striking. It comes in the one letter which the liberals tend to say, "Well, it wasn't really written at all." They like to eliminate 2 Peter, as if it's not a right epistle.

It has some great insights in it, and this is one of them. In 2 Peter it says, God turned "the cities of Sodom and Gomorrah into ashes," in 2 Peter 2, "condemned them with an overthrow, making them an

example unto us that after should live ungodly; and delivered just Lot."
Mind you, He says that Sodom and Gomorrah will be more justified
than those who had Christ and rejected him. God still shows mercy. If
you move over into…it's in many old gospels that where He's speaking
about Capernaum and these places who rejected Him in His miracles,
He said, "Verily I say unto you," Matthew 10:15, "it shall be more tolerable for the land of Sodom and Gomorrah in the day of judgment,
than for that city." So there's *toleration in judgment.* Did you get that?

Judgment isn't so complete as we think. We think, "Oh, oh, oh,
they're finished!" Or they're set as an example because we get the
consequences of what we are…so if you go that way you'll get banged
about. And so they got the brimstone and the fire and they are set
as examples of wicked men, but God doesn't see wicked men. He
sees precious people *going wrong.* He sees some of us going wrong.
He doesn't see perverted Sodomites. He sees *precious* people going
wrong. Why? And here in Matthew He says, "It will be more tolerable
for them in the day of judgment than for you." That's toleration for
all men. That's pretty good, isn't it? We wouldn't say it's so, we'd say,
"If anybody's damned, it's they." God doesn't say so. This is **our** *judgmentalism,* isn't it?

And on Lot then…he goes on and says when He made this example of Sodom and Gomorrah…He "delivered just Lot, vexed with
the filthy conversation of the wicked: For that righteous man dwelling
among them (among the Sodomites) in seeing and hearing, vexed his
righteous soul from day to day with their unlawful deeds. The Lord
knoweth how to deliver the godly out of temptation, and to reserve the
unjust unto the Day of Judgment to be punished." Isn't that truth? So
all God sees about Lot is he is His precious, justified, righteous person. That's not what we *usually* think of as wrath.

We need to have a *new sight* of people don't we? And He judges the
secrets of men; Lot's heart was set on God. Now, in this life he never
got through, only in a very painful way, to deliverance from things of
time and sense. He wasn't governed by them, because they vexed him.

It isn't wrong just to have riches, and so on. That's not wrong in itself. It's not the highest, because we've got higher riches and we live by the higher riches, but it isn't wrong to have them. The wrong of Sodom wasn't because it was rich. It was because they were *perverted*, because they were sexual perverts. That was their wrong...not because they were rich. So it wasn't wrong in *that* sense that Lot wanted to be where it was nice. That's not the highest, but it's not wrong. But where the perversion came, it vexed him.

Now, vexation isn't fun. It's being hurt without deliverance. That's the death of living *half-way*. If you're half-way you get hurt *without* deliverance. If you're *the whole way* you're hurt and you move into deliverance...and get other people delivered! That's why I said yesterday...I think..."By God's grace" I was never bothered by the pulls of the flesh in the army...which were pretty available when you're in the military mess in Britain in those days (it was there) because I had a bigger thing, so they didn't bother me. I wasn't vexed in that sense, because I was witnessing...and kicked out for being a witness! That didn't matter. So if the vexation comes...if you don't like a thing and you're under it, "Now, how do I get on top of it?" Well, better be vexed than give into it anyhow.

So our precious Lot never gave in. He was continually, daily, vexed. He couldn't stand this filthy stuff around him, but *because* he was mixed up his testimony wasn't totally clear. The whole of Lot couldn't come through with power, so he couldn't know how to get his own relatives or anybody else saved. He was still God's precious person...and really we misuse it, perhaps often, into thinking this was a terrible, lost person. No, he was a tricked, carefully saved person! This is a very good illustration *not* of how a person is lost...how they are saved...how *God* kept him in that situation, and *wouldn't* let him go. That's a very strong point for us – to hold onto people, isn't it? God might; they may run into adultery and something, but God *won't* let them go. They're God's! And He put His protection around this just Lot, and did it in secret as he reacted against all this sin around him. But he wouldn't be, couldn't be, a happy person because the Holy Spirit hadn't got the *whole* of him!

And so this judgment fell. *Behind it lay the intercession of Abraham.* Now all we're going to say is that God *causes* us to *stand in the gap* for those He puts across our path. We obviously can't stand in the gap for everybody. Jesus didn't. Jesus didn't *appear* to be a world figure; He appeared to be merely a Jew figure, but He was after the lost sheep of His own. Didn't seem to bother about the world, and yet He *was* **the** *world* figure! So you only reach those who are within your immediate reach. You may have them by the Spirit...that includes everybody... then the *practical*. Now, of course, Lot was within Abraham's reach, so Abraham's truth now was *fulfilled*.

This was the *first known* presentation in the Bible of the intercession from *prayer* action – because intercession involves putting *yourself* in the *place* of those for whom you intercede, and going to any price to fulfill it. Abraham fulfilled that when he rescued Lot, of course, when he risked his whole life to rescue him from those kings. So he really put his life at stake for Lot. He'd do *anything* for Lot. This was the prayer part of intercession. We mustn't think intercession is **just** prayer. It's not! It's a starting in prayer combined to the fact that "I'm available. Anything You can tell me to do that will save that person, here I am," which he had done in this case. He'd fulfilled the physical intercession by his rescue. Now this was the *spiritual* form of the intercession. Being the first presentation of the boldness of an intercessor, Abraham approached it by *stages*. We must remember he was an *explorer*. He was only *finding* the grace of God. He was only beginning to find out this was God operating in him.

How far did he know things like that? It's marvelous what he did know! And of course he *knew* it was God, but how far he would understand what we would claim, what is said now – that it's God *getting* something *through us*...and God intending to do it. I don't know because he made this step by step approach, almost gingerly, but he was determined to do it...so he had the determination. He was going to do it! What he was asked, of course, was to get Lot rescued, because God had said he was taken…these two, it's the angels now… (No, no, it's the Lord) the angels are moving on to see Lot. And He stood. The Lord stood with Abraham, and reminded him that he was the main heir and so on.

Now, at this moment…in the Spirit Sarah rose up and said, "There sometimes must come a division." You see, always the freedom of the Spirit? Sometimes it's wrong; sometimes it's right. You're *not* under law. You're *under the guidance* of the Spirit! And there comes a time it's wrong to have put Hagar out, that pregnant girl, and God rebuked them by having mercy on Hagar and sending her back in a new spirit living among them. Now, the time came when the *true family* was to begin to be expressed, to be seen as a family – the Abraham, Isaac, Rebekah – and the whole way through. Now, this was to be, for special reasons, a separated family. In the life of Moses I discuss how there had to be this *national preparation* with a view to the future *world* nation – the body of Christ. This is the '*had to be*' way in which it began.

So now it became necessary for the next. Sarah didn't always call him lord…told him to obey *her*! So you wives don't always call your husbands lord. Tell them to obey you, because it was Sarah said to Abraham, "Cast her out." I *like* that one because I like *free* women! And don't leave them in this *submission* stuff. You're to submit to the Lord as the Lord tells *you*. That's submission! Therefore, in so far as you have a family, when you know it fits right to you with the husband doing certain things…and the wives. OK, you accept that, because the Lord tells you the family works harmoniously with the husband doing certain things, and the wife and the children, and you *agree together*. In that sense you can call it *submission one to the other*. You can't *submit* to each other! You **cooperate** with each other to run a home, all right. Same on a national level or a mission level. We're *free* to work certain ways in which to cooperate, and agree to this principle and that. No, don't submit to each other; we agree together to submitting if you like to each other to make a thing work. *That's* submission to the Lord, and that's quite a different thing! But the moment the Lord says, "Don't submit," you *don't* submit. The moment you're told to order your houses about, you order them about in the name of the Lord. And here it is...and that supposedly meek Sarah says, "Cast them out now." And she was right! Can't *have* this now...can't have a mixture between *flesh* boasting that it's part of the promises of God. **It isn't!** Flesh and Spirit...divide up. So, in this case, *she* was God.

But, as usual with Abraham...beautiful tenderness. He was grievous. Always *loved*. Beautiful man, wasn't he? Sarah was a bit tough, and this thing was grievous when Sarah said, "Cast them out," but *she knew the Spirit*, you see. Of course, God actually said it to him too... God *confirmed* it here. God confirmed to Abraham, "Don't let it be grievous, because your seed is Isaac, and your seed must be preserved now and in the pure line. But," He says, "I'll bless her and I'll bless her children" (that's Hagar); "I'll bless her." That's God *too*.

And careful, loving Abraham stocked them up with grub and had given her a bottle of water...a wineskin of water, I suppose and bread... put it on her shoulder and sent them out. And there was the Lord, and when they came to a place where it seemed there was no more water (where they couldn't find it before) she found some spring of water...didn't seem to find this time and she gave the child up...thought it would die...wept. God heard the voice of the lad, and came again and spoke to Hagar, and said, "OK, Hagar." And she *saw* all the water there. Whether it was there before, but didn't see it...or whether it seemed not to be...I don't know which. And there she started her life, out of which came the Ishmaelites...and in a previous occasion she'd actually said, "**God** caused me to *see* Him." That was beautiful; that this pagan Hagar...she said, "Thou God, seest me. Have I also here looked after Him that seeth me?" Not she sees God; God sees *her*! Isn't that beautiful? "When God sees me." That's what grace is isn't it? Grace is "God sees *me*. God's loved *me*." That's the grace in the early time when He first met Hagar. This is the second time. We hear no more now of Hagar.

There was one last necessary confirmation – a demonstration of what the purposes of God are...Himself expressed in living form through humans, the two in **union** – *Himself through humans*! He must *be Himself through humans*...not *just* humans...in which God led Abraham to a final act which would clarify for all future centuries the difference between a work of God (which the church is a work of God, but it is a *human* work and can become *just* a human work) and *the real thing*...which is the Spirit of **God** *in humans*...that they're humans, but the Spirit of God *is in the human*...and *that* always has to be preserved!

So the church is not works of God. The church is groups, denominations. They're the Spirit of God *in people*...and the church is always the Spirit of God in people...and *where the people become the people of God* **without** *the Spirit of God,* the rejection has to take place and the division has to take place. That's why there always are "renewals" taking place. That's why we watch with interest these renewal's coming. I'm not so sure whether your denominations are dying or in becoming world renowned...your renewals are coming, because God's not in denominations. He's in *people* in whom the Spirit is, and He has to come in new ways to express – "This is what I am. I am the Living Person, a risen Person in human bodies" and I'm seeing through the human bodies where it's the Living Christ in the human body...not the human body that says it's Christ, and operates **as if** it's Christ...and *it's just become some* **religious** *form."*

Then this was the final height into which He called Abraham. Now, this is 'temptation upwards'. The temptation is up to, not down from. Temptation is tempting me to move up...move up...go on higher! This is what God's after...tempt me up to new callings of obedience and faith...and reproduction which follow. *Our whole life is to be lived on the tempted level – being tempted that* **God** *may do something more through us.* That's real temptation, that part!

See, all of Jesus' temptations centered around [flesh]...although Satan tried to pull Him down...His temptations weren't flesh as we call flesh. He was tempted to utilize God for *personal* purposes. Utilize *God!* "Use *Your* power to turn God's power to turn stone into bread. *You* ought to run the world. *You* ought to be known for who *You* are. Judge from the temple and the people will see God preserved here." They're all up and up...because in Jesus' whole Spirit was elevated. So He was to be one of God's agents...so it wasn't the other things which were pulling at Him. They may have done as well, because He was tempted in all points. The temptation's on *another level* of 'self ways' in which He could complete the purposes of God, and He had to decide between 'self ways' and God's ways...which had to start, of course, by the redemptive process *before* there could be the renewal process.

So with Abraham. God tempted Abraham, "Come up, now, higher." And he was to sacrifice his son as a burnt sacrifice. Loved...Abraham loved, but he always had a *greater* love. So there is a beautiful balance here. We have a human love. There is always a greater love. Our *real* love is God, but we fit our human love into our God love. That doesn't mean there isn't room for the human level also. And so it's said here, that God said to Abraham, "Thine only son, whom thou lovest. I know how you love him. You love Ishmael. How much more do you love Isaac?" He may be about fourteen years of age by now. "Now, take him and burn him." That's something! Not "slay him." "Burn him." That's Baal worship isn't it, burning children? And he was to act like a Baal worshipper and burn his kid. Some temptation isn't it? "Burn him upon the mountains, which I'll tell you."

This is where God's **call** is...may take us *beyond the ethical.* That's why that great book by Kierkegaard, written on "fear and trembling"... the agony of Abraham in the decisive moments of faith in this case... was he a murderer or was he guided? He was being guided to *act* like a heathen worshipper, and burn his own son as a sacrifice to God...or Baal? Was he deceived? Was he crazy? Was it God's calling?

I don't think whether beforehand Abraham had a...... It doesn't record whether he had any other travail before he came to see that this *was* God's calling, and that *God* would provide a sacrifice in place of Isaac. Now that's what he saw. This is a way more purely in faith. He hadn't got one *ground*...the proof he hadn't got one ground – he went to kill Isaac. He took the knife to kill him, so he wasn't trying getting out of it. He hadn't got one earthly ground that it would happen! If God told him to kill Isaac and then burn him as a sacrifice, he would do so.

But, beneath or above that, he had the *faith* that God had a *substitute* sacrifice. How do we know? Because when he got to the mount after three day's journey with the two servants, he said to the servants, "You stay here with the ass. Abide ye here with the ass, while I and the lad go yonder and worship, and come again unto you." "Abide ye here with the ass, said unto the young men, and I and the lad will go yonder and worship, and come again unto you." Therefore it was a settled thing in the substance of Abraham's faith that there was to have been a substitute sacrifice, because Isaac was to come *back*! Alternatively, God would raise him from the dead. It *could* have been...a burnt sacrifice...it *could* have been. But what he did see was the Holy Spirit coming again in a human form. This is the thing. It's a wholeness!

So Abraham took that journey of three days...because I think it's obvious from what is said in Hebrews 11, that Abraham saw the implications of it – that very easily a work of God can become just a work... without God. This can be some *thing* which came into being through God miraculously...the God part of it is lost...and it just becomes a 'thing' which is operating. Now, see, this son had grown to fourteen years of age. That's why I don't think Sarah knew. She was naturally very proud of her son. It was what she had called "Laughter." She had cast out the wrong one so *she'd* got the thing going...and maybe Abraham was touched too. He loved him. But the *danger* was, "This is the son," not "This is God in the son." Now that's it – there's *only God* through humans! Anything else is a lie! It's back to the old thing...it's slipping into the old one again.

And that has to be preserved, always…repeatedly preserved all through history. It's always being missed unless *picked up* again. What starts to be *God* in a person becomes a 'thing'. "Here's *my* church." Certainly of God, but the church has gone just a *dead thing* with this – for its organization – mainly dead. There has got to be *continual* resurrections and revolutions in every church. All that must be discarded. That's why I shout out against churches as I do – because most of them either must have resurrection and revolution…or be discarded, because God is not in a hollow; it isn't a *hollow* body. It's the *Living God* in the body! Now, see, Abraham saw that, and he saw that all that mattered to the future was that Isaac, who was the expression of the Living God and heir, all they could see was the Living God in Isaac… not Isaac. And they had slipped into, at least maybe Sarah, because they were, "Oh, *our* Isaac, oh, *our* precious Isaac." A little slipping away thinking there's only…yes, a detail…he's just a person. What matters is **The Person** in the human.

Now it is God *in* person…it isn't God *outside* persons. It's God related in union. He expresses through persons. So we've got to be in the balance. And so Abraham saw it! And the *proof* he saw it…tremendous! He saw – very well, if necessary he would burn Isaac up. It could even be, because God's already brought Isaac into being out through an impossible couple…parents…it *could be* He'd do something again, and somewhere bring a burned body alive again. Could be! Or he may have seen that because, when Isaac said to him, "Where is the sacrifice?"…"God will provide." I think it meant he *saw* it's not going to be Isaac. "It's all right son, God will provide." But it didn't stop him from binding him up and sticking the knife on him. He meant business! He was a practical…this is practical faith…this is perfect faith, which comes out in business to its *last limit* of God's calling! In that last calling, out comes God! *Tremendous* you know!

And so Hebrews gives us, again, the interpretation. "By faith Abraham, when he was tried, offered up Isaac; and he that had received the promises," against promises as it were, "offered up his only begotten son." The promises were through the son! Now he's going to kill the son through whom the promises are going to come. "Of whom it was said, that in Isaac shall thy seed be called; accounting that God was able to raise him up, even from the dead, from which also he received him in a figure." Because Abraham *saw.* It wasn't a question of the body of Isaac; it was a question of the Living God expressed *through* the body of Isaac. *This* is where he must keep his sight set. And…but it must be through Isaac because he is the promised seed. That he knew! So he got a fixedness to him…He's the promised seed, the promised son…yet he was to kill the promised son, because it must be *seen through all future ages* that it **isn't** the physical son. It's the God through the promised son. It's the God – *we* are the promised sons; it's **God** *through us!*

And all the time this fact to us must remain, "Is this God coming through our situations? Is this God coming through our classes and people? It's God coming through…*that's what it is!*" And sometimes sacrifices must take place. It's a question some of us who are involved in works of God quite rightly may be concerned about. I am about our own, because we're big now…about thirteen hundred missionaries all around the world…all sorts of things. I'm always going for it. And we keep care with our root, but I'm not always too happy…we are putting a little *too much respect* in an organization, and it must be killed. So God has to destroy agencies, and rebuild new agencies which means it's of the Spirit. Then, when they get hardened up, they're the ones kicking *us* out of the mess! *Destroy* that while it's kicking out another one!

And this was what this final act was. And on that act God…again for our sakes, not for His own sake…made the final confirmation with an oath, which also is taken up in the letter to the Hebrews. He confirmed this process with an oath – that this is an everlasting covenant and "through you and through your family" is going to come this blessing to the world which is going to end in a vast family of the world who are His sons…far more than we think…who are His *eternal* sons, who will be the *eternal* Israel – the eternal agency by which God will always be seen through eternity! So He had *confirmed* it with an oath.

God always puts things around, almost as it were, to save us *as if* God wanted to be *sure* Abraham loved him. Well, he knew that, of course, really. But for us all it was necessary for it to be seen that Abraham's love was not his son – it was the Living God, and the Living God's *eternal purposes in people.* So it wasn't really for God to test Abraham, as so many love to say. *He* knew that! But we all have to see it was so in a *practical* fact. So he went through his things…that we all may see when the chips are down…*it isn't Abraham's son, it's the Living God through His people!* And if He can't get through one person He gets through another person, and so on, to fulfill the purposes.

And so we get the final pattern-lesson taught us – watch out! When God has come through and you've been a reproducer of faith, and God has moved in and God has done things…now watch that the *things* that don't take the place of the Living God. The things that are only agencies, and they're only all agencies of the universe…**the Living Person through a living people**…*that's* all there is! And so part of your job, my job is to watch and see that it remains a Living Person through living persons, and doesn't become some organization which would begin to seek to get some pride in organization and operation… and then gradually the *Spirit's seeping out* and the body remains. And we must be prepared to be a carnifex to destroy the bodies when necessary; destroy the temples when necessary…that the **Living Temple** may remain!

And so I, frankly, I want…though I know I shouldn't, because I know I say things which offend my *own* people so much…I frankly want our whole church system – there's something *dead* about that whole business of this Sunday business – this Reverend So-and-So with two degrees appointed by man. Something *boils* within me. That's not reality! Some of them are getting over it, but not many. Some are…

some are…and so you get the *outburst* of youth today, and so on. *Thank God!* Because I *can't help* saying these things. I know if I'm wrong… if I offend, I offend. I don't think, personally, I'd be at ease to be a minister of a church built on those *old* set lies. I don't think I would. However, that's not the point. *The point is what we know through Abraham!*

ISAAC AND JACOB

We are studying some of the men whose lives are recorded for us, who were agents for the fulfillment of *further* stages in God's purposes. We have talked about Abraham. We will take a brief look at Isaac who was the child of the promise. Then we will move on from him to Jacob.

God manifests Himself in different forms and fulfills Himself in different ways by *every* personality because every personality is meant to be *totally* different. So Isaac is an entirely different kind of person from Abraham. Abraham was an originator; Isaac was a consolidator. God was fulfilling a necessary double purpose through His anointed servants which is *still true today*. Part is an earthly manifestation which is in earthly forms, because we are earthly people. But that is only symbolic – an allegory of the truth – for the *eternal* purposes of which these are merely a temporary phase. So He made it plain to Abraham that he was to be the father of a vast earthly family, revealed "as many as the sands of the seashore in multitude," and a heavenly family, "as many as the stars in the sky in multitude." There was to be the earthly family *and* the heavenly family. The people of the spirit *always* saw the heavenly family. The fact that he was forming an earthly family was only incidental to Abraham and Isaac and Jacob.

It was symbolized by the fact that in the land in which this family was to come into being, the land of Canaan, Abraham only lived in tents...he never built cities. Hebrews says that all his life he was "... dwelling in tabernacles with Isaac and Jacob, the heirs with him of the same promise, for he looked for a city which hath foundations, whose builder and maker is God."(Heb. 11:9-10)

It was **not** an earthly Jerusalem, **not** an earthly Canaan, but a *heavenly* city – which is the whole universe – and people to manage by His vast family of sons, who are ourselves. He looked for a heavenly inheritance. That's *very important* because you would think he would look for an earthly one.

"But now they desire a better country that is a heavenly one. Therefore God is not ashamed to be called their God, for He prepared for them a city." (Heb. 11:16)

It was *not* the present Jerusalem, but the *eternal* Jerusalem which includes all this vast family of redeemed sons and all that come out of them. People of the spirit are always heavenly people. They see the ultimate that spirits are persons, a vast family of millions of spirits who have new forms of bodies which are unlimited agents without time or space. They can go anywhere and do anything! The Bible says they will fulfill God's unlimited purpose throughout eternity.

Abraham *saw* that, but he had an earthly commission, also. He was to bring up a son, Isaac, as the next stage in the forming of the earthly family through which God could reveal Himself, and through which His total purposes in the *destruction* of the devil and *all* his works could come to pass...so that the family of sons could come into eternal being. Isaac's calling was to consolidate the beginning of the family in the land. He was not a man of *faith action,* but of *faith determination...* and there's a place for both. There are *exploits of faith* and there are *endurances of faith.* In Hebrews 11 we see the great exploits of faith: "By faith Abraham...by faith Moses...by faith Joshua..." There were also those who died having suffered all kinds of torture without receiving deliverance. *Theirs* was the endurance of faith.

Isaac's was not on that line. The only two statements about Isaac were in some sense passive. One was that he *knew* about his birth. The other was the miracle of his *acceptance* of being sacrificed. That was the moment when Isaac personally experienced who *he* was in God.

He was fourteen years of age. Now a lad of fourteen doesn't lay himself on an altar, let his father bind him, put a knife in him, and burn him for nothing! If he passively gave himself into Abraham's hands to be bound, laid on the altar with the knife raised and the fire there to burn him there was a *yielding there* to something beyond his body, to some purpose and promise of God in him. That's Isaac! It's quite plain that Isaac had an *inner* relationship with God or he *never* would have accepted that. Although perhaps that is the most dramatic positive record we have of Isaac's life. Even *that* in a sense was passive.

The only other thing said of him was that he was a mediator. He was a mystic. When Abraham sent to get his wife for him, Rebekah, the only comment made when Rebekah arrived at the tents of Abraham was that they saw this man out in the fields. It says, "Isaac went out to meditate in the field at eventide." (Gen. 24:36). Evidently he was a person who quietly walked with God.

That's really all that is told us of Isaac's life until we come to the dramatic event in which Jacob took the blessing from his older twin brother, Esau. However, before we look at that incident we need to look back at the birth of Jacob and Esau. This is picked up by Paul in Romans 9 and is often a point of controversy. There it says that before they knew good or evil, God had foreordained them. Historically there was only one statement showing foreordination and that was said to Rebekah in terms of nations coming and it was: "The elder shall serve the younger." (Gen. 25:23). There was nothing said about their *spiritual* condition.

The point Paul is making in Romans with such tremendous emphasis is the *total authority* of God, that what *God says* happens...and that there is only God. Added to that is a statement which Paul quotes in Romans from Malachi, the last prophet of the Old Testament, "Jacob have I loved, and Esau have I hated." That was *not said* at their birth, but was said by Malachi as being God's attitude towards Jacob and Esau. That gives a very good opportunity for the *natural man* to make an attack on God. The natural man includes most of our Biblical theologians, also. They say that God foreordains some to love and some to hate. What a God! If that was my God I'd change Him for a devil! There *cannot* be a God who can do *anything less* than perfectly love everything He makes. Otherwise He is not God! Could you, a person, make a thing to make a mess of it? If you cook in your kitchen you don't cook to make a mess, you cook to make a decent meal. Even a human doesn't produce a thing to make a mess of it, but to make the best of it. It's *ridiculous* to think of a God who makes people to damn them or hate them. It's impossible! He can only make people to love them, because that's **all** He is.

We all start as Esaus. What we have to learn is that we attribute *appearances* to God – not from His condition, but from our *own* condition. For instance, I attribute to God that He will punish me, because I think I need punishment. He doesn't punish, but *I'm* guilty. "Oh, I've broken the law. Surely He has a big stick!" I attribute a big stick to God. There's *no* big stick in God! Take another illustration. Jesus is occupied to the limit in preaching the gospel to crowds in a house. They gang around Him. Then the rumor comes that His mother and brethren are outside of the crowd and call Him to come and join them. (His brothers didn't believe in Him, they thought Him fanatical.) He turns and says, "Who are my mother and brethren? He that doeth the will of God is my brother."

Now that *appeared* to his mother and brothers like hate. Actually it was *perfect love*! If you follow the self-loving way you have chaos in your life because you're cut off from God, and you can interpret *that* as if God hates you. It's because *you* have put yourself in a condition in which God can't do anything else but take that position *with* you. He can't let hellish people into heaven. That's what it means by hate. It's what Jesus meant when He said, "You can't be my disciples unless you hate your father and your mother and your wife and your children and your houses and your lands." That's strong language! You're a Christian and yet you hate your father and mother? Hate your husband or wife? Hate your kids? What it is – that you have to walk *so* with God that if they try to pull you away you act as if you hate them. They *think* you hate them as you turn your back on them to follow the Lord. What *appears* to them as hate is really love because you're taking the way of life as against the way of death. In the way of death it looks *as if* you hate it. That's what hate means in that passage. There's not one iota of real hate in God. We're all shot with the spirit of Esau, but when we get saved we get the spirit of Jacob. Esau is the spirit of self-centeredness and we *all* start that way.

Now we move on to Jacob. Isaac will come back because of that famous incident of the blessing on the sons. All we are told about Jacob is that he was a plain man dwelling in tents. That was not very exciting. Esau was a hunter, the aviator, atomic scientist, All-American. He was somebody! But it was all flesh. If God has your spirit He can use your flesh, but He has to get your spirit *first*...and it is a lot more difficult if you have lots of flesh! Esau was 'sold' to the attractions of the world. He was a great hunter which was the excitement of those days. His friends were pagan women and he got into trouble by marrying one of them. He wanted *flesh*, not spirit, so he was a popular fellow! We need to watch our choices.

I've often noticed in our mission how we miss the best people because they don't look quite so likable as other people. You see that often in scriptures. Jacob lived in a tent with his mother, Rebekah. You can call him a mother's boy, if you like, but he turned out to be a he-man before he was finished. Jacob *knew* the truth. He knew that he was the anointed one with the birthright. God had said it to Rebekah and she told Jacob. He knew the birthright was his right.

When the moment came Jacob was in the kitchen making some lentil soup. Esau had come back from a big hunt totally exhausted. Spirit was contemptible to him for he cared only about his body. By **spirit** I mean the things of God...things of promise. Earth was everything to him. And this nice smell came to him when he got home. "Oh," he said, "I'm about to die. Give me some of that."

Jacob saw his opportunity. "All right," he said, "If you're about to die, and all you want is pottage; I want something else. You're going to die so give me your birthright." In a crisis you'll do what you *really are*, not what you make up in a moment. What was in Jacob was, "That birthright's mine. How will God do it? God said it is mine, but Esau is the elder son. Naturally it's Esau's...but it's really mine! How can it become mine?" You see, Jacob had a set of heart – a set of mind on God. Birthright meant God's promises, but God's promises didn't mean anything exciting down here on earth. It would not bring Jacob benefit now. It was the future promise of God...so only someone who could see God and His *eternal* purposes would be interested in it.

Esau's mind was set the other way on emphasizing the things of the flesh. So he said, "Okay, take it. It's nothing." And the Bible says, "He despised his birthright." (Hebrews 12:16) *God sees the heart.* This wasn't just a little slip on Esau's part. He was operating by *inner* purposes. We don't slip into these things because God operates by inner purposes. These are the purposes of life. So they made a covenant. That wasn't Jacob cheating, but *was* an act of faith – the fruition of faith. Esau had no business playing about with the birthright so when the right moment came Jacob took what he *should* have. That's royalty, not contempt! Never despise him, because he wasn't a cheat. He acted by *faith*!

We know he acted by faith because God justified Jacob. It came about this way: Isaac had a weakness in that he liked Esau more than Jacob. He liked the sport and he liked Esau's meat. Although he was a man of the spirit he had not had his *soul* dealt with yet. We do have weaknesses, but God *uses* weaknesses. *Weaknesses, or deviations, in the saint aren't the same as sins in the sinner.* We **are dead** to sin, but we *can* deviate in the flesh. That's another matter and God can use those deviations. We're going to see how, all the way through, God uses human deviations to fulfill His great purposes. God takes into account our weaknesses, so don't make too much of them. They are God's minor agencies...not major.

There came this crisis. Rebekah knew what Isaac was planning to do. Wives know these things! She knew God had told her that the blessing was to go to Jacob and that Isaac intended to give it to Esau. In those days the blessing was not a light thing, but was a prophetic word of how God was going to deal with that life. A whole lifetime would be a product of that word of faith! It was something like making a will. Isaac's eyes had grown dim and he was old. It speaks here as if he were about to die. Actually, he died forty years later because it says that Esau and Jacob met to bury him in Macpelah's tomb after Jacob had returned from Laban's with his large family. I wonder if Isaac's eyes got dim *because* he was doing wrong, and if he remained blind for forty years?

When Isaac thought the time had come he wanted to make a special feast of it, Esau was to go out and get a good hunt of venison, and at this feast he would announce the blessing which belonged to Jacob onto Esau. Since Rebekah saw this thing coming she was ready when the crisis came. I doubt that it was in one day that they made up this business of putting hairy hands on Jacob to fool Isaac into thinking he was Esau. Every *natural* man who hears this story says, "Oh, what a rotten cheat! What a liar! To say he's Esau when he is really Jacob and even to put goat's hair on his hands." But God justified him. How do I know? Because Isaac got a tremendous shock when Esau turned up and he found that he'd blessed Jacob instead. It says that "Isaac trembled exceedingly." (Gen. 27:33) I expect he did. But what Isaac trembled about was that *he had disobeyed* God, not that Jacob had cheated him. The Bible says that when Esau came in to receive the blessing...

"Isaac trembled exceedingly, and said,' Where is he that has taken venison and brought it to me and I have eaten all before thou, Esau, camest, and a blessing, yea, and he shall be blessed." Gen. 27:33

That's the proof! Isaac was a man of the spirit and he couldn't take it back. That's God! So God was justifying deceit!

Faith does twists. *Faith is not under law.* Flesh is under law. **We** are under no law. We follow the way God tells us even if it does have a twist in it! One queer twist was when *God* told Abraham to murder Isaac. *God* told Rahab to tell a lie and justified it. Rahab was a harlot living in Jericho, but she had a heart for God. She believed God when the others didn't and preserved the spies by lying. Hebrews 11 picks up Rahab and says; "By faith Rahab . . ." So God justifies lies!

Don't judge naturally! We're not under the Ten Commandments, but under love - and love *fulfills* purposes in strange ways sometimes. Isn't it interesting that God had the seed of Christ come through adultery! Tamar tricked Judah into fornication with her and out of that fornication came Perez, one of the forefathers of Jesus. Solomon was the son of Bathsheba, an adulteress. God is not like us. He picks up sins and makes something out of them...so don't make too much of sins. Make more of faith! Sin doesn't belong to our dimension; it belongs to another dimension. *We* are under freedom! Sins have purpose. We don't purpose to sin. We may be tricked into a sin but we don't purpose it.

So don't put Jacob down; put him up! He and Rebekah did the *right* thing in the *right* place. Isaac was to blame, not Jacob. Although Esau received a blessing also, the Bible says that Esau hated Jacob. In Hebrews 12:17 there's a comment on Esau weeping for his blessing, unable to get repentance. That wasn't repentance in Esau; it was that he couldn't get *Isaac* to repent and change. If Esau *had* repented it would have been the admission of God's word, which was that Jacob was to have the *top* blessing. He couldn't change Isaac's mind because *Isaac* couldn't change. Isaac confirmed what appeared like cheating and deceit and said, "That's right."

Esau said, "When the days of mourning are over (thought his father was going to die soon, though he didn't die for forty years) then I'll slay my brother, Jacob." (Gen. 27: 41). Watch how God uses what appears to be a twist of the flesh. Esau's hate and murderous spirit ended in Jacob's being sent off to get a wife from whom he should get a wife – his *own* people, which was his mother's brother, Laban. Out of that came the development of the family of God. The wives and eleven sons and one daughter of Jacob were a product of this 'faulty' situation. If it had not existed he *never* would have gone there and remained so long.

The Bible says that when Rebekah saw that Esau intended to avenge himself on Jacob she said, "Just go for a few days." A few days became thirty years! She *died* before he ever came back. Rebekah thought that if Jacob went on a few days journey Esau would have cooled down when he got back. But Esau was part of *God's* purpose to begin the next stage in the family of God. When Jacob, who went alone, came back from Laban's land he had a family of over forty sons, wives, and grand-children. Do you see that God uses something *we* think is offbeat to be onbeat? God is always *using* the devil. That is the great lesson we have to learn. *God uses the negative to confirm the positive.* If we had not been negative people we would *never* have had salvation confirmed to us. We wouldn't have *had* the destruction of the devil (the negative, forever) except that the death and resurrection of Jesus Christ put the whole business out *forever* and brought into being the eternal family! That can only be possible because we start in the negative and the negative can be put out forever in the name of Jesus Christ – the last Adam, who has come up with a new family. God is always using the devil to bring some further stage in His purposes.

The last thing that Isaac said to Jacob was the final conformation –

"Now Isaac called Jacob and blessed him again, and charged him, 'Thou shalt not take a wife from the daughters of Canaan (which Esau had done) but go to thy mother's father and take a wife from the daughters of Laban and God Almighty bless thee, and made thee fruitful and multiply thee that thou mayest be a multitude of people and give the blessing of Abraham to thee and thy seed with thee, that thou mayest inherit the land wherein thou art a stranger which God gave unto Abraham.'" Gen.28:1-4.

So Isaac himself came right out and said, "*You're* the one I'm blessing; you're the one who is to go."

There were two very wonderful and critical moments in the life of this remarkable man after whom the Jews are named, the people of Israel. They stand out to all who know Bible history, but usually with *negative* judgment. However, it is Esau and Isaac who *should* be judged rather than Jacob...for God did not judge Jacob. The *proof* of this is that God met Jacob.

Let me explain. You see, *faith is experience.* Our step of faith is *only* the way into an experience. Faith is never faith *until it is experienced.* Instead of getting, it is being, having. Saving faith is not that you believe God, but that *God* will settle *into you* as eternal reality. Eternal reality is that He has settled into you...not that you have settled into Him! You have settled into a new level of knowledge. *Faith is knowledge.* I like to use a crude experience on the simple level. Faith is not sitting on the chair; it is the reflex action of the consciousness of the chair. Faith has produced substance which is the *consciousness* of the chair. So faith is faith *because* I am conscious of being held by a chair, not because I sat in the chair. Sitting in the chair is only that which connects me to something which then *becomes* part of me, which is then the chair holding me up. Faith *always* is that you become part of, connected to, or become the thing in which you have bound yourself by faith. Faith is experience. It is substance. Do not mistake the first steps of faith as being the substance of the faith until there is this confirmation – "That's it!"

This is the confirmation to Jacob. It does not say that Jacob had a personal contact with God. But *in his spirit* he had reached out, he had moved over into God. He had accepted that the birthright was his – that *he* was to be God's man in the promise – and that this great nation was going to come into being through him. He had seen the eternal vision and the eternal purposes. He had gotten them more than they had gotten him.

Now God got him in the next great incident which is the Bethel dream. A lonely man had to run from his home. He was a fearful man and we learn a lot of Jacob and his negative fears. He was a running man, yet also a blessed man, and he was alone in the desert. He had made a stone his pillow. And he dreamed of a ladder set up on earth with a top that reached to heaven and angels of God were both ascending and descending. The Lord stood above and said:

"I am the Lord God of Abraham and Isaac. The land whereon thy liest, I give it to you. Your seed shall be as the dust of the earth spread to east, west, north, and south. In thee shall the families of the earth be blest. Behold I am with thee and will keep thee and will not leave thee." Gen. 28: 14-15

He had not thought about the stars in the heavens yet. He was not quite ready for that! Then Jacob awakened and *knew* the Lord was there...though he had not known it. He was afraid. All he had was this sense of a God he *did not know*. When you *know* God you only know love for there is nothing but love there, but until you *do* know God, God appears to you as a dangerous person. Actually, it is *our* reactions that are wrong. We have self reactions and are suspicious of God. Never attribute to God judgment, wrath, fear, or hate for they are not there. It is only *our reactions*. We think that He must be like that because the only God *we* can think of is a God who would beat us back a bit...who would give us a few things back for what we are like. That's *our* misinterpretations of God that comes out of the *distortions* of the Fall.

This was Jacob's first contact. But he was very real and said, "How dreadful is this place." And he vowed a vow, "If God will be with me and will keep me in the way I will go so that I come again to my father's place then shall the Lord be my God." So although he wasn't quite sure yet, he was on to the Person. This was a direct *revelation of God* to Jacob which he never got over. It was *his* new birth.

Esau was on to things of the self; Jacob was on to God. Do you see the difference? In the end, Jacob said, "The Lord is *my* God." That is where Jacob was. That is the real thing! "And of all thou shall give me I will surely give the tenth to thee." That's our first stage of knowing God at a distance with a ladder between us. It is better than not knowing Him at all, but there is a better relationship with God than with a ladder between us. But the first revelation is of a relationship *to* Him. He's my Saviour...He's my Lord...He's forgiven me...He's with me. God is **more** than *with* me...He **is** me! *This* is not a union; it is a relationship...but you *start* there. We have the idea that we have some things that God has given us so we give back to God a little. The whole idea is that I have what I have. God has given it to me, but it is mine and I will give Him back a little, a tenth. At least that is better than not giving anything...but Jacob did say, "You'll always be my God." His heart was right, but it was not any longer he seeking God; it was that God had *found* him. He *knew* the Lord!

In the future Jacob always went back to this Bethel. That is where God had met him. He knew God. This life is *knowing* God. When we first know Him we have some distorted ideas about Him and we have to be dealt with a bit. But the main issue is, "He's my God; He's with me. He promises me things, and He blesses me." When you are *in that* you are out of that world of flesh. You may play with it, but you are not in it. You may be a little mixed, but your main line, the new birth, is right. The new birth means that you are a son. You don't quite know yet all that is implied in being a son...we find out a little later...but now you are a son or a daughter, you don't know unity yet, all you know is a relationship but it is a *living* relationship. The new birth is not, "I trusted Him," it is "He's mine and I know Him. *Nothing* can shake it. He's real to me." Life is knowledge – consciousness – and *this* is it!

This life is revelation and living in the knowledge, the consciousness. It is not obtaining the knowledge, but the knowledge obtaining *us*. The consciousness had come to Jacob through the dream at Bethel that God was his God, and he was totally what is involved in being a son of God – which is God in His son form. He did not know that totally yet because we have to learn where *we* fit and how to function as real persons with our own personalities. We need to be properly trained in how to use ourselves because we are going to be free persons operating as God in redeemer activity through eternity and in universe development in the next dimension, I suppose.

Therefore, Jacob, as we all do, had to go through a further phase where he could at last understand the subtlety of the fallen dimension. *In the fallen dimension our negative human selves operate as if we can run our own lives for our own ends.* In the new birth we discover that we're separated from God by our misuse of ourselves, and we change from seeking our own ends to seeking God's ends. But we still haven't learned that *running* our own lives is the final form of the fallen dimension. What it means to be a person is to make choices, and to have a consciousness. But *we* don't have the resources to fulfill our choices because *only God* can do that. The negative doesn't have the resources only the positive has. Therefore in the fallen condition we're living persons who make our choices and do not have the resources to fulfill our choices. We tried to satisfy ourselves by our false choices in the world of the flesh. In regeneration we are out of that, but we still try to *satisfy ourselves* by 'right' choices. To *try to do right* is as much a part of the fallen dimension as doing wrong. That is a lesson we learn after we are saved. Sometimes people who grew up in very legalistic religions may find it in their unsaved condition, but in the main we only find that out after we are saved.

So Jacob had to find that although he was now for God and God was for him, life was going to be hard as long as he was trying to fulfill it by his own energies. As long as we think that life is "we" doing God's will we do not like what happens to the "we", so we do it under strain and negative reactions and weaknesses. Life is tough because what comes to us just comes to ourselves. We may be in the Lord's service but self takes things hard and the way gets tough. My major sense is duty and committal to God, but the committal is mingled with a great sense of the hardness and unpleasantness of the way…and we wish that we could get out of it. We may have personal reactions to other people and accuse them of causing our difficulties. By all those ways we *finally* are forced by some final crisis to realize that we still have life on the wrong foot...though not as much as it was when we were totally self- oriented. It is a mixture now, of flesh and spirit – God and man. I am a person of the Spirit. My life is committed to the will of God. He's my end and my aim, but I'm living in this live separation from God, which is the **only** thing I can know *unless I am in union*. If I am in union I just know I am in union and there is nothing more to it! Unless I know I am in union I am in the *illusion* of separation. I am seeking to handle life on a self-active basis – as if it consists of myself as a human directed by God to function as a human for Him. *That* is the false mixture.

The circumstances that brought Jacob to the point of seeing God in every situation began by his going to his mother's uncle, Laban. This was important because as one of the founders of the nation of God, his wife should come from the same *faith* family...not from a family who was in no relation to the new revelation of God, which was coming through. One of the *foolish concepts* we have so often is that God is always around the corner to smack us when we need it. We think Jacob was being paid back in his own 'coin'...and that it was because he deceived Isaac that he was deceived by Laban. God does not work like that! This was *not* for the purpose of punishing Jacob; it was for the purpose of being the *means* by which Jacob would find life to be a tough disillusioning service of God. It was not unprosperous and not unblessed, but the toughness and disillusionment was his major set in it. So *he* interpreted what happened to him on that level. What happened to him *had* to be. It was all *of God* for this was how the family came into being!

In those days the social customs allowed for polygamy. It wasn't a sin. Adultery or fornication might be a sin, but not polygamy, so that was not the problem. Leah, Rachel, Leah's maid, and Rachel's maid were his wives by whom the family came into being. But that's not the point, that's just the circumstances of those days so we need not discuss that as a thing that matters.

The *point* was that he felt tricked all the time. The basis of his life was, "I'm a person. I must run my life and it is not fair that I should have to do it with tricks, games and tests all the time." If he had known that the real life was *God* putting him through it, then he would have *taken* what he got from God. It is the *attitude* that matters. He would have said, "Oh well, *God* is taking me through. He is taking me this way and by this means He is bringing me my wives and children." He would be released in his ministry because it would be *God's* way of expressing His own purposes through Jacob. But Jacob did not know that.

You see, **separation** is our problem. Separation is the *consciousness* which came in through the Fall. It has to be...because if I don't know that I am one with God...and that *I am God functioning by me*...I can only be by myself. That is self-life under the Law. Instead of being with God in the union of grace, you are on the other side from God. God appears to you like a law and says you shouldn't be like that. There are no laws in God on the right side of God. There's only God's freedom...because the only law in the universe is love and you live in love, spontaneously a form of God expressing God! We do not see the other because it is *not* there.

Adam and Eve did not know that life when they first started...and they moved into the other one, the deceitful life...and so they became separate. Separation from God means that either you plunge yourself into trying to do what you want and hide away from the fundamental basis of being...or you try to be good and have a miserable life under guilt that you cannot be what you should be. Self can *only* end up being one or the other of these. In this case, the self has come over into Christ...but it has not settled into the *realization* of this new dimension into which it has been introduced – spirit as one. There is a touch of the witness of the Spirit in the new birth – acceptance by Christ and forgiveness, a child of God – but so far, it is only a touch. It has not been what we *really* are – sons in union and operating on this free level. We are still on a *halfway* level. We are His; we've begun this life under new control, but because we have not yet gotten *self* into true focus, we are operating as if we human selves have to function **for** God. Then we find *we* do not have what it takes to do it, or we do it the hard way. That's what Jacob went through.

He was enormously prospered. You can see that God's goodness was *always* there. Occasionally Jacob would see it. Laban and other people could see it. Laban made a very striking remark to Jacob, "For I have learned by experience the Lord has blessed me for thy sake." Gen. 30:27. It was the blessing of God that Laban's wealth increased vastly as he looked after Laban's sheep, cattle, and goats.

Although Jacob had prosperity and the family life was there, there was jealousy because he did not know how to accept *everyone* equally in God. He had favorites. Rachel was a favorite, Leah was not. Leah was physically ill-favored. God knows how to balance things up because *she* is the one who had the sons. The main part of the family came through Leah, but Leah was an unhappy woman. Jacob made her unhappy because he could only see people in the *flesh* and couldn't accept her. Naturally Leah was hurt because he didn't like her and did like Rachel. He wasn't a person in the spirit enough to be able to accept all of God's people on a right level and live not only on the soul emotional reaction, but on the Spirit-united reaction, which loves all. So there were internal reactions in the family situation. Despite that, God blessed him. The great ambition in those days was to have sons... and he had eleven sons and one daughter, Dinah. He had them mainly by Leah and Leah's servant who became his other wife. It was when he had nearly finished his time with Laban that he gained his favorite son, Joseph, by Rachel.

But the sense that Jacob had – that he was hard-done by – is not what I am getting at. Life *is* going to be hard. We are going to suffer affliction as the people of God, but how you 'see' it is what matters. It is what you are *inwardly*. If you know the union, you know you are God coming through you in certain situations. This is the way God expresses His blessing, fullness, and liberation. Although life is hard, you are not seeing the hardness...you are seeing the adventure and the fun and the thrill and the outgoings! Otherwise it is you apart from God – just God's servant. It is tough to be a servant. We are not to be servants…we are to be sons. Servants are under law, but we are *under no law.* That is what grace has taught us. In a sense while you are a servant you are saying, "Oh, I'm God's servant. God would have me do this," or "I suppose I must do this. Isn't this tough," and you are seeing life on a self-reaction basis…and *that* is hard!

At the end Jacob poured out his frustrations to Laban, who was very tough. That was good for Jacob! He was not there to be punished, but for God to use different ways to make, him *find* that self-reaction is a hellish life. It is still part of the grave clothes of the Fall. Independent self is weak. Independent self is under anything that controls it. It *cannot see* that we get good *through* evil so it is always responding with criticism, or reaction, or hurt, or scheming, and so on. That is all it does. His comment at the end was very striking…"Thus I was, in the day the drought consumed me and the frost by night." Twenty years of it! Drought and frost are not too good. It depends on the attitude towards it. We *have* to learn this one thing – we're not in health and sickness, and we are not in cold and heat. We are in eternal life!

Health and sickness are products of the Fall. They are opposites. We still feel heat and cold quite a bit but ideally we do not. When we get into God we do less and less. We know how to *take* things better… but all those opposites are part of the Fall. Instead of health and sickness we should talk about *life.* My precious Pauline has been through a tough time; she is still weak, but I am seeing her in God's *life.* All the time it is *God's goodness* that has taken us through all we have gone through. God's goodness and God's life *are* there, but if you do not see that then you feel the drought and you feel the cold. While God has to put us in places where things change on us and situations are hard on us, while we are in the hardness it means we have not got the union in action. We either do not know it or we do know it and get off it occasionally. But we *start* by not knowing it. We know the relationship… but not the union.

It is quite clear as we go through these men in the Bible that there is this *second phase to perfect us* as people. We are to be *perfected people, released humanity,* not deity, but humanity expressing deity. We are to be ourselves, but *before* I can be myself I have to know *where I fit* in myself. I am a negative. Yet the paradox is – I am not a negative, like a creature is more or less a negative who lives by instinct, and can only go as far as his instinct can take. It's I am a person, like God. So, where a creature just *does*...his creature instinct that is as far as it goes. The *paradox* of our negative is that we are negative, yet we are positive. We are negative, yet we act as a *person* when we are in the right relationship. Through the Fall we were trying to find *how* to act as persons. Everybody wants to be a god...of course we do! We *are* gods. We are all *meant* to be gods. It is quite right that everybody wants to be something. But *we* can't do it. We are inferior. We are either captured by our sins *or* captured by our self-efforts and our reactions. The positive part is really *God* by us. The *two together* make a person...*then* the resources are God's resources by us!

So Jacob went through tough times because he *saw* them as tough. The circumstances *had* to be what they were because, Jacob was to be the multiplier and this was God's way of accomplishing it. God is always using these crises to bring out *His* perfect purpose. The point is how you take it! Although it was a tough time for Jacob, God rewarded him. You see, we get in what we pay out. Now, I am not a shepherd so I cannot go into breeding matters too much. These rods and the water troughs which made them breed certain ways always puzzled me. I must leave you geneticists to understand these things. But he said that God told him to do it. God was with him and there came a time after Joseph had been born that God said that he had enough to go back home with. But first of all he himself said to Laban. "It's about time I had something out of this. I've served you twenty years. You have gotten enormous wealth and now I should have my share, too." That was when Laban told him that he realized that God blessed him because of Jacob.

Jacob devised a plan which looked like another dirty trick. He put aside all the plain sheep and goats to be Laban's. Then he had a way by which he made the breeders breed mixed-colored ones which were to be his. He took Laban's sheep, which he had done for years, on a three days journey. Then he separated the healthy ones and made them breed the way he wanted them to breed. The *point* is that God confirmed it! Faith is *not* what flesh lives by, because flesh says, "Oh how awful! Cheating!" Why he had been cheated twenty years by Laban! Laban had become wealthy through Jacob. It was guile right that he should return to Canaan with a certain amount of his own property. He actually discussed this breeding business with his wives and how the angel had told him to do it. He had the confirmation that God had told him to do this thing, which the natural man would say was another trick. You've got to watch these people of faith. We're funny people! But the *right purpose of God* was going through it and God was sealing it all the time.

Laban must have been a tough fellow...because when Jacob put this to Laban's daughters they reacted strongly with Jacob against their father. It is evident that Laban appeared to take advantage of Jacob, but all the time God's goodness was there preparing the family. The children were coming and the shepherd's life was being prospered both for Jacob and Laban.

After they had begun their return journey to Canaan there was a curious little incident. Evidently Laban's faith was mixed with idolatry and it appears that his daughters were mixed up in it also...because when they escaped the household with Jacob, Rachel had taken Laban's images and put them among the equipment on their camel. I am sure that Jacob never touched them because Jacob was always faithful to God, but apparently Rachel wanted them. However, God knows how to work things out, because the result was that Laban lost his images, which was good for Laban. When he tried to search for them Rachel would not let him search her things pretending she was sick. She was clever. The point was that the images were removed from Laban, and later on Jacob swept the images out altogether.

Laban and Jacob parted on amiable terms. They had agreed that the time for separation had come and Jacob proceeded on his journey. Now the final issue was about to come for Jacob. You see, if you have *only* yourself you only have *your* fears, *your* labors, *your* strains, *your* resentments and *your* reactions. You can't *take* things. We *have* to learn this. All the time Jacob was a fearful man underneath. We all are by nature. He realized that if Esau got him he would kill him. Maybe he stayed at Laban's as long as he did because he knew if he went back he would have to meet Esau, and Esau had become a big man in his own way. *Now* God had told him to return. Jacob always followed when The Voice came to him, because he was the Lord's...but he went back in fear.

This was the great crisis moment. God gives us comforts...so on the way angels of God met him just to give him encouragement. By *this* he knew God was with him and would say so. As he approached Canaan he sent messengers forward to tell Esau that he was coming. The messengers brought back the message that Esau was coming with four hundred men. Jacob had no men except his own growing sons, probably in their teens, and his cattle drovers and hired men. It was obvious what Esau was coming to do, so he prepared the best he could. He made a set of presents for Esau by sending droves of cattle, camels, and goats before him with gaps between them...so one by one Esau should meet with these attempts to appease his vengeance. However, Jacob knew it would take more than that to appease Esau's determination for revenge, When he came to the final brook, the Jabbok, knowing he would meet Esau on the other side, he prayed this prayer:

"0 God of my father Abraham, and God of my father Isaac, the Lord which says unto me, 'Return unto thy country and unto thy kindred and I will deal well with thee', I am not worthy of the least of all thy mercies and of all the truth which thou hast shared with thy servant for with my staff I passed over this Jordan and now have become two bands. Deliver me, I pray thee, from the hand of my brother, from the hand of Esau, for I fear him lest he will come and smite me and the mothers with the children. And thou sayest, 'I will surely do thee good and make thy seed as the sand of the sea which cannot be numbered for the multitude.'" Gen. 32:9

That is a very beautiful prayer because it has *humility* in the middle of it. All the time Jacob appreciated what God was doing. He was overwhelmed by the heat and the cold and the cheating, but underneath it all out came this! This was the *real* Jacob coming out when he was preparing to face what it meant to meet Esau and presumably be lynched.

He sent his family over and they encamped on the other side. It says, "And Jacob was left alone." That was a significant statement. "And there wrestled a man with him until the breaking of the day." Gen. 32:24. This wasn't Jacob wrestling with a man; it was a man wrestling with Jacob, because Jacob was as tense as a self could be tense! *Everything* was built up inside him. He was a strong self; you can see it all the way through. He must have been saying, "What can I do? What must I do?" Now all the time this really was God pressing him. He couldn't see *anything.* When you are obsessed you *cannot* see it. He could not see anything...but his fear, his schemes, his self, and what he would get. He was at the height of tension right through the night, and he never moved.

And then this special thing happened to him! Whether it was a divine stroke or whether it was just that his tension produced a physical reaction I do not know, but it does not matter. The man touched Jacob's thigh and it went out of joint. You cannot wrestle with a thigh out of joint. At *last*...he was there! Jacob had become a tough man and he may have thought, at least I can run. Now he couldn't even run!

There comes a moment when the Holy Spirit has *got* you. This man, whom he now perceived to be God or God's representative, had wrestled with him. It says that this man tried to get away from him and Jacob said to him, "I will not let thee go except thou bless me." This was a revolutionary outlook! It wasn't…how can I save myself? What can I do? It was a recognition that *I've* got it wrong and this man is trying to say something to me! He is trying to show that I'm the one to be blessed. I'm the one! God has it! Tremendous! *That is union.*

He *suddenly saw* that he had the whole *basis* of life wrong – that it was this independent self which came in with the Fall and which cannot do anything. *That* was his problem! He was not wrong, because Jacob was not a sinner. He was not doing it for himself; he was doing it for God. But he had this element that we have in our illusion of the self-reaction…Romans 7. He suddenly saw reality! The revelation is that *God* gives. So it was not Jacob finding God, it was *God causing* Jacob to see that God says, "I'm the One. Your self is no good. *I'm* the One. I won't let you go. It is your destiny." The important point of the whole thing is that this became a revelation, not of God, but of Jacob. It was not that Jacob saw God; it was that God caused Jacob to find who he… Jacob…really was.

When Jacob asked this 'living person' to bless him, He replied, "What is your name?" Then Jacob said, "My name is Jacob," a name meaning "supplanted." The man said, "Now your name shall no more be called Jacob, but Israel for as a prince hast thou power with God and with man." Not *God* has power, but *you* have power! *That* is the secret. He found that *he* was a form of God…a son in the royal household, a prince, with all the resources of the royal house available to him. Jacob's *real* self was revealed to him. *Your* real self is your God-self. That is the key! That is why we stop talking about our weaknesses and so on. We are princes! He is called "King of kings" because we are kings and He is King of us!

When he asked for God's name he was not given it. Why? Because God *has* no name. You move into the illimitable in God. We use convenient names because we are human. He is *beyond* all names. Names are things that are part of the universal. We are part of the universal, but the universal has no name…is just the all. So He would not give His name. He said, "You can *be* a part, but you cannot know."

That is where we move into this final consciousness where we do not know Him – we *are* Him. We do not know ourselves; we can only say we *are* because we are universal. Then we come back to who we really are in the image of God – an expression of the universal God. So we do not know ourselves; we just are…and we move into a relationship as a consciousness that *this* is the truth.

We ultimately know truth…not by outer revelation…not by Jesus Christ who came and died and rose again…not by a bible…but by *inner* consciousness. That is all we *can* know because *all we have* is an inner consciousness which registers the truth. That is how we know the truth. For instance – that is how all men know *love* is right. They know they ought to love. Every philosophy, every political party is based on "we ought to love." We all know that. Truth is what registers within. When you first register "I *ought* to be that," then you know you are not. Now you are coming near…and if you are honest you say, "Oh, I'm not." That is inner truth. "Everybody knows I'm not all love." Now you have two truths inside you. Not by a bible, not by a revealed Jesus Christ, but *inside you*. This is the truth!

It *may* come to some without knowing Him. You find then that the purpose of God is to bring the 'not-God' into reality to destroy it forever. If it had never come into reality, it might come again into reality. When the 'not-God'…the fallen level…has come into reality, and been gone out forever in the death and resurrection of Jesus Christ, *then* it is out. There is no more law, no more guilt. I am back in God and part of His permanent love. I am perfect in His perfection. I have no law; I am just operating by myself. I am love…I am operating. If I deviate a little I come back. That is not sin; I just deviate a little, because I am pressed by the world around. It is temptation. Now this is *inner* truth and that registers.

A Mohammedan cannot find God because truth is *never* outside yourself. You do not find God just by worshipping five times a day. If all you have is a relationship with someone you have to worship five times a day, you are in trouble. You are never held by what is *outside* you. What gets you on Sunday will not hold you on Monday…if it is not God *inside you*. You live by what you are inside. That is all you are!

There was a *time* when in a second revelation by a step of faith a person could say, "Now here is the way." This was the case with Abraham, who without knowing Jesus Christ believed God, and it was counted to him as righteousness. But that was wiped out by Jesus Christ…who wiped out the false righteousness *and* the unrighteousness. *We cannot be righteous now except by Jesus Christ.* Except through Him – we cannot move from the place where we see that we ought to be love, and know that we are not, to the place where we know we *are* love. He took out that whole unrighteous "law of sin" level and brought the other in. If Abraham was counted righteous it means that in *God's* sight he was identified with Jesus Christ, "Before Abraham was, I Am." The *eternal* Jesus Christ was there! We cannot inwardly pass through a death and resurrection without Christ. It is the same thing as tearing myself away from the idea that I have become something and do something. Death and resurrection is when I realize that I am dependent *only* on God's mercies. Jesus wiped out the 'not-love' and put us into the "I am love," which is Himself. *That is the gospel.* That is what we move into, and it is what Jacob moved into.

We move into the illimitable, the unknowable…and yet our reality is that we live by inner consciousness. The proof of our faith is not the Bible; it is not Jesus Christ who died in public. It is because *inside we know* it is true. We will die on it! It clicks. It is that from which I can never be shaken…if I remain true to what I know to be true. I *know to be true* that everything should be love. I *know to be true* that I am not, and that other people are not. I *know to be true* that there is a way in which I have become love in God, that Jesus Christ did the thing which wiped the whole of the old business out, and introduced me in the Holy Spirit to the new one. It registers in me that *I am free* in God's universal family. I do what I like because I am now part of a *divine compulsion of love!* I *am* the law now. *Either you are under the law or you **are** the law.* **God** is the law *and the law is love.* The other is swallowed up…not there!

Now the marvelous *purpose* of God is to have us *all* be the law. But in order to find that, we have to find what it is *not to be* the law...because we have to find 'not-God' before we can find God...or we're not conscious. We have to find that there is that which is *not* God and that there is that which *is* God. That is the Fall. It is *through that* that I find what it is not to be God, and then I find how the whole purpose was that His Son was always going to be the One...who created us...who redeemed us...wiped the old business out...and heads us for eternity – this great race of families!

Note that the *Son* had a second birth. **He was born at the resurrection.** "This day have I begotten thee" refers to the resurrection. He had an earth birth which we celebrate on Christmas, but the *real birth* was not that at all. The real birth is this one:

"We declare unto you glad tidings, how that the promise which was made unto the fathers, God hath fulfilled the same unto us their children. He hath raised up Jesus again as it is written also in the second Psalm, thou art my Son, this day have I begotten thee." Acts 13: 32-33.

On the resurrection a new Jesus Christ came into being – the *eternal* new Son with the brothers. This was the purpose of God through eternity. So we are sons, one. This passage is confirmed by Hebrews 1:5.

I am laying the foundation that reality is *inside you.* It is not in the Bible; it is not even in the *visible* Christ...because the Christ has been there for eternity. It is not in anything outward. The danger of things outward is the danger of our churches, the danger of ministry and all that Sunday stuff. There is nothing in any of it unless it is inside you because you *are* what you *are inside.*

We have *many* of these things wrong. The *only judgment* you can have is that you judge yourself. For example David in Psalm 51 expressed his unworthiness. In Acts 13:46, referring to those who reject Christ, Paul said: "Seeing ye have put it from you and judged yourselves unworthy of everlasting life." That is a wonderful statement! He is saying that it is not that God judges you, but that *you* judge yourself unworthy! Nobody goes to Hell except those who judge themselves unworthy. It is a way of saying that you will *not* come and receive the gift of God in grace, because you judge yourself unworthy of receiving it. This is the *dividing line* between the children of the devil and the children of God – saved and unsaved. This is how inside that dividing line we have to go through these *further processes* to *establish* us in the sonhood...so we may be princes with God.

All these men all the way back to Abraham had this phase. You find out that you have misused yourself, but the misuse was not the sin. The *independent* self is the problem. *That* is the indwelling sin of Romans 7. Sins, the misuse of self, are only the product. That is why to *try* to be important is the worst sin. When you discover through revelation by a crisis, like Jacob, that is really *God* who is doing it, then, although you may slip, you will not be fooled again. You can be a *real* person – *confident* and *kept*! You will not need to worry about failure or temptation...afraid of what people will do. You can be yourself. Be free! Dare everything! Move in! This is the freedom and the life. This is the life Jacob moved into...although it does not come out in Jacob as royally as in the life of Abraham, Joseph, Moses, and David. But Jacob was a very great man.

One other point to bring up about this crisis time in Jacob's life is found in Genesis 28:30:

"So Jacob named the place Peniel, for he said 'I have seen God face to face, yet my life has been preserved.'"

His understanding of God had been changed. Previously, like most people apart from God, his understanding of God had produced fear. *Here* he finds a family relationship – *love*, which is all there is in God. So instead of thinking he might lose his life through the experience, he gained his life! *Faith reproduces release. Fear reproduces fear.* We transmit what we are. If that had been a fearful, frightened Jacob coming to meet Esau, it would have produced a threatening reaction back in Esau.

But when Esau was met by brother Jacob, who showed respect for him by bowing seven times before him and showed love in his whole attitude, the Spirit of God transmitted through Jacob *caused* the same response in Esau! He had come with four hundred men to make a public lynching and *instead* of that Esau gave Jacob a public embrace. He called him, "my brother," and kissed him. This *miracle* transformation took place in a man who for twenty-one years had lived to kill his brother, and whom Jacob had feared for twenty-one years. So you see...*everything* hangs on inner attitude. All life is inner attitudes, inner consciousness. You transmit your inner attitude, your inner consciousness. It not only is expressed through you, but *reacts on others*!

The remainder of the history of Jacob is not as dramatic until we get a little nearer to the Joseph 'situation'...though there was more drama around Joseph than around Jacob. Life is living at ease in God's *appointed* situations. Life is not trying to be anything, trying to achieve this or trying to be that. It is not why am I not like this person or that person? It **is** being relaxed into the *way* in which God means life should be lived.

We saw with Isaac – how his life was meant to be lived just confirming that he was in the land, and digging wells in order that his flocks could live. He persisted in digging them and taking care of his own wells against opposition. He was just to persist in being the person whom God had said he was to be – one of the originators of the family who were to occupy the Promised Land, and out of which the promised Saviour would come. After that, of course, *all* saved people in the world *became* the Promised Land!

In Jacob's case, God's purpose was that he would be the father of a family, the patriarch. He was to have these children, and they were to be brought up and have families and be establishers of the family out of which the great family, the great nation, would come. That was his job. From this time onward Jacob lived a relaxed life.

He had to find a place to settle. God used a strange incident – a sin – to do that. God is particularly adept at *using* the devil for His own advantages. The first place he settled was in, a rather attractive place named Shechem. There was a flourishing tribe or city there with a heathen king and princes and people. Jacob was very prosperous having brought large herds of goats, sheep, cattle and about forty members of his family with him. The Shechemites thought that if they could control Jacob and his family they would be a great asset to them. Then a funny thing happened. The prince of Shechem fell in love with Jacob's only daughter, Dinah, and seduced her. *Then* he wanted to marry her.

Jacob's sons, being very loyal Israelites, were *not* taking that! They schemed up a massacre of the Shecamites and tricked them by telling them that if they wanted to align themselves with the Israelites they would have to be circumcised. Thinking they would then have a share in Jacob's wealth, the Shecamites agreed to do this. While they were going through the circumcision and disabled, Jacob's sons moved and killed the men of the nation.

Jacob then showed a characteristic of his, which was a negative outlook – a product of *fear*. Let me add a word of caution here and say that we must be careful *not to concentrate* on people's negative characteristics. We love to pick out the weaknesses of others, because we have so many ourselves. People criticize Jacob, but we have no right to do that. He was *God's* man, and God sees the greatness…not the evil. Later on in Scripture it is said…"God saw no iniquity in Israel, and yet Israel had had forty years of fussing and disbelieving and rebellion." God does *not see* iniquity in you if you are a child of God. However, we *can see* that certain things can have negative effects, and we have to just mention them. Jacob *always* saw things in fearful terms. He did not know how to see God operating through an evil until *afterwards*. He carried this weakness with him even after he was in union. We all carry with us *some weakness* where sin will pop up…although in the end he acted with the word of the Lord in great loyalty. There was this aspect in him which arose. The thing that bothered him about the slaughter of the Shechemites was that he was afraid that the other inhabitants of Canaan would gather together and destroy him. What God wanted was to deliver Israel from *marriage relationships* with heathen people.

He wanted a *separate* people built up in the law and grace of God. *God* was using this sin and reaction to deliver Israel from a false alliance.

Jacob's commission now was to live quietly and preserve his family. When he died later in Egypt his family was still whole. Though they had troubles and sadness they became godly and what they were meant to be – a family who would ultimately come out of Egypt back into Israel where they could become the Israelite nation and after that the church of Jesus Christ!

Yet we see the same characteristic of negative thinking coming out again and again in Jacob. In noting it we can watch *ourselves*. Can I learn to see a *purpose* of *God's* goodness in a horrible situation? Can I learn that *God meant* that horrible situation, because He has a purpose of His own perfect ways through it? An example of this is when Jacob *refused* to be comforted when the brothers lied to him that Joseph had been killed, and brought back his many colored coat with blood marks as evidence. Although there was a tender relationship there, as all his sons and daughters rose up to comfort him, Jacob still said…"I will go down unto the grave unto my son mourning." We're in a tough spot if we cannot see *somewhere* that God is going to work through our tragedies to something great. Of course in those *pioneer days* they had to see by hindsight, though every now and then someone *did* see. He felt the same when they wanted to take Benjamin up to introduce him to Joseph. He was afraid something would happen to him just as it had happened to Joseph. He did *finally* recommit it back to God and let them take Benjamin so that Joseph would let Simeon out of prison.

Finally, even one of his *greatest moments* was tinged with that same negative attitude. They were brought back to Egypt to be given a special land to live in and received a mighty welcome from Pharaoh. A very *great* thing took place in that Jacob blessed Pharaoh! *God* in Jacob blessed the earthly king! He said, "I represent the King of kings. I bless you because you bless us." That is the great Jacob. Later on the Bible says without contradiction, "the less is blessed of the better." That was one of his *highest* moments, and yet when Pharaoh asked him about himself he said...

"The days of my pilgrimage are 130 years; few and evil have been the days of my life here. I have not obtained the days of the life of my fathers, in the days of their pilgrimage." Gen.47:9.

Notice that he used the word *pilgrimage*. He *knew* this earth was not his home. He was a man of the spirit *always*!

In Jacob's final scene, when he was giving each of his sons a blessing, he was '*fresh* in the Spirit.' We recall that his father, Isaac, was *not* 'fresh in the Spirit' when he was *dim* in sight because he *purposed* to bless the wrong son. In Hebrews 11, Jacob is described as worshipping...leaning upon his staff. God *always* kept before him his lame leg, the *reminder* that it was not to be found in Jacob's self. It was to be *found in **God** expressed through Jacob*. That worship was a *remarkable* presentation of the coming destiny of the tribes descended from his sons. It was keen insight into the *prophetic destiny* of Israel! In the Old Testament we get these great prophecies coming through. The prophesy given on each son was *fulfilled* when they got into the Promised Land and developed. This indication of Jacob's sensitiveness is the very opposite to Isaac who had to be deceived to get God's purposes through.

One *strange* thing that Jacob foresaw concerned Joseph's two sons. Jacob only had eleven sons with the tenth being Joseph and the eleventh Benjamin. At the end, when the sons were lined up to receive their father's blessing, Jacob *replaced* Joseph with his two sons, who lined up *as if* they were *Jacob's* sons. So the final honor given Joseph was that he was to have *two* of the twelve great tribes of Israel descended from him – Ephraim and Manassas. Manassus was the elder son and Ephraim the younger. Somehow Jacob *foresaw* that Ephraim was to be the *great* tribe of the tribes of Israel and Manassus the *lesser* tribe. When they came before Jacob to be blessed Joseph put Manassus under Jacob's right hand and Ephraim under Jacob's left hand. Then Jacob *deliberately* reversed his hands!

"Oh, no," Joseph said. "You're wrong." Jacob said, "I'm not! Of the two, your younger son is to be the greatly blessed one, greater blessed than the older one." It happens *so often* in the Bible that the younger ones come before the older. This was a final indication of the *keenness of insight* in this mighty man of God.

Then Jacob outlined in *no uncertain terms* what would happen to the tribes in their different situations and their different histories. His *great* word was for Judah. There again he had that great insight – for Judah was the progenitor of Jesus! Jacob put it in one of these beautiful little flashes that come..."Until Shiloh come." He *saw* Jesus coming! Moses said, "Until a prophet arises out of me *like* me."

Another of these statements came through the treasonable lips of Balaam..."A star will arise in Jacob, a scepter out of Israel." Micah said this ruler would come whose "being was from everlasting." Isaiah's great one was: "Wonderful counselor, mighty God, everlasting Father, and Prince of Peace." These names were given to the coming Messiah. So they *had* these glimpses.

Jacob was given a tremendous funeral, which was a mark of tremendous *respect* for this patriarch of the Israelite race. The Egyptians *so* respected Joseph that, with Pharaoh's permission, they went in hundreds with the whole family into Canaan to bury Jacob by the side of Abraham and Isaac in the cave of Machpelah. Then they had this *great* mourning. It was indicative of the deep impression that this man, whom we tend to criticize, had upon man *as well as* God. He was called Israel, Prince with God. Let us *see* the same!

JOSEPH

We're going to look together into what we can learn about the ways of God and the ways of the Spirit through a human life – and that is the life of Joseph, as it has been recorded for us in considerable detail in Genesis 37-49. Actually, the *Spirit of God is in operation in all lives from their birth*...as God said to Jeremiah, "Before you were formed in the womb, I knew you." In some instances, maybe including some of ourselves, we are able to trace the operations of the Spirit of God from quite youthful days. Sometimes the real meeting of the Spirit with man doesn't come until later years in recorded form. Joseph is one of those in whom God had begun to do work as a youth – the same as He had done in his father, Jacob.

From early youth, Jacob had identified with the *purposes* of God to pour out His Spirit on the whole world through them, as they walked faithfully with Him. So, Jacob's life is identified with God's purposes. His ambition was to be an anointed agent by whom God would fulfill *His* will. That's why he was ready at the pottage incident with Esau. You can't *jump* into a thing like that. He had a *prepared* heart, ready for the moment when he could possess the promises of God and the birthright which he *knew*, through Rebekah, to be his. So, he moved in.

Joseph was the same. The family of Abraham, Isaac, and Jacob had become established in this area of Canaan, Palestine. It was well known, and their testimony doubtlessly was widely known among *all* the people around. We know that Pharaoh knew, Abimelech knew, and various local heads of tribes knew (and what happened to Sodom and Gomorrah)...and that their testimony was to the living God. The evidence that Joseph knew God was a *disturbance* with his brothers! He was the youngest...seventeen. His brothers were going through a period of the flesh. They were believers, but they had to learn the *difference between* the flesh-governed and the Spirit-governed life. They were the progenitors of the twelve tribes...but they were living, at that time, the life which was *no testimony*...in this area where people are watching to see what *God's* people are like. They were out with the sheep, a good way off...where their father and the influence of home couldn't be felt. Undoubtedly they were plunged into *all* the activities of the world and the flesh and the devil...and maybe, the idolatry in those areas around. Joseph was with them, feeding the flock with his brethren. (Gen. 37:2) But the further evidence that Joseph was *God's* man was the bond of love he had with his father...and as the inheritor of God's Covenant Promises. So he couldn't *hide* the goings on of his brothers from his father. It says that he "brought unto his father their evil report."

Foolish people – who don't see the *depths* of the working of God, would point their finger at Joseph and say he was a kind of sneak, a kind of self-righteous person..."I'm not like them, doing things they are doing; I'll tell my father about them." A person who is building *himself* up in his own self-righteousness can't stand a smash-up for long. Joseph would have cracked up mighty *quick* if all he was concerned with was *his own* self-advancement, because he was to go through some mighty big storms. So all the *evidence* of the life that follows was that this *wasn't* a foolish, silly boy wanting to sneak on his brothers and be better than them. He was a young boy with the *concern of God* on him – which he might be involved in the purpose of God to bring His blessing to the world, as far as he understood what this blessing was to be...as God had promised it. So he brought this concern to his father as a *concerned* young man.

Jacob had been that way himself. He *knew* what it was to *differentiate between* being a man for his own ends – a man of the flesh and a man of the Spirit – because of what he had been through with Esau. So, obviously, Jacob could *relate* to Joseph. Obviously he saw: "Here's one I can talk to, who understands who we are…that God's got some purposes and is preserving us for His world purposes." So he had the *heart* affinity with his son Joseph. It is said that he gave him a special coat as a cover, which marked him as *apart* from his brothers outwardly…as a son of his old age. But I have no doubt that this was a *special* indication, rather like the mess of pottage incident, by which Jacob was beginning to see that Joseph was God's *marked* man. That created jealousy, as it *would* do to the flesh…hatred to the point that his brothers couldn't even speak peaceably to him. They really went for him! (Gen. 37: 3-4)

So now we have the next stage – Joseph not *only* had been concerned with his brothers' conduct…not *identified* with it…but had taken a separate way and opened his heart to his father. This resulted in the brothers turning on him and hating him and making his life a hell for him, yet this only confirmed him more! That's the proof! If Joseph had been just a *self-seeking* young man, he wouldn't have stood this for long. Here he was, *surrounded* by a family who took every opportunity they could to tear him down. Then something happened. A happening which either is total nonsense or truth; an absurdity, a fantasy or imagination…or God! It was Joseph's *first* dream.

We go on to see that *all the way through* his life Joseph knew the dreams were *from God*, and always said God spoke to him by dreams. That's what it means to have the *inner consciousness* of God. You see, *we* live by inner consciousness. We live by what we know *within* us. That's why *my* new birth is when I know Jesus is in me – not merely that I have believed in Him outwardly, but that I have had *confirmation in me*… as Paul wrote in Gal. 1:15-16. This is what Joseph had – a consciousness! The future was to *prove* this. This was that God said something to him – something *so* far out, something which had such an apparent characteristic of total conceit that a person *couldn't* say it unless he believed it! He was to say that in this dream of these sheaves of wheat, *all* the sheaves were representatives of his brothers who would bow down before him and do obeisance to him!

Obviously a young man isn't going to make a dream like that public to his brethren after he had *already* been suffering from them, unless he was getting prepared for a pretty good beat up. That's *conviction* behind that! Faith has a conviction and you've *got* to say it. That's what witnessing is – saying what I've *got* to say. So he said it! Therefore, it says, they hated him the more for his dreams and his words. "You're not going to be head over us, are you?" Now he was coming up to the moment which is a crisis moment in people's lives, when *you* get fixed. Here Joseph became a fixed person; he *never* deviated again.

You're fixed when you're fixed in **unity**…and you know it is *God* in you. Period! It's *always* God in you and God by you – God is in *your* form. That's a fixation. I couldn't prove this in Joseph's life except by the *evidence* of the life that followed. But it is *clear* to me that this happened to Joseph when he *had* to take one final further step. He had *another* dream which is still more wildly fantastic! In this dream, the sun and the moon and the eleven stars do *obeisance* to *him*! Previously it had been sheaves representing the brothers. This was a sun and moon and eleven stars…including father and mother! So this young man had to say, "My own father, my godly, God-anointed father Jacob (his mother had gone by then)…my parents are all going to do obeisance to *me*." You don't easily say that unless God *makes* you. Life is *God making* you. This is this inward consciousness which is *God in you*… operating *by* you. Joseph didn't do it at first…maybe was afraid. It says he first told his brothers, not his parents. (37:9) *Then* it says he told his father and his brethren. Whether they challenged him to *dare* to do so, I don't know. But he finally had to come right out…not only to his brothers who were on his level…but to his father and say *publicly*, "*God* has said you are all to bow down to me in the course of God's purposes." *That* takes some saying!

Now I think *that's* the moment…I would guess by his future life… when *his* God-union became established. He *knew* this was God operating by him. *All* that happened in the future was God operating by him. He knew it was *not* he himself, but the living God. This crisis comes out of the travail of faith…and these are travails he went through. They produce a birth – for faith is a conviction that God *has* said something. "I **know** it!" "He that believeth hath the witness in himself." (1 John 5:10) That's the *key* verse on faith. "He that believeth…" If you believe, *inside* you **know**. So faith is knowledge. Faith is that the thing you *believed* is yours! So a conviction of faith isn't a conviction that I just believed; it is a conviction that I *know* the thing is so…and I *say* so! I suggest that is the *radical crisis moment* in Joseph's life when the relationship between God and him was *settled*.

I might add this. If this *was* God and not phony…and the years were to prove that it wasn't imagination and fantasy, but was *God*…God isn't *likely* to say that to a conceited young man, is He? He isn't *likely* to say that to a self-seeking, self-righteous young man, is He? He *says* that to a concerned man. God doesn't talk to unconcerned people. He spoke to this boy *because* he could take it…he was conditioned. Ah…that's it!

An interesting thing about his father – he acted humanly rightly, probably to cover the family situation when he rebuked his son. (27:10) "Now, steady, steady. Can you say your mother and father are going to bow down to you?" You keep a *little* coolness in the family maybe, if you say that! But what does it then say? "His father *observed* his saying." His brothers envied him, but his father *saw* something…much the same as Mary *saw* something coming for her son. (Luke 2:19) Spirit *identifies* with Spirit. Flesh must fight Spirit because "the carnal mind is enmity against God." It can only identify with its own peers, which are self-loving. But Jacob *knew*. Jacob said, "Listen, that's the kind of thing God said to *me* when I took that birthright and when I deceived Isaac."

So time passed. I would imagine only a few weeks or months. Once again the brothers were out with the sheep. Now, it's quite *obvious* they liked being with the sheep *because* they got away from the family influence – moral or spiritual. If we need proof of that, it is that they were *supposed* to be at Shechem. Actually, they shifted to Dothan, so they got where people wouldn't know where they were. (37:12-17) You can *see* what they were after! Their father thought they were feeding the sheep at Shechem. Undoubtedly with the concern on him for the *consistent* life of the family, which *bears witness* to the living God, he sent Joseph to know how they were getting on. Foresight might have said, "Don't do that"...knowing the brothers' attitude...but he *had* to. This family was God's family, and had to *act* as God's family. The only *key* that the aging Jacob had was his son Joseph who took such a *fearless* stand. Probably Jacob thought, "Well, the *one means* by which God can speak His word of faithfulness and holiness to my other sons is by Joseph." So it says he sent him..."Go, I pray thee, see whether it be well with thy brethren, and bring me word again." So he went.

As I say, they were hiding away, doubtless playing the devil, because Jacob said, "Do not thy brethren feed the flock in Shechem?" (37:13) When Joseph got to Shechem he couldn't find them. He was wandering about and a certain man found him and asked, "What are you looking for?" "Oh," he said, "I'm looking for my brethren." Now, *that* shows they were known. He didn't say who, just "my brethren". So, plainly they were a marked family, watched by the heathen around to see whether *their* God was worthwhile worshipping. These men were *destroying* that testimony, of course. The young man said, "They are departed hence, for I heard them say, 'Let us go to Dothan'." So you see, they slipped away. Probably the reason why they rose up in hatred... the final act of hatred when Joseph *did* find them...was because he found them out. They *never* thought they would be found there! They *thought* they were just playing their own games alone. Then Joseph turned up. Oh, my!

God's purpose is that *freedom fulfills itself,* and we do what we *are* to its completion! So, it was the *inevitable* – the murderous spirit took murderous form! It always does. God *means* it to be, because that's how we find out *who* we are. It took these brethren fourteen years of guilt to find out! *Thank God* they were guilty, which *shows* they knew

God. If they hadn't known God, they wouldn't have given a hoot. But they knew, thank God!

So it boiled up. He found them there. "What'll we do with him?" they said. "Murder him," they said. Judah didn't say that, nor Simeon. "Let's get rid of him. Then where will his dreams be?" Now God always *leads* point by point. Probably if they hadn't intended to murder him they wouldn't have sold him. It was such an *extreme* thing to sell your brother as a slave in those days. They would never see him again! He would go off with some wandering tribe to some distant country... almost *incredible* to think they could do it! They probably couldn't have done it unless they had *first intended* to murder him. Now, is there a way out? *Yes*, there is a way out. "All right, we won't murder him. We'll sell him and then we'll just say he's been murdered, or eaten by a wild beast." And that's exactly what they did! For the moment, they were so *indifferent* to the sin they were committing that they sat down to eat while they put him in the pit. What should they do? It was Reuben who had advised them to put him in the pit...*hoping* he could rescue him. Judah, it was, when these Ishmaelites came by this traveling caravan of traders, who said, "Sell him to them". Judah was the one who gave *himself* up to Joseph later on, offering to take Benjamin's place...Judah, the one who had sold him as a slave! So this *fantastic* happening took place. We know of the agony, *human agony*, of Joseph, because it says he pleaded with them...wept with them...pleaded with them. Years later they said, "Didn't he plead with us not to do this?" "We *saw the anguish* of his soul when he besought us, but we would not hear." (42:26).

So we know the human agony Joseph had, which we shall *have* and are *meant* to have. We are *participators* in the human situation, and we move in human agonies and human suffering. We see how he *pled* with them not to do this. So we can only *imagine* what he felt like...when he had been in a protected home, for those days a wealthy home... *suddenly* dragged off as a slave, marching through the heat into Egypt. Nothing said about *that*. All we know is that he was sold. Of course, he was a fine-looking fellow like David was. Probably his very *faith* had kept him looking healthy too. He was sold to Potiphar, who was captain of Pharaoh's guard, an important and wealthy man with a large household of slaves.

Now all we know of that time, and from then on, was such a *liberated* Joseph! He was happily serving. His *whole heart* was in it to do a top job...and a quality about it which was quite different from the average slave who could only be hating everybody, and cursing his situation. Potiphar *saw* something! Not only that, but it's *quite plain* Joseph didn't hide his witness...though it didn't *look* much as if God was with him...because it says that Potiphar "saw that the Lord was with Joseph." (39:3) He couldn't have seen the Lord with him *unless* Joseph had spoken to him about the Lord, because they were worshippers of Egyptian gods...Isis, Osiris, etc. So Joseph was there with *his* testimony!

Do you see the *point*? This young man has it *so fixed* in him that it's the living God expressing Himself through him, fulfilling His purposes through him...because he had got that fixed when the storms were blowing at home. So, when he was now a slave and had all those *human* reactions, he said, "No, God, You're in everything. You're running this life; I've got Your dreams; You're in this thing. So, if I'm here, I'll put myself into this as where **You** put me. I'll do all I should do here." *That's* the walk of *victory* which can see God in adversity! You can only see God in adversity if you see God in *everything*. You can't see God in everything...happily...unless you know *He means* it. If you *don't* know He means it – "Fancy God letting them do the dirt on me like that!" If you think God *just permits* it, you say, "What did God permit that for?" But God **means** it. (Gen 50:20) Now, that's a *very high* place to come to!

I maintain that Joseph came to *that* with his dreams. God *means* something very great through you. Therefore, your life has a meaning to it when you live on *His meaning* in your life. Now, on *that* level, I can take a horrible situation and say, "God, this is awful. What can this mean? I'm cut off from everybody. How can my family bow down to me? I'm cut off forever from them...wretched slave! Oh, no, God! I've got it clear – *everything* I'm doing is You. *I'm* just an expression of You! It's You *fulfilling* a meaningful purpose! *OK, God.*"

Now we *all* live by inner spirit. When our inner spirit is poised and at peace and free, our operations are poised and peaceful and free...and they prosper. Potiphar doubtlessly quickly saw the prosperity, because of the type of man Joseph was – the reliability, the different quality of man from the other slaves around him. But he also saw his *capacity*. You see, God has His own gifts which come out His own way. Now God was *training* Joseph to run Egypt...so he started by running Potiphar's house, and he showed *immediately* those gifts which could run something – different gifts to different people from the same Giver! This sharp Potiphar was General of Pharaoh's guard and said, "This is the fellow who's going to run my home. Look what's happening since he began to run it. Things run smoothly with the other slaves." Of course, Joseph was a man of *love*; the other slaves loved him. They didn't have the antagonism toward him that his brothers had; they had no reason for it. They found kindnesses, help, sympathy, and understanding with Joseph...and so the whole *atmosphere* was happier. He began perhaps to do a good *spiritual* job with them!

So, we see this situation of this young man – happy in his spirit, free in his spirit – understanding himself to be *God's* man in this situation, and *so operating* that his work was blessed! That's *pretty good* for any of us, isn't it? So there was prosperity. In the Bible ways there is always prosperity. Prosperity comes from *inside*, not from outside. Prosperity comes when *I'm* in a prosperous *relationship* with Jesus Christ. Prosperity will proceed from me in my job. The Bible says (Joshua 1:8), "Then thou shalt make thy way prosperous, and then thou shalt have good success." I've always believed *every one* of us should have good success... *whatever* situation we are in... when we have good success *inwardly*, because the good success inwardly is the living *God operating* by me. Then it comes out in *my* activities!

Now there can be *no greater evidence* of the fixation of Joseph than that of his moral life. You are *absorbed* by what *eats you up*! (John 2:17) If you have a *dual* interest, you have dual appeals. Illicit sex didn't appeal to Joseph. *That* was his safeguard. He didn't care about it because he was eaten up with *being God's man* in God's way! He *couldn't* do a thing that wouldn't please God and wouldn't be right by his boss. So he didn't 'see' Potiphar's wife. She had *no* hold on him. If he had wanted some flesh *and* spirit, he'd have been copped. But he didn't want it! He was absorbed in being God's man. He wasn't against marriage – he had a wife and sons later on – but he was *absorbed* in having God's *way* and fulfilling God's *purposes* and in having God put *first* in his life. *Alternative* temptations didn't touch him. That's *really* the strength for youth, you know.

I must say, as a young soldier in World War I, I never had trouble *because* I was for souls. So I *never* had any trouble running after women and after drink and so on. I had *friendships* with girls, like the rest, of course, and enjoyed them, but was *always* after souls. You see, if you are after the *higher* thing, you don't see the lower. *That's* the victory for young people. It isn't, "Oh, those poor young people in such tough situations." No, they're *not* in tough situations. They're in grand situations if they are *all for* Jesus!

Once again, in the *line* of God's *will*, the evil thing *became* the good! There *isn't* good or evil with God. Good or evil is in the Fall, and *evil is only the misuse of good*. He will *use* it for His own ends! Therefore, Potiphar's wife was the next step in *God's* purposes... Potiphar's wife! She pestered Joseph frequently, pestered him day after day to come and commit adultery with her. (39:10) Finally, she was so *determined* to have him that she grabbed his cloak when he was alone in the house with her. The *only* thing he could do was flee. The Bible says, "Flee adultery, flee fornication, flee temptation." He fled.

Not that he was tempted, but he *must* get out of there! He didn't want it. To save the poor woman's reputation, as well as his own, he made that *great statement* of total trustworthiness. He was a slave, but his boss had put him in charge of *everything*! He said to Potiphar's wife, "Behold, my master wotteth not what is with me in the house and hath committed all that he hath to my hand. There is none greater in this house than I; neither hath he kept back anything from me but thee, because thou art his wife. How then can I do this great wickedness, and sin against God?" I *can't* sin against Potiphar *or* God! God has called me to fulfill *all* I should fulfill, as perfectly as I can...in fulfilling my duties for my boss, to be the perfect servant to my boss. I'm not the perfect servant if I do that...and above that, *God*...I am God's! How can I sin against God? I'm God's man." *That* was his answer to Potiphar's wife.

For the second time he had *severe* sufferings. You can imagine what Potiphar did to him! I *wonder* how far Potiphar could see through his wife. I wonder how far he thought this was *really* Joseph's fault at all...except that at first he was taken in, anyhow. When *she* brought this story to him – that Joseph had tried to seduce her, he jumped into it. You can imagine how he treated Joseph! *Imagine* the beatings and punishment! He was put in irons. That was the time in the Psalms (105: 17-18) where it says that, "God sent a man before them, even Joseph, who was sold for a servant, whose feet they hurt with fetters; he was laid in iron." In the margin it says, "His soul came into iron." So you get the dual suffering. *Soul is not spirit.* Soul is *emotion* and *reason.* Every reason *against* this ridiculous business of being God's...and getting worse and worse! It looked as if God were a devil! *All* his reason and emotions were torn to pieces...the one man who had been *faithful* to Potiphar, *faithful* to God, and this *very faithfulness* destroyed him *again*...not to speak of the beatings he must have had there in fetters, "His feet were hurt by fetters"... pretty tight.

I often think the *best* kind of testimony is in ordinary living. The Lord is just the same. I just go ahead with the Lord and the Lord in me, as me, all the time. That's all there is! Life is ordinary...changeless. In the unchanging quality of life which is Christ in my form, *fulfilling* His perfect will by me with *His* perfect power and perfect peace. He is changeless...and so, *we* are changeless. *We're* as unchanged as He is unchanged!

The prison record of Joseph was a *repetition* of the Potiphar household record which was precisely the same. He started in the lowest dungeon, fetters on him, and probably many beatings, starvings and was regarded as the prime criminal, because he had dared to attempt the seduction of the general's wife. We aren't told how, but the keeper of the prison saw a *quality* in this fellow which *must* have started by his *yieldedness*. It must have started like Paul and Silas in prison by being able to say, "Praise the Lord, praise the Lord anyhow. I'm the Lord's. *He's* got purposes." The jailer had never heard that before! There was a peace about Joseph – a readiness, thankfulness instead of grousing and groaning; thankfulness for what he *did* get. I don't know how long it was before the jailer got those fetters off him...gave him some little duties to do...found how well he did them. *Before we know it,* the jailer put him in charge of the *whole* prison! Joseph became an underjailer *although* he was a prisoner. It all comes from within...*not* from without! Your outer circumstances don't matter...because the whole of this world is *God hidden* away. *Everything* that is, **is God**. God is working through the devil. *Everything is* **God** *hidden away.* When you know this, you don't see *circumstances*...you see *God* in the circumstances. *He's* going to come through in *light* here in *these circumstances!* When you are free *here,* [pointing inside] you're free there [pointing outward]. So the *key* is *always* inside because that's all we are – inside people! *Then* He comes through circumstances in *redeeming* ways. In the next dimension there will be *other* glorious ways. It's the *redeeming ways* down here which includes suffering...and walking it, believing...and being involved in activities which may *not* be the ones we choose. Yet *He's* coming through and His light shines. This is 2 Cor. 4:9-12...daily dying and rising...and life in *others*!

So we pass through several years. Joseph was fourteen years into this *whole* situation. I don't think we know how many of them were in jail, but he was seventeen when he *started* his life of witness. He was thirty-two when he became Prime Minister of Egypt...fourteen years! You can do it if you're *God* in your form, can't you? If you know your *union* and you're not you...you can do it, *because* you're not you...but you've got to know it and you only *know* it if you're *fixed* in it. You do not *know* it by getting *it*. You know it because it...He...gets you! You live by what you **are**, not by what you *get*...for what you get *becomes* you. That's the *law* of faith. I've told you how, in my opinion, Joseph *so* got into God; God into him. So there's no problem except the problem of the *human*...and the *hurt* of the human...and the *reaction* of the human. No, no, no! That's not that negative stuff – that's hell. *I'm* heaven! God's *my* heaven. God's my heaven *in* my prison...and that *cell* is a heaven too! How he was *blessed* and how those prisoners *must* have been blessed! (39:21-23) Well, we *know* it from the two who came to him, and the jailer.

So we pass through other years when God made him fairly comfortable because he was the jailer's 'blue-eyed boy'. I expect he got a few bananas in with his food to comfort him a little. Then *again*, this incident happened, which *couldn't* have happened if Potiphar's wife hadn't lied him into a jail...*and* if he hadn't been in the jail and in a position of responsibility. These two important men in Pharaoh's household, his head butler (who oversaw the dining facilities), and the baker (chief of the kitchen staff), had displeased Pharaoh, who put them in prison...at least temporarily. Now, if Joseph *hadn't* become what he'd been to the jailer (his trusted assistant in taking care of the prisoners), he wouldn't have taken care of *these* men. If he'd been just a sulky prisoner, he'd be in a dungeon. But, because he was *freely* operating for the jailer, his job was to bring breakfast to these two men. So it all fits together! He found them puzzled. After all these years, somebody was bothered with a *dream*. Now here's my proof of a *fixed consciousness*. Unless Joseph had an *inner* consciousness that it was *God* who spoke by dreams, he couldn't believe it fourteen years afterwards. He'd have grown stale.

There's *no* staleness in this life! You haven't got to read the Bible to *keep* fresh. You're fresh *inside*! The Bible just *helps* you to keep fresh, that's all. You *don't* have to pray to keep fresh, because you're *permanently* in union! Prayer just helps you along the line. You don't *become* fresh...you **are** fresh! *This* is the secret...you **are**. *He* is our freshness! "All our fresh streams are in Him." "Thou has the dew of thy youth." So have we! We *have* youthful dew *inside*...even if we have an aged appearance outside. I love that phrase, "Thou has the dew of thy youth." So always freshness. If you're not fresh, you've been *tricked* into listening to *soul* instead of spirit. Your *emotions* won't make you feel fresh. Your *reasons* won't make you feel fresh. If you're running your life by *should*, "Oh, I'm not fresh"...it's a lie! It's an *illusion*. You *are* fresh because Jesus Christ is your freshness...if He's in you. He *is* in you, if you're His. All you say is, "God, I feel as dull as dish water, but I'm as fresh as can be; it's only an illusion." So don't come to a meeting to *get* fresh! Americans use fresh a little *differently* from English, but you understand what I mean!

So at once, you see, he never *hesitated*! Straightway he said to these men, as he was giving them their breakfast and they looked sad, "Why look ye so sadly today?" He executed a *quality of cheerfulness* even in the prison. They said, "Oh, we had these dreams." At once, without any hesitation, what did Joseph say? They had said, "We have dreamed a dream and there is no interpretation of it". Joseph answered, "Do not interpretations belong unto God?" Straight. "Tell me them I pray you." *That's* freshness! We have *no* evidence that he had dreams in between. We never hear of it. But after fourteen years, "Oh, yes, this is how God speaks to me. He may not speak to you like this, but He speaks to me like that and He makes me understand my dreams." He interpreted their dreams to them.

Evidently the butler was a *genuine* man because he was the one who first told his dream – about the vine and three branches that budded…bore grapes…and Pharaoh's cup was in his hand. He put them in Pharaoh's cup and gave the cup into Pharaoh's hand. Joseph said the *interpretation* is – "The three branches are three days, and after three days Pharaoh will lift up your head and you will be back where you were. Pharaoh's cup will be in your hand, and you'll be giving it to Pharaoh." (He added something else which I will mention in a moment.) Now the butler was evidently a genuine man, but had crossed Pharaoh somewhere and was concerned about it, and really looked for some *restoration* in his innocence, and Joseph gave him a good interpretation. The baker, when he saw the interpretation was good, though he *wasn't* an innocent man, saw there might be a good thing for him in it, and immediately followed the butler and told his dream too. But he was play-acting; the butler wasn't. Pharaoh *knew* that…for it was the baker who got hanged, and the butler got restored. So when he gave his dream of the baskets with birds taking food out of them, Joseph pulled no punches! He had not pulled punches with his own parents about what the future was to be, so he said, "Within three days Pharaoh shall lift up thy head from off thee, shall hang thee on a tree, and the birds shall eat thy flesh from off thee." So it happened!

Again, *marvelous*, this level of life! Not that you *start* there. Here, Joseph saw his chance – this was the palace…these men had *influence!* The men had the *ear* of Pharaoh…the butler. "Could you say a word for me? Could you say I don't belong to these people, I was stolen? I'm a stranger. I never did any harm in all the time I have been put in this place" (40:14-15). You see the *human* touch? There was an aching heart *all the time.* It *doesn't* mean you don't feel…"I don't like this, it's awful, yet *it's all right*, God." And the "all right" is what comes out…not the other. The other comes out *occasionally* for us, that's all. But you *live* in the overflow...but *underneath* there's the suffering. There is *that* in this life. But the fact he said that to the butler shows he must *always* have had it in his mind. He said it to the butler, not the baker, for the Spirit in Joseph obviously showed him the *difference.*

Three and a half years? You can't trust *anybody*, can you, if you see from *man's* point of view? How often we say that! Yet, you can trust *everybody*...because God *means* each to **be** what they are! If they're nasty, God *means* them to be nasty. (See Rom. 9:17 about another Pharaoh.) Don't *see* evil! Oh, rotten, thankless fellow, you *can't* trust anybody! No, *this* is God! If that butler, out of human kindness, had told Pharaoh about this incident when he got righted...and he must have been very excited when he saw the interpretation was true... likely, it would have been a forgotten incident after three and a half years. So the dramatic moment came when it was *needed* or it wouldn't have been fresh.

But *now* the moment arrived! The autocratic Pharaoh was frustrated and angry! "Oh, no, my interpreters, my astrologers, my magicians can't interpret these two dreams I've had." "Oh, I remember my error", the butler intervenes. "I remember my fault this day. Pharaoh was wroth with his servants and put me with the baker in ward in the Captain of the guard's house, and we both had a dream; and there was a young man, a Hebrew, who interpreted our dreams and for each it came true." Then Pharaoh said, "Here's a man who can interpret dreams; send for him."

But Pharaoh had to *wait* for Joseph! Joseph *wouldn't* be pushed around by Pharaoh. He was going to change his clothes and have a shave before he went up. Pharaoh had to *wait*. This was a *poised* man. "I'll look decent." He *knew* his stuff. He knew *he* had what it took. *Only* when he had got ready did he come up. Then he repeated to Pharaoh very much what he'd said to the butler and the baker. Pharaoh said to him, "I have heard say of thee that thou canst understand a dream to interpret it." Joseph's beautiful answer: "It is not in me. *God* shall give Pharaoh an answer of peace." You see my proof that this man *wasn't* Joseph – he was *God* in Joseph's *form*. After all these years…you wouldn't say it in a moment like that *unless* you *knew* God did that kind of thing would you? And he differentiated – "It isn't in me, it's God… but God gives it *by* me." (Joseph didn't put that in, I do.)

Because it is *by me*; **God** operates *by us*. But the *first* point is – it's not me; it's God! *Then* he gave the interpretation…this startling interpretation! Seven full years, overflow of corn and stuff, then seven lean years to eat up the plentiful years. It registered as good sense – the same as the butler and baker's dream made sense, and Pharaoh says, "That makes sense. Now what shall we do?" Joseph added an interesting point on the doubling of the dream which is true throughout the Bible…"And for that the dream was doubled unto Pharaoh twice; it is because the thing is established by God". The doubling of a statement in the Bible, "Mary, Mary", "Martha, Martha", means it's His *special* emphasis…so Jesus saying "Verily, verily."

Now I think this is *beautiful* – again, detachment. This was a slave… brought out from his dungeon after fourteen years, cleaned himself up, cool as could be…says to Pharaoh, "I don't do anything, but God does things and interprets dreams. Here are the dreams; here's the interpretation." Well, that's *enough*, you'd think! But what happened? Joseph then turns around and says, "I'll tell you *how* to do it." You see the *organizing* capacity? He organized Potiphar's household, organized the prison household. So it was simple. Oh, *I'll* tell you what to do. *You* do this, Pharaoh. *That* wasn't part of the dream. That was *God* offering Joseph's own personal gifts! Pharaoh *hadn't* even asked him for advice! I *like* that. "God will shortly bring this to pass." Now therefore, let Pharaoh look at a man discreet and wise. "Here Pharaoh, take my advice." I like that! "Come on, Pharaoh, you get the right man to do it." *That's* the way to handle Pharaohs! "Set him over the land of Egypt." Pharaoh could see it!

Well, we know Joseph. I *can't think* it could have come to Joseph that moment that he would be chosen...I doubt it. It's much more likely that he just said it out of his *instinct* for decent organization – *that's* the way you do it. "You're the man! My, my, you're the man." Everybody agreed, or *had* to agree, because it was so *obviously* so. I *love* the statement of Pharaoh. This was a statement from a pagan, *we'd* say. *Are* they pagans? *Do* they find God? *May* not Potiphar have found God? *May* not the men in prison? Because Pharaoh says *this*..."Can we find such a one as this is, a man in whom the Spirit of God is?" Isn't *that* some statement for a pagan ruler...the greatest in the world! He *recognized* the Spirit of God *in* a man! How silly *we* are to say the Spirit of God *isn't* in men of the Old Testament...and is only in the man of the New. He's *there* all right! Way back there Pharaoh recognized the *Spirit of God in Joseph*, not *on* him, IN him...and speaking *by* Joseph!

Now we follow the years of Joseph's *magnificent* management. He was a *top* man, but God brought out of him those gifts which *only* God had brought to light...by *putting* him in these situations. So with 100% efficiency, he handled this huge commitment to build hundreds of barns for corn in the rich years when it wasn't needed by the people... stored it, preserved it...and then, when the lean years began...gave it out, rationed it out bit by bit so the people could be fed. Pharaoh made him a 'big noise', of course. Pharaoh took off his ring from *his* hand and put it on Joseph's hand and *arrayed* him in vestures of fine linen, and put a gold chain about his neck. He made him to ride in the second chariot which he had, and they cried before him, "Bow the knee", and he made him *ruler* over all the land of Egypt! That didn't touch Joseph. He was *already* a bigger ruler than that! He was already *God's* ruler...beginning to rule the universe...so this didn't *bother* him.

Pride and humility *isn't* thinking much or thinking little of yourself; it's *you* not being there at all! *You're* occupied with God. *That's* humility and pride. You're *neither* humble nor proud - you're occupied with God. Humility is only a *reverse form* of pride. Pride is only a *reverse*

form of humility. It's "I'm not" or "I am", but when I'm not there at all...
God is; that's it! It didn't move Joseph. Joseph was occupied in fulfilling *God's* purposes on this new level, that's all.

Now there came the time of the *fulfillment* of the dream and the link-up with the whole family. Distances were great in those days and it was *quite* a big business to travel from Egypt to the land of Canaan. There is *no* reason to suppose that there would be any further link between Joseph and his family. He had married the daughter of the chief priest, Potiphar – priest of On. He'd called his first son "Forgetting" (Manasseh). So it looks as if it *wasn't* in his mind to relate to his family *even* if he could. *Perhaps* he felt he couldn't. There's no sign he was doing so. I'm only saying that, because again and again it was God *engineering* everything! It was the *famine* that brought the family in *desperation* out of Canaan to come and buy some food from the well-stocked Egyptians.

Now, always the *same* things – a *perfectly* cool man, not without the stirring of *outer* reactions, but knowing from his *inner center of Spirit* how to handle things. (Heb. 4:9-12) *Now* he is under *entirely* different circumstances. Suddenly his *brothers* turn up...his brothers who had set out to *murder* him! And there they stood. *That* was when it says that he remembered the dream...as they bowed down before him. "Joseph's brethren came and bowed down themselves before him with their faces to the earth." (42:6) He saw his brethren and *knew* them... and remembered the dreams which he dreamed of them. (42:9 That shows he always *believed* the dreams. They may have gone into the background as something that hadn't *yet* happened...but there they *were*. That was the original *inner awareness* he had of God that *God* had spoken to him by a dream...and that was God!

It is *interesting* to watch how a *relaxed* man will handle the most *delicate* situation. What could he do? If he *announced* himself to his brothers, what would they do? Oh, my! Flee? Suddenly found they were *confronted* with the man they tried to murder! What would they do?

155

How could he handle it so that they would become a *reunited* family? They were God's *family* who were to propagate in Egypt, and become the *great people* of Israel! *Moses* would take them out and the *history* would *start*...which ends in Jesus' coming to found the *new* nation. *How* to handle it? So we see he was *way beyond* self-reaction. Like Paul, in 2 Cor. 4:15, he had a purpose *outside* himself. He *wasn't* a man of vengeance. He hadn't got *that kind* of thing in him, because he had *God* in him. His first thought was that, if he exposed himself, it might *breach* everything. Would they *flee,* or would they just *pretend* - a bunch of hypocrites - that they were sorry? So you see the point. How can I act now? *They* won't know me...I know them...but we must become a *reconciled* family. *We* are God's family; *these* are God's servants.

Now we will see *how* God operated on them...worked on them *through* their guilt. So He took certain...what we call human actions... but actually *guided* actions. The first was, "Let's have a little time, a little breathing space." So, to keep them 'off,' he bluffed it. "Oh, you're spies." They had *no* idea who he was. "I mustn't have them near me because *I'm* not ready. They mustn't find out who I am." "You're a bunch of spies." Sort of put that kind of *fear* on them rather than the fear of the other kind. So they got to protesting. They said, "We're just from our family, come to buy food." "No, you are spies come to see that we have a famine and all the nakedness of the land." Then they told their story. They talked about the family, the father at home. "Ourselves are twelve brethren, the youngest is this day with our father, and one is not."

That part gave Joseph his *next* lead, demand to see the other brother. "Oh, a young brother? That's who I want to see. Here, I'll strike a bargain with you. I'll give you food. One of you go back to fetch your brother. I want to meet him, and that will prove whether you are spies or not, and you all stay in prison." They were there three days. Then he changed his mind, saying that he "feared God" in maybe keeping them all as prisoners, so he would retain one...but the rest could return with the food the family needed. But for them it was three days of *conviction*. It was *as if* they were getting back what they *gave* to Joseph. *This* was God's judgment.

Now *that* shows they were really not, as we would say, lost sinners, but *hidden* saints. For all those years they *knew* they were *guilty* and were lying to their father. Indeed, it was God's *way* of *restoring* them to their right relationship with God. They didn't know Joseph knew their *language*, of course, "and they said one to another, we are verily guilty concerning our brother, in that we saw the anguish of his soul when he besought us and we would not hear. Therefore is this distress come upon us." "And Reuben answered them saying, 'Spake I not unto you saying, do not sin against this child?' and ye would not hear? Therefore behold, also his blood is required?" Joseph turned from them and *wept*. Why did he weep? Praise God, *they* were seeing their wrong. They *aren't* trying to justify; they *aren't* proud, hating people; they *are* guilty people. He wept for *joy* that this was a *first stage* toward what could become a reconciliation. God was at work...but not *enough* yet. You don't *push*, do you? You *go* with the Lord. You *just do* the next thing.

He was conscious that it was *not* time to say, "Come on, you're my brothers", and so he *hid* his weeping. Then he "communed with them." He began to make a fellowship link with them which *wasn't* usual. He began to *show* them something, which you don't expect to find from a Prime Minister who thinks you're *spies*! He began to show an *interest*, which they would *know* would be an interest, and communed with them and talked about things. "This wasn't an ordinary ruler. What's up? He thinks we're spies and he treats us almost like a friend." He took a further step. He *wasn't* going to take their money. This again must have made them wonder, but in their fear and guilt they took it wrongly! *They* thought they'd be caught up in a burglary trick. It was not like an ordinary ruler with his *prisoners*.

When they found the money, the brothers began to say, "What is this that God hath done to us?" So, you see, they *were* God's men. They weren't a bunch of *unsaved* people. As we have said – they were God's servants who had got in the *flesh*, like we do. The Lord was *using* their flesh-way to bring them into *His* way, and now they knew God. I think we can *take it* that their lives had got right...*particularly* when they returned home from their *rotten excesses* after the shock of the Joseph affair. So they went home and told their father.

Jacob was God's special man, of whom Israel was named...a prince with God...but was always one who more easily *saw* the negative than the positive. He tended to see *darkness*. Yet God *used* that to bring something out which was a *key* to the situation. He said, "I can't let Benjamin go. I've already lost one son and I can't have him take my other son and lose him. I can't do it." He *refused* it.

Now there began to be this *further* move of repentance. God had to get a *positive* response of repentance - "works meet for repentance" Acts 26:20 - from the brethren before they'd be *fit* to move into reconciliation again. The *first* step we've seen already - the *guilt*. The *second* step was this – they began to feel *their responsibility* for Benjamin... which they had *never felt* for Joseph...and began to *show* that they were involved in this thing. It wasn't a total step, but Reuben, being the eldest, said, "If he doesn't come back, slay my two sons." That wouldn't help very much. It wasn't "slay myself." You see, repentance is..."Don't slay the other fellow, slay me." He hadn't gotten *that* far. "If we take Benjamin and he doesn't come back, let my sons be the price paid." *Not* a very effective substitute, but a *step* in the right direction. Jacob wouldn't take that.

Finally, they *had* to go, because they were starving! Once again, God's *pressure* was on them...they *had* to go! When Jacob said they *must* go, they said, "We can't go without Benjamin." Then Judah came forward. Now, Judah was the one who sold Joseph into slavery, and Judah said, "My father, I'm in his place. If he doesn't come back, if something happens to him, I'll take what happens to Benjamin on myself." This was what he meant – What *should* happen to Benjamin, I'll take on *myself.* He *proved* this a little later on. He said to Jacob, "I will be surety for him; of my hand shalt thou require him: if I bring him not unto thee, and set him before thee, then let me bear the blame forever." He couldn't, at that moment, quite define *how* he'd do it, but he did mean, "I'll step in Benjamin's place. If something has to happen to Benjamin, I choose that it happens to me instead." That was right, when he had been the very one who'd put Joseph into slavery. On *that* basis, Jacob consented and they went.

Now, once again, Joseph was watching to see *how* there could be the reunion. It didn't feel he had got *quite* far enough yet...and he hadn't heard what Judah said. So they came back, brought the money which he had restored to their sacks and the fresh money for more corn...and *wondered* what they'd get. When Joseph saw them coming, he gave orders to his head of his house to welcome them into *his own* home. Everything was to make them feel at home. This *strange* man who should be beating them up and shouting or hanging them was making friends with them. Yet he called them spies! What's up? Put their money back! What's up? *Normally* they wouldn't have *contact* with the ruler of the country, and here they are in his own home! So immediately they go to the steward, "We want you to know it wasn't our fault. *Please* understand. We came to the inn and, behold, every man's money was in the mouth of his sack and we have brought it again in our hand. What can we do?" The steward said, "Peace be to you, fear not. Your God and the God of your father hath given you treasure in your sacks." *Remarkable* words from the steward! See how the Egyptians were *beginning to find* the living God...how Joseph's testimony was rubbing off? So he brought Simeon out to them and gave them water to wash their feet. Then they heard they were to eat bread there! Well, *that* topped it all...to eat bread in fellowship with this ruler of Egypt. Joseph came, asked after the father, and *then* he saw his brother. That was *too* much for him! He had to go away and hide and weep, for the *final moment* had not yet come. "For his bowels did yearn upon his brother; and he sought where to weep and he entered into his chamber and wept there". (43:30)

Now they had this meal together. According to certain standards they ate at different tables, but had the same dinner together...and with a *special* portion for Benjamin. It got to where they became really *free* with each other. "They drank and were merry with him." Now he had reached the *place* where these men, who *should* have been full of fear or awe, were making jokes with him! Bit by bit he was melting down *barriers* between them. Something was happening...they began to *like* this man! But *how* could he be nice to them? What *sort* of ruler is this who is kind to them, gives them a big feast, gives them money, and takes them into his home? Yet there was still to come the *final evidence* of repentance. *Then* Joseph played his final trick.

I don't know *how* he caught onto this one. We're not told. Certain surprises turn up in the Bible...you can't tell how. *How* did Gideon get the idea of putting torches in pots and blowing trumpets? It was quite *original*. What suddenly occurred to Joseph was a means of bringing them to a *final* point of desperation – to the place of *no escape*! Suddenly it came to him to do *this* thing – to send them back, not only with money in their sacs, but to put what he called *his* silver cup into Benjamin's sack. (The steward called it his "divining" cup, but *Joseph* had better divination than that! He had the divination *inside* him!) Then, when they started on the journey, he sent his messengers after them to say, "You stole my cup." "Oh, we couldn't do such a thing as that." *Utter dismay!* They opened up the sack and Benjamin had it. That *really* tore them apart. They rushed back; they were *caught* in it now. *This* was the time they fell on their faces. That was different from *previous* bowing the neck. Bowing the neck was politeness. Falling on their faces was a smash up! "Judah and his brethren came to Joseph's house," and "they fell before him on the ground." Of course, Joseph looked apparently severe and even pretended he could divine by that stolen cup! (44:15) Then Judah came out. Here was the completion of what Joseph was looking for. The *sign* from God that the moment had come for making himself *known* to them was when Judah stepped out in front of him and told how they had *promised* to take Benjamin back to Jacob, and then he said, "For thy servant became surety for the lad unto my father, saying, 'If I bring him not unto thee, then I shall bear the blame to my father forever.' Now therefore, I pray thee, let thy servant abide instead of the lad a bondman to my lord, and let the lad go up with his brethren. For how shall I go up to my father, and the lad not be with me?" That was it! He had put *himself* for life to be a slave to Joseph or in prison in the place of Benjamin, which was *taking on himself* the slavery into which he had sent Joseph.

Now Joseph said, "This is it! Now we're right through, we have really faced all that was gone in the past, and I've seen the recognition of their guilt and distress, and we've made a bond of fellowship enough for *me* to be able to approach them without a shock. It was *too much* for him. He cried before them all, loud enough for all Pharaoh's house to hear. He sent all his staff out of the room, and stood up and made himself known to his brethren. "I am Joseph," he said. "Doth my father yet live?" They couldn't answer him because they were dumbfounded... but *not* as they would have been without these step by step approaches. There had been a softening of the ground, but, of course, "They were troubled." That wonderful statement: *"You meant it for evil;* **God** *meant it for good."* **This is one of the great statements of the Bible...***proof* that God *means* evil for good purposes! Therefore *all* evil should *never* be seen as evil; it should only be seen as *some means* by which God is bringing out some *manifestation of His good.* Always *see* the goodness of God!

So Joseph said, "Come near to me." He added the marvelous word, "Now therefore be not grieved nor angry with yourselves that ye sold me hither; for *God* did send me *before* you to preserve life and to preserve posterity on the earth". He was beginning to see *God's purpose* in it all. "So it was not you that send me hither, but God."

The kiss of reconciliation settled them when he "fell on his brother Benjamin's neck" and wept and kissed all his brethren. After that, his brethren talked with him. They didn't *completely* get free. There was a *healing* of memories to be done which had to take place later. With some of us, until we've really seen the *completion* of our place in Christ, people can carry that *same* problem of unhealed memories. But there was a *reconciliation*. They saw that Joseph accepted them, loved them and the family. Then there came this period of *great* rejoicing. Pharaoh heard of it, was delighted, and said *he* would send every kind of help and wealth and sustenance to bring the *whole family* into Egypt. They returned and told Jacob his son was alive and that he was to come and see him in Egypt...and the whole family was to move, which they did. There was a great procession with the wagons for transport, and loads of food that Pharaoh had sent.

They came into the land of Egypt and were given the best of the land, Goshen...the *most* productive area. Jacob went before Pharaoh and there he acted as he was...as God's man, God's prince...and he *blessed* Pharaoh and talked a little with him. Then they settled down into their new life.

There's not much more to add. Jacob reached his *final* heights in speaking the word of the Lord when he *prophesied* what would be the *destiny* for each of the tribes. He prophesied how each would function when they came into the land, including the reversal of the two brothers, which Joseph hadn't seen - Jacob put Ephraim as elder; Manasseh, the younger. Jacob was the elder in the Spirit. So he *saw* more than Joseph did. Then he went to be with the Lord with his final vow...that through Judah, "Shiloh should come," – the Messiah!

The family remained and prospered after they had had a great burial of their father in the land of Canaan. But, at first, they were still *afraid*, and, with their father Jacob's death, they still had the *suspicion* that Joseph might turn round and take vengeance on them. So they sent him a message pleading a final forgiveness. He wept when they told him that. They fell down on their faces before him and Joseph then said that final word, "Fear not, am I in the place of God? As for you, you thought evil against me; but God MEANT it unto good."

That was, I take it, where they got the *assurance* of forgiveness. They had said to Joseph, "Forgive, I pray thee now, the trespass of thy brethren, and their sin; for they did unto thee evil." They were *totally* through now. This was confessed sin and forgiveness asked for. That was when Joseph *forgave* their sin. "God meant it for good; you meant it for evil." We take it there was a *final reconciliation* then between them all.

Joseph's last act of faith was to align himself, not with Egypt, but with *God's purposes for Israel in Canaan*. So the last thing he said was, "When I die, I don't belong here anymore than you do; I go back with you. So take my bones back with you and bury them when you come back to the land of Canaan." So his last act and attitude was to preserve the way of *faith* he had walked on...and all part of the *ultimate purposes* of God for the *world's* salvation.

MOSES

Moses was born during a *darkened* period for the growing nation of Israel. God continually does things that way to keep us from assessing things in *temporal* terms and being *deluded* into thinking the devil is a power! The devil is *only* an agent. God puts us in situations so that *we* may know how, as people of the Spirit, to operate as channels by which God brings spiritual deliverances in devilish situations. It is a privilege to know how God can come through, *by us*, in manifestations of Himself in adverse situations. *That's* what your life is...*your* glory and *my* glory!

It started when a jealous Pharaoh who, with his human wisdom, said, "Let us deal wisely with them, lest they multiply." All his 'wisdom' did was to *stir up* faith! *That* is what is happening today! Lenin, Hitler and Stalin said *they* would deal wisely, and now there is *far more faith* in the world today than there ever was in the days when Hitler was here or Stalin was on the go. This is a *great world-era* of faith! The Spirit is *springing up all over* the place in all nations. It's tremendous! That is the response that *God* gives to *move faith into action* in God's people when the devil *conveniently* brings a Stalin and a Hitler into being. Through faith comes Christ! So it was in the days of Moses.

I shall begin with little *details* showing how *common* people could shine with faith. God is always playing *tricks*...and this starts off with a joke...though not a joke to them! The command had gone out that *all* men children of the Hebrews were to be killed. Now, they had midwives...and these midwives *knew* the Lord. We shall find one day that *millions* have known the Lord…and *not* under the Christian name either…who pop up every now and then, as these midwives did. They surreptitiously left the boy children *alive,* and this got to Pharaoh's ear. Pharaoh called these midwives for an interview, and said to them, "*What* are you doing; why are these sons being born?"

"Well," they said "Your Egyptian women are so *slow* in giving birth that they need midwives. The Hebrew women arc so quick that they get sons before we can get there to deliver them." Nice little trick! It was deceit, of course, and not the *real* truth at all. It wasn't that they weren't there in time…they didn't *intend* to be there, that's all. They intended to get the sons born before they could do anything to them. So God *loves* to be a deceiver! In the *ways of faith* you sometimes learn how to practice deceit. In Exodus 1:21, it says that God built them houses. *Normally* they would have gotten prison. Isn't it beautiful the way God *preserved* those women? That was simple people practicing *faith* in a situation. A simple person can be an agent of the Spirit right down to the common things of life…such as childbirth and so on.

It's *likely* that these midwives inspired faith in Moses' parents, Amram and Jochebed. It doesn't *say* so, but it *does say* that they had faith at the birth. Now, faith is *substance.* Faith isn't, "Oh, this is a lovely child, *perhaps* he will get through." It is, "He **will** get through." Faith is, "That's a *settled* thing." There is *no doubt* that this was a godly couple who knew a thing or two. They knew the history of the Israelites and they, without doubt, knew that the time had come of which God had said to Abraham…"After four hundred years I will bring My people back from Egypt to the land I promised them." They are put into the *great* faith chapter in Hebrews 11, where it says, "By faith Moses, when he was born, was hid three months of his parents, because they saw he was a proper child; and they were not afraid of the king's commandment." The king's commandment was *very* tough, but this couple didn't fear the power of an earthly king's commandment. One of the *great* lessons we have to learn is that…**we fear *because* we believe evil *to be* evil**…and it controls us! This couple *transferred* their fear into believing that *God would do* what He said He would do! That's what faith *always* is – *believing God* instead of believing evil! Faith is relaxed and just goes along free of any law, asking, "What is the *next thing* to do in this situation?"

At the end of three months, in their relaxed situation, they saw that it was dangerous to keep the child. The news probably got out that here was this three months old boy. Now they did a *remarkable* thing which again shows that they were *steeped* in Bible history which had come down to them right from the beginning. Moses *knew* it, because he wrote about the Fall. Where did Moses get it from? The Israelite people *knew* these truths, and what this couple saw was that there had been a moment when the *whole world* was going to be drowning…and certain people who *believed God* were instructed by God to make a certain thing…by which they would be preserved. They made it, and were preserved…and the name of that thing was an ark!

So Moses parents build a little ark. They sealed it with the same pitch that the original ark was sealed with. Their *faith* was that in this little ark their baby son would *somehow* be delivered…just as Noah and his eight were delivered. Beautiful! Now they may or may not have guessed about Pharaoh's daughter. They certainly must have known that her regular system was to come to the Nile with her women to bathe. We *can't* say that they *knew* that she would pick the child up, but what did happen was that Pharaoh's daughter and her maids saw, not the child, but the ark. *That's* what caught them! "What's that?" they said.

Building a miniature copy of the ark of history as a symbol that God would *preserve* the child, and then putting the little baby in it among the reeds in the Nile was an act of *faith*. That attracted the attention of the one who became his rescuer. When the ark was opened, the baby cried, and you *know* the effects of cries on mothers. But it wasn't the cries that had gotten their attention…it was the ark. The cry just melted the heart. So Pharaoh's daughter said, "We can't let that little thing die."

Further evidence of an *established faith* on the part of Moses' parents was that the mother sent the elder daughter, Miriam, to watch by the reeds to see what would happen. I think it is evident that she was sent to watch, not out of curiosity, but in the belief that God *was going to* do something. So when the princess took the baby and her maid recognized it as one of the Hebrew children, Miriam was ready and immediately stepped forward and said, "Give him to me. I'll have him looked after," and took him back to his mother. So God made the persecutor of Israel *pay* for the upbringing of the *deliverer*! *These* are the kinds of things which God does! Pharaoh was paying wages to Moses' parents to bring up the person who would deliver Israel from his tyranny! That is *typical* of God. There are many laughs in heaven which *we* can share. So the baby went back to his parents. Think of the *thrill* of being able to train Moses now that they knew who he was going to be! There is a *great* point for us here – this *wasn't* a big, national affair. It involved *common people* as this couple in their home, and a couple of midwives in their job, who *believed* that *God* was going to do something! *These* are the people who are behind destiny. *Any* **act of faith** you and I have taken has an *eternal* flow to it...and is part of *destiny*!

In due time, Moses was moved over into the palace where he belonged as the official adopted son of Pharaoh's daughter. We don't know about his life on the negative side...and I have a feeling that he *never* went very far on the *wrong* side of life because he had this moral upbringing. Those were valuable years because he was trained in all learning in all the wisdom of Egypt. The Egyptians were the dominant race of *that* day and mighty in word and deed. So he was a very fine, outstandingly developed, highly educated young man. God uses all kinds. He starts with a couple of mid-wives and a couple of parents, and continues His great processes through to a highly educated man. In both the Old and New Testament when He wanted to get established truth through, *He* had His Moses and He had His Paul, *both* highly educated men whom He was able to use when they had *been through the crucible and come up on the other side!*

When Moses was forty years old, he came to the moment of *radical* decision in his life...and *totally* turned his back on all the world could offer him. *That* is when God can begin to utilize a life! It may take varied forms, but there is a *total turning*. There is *nothing* left of what this world can offer you...which has *any* further interest to you. It *actually* becomes offensive to you. That's what Paul said in his self-dedication...which can be compared in some sense with Moses' great self-dedication. In Philippians 3, Paul says that he *suffered the loss* of all things when he *saw* the Lordship of Christ; what things *were* gain to him in self-righteousness were *lost* in Christ. There is a *certain* element in which it cost him to give up his position as one of the *topmost* young Jews, but then, he said, "I count them but dung that I might be identified with Christ." Things which 'smelled' a little nice when I gave them up smell offensive to me *today*. *That's* how God takes you! That *old* life becomes offensive to you. You don't hanker after it any longer...and it becomes something you *can't* touch because you've got something *far more* glorious.

That's what Moses had. Moses' dedication was to take the glory of a *cross*, not the glory of a better *human* life. Hebrews 11 is perhaps the greatest presentation of a total commitment ever given. "By faith, Moses, when he was come to years, refused to be called the son of Pharaoh's daughter, choosing rather to suffer affliction with the people of God than to enjoy the pleasure of sin for a season." This was not replacing pleasure by pleasure as we call pleasure, and saying, "Well, God will do me well in this life if I give up certain things." Instead, it was, "No, I can have the glory of being *involved* in all kinds of *tough* spots, and some of those tough spots are God's *power and grace* being manifested. To *suffer affliction* with the people of God is my *privilege*... that I might have a tempestuous life under *all* kinds of tests and trials and pressures...because as I see how *God* comes through those in forms of deliverance. *That's* my glory! *That's* my pleasure...my *permanent* pleasure...instead of the pleasure of sin for a season."

So you see, committal isn't committal to an *easier* life down here…
it's committal to the glory of a *harder* life. Don't ask for an easy life. Ask
for the glory of permanent pressures…because *permanent pressures are
permanent springboards for faith!* They press you into *faith!* From permanent faith comes permanent *deliverances*…and *then* your life is a scream
and a thrill! Jesus said, "My joy I give unto you." Jesus didn't *attract*
people by being mournful; it was because He had such *joy* in what He
did! Yet he lived the *afflicted* life. He said that for the *joy* that was set
before Him He endured the Cross. So you see…He had *another* type
of pleasure! Moses' committal was a positive thing, not a negative, for
it was *replacing* fiddling things by *tremendous* things! How could you
compare being Pharaoh's heir to being *God's* heir…and to being God's
agent in bringing the inheritance into its *fulfillment* on earth! As God's
redeeming agent you can count it an *honor* to be thought a fool. It says
that "He esteemed the reproach of Christ greater riches than the treasures of Egypt." The *reproach* of Christ! The reproach of being thought
insane, being a fool, being rejected, being outside the camp, having
it said, "You're just 'way out' because you are a Christian." Your riches
are to *be* way out with Christ in the *fulfilling* of His world salvation purposes and the ultimate destiny! That was Moses' committal. It was a
radical committal.

Now Moses is *free* for the Spirit of God to operate on Him. God
can't operate where there are *dual* loyalties. The *heart is single*…and
your heart is *single* when you are born again. *Everybody* has a pure
heart; it just depends on *whether* it's pure for God or pure for Satan.
When you are born again, you move back to the *fact* that you *belong* to
God. *Temporarily it appears not to be so*…and in order to get the thing
established you have to go through negative *processes*.

I went through negative processes just after I was born again, because I was very fond of a girl. We had a good relationship, but although she was a *church* girl, she wouldn't get saved. Suddenly, the Holy
Spirit said, "You drop her." Why? "You can't have both Christ *and* her…

and she doesn't want Jesus Christ." That *cost* me more than my salvation! That cost me a nice little three weeks of *hell*. I was just preparing to go into the British Army in World War I...and as I was preparing my uniform, all the time I was hearing, "You can't have both." I won't go into detail now, but I had a *very wise* mother who finally told me that *what God says* is usually right. I made the cut. When the cut was *made*, I didn't feel it! I have visited the lady since. She is an ancient lady now... about *my* age, married to a school master...and I go and talk with her. I am glad for her sake we *didn't* marry...and *also* for my sake. I made the cut and it *released* my heart.

Therefore, the next *stage of the preparation* of the Spirit in this man... by whom *God* was to be great...was to go through the negative process. That was to be the *final* form of the *self*-operating. You see, it isn't *God* in the foreground through eternity; it is *man* in the foreground...**God manifested by man**! The Father is manifested *through* the Son and *we* are the sons...and for all eternity we are to function as *real* persons. We are *free* people and we will think, will, and *act* as real people! If we are going to *be* real persons God has to take *considerable* pains for us to find out how to function as *right persons* so that we may be perfectly free, right persons. Then that right person isn't really *you*; it is really the One to whom you are joined, expressed *by* you, and *appearing* to be you. *That* is the paradox!

The *final* form of sin is self-sufficiency – self-love that says, "I'll run my own life. I'll do what I want with it." To get our *personality* into focus, we have to find *first* of all that we are the wrong kind of people – lost sinners – and then we get right with God. *Next* we have to find our helpless selves – because the *real place of the self* is to be the *agency* of the deity – it is the negative to the positive. The positive operates *through* the negative. The symbols given to us in the Bible are the branch to the vine, and the body to the head. The *resources* are not in the human self but in the Divine Self...for He is the all, operating *through* the human self. The human self has very wonderful abilities which are here to be utilized...as the power of the mind...the power of the will...and the power of the emotions. Humans can produce a good deal in the midst of this distortion of the world with these powers, but it is all geared to self-interest...as the self *is*!

The purpose of God is that we *humans* with our resources may be put into the right focus – so that the resources are being used under the *right* motivation. When they were used under the *motivation* of the spirit of self-centeredness and our resources were *centered* in the world geared to self-interest and self-aggrandizement, sin and bondage were the result. By coming to Jesus Christ we have gotten *delivered* from sin and bondage and the guilt that would send us to hell, but we haven't *yet gotten delivered* from the *sense* that **we** can live life by *our* resources... now with the *help* of God. Our motivation is different because we are being motivated by God but the *emphasis* is, "Now with **my** resources *I* can fulfill God's will."

In order to *discover* what he is and who he is as a *true self*, every human has to go through *another phase* of self-education – and that has to be a *total* frustration with self-activity! These are not wrong forms of activity because, though he may slip, he is **not** *living for* sin as he used to; but he is frustrated because his concept is that he must now do the *best he can* for God! He must battle, and take the strain, and handle things as best he can...maybe with God's *help*...but his main emphasis isn't so much God's help as his *frustrated* but *dedicated* **self**. He has to be brought to a *final recognition* of his frustration, *precisely* as he had to be brought to a final recognition of his sin. He had to see himself as a *guilty sinner* going to hell...then he has to see himself as a *helpless saint unable* to fulfill the will of God...or only fulfilling under the strains and distresses and fruitlessness which he *can't stand* any more!

So this was the *next phase* through which Moses was taken. It almost seems, looking at it now, that it *had* to come. This man had the vision now and was totally dedicated to God and his calling. Stephen, in his speech before the Sanhedrin (Acts 7), makes it quite clear when he said that "It came into Moses heart to visit his brethren for he supposed his brethren would have understood that God by his hand would deliver them." Moses knew that *he* was to be the deliverer. But what could he do? *He* had to move a nation…*he* had to change the mind of Pharaoh…*he* had to deliver a helpless people who were just farmers and being persecuted and treated as slaves now, and get them out of the hands of their bosses, and march a couple of million people to their destination. *This* was fantastic!

What *did* he do? He killed one of the Egyptians in secret. That's all *he* could do – kill one of the Egyptians. Now, you can't rescue a nation by killing one of the Egyptians, and hiding him because you are *afraid* you might get found out! This shows right away that he was under the fear of the power of *man*…not *under the faith of the power of God*! *That* is not sufficient effectiveness to deliver a nation! It looks silly now, but it was, in fact, *beautiful* – for it identified him *with* the Hebrews. He acted *rightly* to defend his people by killing the Egyptian who was persecuting the Hebrew. That's all he *could* do! All *his* power could do was to use his physical force to kill a man, and then be sure no one saw him. And so he *lived* in fear of the power, which he *had come* to overcome!

The *ridiculousness* of it was seen the next day when he found one Hebrew beating up another one. He must have *thought* that because he was from the palace and was a learned, unusual person that he would be *respected* by his fellow Hebrews when he went among them… but when he tried to break up the fight, the response was, "Who are *you*? Are you trying to kill me, the same as you killed that Egyptian yesterday?" He didn't know they knew…and they were laughing at him! "All you can do is kill people and seek to hide their bodies." *That* is not much of a deliverer! So he was held in *contempt* by his people.

That is when he saw that there was *something* lacking. *How* could he make these two contrasts meet? He was to be the judge and deliverer of his people…but *he* couldn't do it! He had tried it out. He *had* to try it *because you always have to try the negative to find the positive*! Killing the Egyptian and being held in contempt by his brethren were quite right because he had to be *shown up* to himself. You can't see a positive replacement until you see a *total negative false condition*…and are *para-lyzed* by it!

All he could do was run…so as *soon* as he heard that Pharaoh had heard and was sending his police after him to kill him he fled. All he had was a helpless body. *His* mightiness in word and deed wouldn't do *this* job. *Now*, it is obvious that Moses had given himself up in **outward form**…but not *inwardly*. He fled to the desert, and did a kind 'act' for the daughters of a priest of Midian. They were trying to draw water for their cattle, but the other shepherds kept pushing them out because they were women, so he stepped in and watered the cattle for them. This was the *real* Moses coming out. He *had* that saving streak…even on that level. So he gained acceptance from Jethro, the priest, who appointed him a shepherd. *That* was really giving *himself* up…because shepherding is the one thing the Egyptians held in contempt. It says that he was *content* to dwell there…and he wouldn't have been content *unless* he was really giving himself up. He had a real *inner* paradox, because *God* had said to him that *he* was to deliver Israel and he had said, "Yes."

Now here he was completely cut off! How could he make the two meet? He didn't make them meet in practical outcome. The *proof* that by faith he made them meet was that when the right time came, *he* could *see* the burning bush! He wouldn't have been *able* to see the burning bush unless he was *conditioned*…because natural bushes don't burn and *keep* burning! It's only when they are *supernatural* that they do that. It may or may not have been a vision, but certainly it was *not* a sight that just *anyone* could see. There are sights that *only* those who have 'eyes' to see can see…as Jesus always said. Unless Moses had been *quickened* in spirit and ready to *hear* the voice of God, he *couldn't have seen* that bush. That is the *evidence* that he remained all those years in an *inner faith*. Maybe it took forty years because *he* was such a dynamic person. He had to let *loose* of that dynamic personality and drop it from the scene before God could *use it* to have *him* become one of the great men of history!

One of the daughters of Jethro, Zipporah, was given to him for his wife and when his sons were born he *did not* insist on having them circumcised, the *token* God had given Abraham for the Hebrews. Whether he should have insisted on this at birth or whether, in a sense, he had *given it all up* and let it go for the time being, I don't know, but it turned out all right because when the right moment came, God dealt with him and he *had* to do it. God said, "You must conform your sons outwardly to the nation which you are going to lead." When it was done, Zipporah became very angry and left him. She came back later on and joined him in the wilderness. This is all we know of those years as a shepherd.

We know that the wilderness worked the *necessary conditions* upon Moses because his *attitude* changed from the time of the burning bush onwards. The burning bush is a *remarkable symbolic illustration* of this real **God-man** *life* – the God *united* life – and it's plain that Moses *saw* it as that. What he saw was like *no ordinary* bush which burns and dies down and finishes. This *kept* burning and when he went closer to investigate. The Voice came out of the bush...out of the flame...and told him to take his shoes off his feet, because the place *he* stood on was *holy* ground. Those were still the days when God was only manifesting Himself *partially*...as He did before the birth of the church...and so some places were holy and some places were unholy. Of course, now we know *everything* is holy and we don't have to take off our shoes on holy ground because **we** are part of the holiness...so where *we* are **is** holy ground as much as *any* place that is tread on. Any idea of a special *building* being holy **disappeared** at Pentecost...and now we know that everything is a form of God and *nothing* is unclean of itself.

In that sense, everything can be worshipped because *everything* is an expression of God, but nothing in *particular* is an expression of God...*except* **God Himself in union with us**, whom we worship in spirit with whom we are co-gods. But those were still the *childhood* days when God was getting His truths through *stage by stage*. So He spoke like that to Moses. The *point* was that Moses suddenly realized that the Living

God, speaking by His *living* voice, speaks through a common bush. The burning of the bush is **God** *speaking through a human agency*. *As* He speaks through the human agency He *renews* the agency. The bush not being consumed was because it was *refueled*, as it were, by God. The vital truth conveyed by this strange sight was that *God dwells in and manifests Himself by man!* This was a *new* revelation to Moses.

What Moses went through was the end of that *illusory separated* relationship to God. Through the revelation of the burning bush, the *truth dawned* on him that the Living God speaks through human agencies…pictured in a common wilderness bush…because God *does* speak by common people. *This* was when Moses graduated out of the *school* of faith and moved into the *life* of faith. The school of faith is where we are learning what the completion of that faith relationship is. This is that by which we receive, recognize, and experience who *we* really are…not who God is…because we have had these *mistaken* concepts of *ourselves*. We have now moved into a properly focused consciousness when we discover that a *real human* is in a *permanent inner union*. This is *not* a union which destroys his personality, but *liberates* it…so that he is *conscious* that the One who is really thinking, willing, and acting in him is the Living God in **permanence**! There is a *consciousness* of something which is indissoluble and *nothing* can ever change it or shadow it. The *shadows* are only in *our* imaginations or in *our* false senses of guilt. That is the real importance of the impartation of the consciousness of union. *We are spirits so we live by consciousness.* Consciousness is what we just know to be a fact about ourselves. You don't have to *find* a consciousness; you just **are** that and recognize it, if necessary.

Now Moses had passed through what we might call the three phases of consciousness. **One** was a consciousness of just *being a person*. That is the unsaved condition. Perhaps we are not even conscious of being whatever we call a *self.*

The **second** phase is when we **are** conscious that *we are redeemed* selves…and it has been imparted to us because faith is knowledge. *Faith is only faith when it becomes that to which it has committed itself.* It produces a **union** with that to which we commit ourselves. For instance, you are in union with the food you eat...or anything else you do...and become conscious of it. It is a *consciousness* which is perfectly natural and which you are perfectly at ease with. You never have to think about it again except to delight, if you like, or remind yourself of maybe if in this world of pressures we may for a *moment* forget who we are. The point *isn't* that it had been a fresh revelation of God to us. It *has been* a fresh revelation of who *we* are – God in human form in an *unchangeable permanency*! Living, as we do, by inner consciousness, all we *ever* have to do is recognize it when necessary, but largely we can just forget it. The point of 'being' is to forget your consciousness and **be**! You function on the basis of being a person. The point of life is to have what we may call a **subconscious** *permanent realization*...which we forget because we are *involved* in that to which our lives are being given. To a large extent life is forgetting self and forgetting God *because* He is me and I am He. *It is a permanent fact!* When necessary, I remember that it isn't really I. It is **He expressing** *His mind through my mind* and *His will through my will...His emotions through my emotions*! We are free people because we are living out the God-relationship...which is ours within. It is into *that* that Moses now moves. It was necessary that he become conscious of his total inability – the total negative – in order to have the *full-orbed revelation* of the positive, which is God's total *ability* in a *permanent* relationship.

The **third** phase occurred as Moses moved out from the *school of faith* into the *life of faith* and the way in which the inner spirit began to speak to Moses was by way of a commission. The life of faith is always a *commissioned* life because it is an outgoing life. We are here so that *by us* God may do some of the redeeming work that He has *already done in* us! He came that the whole world might find redemption and His purpose is to fulfill some phase of His redeeming work by *us*. God is saying to us, "Now, there are some ways in which I purpose to unveil Myself as Savior to this certain person." Or "Here is someone who already has the Savior, but needs building up in Him." *Because* God is self-giving love, we are rooted and grounded in love. If the first part of that prayer from Ephesians 3 is fulfilled, then "Christ dwells in our hearts by faith and we are rooted and grounded in love with Him so that we comprehend with all the saints the height, length, depth, breadth and know the love of Christ which passes knowledge, filled with all the fullness of God." This is the outgoing Christ in His universe!

In His commission to Moses God explains how He had always had in His inner heart His concern for His people in their oppression under the Egyptians, and how He is now come to deliver them from the Egyptians and take them into this land flowing with milk and honey. He immediately gives Moses his *rightful* place when He says, "Come now, I will send thee." That's always what God does! He says He will deliver and will send Moses. In Exodus 3:10: "I will send thee unto Pharaoh that thou mayest bring forth thy people, the children of Israel, out of Egypt." This is a *staggering* sentence...a commission to Moses, who had to hopelessly and helplessly flee forty years before! There wasn't a finger he could raise against Pharaoh, and when Pharaoh threatened his life he had to get out. Here is this *same* man now being told to go back to confront Pharaoh and all the might of Egypt to deliver this huge, helpless slave nation. There was not a soldier or a disciplined person among them...and *he* was to bring them out of Egypt and into the Promised Land. So we see at once the *extent* of the change of consciousness Moses had. The Moses who couldn't *dream* of such a thing forty years ago could *now* talk it over. Now he saw how it could be done because this would be *God in all His resources operating* by the hand of Moses! It's always by *our* hand. So they entered into practical conversation, as they *should* do.

Faith is *entirely* rational...faith isn't irrational. It's *beyond* reason. However, its rationality only takes shape for us *after* we have first experienced it. It's the *explanation* we have...*after* we have entered into a relationship which we receive to satisfy our *need*...not our reason. Salvation satisfies our *need*, not our reason. In coming to Jesus we bypass reason, and usually haven't got very many sufficient reasons by which we can prove why we can say Jesus is **our** Savior...except a complete sense of our lost condition, and a complete sense of the presentation of the gospel of grace given to us through Jesus. So we move... and *having moved in,* faith *then* becomes knowledge and we know it to be so! Now reason will come along and explain just why it *is* so. It is right to know...for truth is not to remain a mystery. We are to share *God's* mind...and to *know* the mind of Christ. We should be able to know the whys and wherefores, both of God and ourselves, for we only really act confidently when we do. There always should be an examination going on of what it all *means*...or of *how* we are to function if it's a question of a practical situation. This is what was happening in this dialogue between God and Moses in the desert.

Moses started in quite normally and humanly saying, "Who am I?" He had *had* to say that because he previously had said, "I am I," and "I am the person to do it," and then collapsing. It was necessary for him to say, "I am quite sure I am not the person." That doesn't mean he was *doubting* the union, but just that he was settling into what that relationship really was – and it certainly wasn't in him! He wanted *himself* to know that...and God *already* knew that. So he quite rightly says, "Who am I to do that...to go on to Pharaoh and bring forth the children of Israel out of Egypt?" God gave him the confirming word, and He put it in *external* terms, "So shall I be *with* thee." However, He knew that Moses knew *more* than that or he could not have functioned, so a little later on He said, "Moses, you are God to Aaron and a god to Pharaoh," **or** "I am thee." He was saying, *you* are actually Me in the *human*...but at that moment He just put it in these terms, "I am with you and you will do it."

The proof that Moses *had* moved into this easy relationship was that he then said, "*When* I come to the children of Israel what shall I say?" He didn't say, "Shall I come?" but "When!"......which means he *accepted.*

That was a *tremendous* acceptance! He hadn't the *faintest* notion how it would happen – this is the *thrill* of a faith which says as **fact** what is *perfectly ridiculous*! It is a wonderful basis to living as a *true* person. He asked for certain confirmations...not for himself, but because he had already *had* a bang in the eye when he had previously gone to Israel proposing himself to be a leader, and they had laughed him to scorn because they saw his weakness. Therefore, he needed to know on what basis he could go back to persuade them that *he* was to be their deliverer.

The first confirmation was that God revealed to him a strange name. This new name, the I AM, is the name that Jesus took, "Before Abraham was, I Am" and then He tacked on to it, "I am the way, I am the truth, I am the life." "**I Am**" really is a *statement of being* to which you tack *any* name...anything you like to it. I AM everything! This really is God saying, "I AM the universal, and you are now operating on the resources *of* the universal." The universal I AM is present tense because there is only one tense. There is no past or future for those are only *human* conveniences...just the *same* as there is no here, or there, or space, or time. They are simply Einstein's tricks, conveniences. There never has been with God – only the eternal now. I AM. I AM the sufficiency *now*. That's why God tells us not to take thought about tomorrow... because there is no tomorrow. It's a phony. It's a joke...because when you get to tomorrow, it's today again! You never catch up.

Don't fuss about a possibility; in actuality what happens tomorrow *is* a possibility. Don't fuss about possibilities...*today* is the actuality. Jesus said, "Sufficient unto the day is the evil thereof," *because* this world is evil, it comes to us in evil form. *You* turn it to good. *You* can turn into good the evil which is in reach of you by saying, "Oh, praise the Lord, You are handling that." You turn something which you don't like *into* a place of praise and acceptance, and doing something with the love of God *because* it is within *your* reach. So live in today and be sure you don't see as evil...what always is in this evil world coming to us *as* evil. Be sure *you* turn it around and see it as only an expression in which *God* is showing you *some new phase* of His goodness! Through the spirit of praise (which I lack plenty myself...we often do in these sudden situations) and peace, *you* may do the works of God! That's the I AM! So the I AM is the *eternal now* and the eternal *total* sufficiency – because you can tack any name you like after I am, just as Jesus did. We are now the 'I am's.' He is the Father I AM; we are sons I am. This is the wonder of the *liberation*...I AM! And, of course, I have found the secret now! My 'I am' *is* His I AM, expressed by my 'I am.' *This* is the hidden paradox. That's why I could never really be understood by those who have to experience *first*. Often people say to me, "Oh well, doesn't that sort of make me passive if I am just a vessel or something?" People talk like that when they *don't know!* Put in natural terms, it's not you, it's He...but it *is* you! What does that mean? In *rational* terms, it's silly. You don't have to reason **until** you first *know* because reason is to *explain* what you know...not what you *ought* to know!

Therefore, God gave Moses this new name of Himself to present to the children of Israel with this new revelation of the unlimited, immediate presence of the God by whom the deliverance was to come. Moses, however, asked for something a little more practical. He said, "Well, even if I say that the God of Abraham, Isaac, and Jacob has met me and revealed Himself to me in a new and living way, they may say, 'That's just talk.' Can there be a practical demonstration?"

Now this was the moment when Moses was taught *practical faith action*. No one else previously had been taught this – as a kind of *philosophy of life* where you take action on something, move into it, and have it turn up. *This is the word of faith completed by the action of faith.* In Moses' case, God said, "You have a shepherd's rod in your hand, throw it to the ground." When he threw it to the ground, it became a snake. Now, everyone runs away from snakes, and so Moses fled. Then God said, "Pick that up." How *ridiculous* to pick it up! He did say to pick it up by the tail, not the head, but actually that's worse because the head can come around and bite you! Now, this is *practical* faith. "Do that Moses."

And when he did it, he found the thing which had a snake nature, a biting nature, became *his own* rod...the rod he could use in his shepherding and which became to him a *symbol of faith*...and that God *does* things! God gave him a *second* demonstration...this time by the hand that would hold the rod. He said, "Put *your* hand in your bosom. Take it out." He took it out as a leper. He put it back again, and it was clean! This is the same idea – *believe* God; *act* as believing it!

From Moses' example we can learn the lesson of the *practical operation of faith*. This is not merely the theory, but how to *operate* in life by moving into situations which are all wrong and confusing. As we *act* in a situation in which *God* has put us, we act on what *appears* to be a diseased condition and it becomes a whole condition! This gave Moses a little first *private* practice in what he was going to do in a *tremendous* way in public! It set Moses going for this *great* event of history when this *one man* was to shake a nation to its roots...even to the point where the nation *poured* its wealth into this slave people to get rid of them. Fantastic! The wealth which the *slave nation* would take out, the jewelry the Egyptians just poured on them was the wealth of Egypt! It built the tabernacle and maybe even the temple, because we must presume that these Hebrews had no wealth of their own since they were slaves.

One other fact to mention at this time was that Aaron, his brother, joined him. Moses *desired* to have a companion. Moses had told God, "Oh, I can't speak. I don't have that public gift of gab and I can't do that, so will You provide somebody who can do the public speaking for me?" It was all right for Moses to do that. Remember, God meets us in our *freedom*. It isn't a *law* of life that you have to go by yourself. We are *not under law*. We do what *we like* and God adjusts Himself to what we like and turns it into good! God was a little annoyed, but that didn't hurt anything, either.

God said a good word as a consequence...a *very good* word! Do you know what He said? "And the Lord said unto Moses, 'Who made man's mouth? Who maketh him dumb or deaf, or seeing, or blind? Hath not I, the Lord?'" So *God* makes blind people. *God* makes dumb people, because God makes *everybody*...and because the physical is *nothing*. The physical is a very convenient *way* in which we find God... though often the more inconvenient it is, the more we are *pressed in* to find God. Disease is not our problem; it is how we *take* disease that is our problem. That is a strong statement to make about the kind of Person God is – because the *spirit relationship* of a person and the purposes of God by spiritual persons is *infinitely higher* than the physical condition – and He actually fits the physical condition in! It becomes the agency by which *He manifests Himself* in certain forms. So you can include blind, or deaf, or dumb, or what you like, which are products of the Fall...and see that God utilizes them for *His* ends of grace! So Moses left that place and returned to Jethro saying, "Let me go and return to my brethren which are in Egypt and see whether they be yet alive." This is Moses moving into *action*.

The Israelites gave Moses a great reception. Evidently the *liberation and the authority* with which he spoke, and the *evidence* he gave caused them to take him. It may be that all these forty years they had wondered what had happened, because they knew what had been said of him...what he had been declared as being...and yet he had *disappeared* from sight. Maybe they were therefore *prepared* to accept him back with this kind of word...and this kind of evidence...and this kind of authority. When Moses and Aaron had gathered the people together, Exodus 4:31 says, "And the people *believed* when they heard the Lord had visited the sons of Israel and that He had looked upon their afflictions, and they bowed their heads and worshipped."

There is a whole world of difference **between** belief in an *external fact* and the *inner consciousness* that it is a *fact* to you. That is why *faith is not faith when it is related to external facts*. External facts are only to *inspire* internal faith. You are an inner person and only when your faith imputes *inner* knowledge is it *real* faith. So to say they believed God meant nothing, because the next day they were *not* believing Him... and doing it again. *That* is not real faith. Faith is only a real faith when it produces an inner awareness that *this* **is** *so. Then* you are not shaken! That is the difference between the faith that Moses had and the faith the people had.

When Moses and Aaron went and made their *first* bold confrontation with Pharaoh, they told him to let them go three days into the wilderness that they might worship God. His reaction was to pour scorn on a statement like that, retaliate by doubling the burden of the people, and give instructions that they should not even be given straw for their bricks but find their own straw! That brought out the *difference between* a professed faith in an eternal fact and a *living* faith which has its inner reality...because they then turned around and jumped on Moses as they did many times later on and said, "You only made things worse for us. All you have done is to make Pharaoh increase the burdens on us." The difference between their external *so-called* faith (which will wilt) is that Moses went back to God and said, "What about that?" He *challenged* God. That's different. He went back, turned around and said, "Wherefore hast Thou so evilly treated this people? Why did Thou send me?" He sort of hit God between the eyes...and God likes that kind of hitting! "Since I came to Pharaoh to speak in Thy name he has done evil to this people, neither hast Thou delivered this people at all." He threw it back on God!

That's faith! That brought forth the *final* confirmation. These negatives are *always* used as positives – confirmation from God to Moses of the *drastic and complete* work He *was* going to do for their deliverance. Moses *never again* challenged after that. In Chapter 6 He piles on the "I wills" – "What *I will* do to Pharaoh you will see"..."*I will* do it by My new name they had not known before, by My name Jehovah, I Am"..."*I will* bring you out"..."*I will* rid you of their bondage"..."*I will* redeem you"..."*I will* take you to Me for a people"..."*I will* be to you a God"..."*I will* bring you into the land"..."*I will* give it to you for an inheritance"..."I am the Lord". So it brought back to Moses' spirit by an inner voice – this pile on pile. "This is what I am doing, now go." It turned out to be a final confirmation – a strengthening to Moses of the faith which was already in him.

Incidentally, God had said, "The evidence to you, Moses, that I am in all this is that I shall meet with you at Mt. Horeb." That is where the *real* purposes of Moses' life were going to be fulfilled. He said, "Certainly I will be with thee, and this is the token that I have sent you, that when thou has brought forth the people out of Egypt you shall serve God upon this mountain." It was then that Moses would have his commission *fully fulfilled* and know it was of God – the purpose for which he was to bring the people out.

There followed the extraordinary presentation of the ten plagues. They are the kind of manifestations of the power of God which we don't see happening today on that level. I would say that carefully be- cause a good many things do happen, but they are not the kind of things we can easily line ourselves up with and say, "This happens to us or this could happen; this happens through *our* faith," because our calling isn't that...although it *could be* that. It can give us inspiration and a drive forward in the bold calling forth of faith because in each of these, Moses came out, spoke the word of faith, stretched forth his rod, and these things happened. We can learn that from him and practice. Some of us have, and in our own smaller ways, seen God do- ing things which are wonderful in *our* situations. I won't go into more detail on the plagues. I don't know if we should get anything more from them except that if we have begun to operate in *our* situations by the declared words of faith and the actions that follow, we are living lives of *that* type.

One question that arises concerning Pharaoh and the plagues is the same one that arose over Jacob and Esau, and again is brought up by Paul in Romans 9...and that is the hardening of Pharaoh's heart. You see Paul, *by the inspiration of the Spirit*, makes plain to us the *abso- luteness of God in every form*. Whether it is good or evil, *everything is **God** in action*. When it involves human freedom, which it does, then God's actions are to *confirm* the human freedom, but they are still God's actions – because human freedom *is* God's action. *Everything* is God! If we are free people, it is *because* we are forms of God – therefore our freedom *is* God. It's the paradox because it's *also* ourselves. It's God's freedom we are utilizing, yet it is our freedom! Therefore if we *misuse* our freedom, God's will is that we get the *products* of misused freedom, but it is still God doing it, because everything that happens *is* God!

So Paul is laying down this foundation that everything happens *in* God, good or evil. Because of this...though he was a *candidate* for grace like everyone else, because God is universal in His offers of grace... Pharaoh's heart was hardened. Pharaoh could become a son of God as well as any of us could, but when you persistently oppose God *you* get the consequence *in you*...not in God...which is hardness. You become more and more set in your ways. *Moses* became more and more set in the *ways of faith. Pharaoh* became more and more set in the *ways of defiance.* Moses gets hardened as a *believer* they can't shake. Pharaoh gets hardened as an *unbeliever* that they can't shake. They are *both* God! That way it can be said that God hardened Pharaoh's heart **or** God confirmed Moses' faith, *whichever* way you like. *God* made Moses a strong believer; *God* made Pharaoh a strong unbeliever, because each is channeled through *our freedom* because everything is God!

In the passage in Romans 9 where Paul speaks of Pharaoh's heart being hardened, he *adds* two facts. One is that God has *foreknowledge.* He foreordains us to *freedom* and foreordains us to have what is the *product* of our freedom – grace or the lost condition – vessels of wrath or vessels of mercy. That is foreknowledge *because* there is no past or future with God so, *of course,* everything is known of God, by God! The other fact that Paul brings out which affects us here is that when a person is set the *other* way, it can be said that God set him. It's *put* that way to *assure* that we understand it is God. "Very well," God says, "If Pharaoh is this way because he has gone that way, it can be said that I hardened his heart...because I *mean* that Pharaoh should be what he is. If Pharaoh *chooses* to be hardened, he is hardened and I hardened him because I choose people to *be* what they *are*. I will now use him. I *have* to use him negatively...by the judgments on him, by these distresses...until finally he is forced to release the children of Israel." It is upon his opposition that there comes the deliverance of Israel, the going out from the land, the Passover, and the wealth they poured on Israel. So that is the *explanation* of the statement that Paul made about God hardening Pharaoh's heart.

Another striking fact concerning the plagues is the Passover. This was the *first* revelation of salvation being given us in terms of the *blood* of Christ. It was through Moses that that revelation came into public statement. "When I see the blood I will pass over you." This is *part* of the revelation which He gave through Moses – the sacrifice of the Passover lamb which proceeded all through Jewish history, and was replaced by the Lord's Supper in our day. It symbolizes the blood and body of Jesus, and the destroying angel that *didn't* touch the Hebrew families if the blood was on the lintel and the doorpost, while inside they were feeding on the roasted lamb...the Passover lamb. These are the *two* forms in which we experience God's true deliverance through the true lamb, Christ.

The blood is the term used to symbolize the outpoured *life*. Leviticus 17 makes that plain, for here Moses reveals that telling them that when they made a sacrifice they should not eat the blood, because the blood **is** the life and therefore sacred. The shedding of the blood of Jesus meant the *outpouring* of the life of Jesus – therefore of His death. It is, again, one of these strong terms the Bible uses, such as the wrath and the hardness, because strong terms make things *clear* to us. We talk about the shedding of the blood of Jesus which means the life outpoured. We have explained why – because our life ends in an eternal death. After our physical death...which is nothing but just leaving the body behind...we move on into the dimension to which we are destined *after* the physical death. If we are still in our fallen conditions, our destiny is the fallen state presented to us in the terms of the spirits in prison. If we are redeemed people, we move into the Mt. Zion where we are spoken of as spirits of just men made *perfect*...waiting for the resurrection.

Now the outpoured life of Jesus meant that He *voluntarily* took on death...the product of sin...which *never* should have touched Him... never needed touch Him. He took it because death is the *outer* form of a destiny which He took upon Himself...and then went *into* the destiny. The Bible says, "Thou wilt not leave My soul in hell," which was the prophecy which Peter used when he first preached at Pentecost. So Jesus Christ went to hell, the term used as the place of the spirits in prison...who are ourselves if we are in that condition. That is where Jesus went representing us, and then because it was impossible to contain Him, He came up into the *resurrection* life – which is *restoring Him and us in Him* to our spirit-union with God. That is the total meaning of the **blood** of Jesus, the outer term used to explain the taking away by Jesus of *all* that came to us through the Fall. It *annulled* any claim or power the devil had over us. The Bible says in Hebrews 2 that "through death He destroyed him that had the power of death." He had no more power over us because Jesus had taken that death away. Physical death is nothing because *it isn't the real* thing, and he has taken away all that is involved in the consequences of being fallen people – which is being destined to the fallen condition. It has disappeared! Feeding on the lamb means *we* are identified with the crucified, risen Lord. The blood was struck on the lintel and the doorpost...and we are not identified with that. That was *His* precious blood...His unique life given to death for us. He trod that winepress *alone*.

It is the **body** of Jesus that we are identified with. That's why, in the account of the Lord's Supper in I Corinthians 10, it says we are *one bread, one body*...not one blood! We take the cup of blessing, then take of the bread. One bread means one body. Now *we* are part of the one bread, and so they ate the sacrificed lamb in their rooms and identified with it because the identification means our *re-union* with Him in the spirit. This is the union of God! This is the *re*-union. *We* are identified with the One who was crucified and risen, and *we* eat Him. *We* are part of the body which died and rose. *We* are that body!

So now in this case we come into the *identified union* with the Spirit eternally. That's where we have come right out of that *old* stage of "Thou shalt not." *We are no longer under the law;* **we are the law**! We are identified with the law...the **law** of *love.* We are in this *new* union. So this was the *first* revelation given in those days by symbol of the ultimate redemption which was purposed for the world...out of which would come the *family* of the sons of God.

I hesitate to pass over in a few moments events which are *so tremendous.* This extraordinary story of the way in which God forced the release of the children of Israel, finally, by the deaths of the firstborn, the shocks of the nation, the final shock in which we see every family, from Pharaoh down to the lowest slave crying to the children of Israel, "Get out!" Not *only* did they send them out, but they poured their wealth on them. The Israelites "borrowed." I always like these Spirit jokes, "They borrowed the treasures of Egypt," but they had a *right* to them! After all, they had been made slaves. They had not been paid. They had better have some repayment! I keep saying, *"See things always in the spirit."* The terrified people poured their treasures, their jewelry and their gold on the people. They went out laden with the wealth of Egypt. Tremendous!

Now God had purposes in which Israel must function as an efficient nation. It must have a *national image* and be a nation. At present they were nothing but a bunch of slaves...probably about two million people. It's difficult to imagine this huge group pouring out of Egypt. They couldn't possibly settle into Canaan like that where they would have to meet the various tribes that were already occupying Canaan. There were *educations* and *disciplines* and *orders* which had to be brought *into* them to form them as a nation. So the Bible says that God didn't lead them by a short cut. They could have cut through the land of the Philistines up near where Israel is now, on the coast, and in a day or two they could have gotten into the land. However, He led them through the wilderness to Mt Horeb, for God said, "Lest peradventure the people repent when they see war and they return to Egypt." That brought them up against the Red Sea…which they had to cross to get in along the established route towards Mt. Horeb (Sinai) in the wilderness. Here we begin to see the way the children of Israel went into a tailspin *whenever* they came across some dangerous condition.

They aren't the only ones who go into tailspins. We keep saying, because it's **all** we can say – *that people are controlled by their inner consciousness*, because that's what you *are*. If, from your inner consciousness you *see evil as evil and believe it*, you are *controlled*. You *immediately* are terrified that something is going to overcome you. What can you do? That was the condition of the children of Israel. They only had an outward relationship, although I must say it was a *real* relationship, because they were under the blood. Certainly there were those among them who also had the inner relationship, as we shall see later on, but on the whole they had an *outer* faith. They asked Moses to interpose between them and God. You could say that the outer passes into the inner, but you *start* by a trust in someone who is a *symbol* of God to you.

That is the *danger* of outer forms. Paul says they were baptized unto Moses, *not* unto God, and to most of them, Moses was practically like their God. They would say, "Moses, *you* talk to God for us; *you* interpret God to us," It isn't *wholly* a false faith when the person you are attached to is expressing God to you. It's not like attachment an idol or something, but it is a kind of stepping stone. Paul would say, "Follow me as I follow Christ." Jesus on earth said, "Follow me." *We* don't *follow* Jesus – we are He in human form operating *as* Jesus – and we are not altogether in the New Testament experience. However, he starts by saying, "Follow me," which is external. That didn't work very well because you can't follow anything outward. It **has** to be something inward! So you get this continually occurring with the children of Israel.

The *first* time this happened after they had gotten out of Egypt was when they were up against the Red Sea, and Pharaoh changed his mind. He saw the loss of his huge slave population who were building his pyramids…or whatever they were building in those days. He said, "Let's get them back," and sent his army after them.

There was a little bit of drama here which can be very *educating* to *us*. You see, *fear isn't wrong*; it is how you *use* your fear that is the question. No *temptation* is wrong if you stop while it is *still* a temptation. It's how you use it. Now the trouble with the children of Israel was that they *turned their fear into rebellion*! They turned their fear into an *attitude* for evil *against* God…or for the evil they thought was coming on them; *that* was the sin. Now when they were in this very disturbing condition with the chariots of Egypt thundering after them (and we may presume they can see them coming in the distance) and here they were up against the wall of the Red Sea. What could they do? And so they said to Moses, "Because there were no graves in Egypt has thou taken us to die in the wilderness?" You see the defiance? "Wherefore hast thou dealt with us to carry us forth out of Egypt? Is not this the word that we did tell you in Egypt, saying let us alone, we will serve the Egyptians? It would be better for us to serve the Egyptians than we should die in the wilderness." Now *that* is turning fear into defiance!

Then Moses said, "Fear ye not, stand still and see the salvation of the Lord which He shall show you today, for the Egyptians whom you have seen today ye shall see them again no more forever. The Lord shall fight for you and you shall hold your peace." This is a man speaking the word of faith! This is a man who was speaking from the union…the same man who stretched forth the rod to Pharaoh. He gave it to them *again*, "The Lord is doing it." You see this is the *real* word *as* God. *We* speak the word *as God*. You will see it happen! He recognized it was *all* of the Lord, because he knew that now the Lord would fight for them and they were to hold their peace…because *everything* was the Lord. That is a *perfect* word!

Now the little bit of *education* we can get from this is that Moses wavered for a moment…and the moment you waiver you have got to have the Lord *put* you right. It isn't sin; it is just a little kink which can be used for adjustment. We know about it because *when* Moses made that statement which is found in Exodus 14:14 and quoted above, the wavering stopped. In the King James version there is that little paragraph mark which means that the incident is finished. Verse 15 says, "And the Lord said unto Moses, 'Wherefore criest thou unto me? Speak unto the children of Israel that they go forward, but lift thou up thy rod and stretch out thine hand over the sea and divide it, and the children of Israel shall go on dry ground through the midst of the sea'"

Well, can you *have* a stronger word for a man to operate as God? God said, "*You* do it Moses," and He rebuked him for praying. That is why I often make fun in meetings and say, "Stop your praying. You are wasting time. It is sin! You are praying when you should say, **'God's doing that thing, and I am saying in God's name it is done.'"** *That is our authority*! We are *sons* with authority. We are not a bunch of kids that have to keep *calling* for something! God has *not only* put Himself at our disposal, He has made us *into* Himself! We are Him in *son form*. He expresses Himself through His sons…**as** He expressed Himself through His Son! We are all one and He says, "Go to it. Operate as Me in the situation in which you arise. *You* now say, "God's doing so and so, this will happen." This is this word of faith, the law of faith, and as in the material realm, what *you* **say** becomes *real* to you!

If you relate yourself to something it comes back to you as substance. So you relate yourself to what God is doing and it comes into substance. So He said to Moses, "*You* do it. *You* open that sea. *You* lift up your rod. *You* see them go across on dry land." And Moses did it because Moses had done it often. This is just a little kink, that's all, but it is valuable to us – the little touch of differentiation there *between* the prayer of supplication and the prayer of faith, the word of faith.

So they went across. The sea came back behind them. The chariots of Pharaoh got all bogged down, and the army was drowned. The implication was that Pharaoh drowned, too. The famous song of praise in Chapter 15 was a song of deliverance sung on the other shore of the Red Sea by Miriam with her guitar and timbrel. "Sing to the Lord, for

He is highly exalted; the horse and his rider He has hurled into the sea."

Now we move into the wilderness life with this great company of illiterate, helpless slaves...who were yet believers. There is a *level* of believing when you are believing something external which is not real believing...because real believing has its own *evidence*. The Bible says, in I John 5:10, "He that believeth on the Son of God hath the witness in himself." That is one of the *key* verses on faith. You are inwardly conscious that what you are believing is a *fact*. Faith isn't believing in fact; it is **knowing** fact. In this case we are talking about Spirit facts. Spirit is *all*. Spirit is the almighty God, but it appears phony. To our un-enlightened minds the *world* appears real...the Spirit appears unreal. The truth is the very *opposite!* We are just beginning to learn to live by the *true* facts of the spirit – facts which are conveyed to us *through* our faith. When we have moved into faith in our Lord Jesus Christ, we have conveyed to us the inner consciousness that He is God...He is my Savior...He is my Lord...and we are in the union. *He* is the one who operates by me. I must reluctantly admit, however, that God, being a little more loving than I am, sometimes puts it through even where there is a faith which hasn't *yet* had an interior witness.

However, it is a very *weak* thing because you cannot be governed by the externals. *Nothing external governs you...* neither the Bible...nor the church...nor the standards...nor anything! Your only concern is what you have *inside. That* is where you live. The others are just passed to and fro and you pick them up and drop them again. So a faith which starts externally and hasn't yet become internal is *not* the real thing. It is *uncertain, inconsistent*...because it hasn't *become* me.

That was the quality of faith the Israelites had. They were God's redeemed people. They had been under the blood, the blood that was on the lintel of the doorpost. They had eaten of the slain lamb, the Passover. They were God's people. Stephen, in his speech, called them the *church in the wilderness*. Where it says "they died in the wilderness, doesn't mean they went to hell, but that never moved into union life – the *really operating life* where God is magnified by us, and *we* can operate and work His works for Him. I think we may say there may be many who will die in the wilderness life. They are God's people, but their faith has never become internalized.

The Hebrews began their wilderness period loaded with the wealth of the Egyptians…having more earrings than sense! This is the critical time when they were formed into the nation into which Jesus Christ was to come *as the true Israelite* – the hoped for Messiah – and out from Him was to start the *true Israel*…which is we! So these are very important days. The miraculous happenings in Moses' life, though very wonderful details, were *not* the most important thing. The center and heart of Moses' life was Horeb, because God had said, "My seal on my calling to you is the **burning bush**. The evidence I give you that this is My call is that you will worship Me at the mount where the burning bush was, Mt. Horeb" (or Sinai). That was where God's purposes were going to be *fulfilled* by Moses in fixing this as God's earthly nation.

En route to Horeb and afterwards there arose disturbing events… products of the compulsive human belief in human situations…which are evil. If you haven't got an inner faith in an inner God, your inner faith is in outer circumstances! So they were moved by outer circumstances…and there is where Moses' trouble arose. The people were *continually moved* by outer circumstances…and they distressed him… and they feared…and they grumbled…and they then became rebellious and defiant. As we said before – to fear isn't wrong, to tremble isn't wrong. To defy *is* wrong! When I fear a thing and tremble about a thing – if I say, "Wait a minute, my fear can become a stepping stone to faith. It has been the *means* to move me off from attaching my faith to the external which is 'bothering' me, to the Living God who **is** the *supply*!" That's what they did not know. It *became sin* when instead of *recognizing* that God had the situation in hand, they *moved into* rebellion and angry words about God.

The three main incidents of that type, which, as I say, were not the main line with Moses, but were on the circumference, were concerning life's economies – bread, water, and enemies. These pretty well affect us all.

The one about bread comes in Exodus 16. When Moses was confronted by a shouting multitude, "We are starving, send us back to Egypt where we can get our leeks and onions and so on," he always shut them out by falling on his face and calling to God. Many times he fell on his face and shut out their noises to hear another Voice. That is the first step, shut out the impact of, "Oh, what shall I do with this situation?" Moses *started* with a disturbed heart. Anyone would be disturbed when there is a raging multitude around you telling you they are starving and it's *your* fault, but he met these disturbances by moving to a 'place' where he could be quiet enough to listen to God. That is the *strategy* of faith.

The next phase of the strategy of faith is to *know* what God will do. The word of faith is that there is a *confidence* that this is what God **is** doing. That is why I always made **prayer** *supplemental*…**faith** *fundamental*. Prayer is the circumference…faith is the center. We have gotten that wrong *because* we don't know how to **believe**. We say, "Oh, God, do this, do that, "and "Oh, God!" We call *that* praying. Pretty unproductive stuff! It doesn't produce anything in your *own* heart except to *leave* you where you started! *Prayer is to settle me, not to change God.* It is that God may get through to me what *He* wants to do. The *prayer element* is the element Moses had when he fell on his face or when he cried to God. Now, that is the element when he is settling *his* mind that God may convey to him *God's* mind. So prayer isn't conditioning God – it's conditioning **me** to catch on to what *God* is doing! That is supplemental *or* circumference.

The **heart** of prayer is found in what is perhaps the greatest scripture on prayer, Mark 11:24, which ways, "Whatsoever you **desire**…when you pray" – that's the *circumference*. "**Believe** you received it" – that is the *center*. The tense of that in the Greek is that queer tense called aorist, which means a thing is **done**. It should read, "Believe that you have received it and you shall have it." That is effective faith-prayer-action.

You can call it the prayer of faith if you like, which is the phrase used by James, but the **point** is not prayer, but the *faith* – because faith is bringing something into *existence*! Faith on the human level is that you are bringing an experience into existence.

You came here tonight by faith…your faith was, "I'll come." That is an *inner* act. You then came. So your faith brought you into existence through your automobile, and now you are experiencing being here. That is a faith which produced a substance. Now in the Spirit level it is not *you* who do it. On the natural level you can come in your car and be here. In the Spirit level you are talking about something which is *beyond* you. But Spirit is ALL – Spirit is a universal God with universal resources…and *you* are a part of that…*you* are now in this joint union with God.

When in my inner self I say, "God, You are doing that. I am setting *God* in motion. I am releasing God. I am the agent by which God now is…it's really *God* pressing Himself through. I am the one now turning the light on by which God comes through! God is coming through along the level of where *I say* He is coming through. He puts Himself at my disposal!

It is Spirit-faith when God has to do it, because it isn't a thing that the human can do. To be up against all sorts of situations which disturb you requires effective *authoritative* action. You start with a beating heart and a confused mind. Then you turn from that disturbance by having a quiet place where you say, "Now." You needn't even turn, Jesus never even turned…He did it on the spot. He could turn five loaves into five thousand just like that! *We* can do some of that, also. By some means or other we can transfer our *fear*, which is *negative faith*, from this to God. "I am waiting for God. God's in this thing!"

The second stage is to find out what God *will do* in the situation. God speaks mainly through *our own* minds. *We* have the mind of Christ. It is only quite rarely that there is an external appearance by an angel or something even in the Old Testament. Usually, "Thus saith the Lord," means *inside* the mind. The Lord told them something which convinced them that is what God *would do*.

Now in our own normal lives what happens is that something comes up that we would like to see happen. That is covered by the word of Jesus which says, "Whatsoever ye desire when ye pray..." So what seems to me to be the thing I would like to have happen, that is the thing I am to say, "Now *this* is the thing God is doing." God conveys His will through my desires when I am in tune...when I am in His tune...when my listening ears are out to hear Him.

I am talking about something that some of us have practiced. In our mission we have done this for years. We have gotten hundreds and hundreds of consignments of men, workers, money, buildings, and fields for fifty years *by knowing that what we desire is what God is giving.* Watch it come, and there they are!

In this case, it was bread, and Moses was able to give them certain instructions. The main point was that Moses wanted to tell them *how* they were going to live in the wilderness. He didn't know it would be forty years instead of a few weeks. He said, "During the time you are in the wilderness, God will provide you with a certain bread called manna. God will provide it for you daily." Moses never repeated that word. Exodus 16:4 is a key statement where he tells them that God would supply them with a certain amount every day and it was never repeated through forty years. Every day for forty years that manna turned up and the Bible quietly says that when they crossed the Jordan with Joshua they ceased to have the manna and began to eat the old corn of the land.

You see how little we need to *trouble* about daily bread? You see how fussed we are about inflation, the loss of jobs, and so on? Only because we are *believing* that to lose a job or inflation has got *more* negative troubles in it than *God's resources* can take care of. I think God's resources are slightly bigger than inflation and the loss of a job! Turn your faith where it belongs. Say, "I lost my job. I know I lost my job...God is my provider...and forever every day inflation or no inflation He just gives me a chance to say, 'You watch how God gives. You watch how God provides daily bread.'" This is a very great lesson on the *quality* of faith which needn't be repeated once you have made it. If you have it *settled* now, that you are God's man or woman, God will provide on the basis of His Statement, "Seek first the Kingdom of God and His righteousness and all these things will be added unto you." Take no thought for the daily bread and clothing, they will be added unto you. We needn't waste our time on praying for daily bread when it is *there*!

The Lord's Prayer is a *child's* prayer. It's a beautiful prayer which people who don't know much can use, but it is *not* the prayer for the spiritual. That is why they pray the Lord's Prayer at the football match or something. They do that in England. Well, bless them. It is a little touch of faith, anyhow. I would rather have that than gambling... wouldn't you...which they have also. So that is a child's prayer because a child's prayer can say, "Father give us this day our daily bread"...but *we* can just say, "Thanks, it's coming every day" because we have moved beyond. So drop the Lord's Prayer and try a *better* one!

These exploits of faith were repeated concerning water, and with their enemies. The most important incident concerning water came about when the Hebrews cried to Moses one day that there was no water, and God told Moses to strike the rock with his rod and water would come out of it. Now, *that* was some guidance! The rod was *equivalent* to a word of faith. The point to learn is to *step out* on the faith once you have said it, and as the thing is happening, make provision for it. The outstanding fact about this incident was that Moses struck the rock, as God had told him to...so faith is *followed by an action* that is happening. It means I am acting, and that is happening. I am to *see* it as it is happening. I am acting *as if* the thing is happening. I am acting on that basis, so action must exemplify our faith – it must materialize our faith. So you see – faith is that we get it clear that it is God doing it! God says what He will do and you say "God's doing it," and then you will say, "Therefore it is done. I am going to act as though it is done!"

Quite a lot of our missionaries have booked passage without the money to pay for it and have even gone so far as to go to the boat without it. They said, "If we are going, if God is sending the money, then *somehow* by the time I get there the money *will be there.*" I have experienced that kind of thing myself and if any of you want to really read some of the principles and exploits of faith, read my book on Rees Howells from whom I learned faith.

Incidentally, this water turned out to have a marvelous continuity like the bread. There is a little statement made in Deuteronomy 9:21, "The brook that descended out of the mount." So that gush of water out of the rock became a brook – a stream which never ceased – and *all* the time they were around the mount there was this stream which had come from the rock. Paul brings this up very interestingly when he says in I Cor. 10:4, "They all did drink that same spiritual drink, for they drank of that spiritual rock that followed them; that Rock was Christ." In other words, the stream *followed* them, it made a river which didn't go underground, I presume, which is *unusual* in the desert.

That was a *remarkable* statement for Paul to make! Christ was known in His **eternal form** *before* He ever came out in His **historical form** because there were some who could *see through the symbols to the reality*, seeing them as forms of the abundance of the Living God. Christ has *always* been there. He was there as He sees all men. Christ is in *all* men! You just have to find Him. You don't find Christ out there... you find Him inside. There were men before Jesus' birth who found Christ...who never knew Him by the name we know Him – the Jesus name – because Christ is His *eternal* name; Jesus is His *human* name. He wasn't Jesus Christ before Bethlehem. He was Christ through eternity, the anointed Son, and in God's sight *always* had been crucified and risen! The Bible says in that remarkable phrase in Rev. 12:13... that He was "the Lamb Slain from the foundation of the world." So in God's sight, where there is no time factor, He always has been the Savior...even before there was a world to be saved!

Next, we get to the question of the enemies. This was another form of outer impact. We must remember that we are dealing with an earthly nation...which is *quite different* from the heavenly nation. That puts into focus the killings of people and the wars. An earthly nation can *only* be controlled by law. The *only way* an earthly world can be kept in order is by law and punishment and oppositions...*because* it is in chaos with jealousies, and fights and seizing of people's land. God was *bringing into being an earthly nation* and therefore this earthly nation *had* to use the normal forms of protection, and so on certain occasions they had to fight and kill. That accounts for the differentiation between a war in which a nation is involved and *personal* animosity. Murder is personal animosity. Murder is when I purposely mean to kill. Judicial slaughtering, whether it's a hanging or in a war, is not murder. Paul underlined that when he said that they were to respect governors who beareth up the sword in vain. The sword cut the heads off in those days.

The *difference* between an earthly nation and a heavenly nation is that in the heavenly nation your enemies cease to exist! That's why you *love* your enemies. You *have* no enemies...because every enemy is only a distorted son. You don't see his *distortion*; you *see* his son-hood. *Every* single person is a son of God who has missed the way and thinks he is right when he is wrong...and thinks he is right in being a man of the flesh. All the time he is really one of God's sons and doesn't know it – a prodigal son. Now you had better love your prodigal son because he is also your brother, isn't he? Under blindness and ignorance and false conviction he is doing this and that which hurt you...but he is not your enemy...so you don't take notice of those things any more than *God* takes notice of them. So you see, the church of Christ *has* no enemies and no tribes! We are One Holy Nation, interspersed in the nations of the world. *God* told these people to take life. *Human* life isn't reality. *It is eternal-life that is reality!* *We* have no enemies as people of God... but as nations we do have enemies. If I make a war – I take it's God's way – and in God's faith in most cases it never turns out to be a war at all! Something happens by which somehow the enemy *dissolves*. The Bible is *full* of that.

The first illustration of it is when Amalek attacked Israel. God gave orders from that time on that Amalek was always to be destroyed...

because Amalek was the virulent foe who wasn't just a passing tribe. He *intended* to destroy Israel! God's nation was to be protected as the nation through whom the world would get the gospel, so Amalek was *always* to be destroyed. Others he would spare depending on the situation.

The encounter with Amalek was the first step in Joshua's 'education' when he was going through his *school of faith* under Moses, learning to be Moses' successor. Once again God used negative actions for some furthering of *His* purpose…which was at that moment to select his coming military leader who would take them into the land. So Amalek stirred Moses up to select the man elected to have the military know-how. God is always using the negative for positive ends. However, Joshua had to learn that it **wasn't** military powers which won the battle. It was the upraised hands of Moses on the mount! Upraised is the sign of surrender. When the hands were down, Amalek prevailed. When the hands were up, *God* prevailed. So Joshua was learning a very vital lesson, that the answer to wars *first* is **faith**!

We now move on to the *heart* of Moses commission – which was to establish a nation which had all the revelation God had then given of Himself as their living God to whom they could attach themselves in all their weaknesses and failures…and from whom Jesus could become the *true manifestation of the living God in His love.* He could pick up on the living God the Israelites knew…and not have to find some strange new tribe to relate to them who He *truly* is – the God of love and the God of Salvation. He did that by a remarkable process which *had* to be…and which was to reveal the depths of the sinfulness of self-reliance.

This was the *first purpose* of the nation…and in order to get that into focus, God presented to them what He really is – what His *purpose* is. When He first spoke to Moses on the mountain (Ex.19:3), there was no thunder and lightning and burning. It was simply God speaking *by* Moses' voice. Quietly, God told Moses to say to the people something very wonderful…"You have seen what I did to the Egyptians, how I bore you on eagles' wings and brought you unto Myself. If you will obey My voice, indeed, and keep My covenant, then ye shall be a peculiar treasure unto Me above all people, for all the earth is Mine. And ye shall be unto Me a kingdom of priests and a holy nation."

Now we get the *facts* of the revelation. A kingdom of priests is not a priest in a kingdom; it is a kingdom in which *all* are priests. A priest is for others and gives himself that others may get their benefits and have their needs supplied. The *purpose* of God is to have a vast family of priests. That is what *we* are, of course. Being a priest who fulfills the law of intercession means *we* are given for others. This is God's pattern...and it is what He is doing now! *We* have begun to be a *kingdom* of priests...not *a* priest. Now there is a catch in this. If you are *one* with God, it is not "if" you obey! You are spontaneously God's and you *are spontaneously* going God's way which *is* obedience. Obedience is not obeying; it is that you *just can't help it*...because when you are in God you *just go* that way! The best word I know on life in God is said by Ezekiel when he says, "I will put My Spirit upon you and **cause** you to walk in My ways." Note the word "cause." Not that you *have* to walk, but **I will make** you walk. *That is the beauty of the free life.* Obedience is just doing the next thing! So when you are in this life there is *no question* of "ifs." The fact that there is an "if" means that you are *not* in that life.

The self-exposing word was, "If you obey my voice, and keep My covenant, then you will be ..." Now, the new covenant has no conditions **except** to *receive* Jesus Christ...which we have done. **That is all.** We *have fulfilled* the only condition of the universe, which is love. When we deviate, we always come back. So God's *ultimate* Covenant has no conditions...and when the new covenant is given us in Hebrews 8, no conditions are with it! He says that He *puts out* the old covenant with the conditions. Now law *is* a condition. Where it says, "If you are, or do, something, then I'll be so and so...," that means you are *not* in it and you will be *if* you obey. Finding fault with the old covenant, he says, "I'll make a new covenant with the house of Israel." It was said by prophecy by Jeremiah, and it was picked up in Hebrews: "This is the covenant I will make with the house of Israel after those days; I will put my laws *in* their hearts. I will be to them a God, they shall be to me a people, they shall not teach every man his neighbor, and every man his brother, saying, 'Know the Lord;' for all shall know Me, from the least to the greatest." Do you get the point? We are in the **conditionless** dimension…the heavenly dimension because we *are* it. *We are it!* No man need *teach* us to love the Lord. We all know Him…from the least to the greatest. **This is the new Israel**!

Now, when Moses had spoken to the people what God had said, (Ex. 19:4-6), then the people answered together and said, "All that the Lord has spoken to us *we will* **do**." Silly, blinded people! That is the very thing we *don't* do…we don't keep God's covenant! We don't want to keep God's covenant. We pretend we do because it is *respectable* to do so…because we want the benefits. We don't want to keep them. We want to keep our own covenant in our own way. Do you see the blindness?

The *purpose* of this covenant with a condition was to *expose the self-sufficient self.* One thing we need to watch against is all the psychology which speaks about *improved* self. *There can't be an improved self.* It is putting a cloak over what we really are! So now the first necessity of God's self-revelation to this nation…who was to be His agency of revelation in the world…must be law. He must plant on them the law of what they are *not* to be, and spell it out in black and white so that everybody could *know* now – because where there is no law there is no knowledge of sin. Where there is law there *is knowledge* of sin. He had to change his approach…and now it says, "The Lord said unto Moses, 'Lo, I come unto thee in a thick cloud that the people may hear when I speak with thee and believe thee forever.'"

He came to them in a thick cloud because this fallen self *cannot unite* with God. *If* the fallen thinks it isn't the fallen self, then it has to be 'buried'. It has to find out it *doesn't* **know** God. That is what we can find with legalism…whether it is Christian legalism or legalism of other religions! They can't **know** God because God is not legal. If you

know God you just are *automatically* what He is. If there is one iota of legalism, you don't **know** God. *There is no legalism in God!* It means you are not there, and therefore you cannot **know** Him. You can only have certain *religious viewpoints* and *ritualistic loyalties* and so forth. That is what all the religions of the world are...and a great deal of Christian religion is also!

So God now had to *change* His form of self-revelation, and had to manifest Himself in a thick cloud with thunder and lightning and burning of fires...because it had to symbolize the fact that self-reality is burning itself. So the law was "Don't let a person touch that mountain or they will be struck and killed." That is because **all** that self can have is *its* self-effort. Self-effort is the fallen world, the fallen condition...which is the fires within. This was symbolized by the fact that they must not touch this mountain, because this was the mountain of God. Moses could live on the mountain and in the fire because *he was part of it!* We live **in** God when we are a part of Him. We are one love.

In John and Hebrews God is represented symbolically in terms of fire and light. Hebrews 12:29 says, "Our God is a consuming fire," and John 1 calls Him "the light of men." Now the relationship is very interesting. Light is a product of fire. Fire consumes, light blesses... and yet the light is a product of the fire because there is a *death* in the fire to give the light. The fire is consumed to let out the light. We see that in the sun. It is known that the sun is made of hydrogen atoms under intense heat. When they fuse they become heat atoms. In the fusion energy is released, that is light. So light comes out of a burning sun by a death. There is a death in the sun when it dies to its original consistency of the one form of atom to another form of atom and releases that which *becomes light* to us. So you see, fire only dies to itself and produces light for others. When fire remains in *itself* it consumes itself. That is why God is a fire and a light! If we remain in ourselves we consume ourselves. That is the burning.

That is why the Bible says we have hell inside us. James says that if you have an evil tongue, your tongue is set on fire of hell. An angry tongue is a hellish tongue, so hell is here. Therefore a self lived *unto it-self* consumes…and that is the fire. When our self is given up…through Christ for others…it becomes light, a blessing. This is what *God* **is**. So if we are on the wrong side of God, we are consuming fire; we are part of God which is the consuming fire. If we are back in the relationship to God which is being fulfilled to us through Jesus Christ, we will become a light which is a blessing to us and a blessing to the world.

So the Israelites mustn't touch that mountain…it didn't belong to them. It had to be *symbolized* that way or they would get burned because their condition was really a *self*-burning condition. Now Moses lived in that fire, got light, and came out with a face so radiant that they had to hide it under a veil. He poured light out in what he *gave* to the Israelites. He poured out the tabernacle and the grace of God. What we see here is one man who had *become part of the fire*…and because he left it up to God, he became a manifesto of light.

You see, now, what happened. God had announced His ultimate *purpose* – which was the holy nation, the kingdom of priests – knowing that *that* could not come to pass yet because man had not found himself in his ultimate evil. When he finds ultimate evil and finds that he is a lost person, he can then take the ultimate gift of good which is given to him in Christ. So the *law* comes. It becomes *part of* the revelation…the necessary part…to show up sin. In 1Corinthians 15, Paul says a strange thing. He says the *law* is the strength of sin. Why is this so? Because the law says *you shouldn't* do a thing. Satan in you says, "I want to do it." So the law gives strength to sin. That is how Paul found out. Paul said, "I found a law which says I shouldn't covet. When I said, 'Oh, I won't covet,' then I found myself *full* of covetousness." So the law which says you shouldn't covet stirred up, or revived, sin in Paul. The sin of self-centeredness, the sin of self-gratification, and self-requirement revived in him. So the law is used by sin to express its real self. That is the value of law. By saying you *shouldn't* do it, it causes sin to say, "I *will* do it." That is how sin gets *exposed*! This is the way in which God *forces* humanity to find themselves.

Now it must be noted...because it is so often missed...that the occupation of Moses was *not* to give law. It was to give *grace*! The *whole occupation* of the chapters of the revelation given us in Exodus, Leviticus, and Deuteronomy is the *outpouring of God's grace* presented in the tabernacle. It is only in the first few chapters of Exodus that He gives the Ten Commandments and runs through a few very valuable social instructions of what is good to eat and what is not good to eat and so forth. Then, God begins to announce grace!

Let's get it straight – **God is nothing but grace**! Law is what we have to have *if we are not in God*. It *appears* to come from God. It does come from God in the sense that everything comes from God... though if you are on the *wrong* side of God...*that* still comes from God. It isn't in God's nature whatever! *There is no law in God's nature.* There is no wrath; there is no judgment...**only love**. The wrath and the judgment is what *appears* to us when **we** are related to the wrong side of God.

That is the same as the family. The kids think we get pretty tough with them. It is the only answer they *must* have when they do the wrong thing. In this case, we may sometimes inflict the hurt...but we know it is not an angry thing at all. It is a form of instruction. In a tiny way it is the same principle. So we must *eliminate* the whole concept of a God of anger and wrath. It is not there! It *appears* to be because we are all forms of God, so what goes on inside of *us* can be said to be God's wrath. In the hardening of Pharaoh's heart we saw that this was in Pharaoh, *not in God*, but because Pharaoh was one of God's *distorted* sons...like we *all* are in God's being. It may be said that his hardening himself was *God* hardening him...because in his *freedom* he was hardening himself (and the freedom comes from God) and then God used him. God lets *us* say, "God did it," to make it simpler for us...and also because these were 'childhood' days. So God *lets* it be said that He is angry, because it is easier to see God angry. He isn't really angry at all...but because we are not yet *conditioned* to see our inner conditions and see the real balance of truth...He has to put those kinds of terms on them. The black-souled man wants an angry God. He wants to be able to hit God back a bit and put God down...not lift Him up.

You see, it is a *very dangerous* thing to have a God who gives you *no laws* and you can do what you like. It's *easier* to have somebody who gives you a few laws, and keeps you a little in order. That is why *man* made a religion with the law! We're afraid of ourselves until we *have* God... *until we are in God.* We run into this or that sin and we'd like someone to tell us that we shouldn't do it. We'll go and do it on Monday, but it won't be quite so bad, because we know on Sunday that we shouldn't do it. So we like a *little something* of God's forgiveness and comfort to cover us and keep us in our *self*-condition...and in our fears and wrong doings...but enough covering to help us **pretend** that we are related to God in some ways. *We* don't want a God who has no laws. *We* don't want a God who says, "Be free, I am in you and you can do what you like." That is dangerous talk! So we try to *keep* God as a legalist...the punisher...but it's all an illusion.

We now find God beginning to teach them that sin must be removed...must be atoned for. Atoning means that somebody must take away the consequences of our sins *or* we get the consequences ourselves...and we are *eternal* people. That is where the teaching about blood comes in. In Leviticus we learn that the blood is the life of a person and so the shed blood of Jesus means the life of Jesus poured out. The life of Jesus meant the death of Jesus. The death of Jesus meant going to hell. The Bible says He was in hell three days, and they couldn't keep Him because He had *never* been the devil's man. *He* was free and when He came up representing humanity He brought the whole human race out with Him! There *had* to be that or we should simply be *caught inevitably* in this binding of Satan and law and wrath and judgment. So the blood is the symbol used for something which can *release* us from the *consequences* of our sin. It is the first simple teaching given them. All He *had* done was to give a few commandments and a few healthy instructions – social instructions about how to handle your animals and a few things like that.

Then, in Exodus 24, Moses calls the elders of Israel together and speaks to them a word about the offering of blood, burnt offerings, and peace offerings. Then Moses took half of the blood and put it in a basin and half of the blood he sprinkled on the altar, and then he sprinkled *everything* with the blood. This is the *first revelation* of the God of grace – Who intends to relieve us of our sins and already does so in symbol. The symbol is the outer blood which he sprinkled that began to teach them that there is a forgiveness with God...a reconciliation with God. You can come back and *get forgiven right away* **even** if you *do* make a mess of things. He had begun to teach the first elementary lessons of the kind of Person God is and the kind of relationship God really has towards His great earth family. This comes after all the *fires and thunders* in which Moses had received the law. That was because the law, if it is broken, has in its effects the fires and thunders!

From that point on he is occupied with this marvelous presentation of the *pattern* of the tabernacle. There are certain men who go around in your country and doubtless in my country, England, also, and explain the tabernacle. They have a model of it in every detail and they show you what everything in it is. It is most fascinating – because they all relate to the expressed *mercy* of God, the *presence* of God, and the *approach* which can be made to God through the sacrifice and through the blood...which was as near as He could give it to them in those days. This was the *pattern* shown him on the mount – the pattern of the full grace of God which was completed in the One Person of our Lord Jesus Christ, in the one act of His death and resurrection which put the whole thing into **One**. First he had to begin to teach them that God was *available*...but on a certain basis which there must be a recognition of sin and atonement for sin. In those days, the atonement had to be the shed blood of animals – a symbol.

So the tabernacle came into being with its center in the holiest of all – where the mercy seat was. This is a beautiful expression – the mercy seat, the seat of reconciliation, with the veil in between, because the Messiah had not come who would tear that veil out *forever*! We humans could not enter the holiest. We have to learn sin. We have to learn holiness. We have to learn right and wrong. We have to learn that wrong has to be atoned for and removed. These things had to be *gradually seeped into the consciousness* of the nation. So they began with the law which, naturally, they often did not keep...and then they were given the tabernacle which is the *presence* of God in their midst, the presence of the *God of mercy*!

This God of mercy was always to be approached through certain sacrifices which symbolized the *ultimate* blood which was to be shed – the blood of His own Son to remove the whole curse and open the door into *your* destiny as an immortal person. The destiny you move into as belonging to the self-centered dimension is in the self-centered location in eternity to which we give the name of hell, which is occupied, we are told, by spirits in prison. You are *imprisoned* by yourself! Self-loving self is prison, and the *only* prison you ever have now is your self-loving self. There isn't a single prison in the world **except** *how you react*. If you react to it as a prison, it is a prison. It is when you don't like it...and are self-interested...and want what you want, not what other people want... that you are living "spirits in prison". *That* is hell. *That* is what The Redeemer took upon Himself, and therefore He is presented in this *external form* by the blood, and the blood is presented before the Lamb Himself had come – by symbolized lambs, the sacrificial lambs. That could not be done at that time so there had to be priests to represent them, high priests who would perform these sacrifices. They brought animals to sacrifice on certain occasions so they could know their present sins were forgiven. They didn't know the *permanent* forgiveness we know. *Temporary* forgiveness was there all the time by *temporary* sacrifice, but they couldn't get the **permanent** assurance of forgiveness we have because the veil was there.

All these marvelously illuminating presentations are given us of *the ways* of the *living relationship with God*! That was the mainline occupation of Moses. To get the *pattern* on the mount took him forty days. Every tiny detail, every knot, thread, and color was given. It was beautiful, marvelous. There has not been a more marvelous building than the tabernacle. It was the *genius* of God! That is why it is a very wonderful thing to be able to see what he presented in *symbolized truth* in all these different materials of which the tabernacle is made…the objects in it, their uses, and so forth. The tabernacle was the means by which they could keep the relationship **until** the *whole thing was swept out in one simple act* – when the veil was rent in twain by Jesus. *He* is the whole thing…and through Him we move into the single eye and *living* **in** the holy place! The tabernacle is an amazing presentation of God in *His presence of grace*…and how *He* could be approached, related to, and communicated with, *and* how He is there to bless and preserve His people and build them up. Moses finalized the presentation of this great revelation…the *greatest revelation* this side of the Messiah coming!

The Bible says, "The law was given by Moses and grace and truth by Jesus Christ." But Paul said the *law* had glory…the *negative* had glory…because exposure to it *conditioned us* for the positive and *in* the negative is the positive! Wherever there was the negative, God said, "I am here in grace. I am here if you understand and admit the negative which is your wrong condition. I am here." So *always* grace! He couldn't put that forward too much – because we must learn that we are under law *before* we are *conditioned* for grace. There had to be a total recognition of guilt *before* there can be a total recognition of justification. Until we have really seen ourselves not just having committed sins…but *sinners*…we remain *self-believing* selves. The ultimate sin is what we *believe in* (because we are inner people) and we *are* what we believe in. Our ultimate sin is that we *believe in* the fallen self-loving self. When we have that *total revelation*, then we are conditioned to see, "Oh, look what *He* did for us. He *took the whole* blame for us!"

A number of chapters are given to building the tabernacle and how God put the spirit of wisdom in men like Bezaleel and others who could handle the molding of gold and making the tapestries, cloths, and instruments in the highest perfection with the wealth of Egypt, which had been poured onto the Israelites when they were turned out in desperation from Egypt. The final scene when the tabernacle had been erected was a day of sanctification and offering of it to God. The last chapter of Exodus tells of how the Shekinah glory fell and Moses couldn't bear to be in the tabernacle himself because the glory of God was there!

That completes the true *center* of the purposes of God through Moses to fit the people to be a nation in the land of Canaan and to live those thousand years, preserved as God's nation in the Promised Land in preparation for the true head of the true nation to appear. So Moses was God's preparatory agent.

There, are just one or two further incidents which are outstanding in Moses' life and are important in the finalizing of God's preparatory purposes in the wilderness. The first was the golden calf incident and the significance of that was to expose whom we *really* worship. Man *must* worship. Man is *made* to have some center to which he is attached and from which he molds his life...because man is a central person like God is. Only those who have had the spiritual rebirth can have their *center* in the living God, because living God is Spirit. You can't see Spirit. When this becomes *knowledgeable* fact, they move in and find their living center *in* the Living Person and can themselves be expressions of that Living Person! They are thrilled to be part of this One Person who is the ALL – the Self-giving *heart* of the universe!

Faith is knowledge only when faith has produced an experience of that to which we relate *ourselves*. Faith is the *evidence* of things not seen, the substance of things hoped for. It is not merely my putting myself into a relationship; it is the relationship becoming real to *me*. My faith is *my* knowledge and then I live *in* my knowledge. Knowledge is union! The word "knowledge" in the Bible always means *mixed* with. Anything you know, you are mixed with. Any profession you have, any capacities you have, you know because they are *part of* you and you are simply able to function on that level. That is what knowledge is! Only those who have that *knowledge* can therefore spontaneously live in the presence of God...even when He doesn't *appear* to be present. *Only* when we discover that the true deity is geared to *us* and we become forms of the deity can we walk steadily in this life geared to its true deity. This is the heights we reach! *Until then* we have to have some 'form' of deity.

There is a significant term that Paul used of Moses which says of the children of Israel in I Corinthians 10...that they were "baptized into Moses in the cloud and in the sea," *not into God!* Moses was the outward manifestation of the living God, and though some could see *through* Moses to the One of whom Moses was the expression, the majority probably didn't, because Moses was like God to them. That is why at certain times they said, "Don't let God speak to us," because self only knows no-God, and self-loving self can't know the true God – Who is self-giving Self. It only knows no-God, as if *He* is God...so He is fire and thunder to them *instead* of grace! The no-God puts you under curse, so they didn't want to touch the fire and the thunder – which were the forms He had to take on Sinai to express to them that *until* these things had been *exposed* and *remedied* they couldn't touch Him, although He wanted them to. Moses could, because he was part of God. Moses *lived* in the fire. He *was* the fire which becomes the light. The true meaning of fire is that it *becomes* light. If it turns into *itself* it consumes, and that is what we are...self-consuming fire...in our fallen condition. When we are yielded in the death and resurrection, we are light. We become light in ourselves...light to the world!

Our fire is the fuel of light. That is why God is both fire and light... and we're not meant to be fire. Fire is the *hidden* thing. We are meant to be light. Moses was that – so when he had lived in the light for forty days he came out with such a radiance to his body that he had to put a veil on his face. They could not take the beautiful light shining out of Moses' face. "If your eye is single your very body is filled with light." When our eye is single *our* very bodies express God!

Because of all this, Moses was the only God they *knew.* He had gotten them out of the land and now, where was he? They were beginning to feel a bit lonely out here in the howling wilderness with 'their Moses' gone forty days up on the mountain. You would feel a bit lonely, too, wouldn't you? They had the protection of the gods of Egypt and all that, and they looked back at what they projected onto the pleasantness of Egypt with its leeks and garlic...sounds very unpleasant to me, but you may like it...onions and things like that. So we can't blame them when in his absence *rebels* took over. "Come on, let's drop this business. Get some god we can understand. As for this Moses he has disappeared." And so we get the first break-in of the self-exposing self, right in the wilderness, in the making and worshipping of the golden calf for which Aaron was an agent...though not responsible. Aaron was a right man, not a wrong man. He was an agent for certain reasons, but not responsible. However, he *was* responsible in a sense that he did it and brought it into being.

Now gold meant they worshipped wealth. Wealth meant worshipping luxury...the kind of luxury they knew in Egypt (flesh indulgences) because your god symbolizes what you are and what you wish to be. Gold meant luxury and self-indulgence, and all the rest of it. So surrounding the golden calf was the worship of the flesh. It says they were even naked dancing around the golden calf, because it excited them to flesh indulgence since it was a flesh god. (Idolatry is building up a flesh god, so that you can indulge the flesh to the level of the god.) You have put your *faith* in your imitation. This was their condition. Now, the flesh *must* be exposed! Watch how God, by His Spirit, stirs a man – stirs men to be the mediators or saviors...the intercessors, His agents for salvation. God *operates* by man – by His man Jesus Christ... and men! It is *through them* that everything is done. They are the ones who are *bringing into being* His purposes. So now you get this remarkable relationship between God on Mt. Sinai and Moses, and God kind of veils Himself. That is where the *flesh* misinterprets God. They saw Him as an *outer* God. He appeared as if He had a veil. An outer God has to say, "You get what you get."

The first reaction in this account given us of the golden calf was Moses' up on the mount. "And the Lord said, 'Get thee down, Moses, for thy people whom thou brougtest out of the land of Egypt hath corrupted themselves. They have turned aside and made this molten calf and are worshipping it. I have seen this people and behold it is a stiffnecked people; let Me alone that My wrath may wax against them that I may consume them and I will make of thee a great nation.'" God was saying that if this nation continued in idolatry, then they just weren't God's nation, and they would have to be wiped out. It *wasn't* that God was angry...He was simply stating a given fact that they had ceased to be a God-centered nation, and instead became a golden calf-centered nation. It was God's way of *getting things into focus* – to act as if it was God's doing and feeling like that. No! God's feeling was that they are His *precious* people. He **had** to save them... but He had to get the *agency* of salvation, His representative man into operation!

God operates through His agencies...His representative men. That is how *we* become soul winners...we ourselves being won by men. That's how an ex-Army officer in England first won me to Christ. A *man* led me to Christ! So we see – God operates through His agencies to get His *redeeming purposes*...instead of damning purposes...into being. But He leads people into *feeling* that they are damned...that they couldn't be God's nation...that God must reject them and make another nation. He starts by a little trickery. God is always playing tricks! He said to Moses, "*Thy* people."

Now *that* aroused Moses. *Now* he could say, "Oh, Thy people"... Moses rounded back. God used a little psychology! You *want* to do what you are told not to do, so the moment God said, "Let Me alone," Moses didn't intend to let God alone. The negative operates! "I don't want to let You alone." And in boldness for God, he said, "Don't You say that, God; they are Your people, not my people. And God, how can you talk like this! Didn't You rescue them with Your mighty arm? Haven't You shown the world the magnificence of Your deliverances through the trials of plagues and so on? Now that You have got them here, are You going to make them a public mockery by destroying the nation? They will say You couldn't do it after all, You were just playing tricks."

Moses was aroused! Moses was the redeemer, you see. He *must* be aroused about the need of the people to whom he is responsible. *This* is God's purpose. It wasn't that God was angry. God was only saying what they are. Therefore the anger is what you get inside you…the effects that would take place in the corrupt nation. But what He really was, was the *Spirit of love* in Moses. Moses was His *human* manifestation. Now Moses is aroused and you see the *perfection of the spirit* in Moses. In the school of faith there is a certain amount of self…whereas in the life of faith you are in union and you *simply flow* with God. Because Moses flowed with God, he never thought of picking up God's word, "I'll make of *you* a great nation." If there had been any iota of self-interested self, Moses would have said, "Well, come on, I'll be the new Abraham." He didn't even see it!

I don't believe we *see* temptation…a lot of it…when we are in Christ. I don't believe Joseph saw Potiphar's wife. He wasn't living in that realm. He was only geared to God being glorified in his life and doing what was fair and right by Potiphar. Moses didn't see *this*. He was out of that realm, and not interested in it. He had enough trouble already without ruling some other nation. So he passed it by and turned back on God and said, "This is Your nation." God likes repenting when we get Him to repent, because He always *was* repented really. He was just pretending and He is very glad to repent! It says, "The Lord repented."

"All right", He says, "I won't destroy them. Now get you down." Then Moses said, "Okay, I've got it clear. I'll deal with this now." Now, this is the man of God in action, tremendous action…action of a total boldness outwardly, action of total self-giving inwardly…the great human mediator which, of course, was *Christ through the human.* He was total uncompromising action outwardly. Now we need that. In Moses there was **no** compromise! He went straight down. He broke publicly these tablets of stone before their eyes. He broke them; his anger waxed hot. He moved right in and he seized the calf, ground it to powder, strewed it in the water which was the water coming out of the rock, and made them drink it. "Drink that gold stuff you were worshipping. I want to expose to you what those things were. Drink it!" Think of the authority! See a man asserting his authority. And they listened to him...or wanted to kill him! But he didn't *care*.

Then he turned on Aaron. Now he loved Aaron. Aaron was a godly man. This was Aaron's *graduation* into the life of faith. You see, Aaron *did* know the Lord. He had been with Moses all the way through with the rod and the plagues. He knew the Lord, but still in the *divided* sense. He was still Aaron...and he was operating *as* Aaron. *Aaron* couldn't stand against rebellious people. Humans are weak, and so normally Aaron was a weak man. Moses was strong because he was God's man...and because he *had* God...not because he was strong. Moses had shown his weakness before when he ran from Pharaoh, but Moses was strong now because the *real* Moses in this union was God... Moses operating, and that is *God* operating!

Aaron hadn't gotten that. He still had the separated concepts so when they had come to him saying, "Oh, stop this Moses stuff and make us some gods." He didn't have what it took to stand against it and even went a little farther. I feel sure that Aaron *knew* that Moses would turn up because Aaron knew Moses...and he knew God. I think he was playing compromise, which is what you do when you don't know the flat-out life. So he made a calf, and molded it himself. Certainly he knew the old worship because he had been in with Moses in the old Egyptian days. He knew these sensual games and so on. So when he came and Moses challenged him even his answer was weak, but Moses knew he was not *identified* with the calf worshippers. So Moses said, "What did they do unto thee?" You see, he knew Aaron...that he was God's man...so he didn't say, "*You* did it." You see the subtle difference? Then Aaron's answer, "Let not the anger of my Lord wax hot, thou knowest the people that they *are set* on mischief. And they said to me, 'make us gods.' I said unto them, 'who has gold, let them bring it.'" I love his way out. "And then I cast it in the fire and there came out this calf." A little bit of runaway self, but he was not identified with the people. That is all Moses ever said to Aaron. Aaron *never* did that again.

There are great moments later on when Aaron stood the stoning with Moses. He is identified with Moses through stoning and dangers and so on. I am sure that this was inwardly the moment when Aaron had the *real* light on the helplessness of the human self, and that he was not a human self any longer – he was God's priest! God appointed him as His high priest and God caused his rod to be put in the ark and to bud...to have leaf, fruit, and flower in one evening. It was a miraculous presentation to the people that this was *God's* man, *God's* priest. Plainly, God saw *Himself* in Aaron!

Then Moses went into the positive. He was out to get a 'confessed' God's people. It wasn't enough for Him just to wipe out the ungodliness and in that sense to put fear into those who were beneath feeling responsible, who had egged Aaron on. He went the other way, He said, "Come out, now, and let us see who will stand for God and pay the price." Come out! Who will stand for God! The Levites did, about seven thousand of them. It was a risk because the people might turn on Moses and kill him and go back to Egypt. Now Moses said, "You go through the ranks and take your swords and slay every man his brother." He meant that even if it was their own brother they were to slay him if he had been one of the instigators. And they went, sword in hand, and killed three thousand who were the instigators. These were the days when punishment took physical forms because this was a physical nation, an earth nation. It doesn't do that in the heavenly nation. We have other forms, but they are symbols. In *those days* God's laws were implemented physically.

Moses had now taken the first stages in rescuing the people. These were *God's* people and they were to be rescued. They were to be put back on line where they could be God's people through whom God could *continue* to manifest Himself through the centuries in *preparation* for Jesus Christ. The first stage of the great rescue was to clear the rotten out...clear out the people who instigated rotten things.

Then he went back to the mountain...to God. When he went back, he showed his *inner* heart. This was love...though you might think it *looked* like hate. Love does look like hate when it *has to meet* certain oppositions! When Moses went back into the presence of God, he said, "Now God, forgive these people. At heart they are weak and foolish and childish and we have dealt with the real instigators. Forgive these people. I am identified with these people. If You don't forgive them, don't forgive me. If You blot them out, blot me out." Do you see what he did? *That* is intercession! That is one of the great events in history outside Jesus Christ...an intercession. "My life is *involved* with these people. I exist to see Your purpose fulfilled. I am on the altar. If in the process of getting them there I die, I die." That is that sense of *identification* we have with certain given purposes.

Some of us here have had it in *our* lives. The man I lived with in Africa who had a great effect on my life...C. T. Studd...gave *himself* to die for the Africans. He went out and would never come home. He lived the last sixteen years in those raw conditions. He saw his wife for two weeks the last sixteen years of his life because his wife stayed behind to get the young people to get the gospel out to Africa. I was one of them! And so she poured herself out and died getting young *life* to come out and begin the work of salvation in Central Africa. Her husband remained on the field and everywhere he went he called these people his "black gold." He said of them, "They are here...and here to a *purpose*...for Jesus died for them." Do you notice the purpose? That is the intercession. Not, "They are just here," but "they are here and they'll get it." That is intercession. And he died.

This is a condition in which God takes some of us in different ways. In some partial sense He has taken me. My life is a distinct series of places where I *had* to *put something through*. I went through certain sacrifices in my college days and that is when God put through the birth of the Inter-Varsity Fellowship. He gave me the vision of the Inter-Varsity Fellowship, which since has spread all around the world! That was fifty years ago. Then He put me in with this commission with

Studd. Studd's commission was not only Africa, but any part of the world which hadn't gotten the gospel. When Studd died all that was left was my wife, who was his youngest daughter, and myself at home... and the Lord commissioned us. And we gave our lives for that. We made certain definite sacrifices which *fixed* us in this business, and all my life, until just recent years, I have given my life to it. We are in forty different fields around the world now.

Mind you, these are feeble illustrations. I don't think I had better stop to give more though I am tempted to give Rees Howells because that is where you learn most *about* intercession. These are still people who have laid their lives down on the altar to be intercessors for the gospel, even to the breaking up of their marriages. Years ago they stood throughout the war that Hitler and Mussolini would never win, because the world must become *free* for the gospel. It remained free and since then the gospel has been pouring out over the world. They have been seeing with their eyes the things they had given their lives, their marriages, to fulfill. God doesn't call everybody that way, but there are different forms in which the Spirit of God reaches the Spirit of Jesus...which went to death that we might live.

It can take us, too, and some of you may know it. God may reveal to you that He has put *you* in something and now you are to get through with this...you are to see this thing through now. An intercessor is a person who *must* have it! A prayer person is a person who *may* have it. You may pray; you can pray for *many* things. You intercede for **one** thing. Intercession is standing in a gap. It says in Ezekiel, "God looked for a man to stand in the gap." A gap is a *certain* gap. Intercession is, "God has put *me* here; now it is going to happen. The thing I have come to 'see' is *going to come* to pass. *I* am on the altar for it! Whatever may be done in the way of drastic open action or secret intercession or boldness or meekness...whatever it may be...I am involved *only* in this being fulfilled. This is perhaps the greatest illustration in the Bible, outside Jesus Christ, of God operating through persons. God operates through persons and *this* was the person. This was *God's* action. It wasn't quite finished yet. The people must know the sinfulness of sin.

You see, these were the *early days* when these things were being exposed by law and by judgment. These were the beginning days, and so the next stage or the final stage was when God said to Moses, "Okay, they are My people, but I can't go up with them. I will send an angel. I will take them into the land and give it to them and an angel will come with them." Now, an angel isn't God. Don't have **second** routes. Don't have theosophy, theology, *or* Bible. Bible isn't God. Don't hang yourself on a 'thing' of *any* kind. *Only* the One Person can satisfy. His representative can't satisfy – unless you can see through the representative to being a representative of *Him*. When He said, "I'll send a representative," Moses took that for a purpose. He went back to the people and said, "Now God has accepted you back. He has forgiven you, but He will not go with you." To symbolize that He wouldn't go with them He put the tabernacle outside the camp. This must have been a kind of first form of the tabernacle or something, which represented the presence of God to the people. Now this was to bring out the truth....and they mourned.

The key, then, comes in chapter 33:4..."And when the people heard these evil tidings, they mourned." *Now* they regretted that they did the thing. They put away all their ornaments and all their jewelry for a whole week. There is a beautiful contrast here. The person who has found himself, and then had his *human self replaced* by God's Self is now the new kind of human self that knows it *is* the God-self and doesn't center around itself. A person who has identified with his people saying, "I am just weak and sinful like you, but God has shown me that life isn't really me now, it is He in me," can cause this change to take place. In intercession you don't lose the sense of who *you* are. You don't have a sense of superiority because you know yourself...and you know what you are *by* yourself.

The consequence of that was very interesting. Moses lived with a separated people. He didn't remain in the tabernacle. He remained among the people. Every day he got up and went through the tent and the people stood as he went and met with God face to face in the tabernacle outside the camp. But he didn't live with God outside the camp. He lived with the people! That is God, because God is with people. He is here to renew, rebuild, and *make* people. He doesn't live *outside* people.

When Moses finally went back to the presence of God he got the final acceptance which God *always* meant to give. He did it, He said, for Moses' sake because he had seen the thing through. God does things *because* we have seen them through! That is in chapter 33 where Moses appealed unto God and where it says the Lord spoke to Moses face to face.

There are stages of face to face. At the end of the chapter He says, "You can't see my face." Yet as far as Moses was able to, he could come face to face with this *perfect God of love and grace and truth*. But there was mixture in that God also – the God of punishment...who isn't really there. *That* God is not real. Punishment is what *we* project on Him. But this is the one Moses knew and so it says, "The Lord said unto Moses, 'I will do this thing also that thou hast spoken for thou hast found grace in My sight. I know thee by name.'"

Then there was the time Moses turned and said, "Oh God, show me Your glory. I have seen Your mercy. I would like to know all You are." He *couldn't* know that. We don't *wholly* know yet. We are still looking in a glass darkly. We have gotten a little closer than Moses, because back then a man knew nothing. There had been no Redeemer...no Cross...no resurrection. He had a pattern. We don't know what he saw through the pattern, but he obviously couldn't have seen the kind of details we know, and the salvation we know. The hunger of his heart was, "Your glory is Your totality. Show me."

But God said, "I can't do that Moses. I have revealed Myself to you as the Living Person on the level you can take Me." The level He could show was a merciful, forgiving, long-suffering God...but also a judging God on those under judgment. Those of us in Christ are not under judgment, but while there was this mixture there among God's people there *had* to be judgment. It was not that *God* punished... but that they did it to themselves! That is the best He could reveal Himself to Moses. He said that there are effects, "visiting the iniquity of the fathers upon the children," because our freedom is God's freedom! What really happens is that we project *consequences* on our children. Because we are all forms of God we may say God visits it... and because this is the consequence of sin, it *does* affect children. That doesn't affect the *plan* of God. The fact that through our humanity we visit disease or something on our children doesn't necessarily hurt the children, because people aren't outward. It isn't the outward hurt that matters. It may be that those very hurts may be the way they are *prepared* to listen to God!

But that was the best Moses could see. And God said a beautiful thing, "Moses, I will put you in the cleft of the rock up in the mountain and I will pass by you and you will see My hinder parts." His hinder parts were His grace and His law...and in His grace was His redemption. In the cleft of the rock was, "You are hidden," so wrath can't touch you.

There are these intimations that came through to Moses every now and then – such as the blood at the Passover and the cleft of the rock – of what would be ultimately fulfilled in Jesus Christ. Even now, we are still in the flesh so that we can't *wholly see* God as we should see Him. Paul says, "Now we see Him through a glass darkly, then face to face."

The other basic crisis in this wilderness period, about which we will touch, was the sending of ten spies. They had moved from Horeb, completed raising the tabernacle and the tribes had begun to move. In the book of Numbers it tells that they were put in different categories with a certain way of marching with the Levites carrying the parts of the tabernacle. They had begun to march towards Canaan, and as far as Moses could see they would get into Canaan, the Promised

Land. They approached a place called Kirjathjearim at the edge of the mountains which moved into Canaan. Now, because God is watching and *preparing* His people He told Moses to send twelve spies from among the top men to go and have a look at the land they were to enter. He knew that when they entered the land there would be warfare, because *His planned purpose* was that certain idolatrous tribes were to be put out of the land that was to be occupied by Israel. The Israelites knew nothing about soldiering and operating as a disciplined army, and He wanted them to be prepared.

Of course God knew what was going to happen. The spies spent nearly six weeks. We will take it that they were God's men, but they were men who only saw things *as the flesh sees.* Their outlook was what would *appear* to them on the *externals.* What did appear to the externals was the amazing fruitfulness of the country. They brought back one bunch of grapes so big that it took two men to carry it between poles. They were staggered with this land flowing with milk and honey. But they were still *more staggered* by the tremendous giants, called Anakim, and the great walled cities that they found! Perhaps we wouldn't call them great in our society, but in those days they seemed great. And they occupied the strategic points...the mountain tops and so on. So they said, "What can we do? These people will eat us up. We are grasshoppers in their sight." *That* is how flesh sees it. So this is the word they took back to Moses. Now this was very important for the *operation of God* that was going on within this incident. *Negative instances have positive ends* and we need to *always* be in the habit of saying, "This negative situation is only the back side of better things coming!" *God is always using negative incidents...set-backs for go-forwards!* One of our great keys to life is when we learn to see that set-backs are *only* the reverse side of the coin. The reverse side is the go-forward, and God is meaning to go forward through what *appears* to us to be a setback.

This is the way it happened. There wasn't yet an *appointed* successor to Moses. He had his eye on Joshua. That came out through the first attack made on Israel by the Amalekites in the early days.

For some reason, Moses had put the army under Joshua. Perhaps he had seen something in Joshua during those early days in Egypt that made him think he would be a good military leader. So he took Joshua back to be his servant. Now, Joshua didn't run about running armies. He just washed Moses' hands for him and shaved his beard and wherever Moses went, Joshua went. He just had a humble job. At the same time, it is interesting to watch little forward flashes coming in Joshua…leadership flashes…but still in the *self* realm. He was God's man, but he was still in the area where he thought he must be his *own* self and operate…and God would bless him. He was on the level of a self-expressing self. It had expressed itself in three ways *before* this moment.

The first was when they came down the mountain where he had been with Moses at the time of the idolatry of the golden calf. As he came down the mountain and heard the singing and dancing and shouting, immediately the military instinct of Joshua arose and he thought, "Now is my chance. Now I can do something. That must be battle."

"Oh no, that's not battle," Moses said, "That is evil worship. That is sensual dancing, not battle."

The other touch came after the golden calf incident. He was trying to be a better person himself and condemning those who weren't better persons…so he stayed in the tent of meeting and wouldn't mingle with the others. We do that, also, when we say, "Why are they doing this? Why are they doing that idolatry business?" He didn't yet know the difference *between* independent self and God…so he tried to judge independently, because he was trying to be somebody. When you are trying to *be* somebody you judge those who aren't! So there was a certain judgmentalism there. He hadn't cracked up yet to where he himself was just an idolater at bottom. *He* was just as much a sinner as anybody else that *believed* in flesh. Idolatry is believing in flesh, in the material, instead of believing in God. Moses *knew* better than that. He knew he was one of those people; he was just a little picked up by God, that's all. So he wasn't bothered. He was just as much an idolater as any of them because he had been an idolater for forty years with Pharaoh, and so he could live with them and then represent them. That is the *true* intercessor!

One more incident turned up which was very interesting. You see, Joshua saw man and man's abilities, and man's magnification – and Moses was the man! He hadn't yet caught on to the *broken and renewed* Moses – the burning bush Moses. He did not yet recognize that though Moses was a man it was really *God* coming through. He was still occupied with the man, Moses. Perhaps he already saw himself as a possible successor since he had already been appointed captain of the armies in the battle. Now suddenly there came an incident where the people were grumbling and pressing on Moses, and Moses lashed out. This was one of his spots where he could lash out. (I like lashers, being one myself!) So he was thoroughly annoyed and said, "Oh God, I give up on these people. I can't carry them any longer. You take the people back. I can't do it!"

So God said to Moses, "You have taken on a tremendous thing. I will give you seventy men who can take a lot of the details off you. I'll put My Spirit on them, and they can be co-leaders with you under your main leadership." When he called the seventy, only sixty-eight came. The two who didn't come, Eldad and Medad, remained in the camp. I don't know why. When the others met together the Spirit fell on those two as well as the others. They all were praising God and worshipping and enjoying the Lord. Joshua, being concerned for man, was a little annoyed that these people had put themselves with 'his' Moses, and when he heard that the two who had not come had the Spirit also, he grumbled to Moses about it.

Moses' reply to him was, "Enviest thou for *my* sake?" Catch that? What he was saying was, "You have personal envy. You have likes and dislikes. You like a Moses, but you don't like somebody else. You don't understand that Moses is just a manifestation of God." You see, there are different ways in which we all have to go through forms of independent self. Self has the element of self-sufficiency that Joshua showed, yet he was God's prepared man! This is the school of faith. Now the school of faith has its *graduation* in a final negative self-revelation to prepare for a positive self-revelation! The negative revelation is, "Oh, I'm no good, it isn't in me." Then when it becomes, "Oh! It's in *God*," you are capable of seeing the *inner* union! It's not God of 'somewhere' because you already *are* God's. Actually He is there already... you just don't *know* it. It is getting to, "Oh, *that's* it...it isn't I who am (the one operating) *I* am the agent by whom *God* operates"...and your central recognition has passed from the self-acting self to *God acting* by self. Self goes into action, but now I know inside it isn't I. Now that *always* is a crack-up. That is the *graduation* in the school of faith when *somewhere* you are *at last* caught out!

This was Joshua's catching out. It was very subtle. He was one of the twelve spies. When they came back, one of those noble spies whose name was Caleb made a magnificent stand by himself. All of them were set up and moaning and crying and disturbing the children of Israel until the whole nation was crying..."Oh, we can't. There are giants that will eat us up...we were as grasshoppers...there are walled cities. What can we do?" You would have been just the same! *Everybody* talks like that. So there were deep disturbances right in the very center of the nation. *One man stood* - Caleb.

Caleb's was a magnificent statement, which we in our missions have used again and again. He stilled the people before Moses and said, "Let us go up at once and possess it; for we are able to overcome it." **We**...not God! That is the great secret. Again and again I have said that to my fellow missionaries. "Don't say, 'Oh, *God* does-it,' say, '*We* do it.'" We are God – operate *as* God! Our fellow missions have done this in opening the Congo...and all the other places where we found that we couldn't understand or speak the language. We said, "We are well able *because* we are God. *We* are God expressed through our human form." Caleb knew it! So all the way afterwards it spoke of Caleb as one who *wholly* followed the Lord.

Now the significant thing was that Joshua was one of these twelve spies. Therefore Joshua was with the unbelievers. You see, Joshua was a military man, and when he assessed those giants he agreed with them that they couldn't be touched. His militarism had caught him out. He didn't have what it took to handle giants so he sided with the eleven on the *wrong* side. Now this was Joshua's *great crisis* and *great graduation*! The whole nation was disturbed so they had a very disturbed night. They were preparing to stone Moses and Aaron. They felt hopeless. "What are we to do? Go back to Egypt?" If you have **only** got yourself and your self-reactions to look at, you feel like that! They cried all night.

The next morning Moses and Aaron stood alone against the congregation. At first the people murmured against Aaron, and then they went all the way and said, "We wish we had died in Egypt or in the wilderness. Let us find another leader and return to Egypt." This was a real revolution! Now Moses and Aaron did what they always did and fell on their faces in order to hear what God had to say. While they were on their faces with this raging crowd around them, Joshua and Caleb arose. Joshua had swung around! He had made the change, and now he sided with Caleb and Moses and Aaron against the people. In the night he had seen that it wasn't a question of *his* military capacities...but a question of *God* having told them to go, and therefore they could go! So he took the stoning with Caleb, Moses, and Aaron. That is the Joshua committed now in the condition to be a leader. He knew his military faculties were *secondary* to *God's* enabling and *God's* leadership!

This incident set the people back forty years. But God doesn't play about. This *awful* idea we have that God is a bit tough and mean is not true! We have a mighty, good, kind, loving God. Look for goodness in *everything*. No matter what happens to you...*look* for goodness! In my own, life recently, my Pauline who is eighty years of age has been through this very severe surgery which you don't usually go through at her age. All the way through we have seen the goodness of the doctors, the goodness of the hospital, the kindness, the benefits. Even Medicare I am very thankful for! They give Medicare to an alien – that's a pretty good country, this one! Goodness, goodness, goodness...and the Upholding Life which has brought her through. She is back home, though weak...and still in the Life of God. These are little things, but what a *difference* it makes when you are in a tough spot to say, "This rough thing is just *some manifestation* of the *goodness* of God." Get out of thinking *meanly* about God.

For forty years He hung them on – one year for each day the spies had spent investigating the country. Actually what it meant was the forming of a nation who could act with Joshua as a disciplined army – a disciplined people. *This* was the disciplining. During those forty years they began to move towards the land stage by stage. They became socially and nationally an ordered people with laws and God's grace. They needed to be militarily equipped to fulfill the next stage of occupation of the land so these years were *necessary*.

There were two more rebellions which Moses handled beautifully. One was a domestic rebellion when Miriam and Aaron objected to his colored wife. That is very relevant for the day, isn't it? Moses never said a word. This is what is meant by saying that Moses was the meekest man on earth, because Moses would never act for *personal* reasons, though for God's reasons he would always act! Just as you always find the pourings out of prayer for destruction in the Psalms are never for *David's* enemies, but for God's enemies...so it was with Moses. Obviously there was tension, but he never said a word. God exposed it and rebuked Aaron, and Aaron came through again, "I am sorry, we shouldn't have done this." We all have a weak spot, but don't measure on the weak spot, measure on the *strong* spot. *This* is what God sees!

The other more serious incident was a political and religious rebellion. Korah rebelled against Aaron and wanted to replace him as high priest. Dathan and Abiram rebelled against Moses as the leader, and dared to accuse him of becoming the kind of king who would put their eyes out like the old tyrants of that age. He himself hoped to get a change of leadership. God dealt with that very strongly *because* this was against the public order. Privately, Moses never said a word. Publicly, Moses dealt…and God dealt through Moses. That is when the earth opened and he made that remark which is not made anywhere else. He put himself out on a limb and said, "You will know when this happens that this has not come from my own mind." That is a very striking remark there which showed that he differentiated in guidance between *his* mind, which could think all sorts of things, and what *God revealed* to Him as God's mind. **Really**, they are only one. That is in Numbers 16.

There are two other incidents I will touch on. One is the beauty of the prophetic word by Balaam. This is very curious, and we have to admit that it was clairvoyance. That's all right; it isn't a wrong thing…it is just a capacity. Every now and then there are exercises of *God's gifts* by those who are not God's people. Because it is a gift is *not always* an indication it is from God. A very outstanding incidence is Balaam. Balaam was *possessed* by covetousness. He sold himself to get the money. Yet there was this strange ambivalence, because he continued to say, "I can only say what God gives me." This Spirit on him *compelled* him to say what God gave him, and so we get these remarkable statements by Balaam which so perfectly fit God's point of view! Balak, the king of Moab, who was afraid of the advancing Israelite army, paid Balaam to curse Israel…because he felt that would give him strength for opposing Israel. But Balaam *had* to bless Israel and in this case he said, "God is not a man that He could lie, neither the son of man that He should repent. Hath He said and shall He not do it, or hath He spoken and shall He not make it good? Behold, I have received commandment to bless; and He hath blessed, and I cannot reverse it. He hath not beheld iniquity in Jacob, neither hath He seen perverseness in Israel."

Well, we have seen *nothing but* perverseness in Israel! What a difference! We see it in our brother. Don't 'see' what we think is perverseness…forgetting our own perverseness. *Don't see the kinks…see the perfection of God coming through the person.* Live here…affirm that…accept that…and then just bypass the other! God will deal with that in them as He is doing in you. That is this attitude, the union attitude. Isn't that marvelous that God would say, "He hath not beheld iniquity in Jacob." It is laughable! Then he says, "The Lord his God is with him, and the shout of a king is among them!" I like that phrase. We use that in our mission quite a bit..."The shout of a king." The royal person with authority is putting something through, managing, reigning, or *something.*

The other statement is *so glorious* that it shocks them all over again! This is in vision..."He hath said which heard the words of God and knew the knowledge of the Most High, which saw the vision of the Almighty falling into a trance, but having His eyes open, I shall see Him, but not now: I shall behold Him, but not nigh; there shall come a Star out of Jacob, and a scepter shall rise out of Israel, and shall smite the corners of Moab, and destroy all the children of Sheth." Of course, he got that a little wrong. He didn't come to destroy; He came to redeem! He didn't know that much, but he knew He had to come. Isn't that beautiful? The last incident, bypassing several (even the brazen serpent) that we'll touch on is this last outburst by our *human* Moses. We saw the outburst in the *human* Isaac who for the dictates of his own tummy wished the best to Esau instead of to Jacob and all those things, so some of this has come out.

This is the last outburst in Moses. Very significant! Remember, a person in leadership is especially responsible and in a sense there must be special reverse action when they do the wrong thing. James makes that clear when he says, "For in many things we offend all. My brethren, be not many masters (teachers) knowing we shall receive the greater condemnation." In other words...a greater assessment of our leadership. So a leader who goes wrong may be putting multitudes of others wrong, and there is likely to be a quicker reaction. This was so with Moses. Moses had a custom for years of the *external.* The Israelites only saw this man operating his rod, and to them this rod had some mystic powers – like we have *foolish* ideas that the sacrament or the baptism have some mystic powers. Even the Bible hasn't mystic powers!

It **conveys** the Spirit. The *Spirit* has the mystic power – the Spirit is the Person!

So the Israelites, who saw again and again Moses using his rod bringing the water, and getting the manna and getting this and getting that, got the idea that *God* came through the rod. Now this is near the end of Moses' life. He is going *behind* other people. Faith must take him out. They must not be wrong-minded, but God-minded...word of faith minded. It is the *inner word of faith* which is the recognition that God is operating in you...*that* is where the power is! The rod is only a symbol. (God does give *symbols* – such as the Bible. The promises are for *symbols*. Power isn't in the promise; *it* is the God who fulfills the promise. Anything can become a symbol.) Now in this last occasion, once again Moses is irritated. After all these years they were again grumbling...they hadn't any food, they hadn't any water, and sometimes it got to him. In this case they didn't have water. So he rose up and said to God, "Oh, this is the limit."

God spoke a very subtle word to him, "Take the rod and gather the assembly together and speak to the rock." (Numbers 20:8) This was a naughty little twist of God; it wasn't very kind of Him! It *really* caught Moses out. Oh, the rod. *Speak! No, rod!* And Moses used the rod. Now that presented a *wholly false basis* to the *principle of faith* for the whole tribe, for the whole nation...for Joshua and all of them. If they caught the idea that the last thing Moses did was to get water by that rod, then when they had a need they would think, "What am I to do, I haven't got a *rod*." That wouldn't do. So God *had* to judge it!

Actually Moses had had enough. He would have been too old at 120 years to get them marching across Jordan and taking Jericho and things anyhow. We old folks are best out of the way quick! So it was okay...there was no harm. And there is this beautiful ending where He said, "Moses, you can't." He put it in that line because He had to teach the people! Moses had to *confess* it. In Deuteronomy, he confesses it. Deuteronomy is when he gives his last talk. Deuteronomy means second law. He is reconfirming things to Israel. He had to make this public once or twice over..."God said I couldn't go into this land because of this. I did something which put a wrong emphasis on a rod instead of on a word of faith."

So God "took him up to Mt. Nebo for a survey of this land that he *longed* to be in...this Land of Promise into which the Messiah was to come. He *saw* beyond the land, beyond the people – to the other prophet coming, the Messiah...whatever that meant! They didn't *fully* understand about the One whose blood would be shed...who would finish the redemption...who would bring out the new nation. He *saw* that vision!

He gave one last sentence that is very precious to us all. It is interesting that every now and then Moses would shoot out a word which showed how *much more* he knew underneath. For instance, he gave so much of outer activities – circumcision was a physical outer symbol in the people...the ritual of the sacrifices...and the tabernacle – *all* outer. Then, suddenly, in Deuteronomy 10, he says, "Circumcise the foreskin of your *heart*, and be no more stiffnecked." Oh, that is something else! Have an *inner* circumcision! You see what he saw through? So underneath, Moses saw through it every now and then. He didn't say much; perhaps he didn't know *how* to put it into language very much. Paul picked up the bit about having *inner* circumcision when in Colossians he speaks of the "circumcision not made with hands."

Another word of Moses that Paul picked up on was from Deuteronomy 30: 12-14, "The word is in you, in your heart and in your mouth." So Moses knew the *inner* relationship! And the word of faith is in you...you simply speak the word of faith which means you are *affirming the fact which is here*! Word of faith means, "I am saying this **is** here." Confessing with their mouth the Lord Jesus – the word of faith which He preached. And then he says, "He is thy life." The final word which has echoed down the ages to us and we will close this account of his wonderful life with his "The eternal God is our refuge and underneath are the everlasting arms." Deuteronomy 33:27. It was almost the last thing he said.

Every now and then he had a flash of *substitution*. One was the lamb, of course, the blood on the lintel of the door, the Passover. The blood was substitution. Again, came in the actual fact of the sin symbol which was the serpent being nailed to the cross, so the sin itself would in some way be borne on the Cross. It was taken out of the way by being on a cross – nailed to a pole and if you looked at that, your disease went. Sin here symbolizes disease. They were bitten by the serpents. Sin was like a serpent. If they were bitten, they were poisoned.

It was a little shadow again which is taken up in John 3, "As Moses lifted up the serpent in the wilderness, even so shall the Son of Man be lifted up." It is picked out there as a very clear indication of the fact that Jesus Christ *became* sin. He did more than bear our sins…He was **made** sin. He *became* the serpent in God's sight…and died as a serpent…and left the serpent behind because the serpent was something He took on Himself, and He couldn't be held by death! He came up again the new man with a new race, in the resurrection. That is the nearest. But there just come these little flashes every now and then through the Old Testament of what can only be *dimly* seen by them and what can be *clearly* seen by us. That is all…and *that* is Moses!

GIDEON

Well, we're looking at one of those *dramatic* instances we can pick out of the Old Testament where we can get a great understanding of the ways by which God operates *by a human*...and a human is *God* in action! And as a human moves out *as* God in action these miraculous things happen, which happen today in their different forms. And this is a very *dramatic* and *startling* one that stands out by itself in just two or three chapters – that is mainly the life of Gideon, who went on to be one of the judges of Israel for 40 years (and days before that kings) to be found in the 6th chapter of Judges onwards.

The conditions in which this happened were the typical conditions, and people are always saying, "What you sow you reap." Right away from Moses time onward He says to them..."If you attach yourself to Me – I'm a *living* God! You have a faith in a *living God*. I'm a God that does things and will work *for* you...that will put a quality in *you* that will *do* things and work *for* you (like Israel today) and *you* put it through. But if you turn from Me, you're really turning on your own self. Your false god's kind of a self-image – a fleshly, self-gratifying, self-seeking person. You make a *god* like that. Well, there's no conviction in that... it's just yourself. You *know* in your *heart* that's not a living God at all! You've got no *center* to your faith which puts muscles into your operations and so you sink under them and then the people you oppose. You've adopted their false gods. You've got no foothold to then stand on. They're stronger than you; they'll eat you up!" So He says, "I warn you…if you exchange Me for one of these heathen gods, down you go with them! They'll destroy you, and it'll be *good* you'll be destroyed… it's how you'll know you've gone in a false way."

That's *always* the history of Israel. It's really the history of *all* self… unredeemed self, of course, in different forms…but here it takes a *national* form. And in this case they'd slipped into Baal worship. You'd think with all the corruption and horrors centered around Baal (Jezebel was a prophetess of Baal) and as a *consequence* they'd lost their spiritual muscle. They had no *faith* to operate, and these surrounding Midianites ate them up! They were a very populous people. They said they were like grasshoppers in multitude and they *so* oppressed Israel for 7 years. They hid their dead in caves…were run out of their homes to hide…and to make it worse, the Midianites would come at harvest time and burn all the harvest, so they starved them. They were terrified and hidden away. There wasn't a weapon among them…and they were in *this* condition.

Now they *did* know God. These were not sinners of the Gentiles. They were God's people, so they *knew* how to cry to God. We read after 7 years, they were crying to God. Well, this is the *first* step. They were turning back…noticed the idolatry…hadn't cleaned it up yet…but in midst of it all, were saying, "God where are You? Help us!" So that was big the condition for *God* to begin to move in among them!

Now there was one young man, in whose heart obviously this was a *real* cry and a real argument. What's up? Therefore, He had a basic faith – if God was the kind of God that took us out of Egypt…why doesn't He work today? Is He dead? You know how you begin to criticize God and resent and judge God. *This* was this man, Gideon.

There had also been, during this time (which everything had to be found outside Gideon) a prophet. I will not give you his name. These are *bold* men; these are great men. They *speak* things out! Of course, very often they were tortured and destroyed for doing so.

They spoke the truth…and he came out and said you got what you deserved. He spoke to Israel. (They came out of laws instead of prophet.) And He said, "I told you. I got you out of Egypt didn't I? I told you if you detach yourself from the living God and take on these false gods – which are only mirages and you're really back on your old self-loving self – you'll collapse." So He didn't give them a remedy, but He said, "You've *not* obeyed My voice." Otherwise He pinpointed the reason why they were in this appalling condition and being trampled under by these Midianites, these 'hosts'. That must have affected Gideon.

And so the day came when God knows a *conditioned heart*. Any heart can be conditioned. We aren't allowed to know the *ways* of conditioned hearts when God can begin to speak to us. And this came in the form of an angel…appeared! (Well, that was presumably probably a visionary one…we don't know. Or whether in some sense he came in an actual physical form…it doesn't matter to us.) And Gideon was in a final condition of terror. He *pretended* to preserve a harvest. So he threshed his wheat in the wine press…hidden away in the wine press, so it wasn't wheat at all. (He was preserving his daily bread.) He was hidden away in the wine press. And this angel of the Lord spoke to him and said the startling words…too much for him to take at the moment…he just said to him, "The Lord is with thee thou mighty man of valor."

That's what *we* are - but we have to be brought to the place where we recognize *why* we are mighty…and we *are* mighty…*we* are mighty! This is what we've got to relearn. This is a person who's *found* the secret of power – I *am* mighty! I *can* do all things! This is a little too much for Gideon at the moment…but it startled him. Straight away, "The *Lord* is with thee." That's the reason *why* you're mighty! You're mighty as a consequence!

Well, Gideon reacted because he was an honest man. He couldn't see at the moment, but he turned around. But he *did* show he was in the controversy of God. If that's so, then why didn't You rescue us?

He turned back on Him. He says, "If the Lord did all these miracles, where are the miracles today? He says, "You say...if the Lord's with us." He didn't say with *me*...didn't get that far. He answered the angel, "Oh my lord, if the Lord be with us, why does this befall us? Where are the miracles?" So he's at a *rightful* controversy with God. God even has a controversy with regard to them! But you turn that the other way around. But *this* is a *conditioned* person...alive...with this battle of argument going on within himself and this controversy with God.

The angel? Never deals with reasons, he deals with faith. God doesn't deal with reasons...bypassed it. God didn't attempt to answer...turned right back, and said more this time. He said, "Go in this *thy* might and thou shall save Israel from the hand of the Midianites." He said, "The Lord is with you. You're a mighty man of valor." He bypassed that and turned to "us" and said..."I can't take that out...why has the Lord left *us*?" The angel disregarding "us" to come back to *you* – because that's *all* we ever have is ourselves. God only operates you by you, me by me. Maybe we can be cooperative, but we never get through this thing, except as *we* are the person God uses. Each of us are the *we*, the *I*, whom God uses. We've **got** to get that clear – then it comes through us. It may cooperate with others, but that's the *main* point. That's where God comes in *effectiveness* through humans...moved past this reasoning and arguing and said (this *strong* point is very interesting in saying that)...said the Lord *looked* upon him (verse 14) "Go in this *thy* might and thou shall save Israel." *Looked* upon him – now he caught *His* eye. By that meant the Lord is the angel of the Lord. We see the angel of the Lord talked inside of Gideon. I presume this still came through the angel, I suppose, I'm not sure. He caught his eye – "I'm talking to *you*...I'm saying it to *you*." That caught him! He was conditioned. He first tried to escape...well, you do. But he didn't really escape because he'd been arguing with God. He was the one man who was bothered about this...and so you were conditioned. God said, "Now I'm coming to *you*. I have settled with you." He said this to Gideon, and Gideon began to take it. He said, "I say to you. I look upon you, and I say to you, 'Go in this your might and you will save Israel from the hand of the Midianites'".......this *one man* hidden away in the wine press, and the Midianites, like grasshoppers in multitudes... "Have not I sent *you*?"

And now we get further on...a little further. And Gideon *did* take it. But then he began, "How could it be?" Just as in Moses...where He turned up to Moses in the burning bush and He said, "Come now I send you." "Okay...but how can *I* do it? They won't listen to *me*. They've already rejected me once. How can I prove it's You who spoke to me? I haven't got any voice; I'm a poor speaker and such." Alright, that's good. That's a *human* argument...negative-positive. Settles the positive! You must have the negatives out; gets replaced with the positive. Moses was like that.

So Gideon says, "Wait a minute, wait a minute...my people are just an insignificant family in the town of Manasseh. I'm the least significant in my father's house...I'm the least in my father's house. There's nothing had to be (which if You look on my family and me) which means *I* can save Israel (It's *laughable!*) from the hands of the Midianites." Still He stuck to the *one* man – you've *got to get it* – not worried about Gideon. "I'm not taken about that." Again no answer on his family being too poor, or being insignificant...back again on himself **from reason to faith**.

He said, "Surely I will be with *thee*, and thou shalt smite the Midianites as *one man*...a vast host! No, it's you and they – they're going to be the one man; I'm going to do it by you." (I don't know how You'll do it!) "I'll reduce that host to one man as it were...and you'll knock the whole host out in one blow. That's something! You are the man! It's going to happen *by you*. And something shall happen by you which shall put the whole Midianite army out of action." That's something! We're catching more and more, *we* have to do it. *I'm* the one God said…it's got to come through me. Now others may be in and out of it, but for myself…each of us, when we see it…have it in our own 'couldness'. That's through *me*. And it kept him nailing down… it's through you, Gideon…you're the *man*; because the Lord's with you, you're the man. Finally got him! He'd got him!

And so now Gideon turns around and says, "Well, I'd better have a sign on that, angel, lord. I need a sign. (This is ridiculous, but he began to get it! There's something here…I'm to be your man.) Well, I can't do it unless you make me sure of it. You'd better give me a sign." And so he made him a bit of a sign. He said, "Look here. I don't know what you intend to do with it, but I'm going to make a meal – a kind of sacrifice I suppose." And he says, "Will you wait here? I'll go and bring forth my present." He called it "my present." And the angel said, "Alright, I'll wait" and he went in and roasted a kid, and got some unleavened bread…took some time, I suppose…flesh and so on…brought it in a basket…and put it under the oak where this angel was there. And the angel said to him, "Take it now and put it on this rock, and pour out the broth…as a kind of sacrifice, I suppose. And what happened was a miracle – fire came out of the rock and burned it up. (That's alright…I mean God has His own ways of confirming to us…we just say that's the way it happened *then*. We *also* can have confirmations.) And then the angel disappeared. And *that* confirmed to Gideon of having God spoken to him.

But now Gideon had to move into a place of *familiarity* with God. See he only had flesh. Flesh always says God's awful…He's judgment… He's wrath…He's dangerous…I'm afraid of Him…if I meet Him face-to-face I'd die. All that's sort of the flesh idea of God…came through law without grace…didn't know grace. You've got to *pass from* law to grace. Gideon's rational, "Oh, I shall die. I've seen God face-to-face" and this is the first time it says God spoke…not an angel of God now (he's disappeared)…this is the Lord *in him*! Now we can bring to life, *our* life, where the Lord *in* Gideon says this to him – and it says the Lord said to him, "Peace be unto thee; you'll not die."

This meant to Gideon he was settled...because He'd produced a new name, which is used today – Shalom. This came in here. And God in Gideon built an altar and called it Jehovah-shalom, which is peace. It's the word we use today after the Jews. Peace. Peace meant – Oh, it's okay. I needn't be afraid of God. It meant God and I have a relationship – we're in with each other! We have an 'in' now. (Yes, it's what we call union!) In *those* terms you could be on good terms with God. Now this fear stuff, this distance stuff had gone. It led to what we call **union with God**.

Now, it's all a relaxed life...he'd got it now! Something had happened! What *could* happen...this *fantastic* situation! What *could* happen? Now you don't push this life because, of course, *God's* the pusher... He's in you! So we don't *know*...we don't go pushing...we just find – the next thing happens! And this happens: That same night, again the Lord spoke to him, and touched him on a spot. "Look here, Gideon, you can't be my mighty man, and I'll do things by you while you're co-idolater...and your own township (Abiezerites, Abiezer) they have an idol to Baal. They have a high hill (a temple to Baal) who are supposed to be godly people. You can't let that stand. You are to go at night and destroy that thing."

Now you see...now in this life there **is** a death. There's a death which you die; (that's the *other*) you die in yourself – crucified with Christ *now* to those who're facing ministry. Now I wouldn't make it up, but there *is*...you'll always find *somewhere*. There's somewhere...I tell it in my *own* life where you take a step (which puts you out of step) maybe in the world...even with your fellow Christians someday, which has a danger in it. You're risking something, and you will find it goes all the way through the bible like that.

Abraham had to sacrifice Isaac and be delivered and had to cross away...all these things, there's *risks* in them! So we don't make it up, but you'll find as we follow, there are some things which push you differently – something that makes you a peculiar person – and this of course risked his life! He knew it! And he used sense...you can use sense. He took ten men. He had servants. They must have been quite wealthy people. (He said they were poor...they had ten servants!) And these men, either willingly or because they respected Gideon or something went with him at night. Now you see he...like *all* men...he had fear. He was a man of fear. *Faith comes out of fear.* Faith then conquers the fear...because *fear is negative believing.* Faith is positive believing. Fear always means I believe in the evil thing. It paralyzes me! *Fear is faith.* It's really *faith in reverse.* So all men are fearful. Watch negative, believe negative – fear. Turned around and it's turned into faith... while you're believing its God! Fear is faith in reverse, or faith is just fear in reverse...whichever way you like it.

And he feared, but he did sensibly. And while he knew he *couldn't* do it by daylight, so he did it by night. Because he feared them...because he feared the household he couldn't do it by daylight; he'd do it by night. Sensible caution...he was fulfilling his commission and he destroyed this thing, and built an altar to the Lord!

Now, here we get to the next stage. (*Who* can tell? You can't tell. When we follow the Lord we *can't* tell in what way the news will come.) Because he *did* face the fact that they were sure to kill him the next day if he destroyed Baal which was the center of their worship, so when they found next day that their temple had been destroyed, and an altar had been raised to *God*, these men said, "Who did this?" They found that Gideon, the son of Joash, did it. They said, "Take him up, we'll kill him. Bring out thy son," they called to Joash, "so he may die! He's cast down the altar to Baal and cut down the grove that's by it!"

Now this miracle happened because these men were, underneath, men of God. We see later on the whole Abiezrites went with God. The whole town turned around because the roots were there, but it came out this time in this very bold statement – this very wonderful statement with *wisdom* in it from Joash! Evidently Joash had a conviction that he had allowed this idolatry to take place and he saw his son (maybe his son had already said things to him, I don't know). His son was being *led* of God, and was *speaking* in the *power of God* and *operating* in the *faithfulness of God*. He rose up! He said a very clever thing. "Okay, if my son has destroyed the temple of Baal in the name of the Lord...if Baal is a *real* god, let him come back and pay his own price... let *him* take vengeance. Let *him* do something to Gideon. Don't *you* do it. Let Baal do it!" Very much the same as Elijah. Elijah said, "*If* a prophet of Baal...call on *him*. If he's real, let him come and send fire" That's the same idea...and that *so* shook, and probably got underneath the convictions of the Israelites. They didn't touch either Joash or Gideon! They did nothing. I think they began to know where truth lay.

The effect of this was you see again the stark living is *by you*...is costly, you don't make it up. It's because God calls *you* to **do** it. You move into something...perhaps in our own way...some small way, a typical way. (That's how God had Bill Volkman start Union Life!) Little things, something startling, which makes something become *known* and this very sort of thing...it *ran* around! This city, this family and city destroyed Baal...turned him out and put God back. It ran like lightening, not only ran like lightning through Israel or at least the northern part of Israel, it ran like lightning through the Midianites! They heard, and it shook them, that Israel was rising up! They were going to defy this Baal and stand in the name of the Lord. So the next thing that happened was they called the army together. And it says...verse 33... "All the Amalekites and then all the Midianites, the Amalekites (they were the old enemies) and the children of the east, the whole lot would gather together...the children of the East...135,000 of them. And they were pitched in a certain valley." They were to come back and reaffirm their enslavement of Israel.

And now you get this *wonderful* statement. It says, "The Spirit of the Lord came upon Gideon." Verse 34 – the *exact* translation..."He *clothed*

Himself with Gideon." *That's* a beautiful expression, because that's *exactly* what **we are**! The Spirit of the Lord is *clothing* like in Gideon... that's exactly what it is! *We're* the **clothing** of the Spirit of the Lord! In a *specific* way now He *clothed* Himself with Gideon...he *was* the *Spirit operated by Gideon! There's no other place in the Bible where that phrase is used.* In my translation it says that the Spirit of the Lord came upon Gideon, but the margin is that *He clothed Himself with Gideon!*

This now moved Gideon. He had to come into action. He got *forced*...he's for it now! He had this role which he accepted. He was to smite the army as one man. He was the man who had the power to do it...better get on with it now! So you get to the place where the Spirit forces you into action. First it is local action...cleaning things up in their own situation and we see here as he called people together the *whole* Israelite people came with him...so he won the whole town. He blew a trumpet, which is the way they did things in those days. Must have been some way like we did it in Africa. We did it by the hollow drums. The drums would call village to village. You pass the message by the drums. Here they did it by some way...one trumpeter to another trumpeter and so on through Israel...calling the people to action. And he called the people of Manasseh...his own tribe, Asher, Zebulun, and Naphtali. If you look at a map they were the northern tribes which was a northern area of Israel, and they were gathered together with him.

And I'd forgotten that where it says – when the Spirit of the Lord came upon Gideon, the Abiezerites were gathered with him...his own city...and they stood right with now! And with him came the large number of the other tribes, up to 32,000 (a big number) but the others were 135,000! Some *difference*...and as far as we know they hadn't one weapon among them. They'd hid in caves and hadn't one weapon among them! The others were armed...a *hopeless* situation. Now then Gideon, (he was a released and detached man) he went cautiously, and there's a place we should go cautiously. He still thought on this side he needed another sign...at this distance he needed another sign...at this juncture.

That's famous...that's the sign of the fleece. Christians use it all the time...put out a fleece. Now, I don't know why he did except that in his *mind* he only wanted something which related God *particularly* with *him*. Apparently that's why he did it. So he put out two ways round in some way. The first way – I'll put it there, and then (meaning) You can do it. There *is* a place we can do it...many of you've done it, maybe. Alright you can do it! We're humans and in situations perhaps it pleases God that we should move in to confirm ourselves with signs. That's not wrong...and the sign he asked was...I'll do a thing...which again, impossible – I'll put out a fleece, lay a fleece on the ground. I say to You God, "If tomorrow morning, there's no dew on the ground around and the fleece is full of dew, I'll *know* that You're with me."

And it happened! And he even then wasn't *quite* strong enough, so he reversed it. He said, "I'll do it once more." That's all right. God loves us to push things through when we're His servants...to get our confirmation. That's alright. And then he said, "I hope you won't be annoyed with me. Let not Thy anger be hot against me." I'll reverse it, he said. "This time let the fleece be dry, and all around it with dew." And it was so...and God did so that night. It was dry from the fleece only and dew on all the ground.

So that was to Gideon a confirmation in this unique way God was with him...he was expressing God. The others hadn't got God. That was the idea, I suppose, dew and no dew. And in the other case...no dew and dew. In each case he was a peculiar person...and a thing happened to him which didn't happen to the others...and he was a peculiar person to whom *God* would do it. Well, that's a good confirmation!

So now they move in, and he gather's his army together. A bunch of farmers had come out of their holes and caves and we see, as far as we know, not a weapon among them...32,000 of them....and they're [Midianites] up in the hills here and this *vast* army...135,000! Their camels all lay in this big valley. Here the Israelites with Gideon were overlooking this crowd in the valley. Now God again, very significantly in some ways, in which it must be confirmed – that what God did, *God did*, and not by the powers of man. And, also, I suppose it works out that way...a number like that you would have (camp followers) who come along with him hadn't got the same quality of faith. How could they have the same quality of faith as Gideon? Some had said they'd go with him, but they'd had doubters. This is sense – how on earth! We'll be *destroyed*! So they follow. All right, we'll follow; we're called, we'll follow, but we can't say we're really *in* this thing. Maybe it was that Gideon could discern that. Maybe Gideon must have people who really mean business, because we're going to have business. We need people who can be *bold* and will risk their lives as you're risking your life. We can't just have hangers-on. And if there are hangers-on come to the camp, they may take all the credit...and we *all* did it.

So this guidance came (may have come through Gideon's common sense) and the Lord said, "Make a division and be quite free." And he said to the people, now look here, "This is a *big* thing, and you'll join me. Now you may not all quite see as I do...that God's going to do this thing. (I presume he said to himself...but somehow or other God's going to *do* it.) If you can't, see that its better you go home if you can't be *so* involved that you can take this *risk of faith* with us, and somehow God will put us through. So if any of you are afraid, OK, go home." And then he said, "Whosoever's fearful and afraid, (Chapter 7, verse 3) they can return and depart there from Mt. Gilead...and there returned 22,000 and remained 10,000. Of course most of them and Gideon had it fixed now, that somehow God was going to do it. Gideon was a man of faith. His faith had to be confirmed every now and then, but basically it wasn't failing. None had any idea what had happened, like usually...almost like one of God's huge jokes! He couldn't see it. There's no evidence he could see it. You only go step by step. He had the confidence somehow God's in this thing. Now he only had 10,000!

That's a considerable number, but not much against 135,000. And *again* it came to him. In this sense, I think again he could see it. He was going to be called to something to which he must go into action, and risk their lives! Not just *passively* be in this thing, but be ready to jump in the action…and be ready for action! Something God's going to do *by us* in action! So he's called… God led him to a further step – very practical, simple, testing step. They were on the march apparently… hadn't got there apparently. There wasn't water; they were thirsty and this crowd of 10,000 came to some kind of stream. He said, "Now I'm going to test them for you." He says, "You watch. Those who are not all that set on *getting* this thing at any price – they're with you. They want you to *think* they're getting into it, but at the moment they're thirsty. So they'll get down and have a good old drink. They'll lie down and put their mouths in the stream and get a good old drink, but they are thinking more about their own sustenance than they are about how they'll go to put this thing through for God.

Some among you aren't thinking about their sustenance and thirst. They're thinking, "We're ready! We're ready! We'll go *in* on this thing. We're going to *dash in* on it, and they *won't* lie down and drink, because the enemy might turn up or something! Those will just take a drink with their hands and go on. *Those* are your men! Three hundred. Let the others go. Have only those whose whole *center* of their being is 'We're with you; we'll go right with this thing. Whatever God shows, we'll do even if we *appear* to be the ones who'll die……'cause they won't die because they believe in God!

So there came the next series in which they were brought down now to 300 men who *did* mean business…were ready for action. Now once more, now they got…now they're back over in the hills in the Syrian hills overlooking this *vast* mass spread out in this valley with their camels and so on. Pretty casual, not doing much to knock the Israelites out, I presume. Not quite so, as we'll see in a moment. Perhaps the majority had that idea.

Now once again, you get this cautious man with his human fear. He didn't know what *to do*…what *should* he do? What *do* you do with

300 unarmed men, with 135,000 behind you waiting to slay you? What *do* you do? The Lord had said now to Gideon (verse 7) "By the 300 men that are left will I save you, and deliver the Midianites into thine hand, and let all the rest go." Now they took vittles in their hand. It turned out they had pitchers. (Whether it is that they put their food like we did in Africa in a kind of a pot to carry it with them...or whether it means they had a pitcher of water as well as the food.) And *all* they had was trumpets in one hand and this food, presumably a pitcher with food in it, in the other hand. That's all they had...not a sword among them! This is all they had with them. And all the rest went.

And there were these...look! There's the host of the Midian down in the valley. So quite naturally, you'd think...what next? There's no sign he *knew* what. What's next? What can I do? Another guidance came...again as it were, to meet fear. God said, "Here Gideon, go down at night, in the early part of the night, outside the host. Listen to them. Catch something they are saying. Get on the edge of this great (probably casual) mess chattering together in their tents...in whatever form their tents took in those days. Go on here.

And so it says he took his servant Phurah. The two went down the hill, and there near some tent, some people he heard a conversation – a remarkable conversation! The nearest you can get is like Rahab in Jericho. He says one of these men, these Malakites...these heathens, these men...they're like grasshoppers he says. They lay along the valley sleeping, I think, casual sleeping. Like grasshoppers in multitude and their camels without number as the sand by the sea. A sight! That's what they looked like to Gideon – a *great crowd*, sleeping. And when he came down he listened to a man who said, "I just had a dream, and in this dream was a great big cake of barley bread." (That means a great big thing like they baked in those days, not like little cake as we call it, but a *big* thing rolled down.) "This great thing came rolling down on us." (What he called tumbling... it tumbled. It didn't come *meaning* to come down; it rolled down...

wasn't man's action, it just rolled down. That's an important word, I think, to Gideon.) "It came rolling down and hit on the tents and the tent collapsed. (Presumably with the people with it!) This was my dream!"

This *remarkable* man showing there's believers right *among the heathen* all the time! There'll be more in heaven than we know of! This man, this Midianite, said, "I'll tell you what that means." He *knew* of Gideon. He evidently *heard* the word of the Lord! Gideon probably made a boast in the Lord…and they destroyed the temple of Baal… and this man definitely knew *this* is the living God! He perhaps went back to Moses and saw in his mind, I don't know. And he said all the people know it too! *Faith* **does** *do something* and this was a living faith… *living* faith! And this man knew it! He said, "I'll tell you what that was, that's nothing less than the sword of Gideon, the son of Joash, a man of Israel: for into *his* hand God hath delivered Midian, and all the host." Isn't that something! This soldier…like Rahab in Jericho…says, "I *know* it's his God; I know its God…and this man of God lifts his sword and God delivered the Midianites into this man's hand." Somehow he knew it! So whether Gideon had made that public boast – God is going to smite the Midianites by *me* – I don't know. It sounds like it. And this came back from the host: "Oooh…"

What Gideon did – he worshiped. He worshiped. "Oooooh," he said, "This is God!" He forgot the host; he forgot what to do. *It put him on his face.* It says as Gideon heard the telling of the dream, *simply he worshipped.* Joshua worshipped when he'd been plotting around Jericho…what should he do as a military man….the captain of the Lord *came*; he worshipped, and *there* in *that* God speaks to you.

You're *free* now…you're not plotting. Your worship is – **God's** in *me*, and *as* you do that *something* comes to you which **is** God. This is what came to him – and I think it's quite obvious. At that time, I think he saw *in that moment*…don't do what you were. We haven't got swords to fight with…you have got trumpets. The trumpets can make a noise. And somewhere it occurred to him. (It doesn't say so.) They had torches of some kind with them, or could make them…and they've got pitchers. What we *can* do is *shout* the Word…and he saw the trick! In the middle of his worshiping, he saw the trick!

Its *night*, and they waited as the guard was changing, a fresh nervous guard was taking on (just coming to this camp now…changing guards) and he gathered his people together (must have been pretty sharp…the same night…because they must have got their torches ready) and said, "We will divide into 3 companies. You go on that hill there; I'll go here and you all have trumpets." (Probably they all had trumpets in those days…it's the one weapon they had.) They had *big* trumpets, (like they blew around Jericho – they blew the trumpets) and you have your trumpet in one hand, and you have your pitcher. Inside the pitcher you'll put a lighted torch. Now we want the thing tumbling down…we won't do a thing, but something will tumble down…we'll *shock* them into flight! We won't go down; we'll stand where we are. But when I give you the signal, when I blow my trumpet, you will all make a great big blowings of your trumpets…three hundred of you all around the tents…and your show your lights, they'll say, "You've got us this time" – because they are terrified heathen! There are people like that; they don't know a thing, and that's all they did. That's all they did! Three hundred men came outside of the camp at the beginning of the watch…outside…and they knew they'd upset the watch and they blew their trumpets. And they'd break their pitchers in their hands, and the three companies blew their trumpets and broke their pitchers, and held the lamps in their left hands and the trumpets in their right hands, and cried, "The sword"… (not the sword of Gideon…that *man* said the sword of Gideon)…"the sword of the **LORD** and Gideon!" Gideon knew Who he was! So they shouted "The sword of the **LORD** and Gideon!"

Now it looks as if that rumor had already gone out because this man knew it, and it said Rehab says the people of Jericho were *terrified*.

They *know* the LORD is with you and they're *terrified*! They aren't go-ing to repent...but they just want to get a way out. It *looks* as if there's God among the Midianites. They'd heard this rumor – this **living God** had done things through Moses and all this kind of business. This man is now moving among us...looks like it! Anyhow when they heard that shout, "the sword of the *Lord* and Gideon," saw those lamps...they got *terrified*! They were going to fight each other...or just ran! (Under Jehoshaphat, before Isiah, they sang...they heard the song and they got fighting among each other, but that's several different tribes fight-ing each other...got mixed up.) It says that as they did that they stood every man in his place round about and *all* the hosts ran and cried and fled. So three hundred *did* that!

So this is what he caught...I think he caught – I think he caught the 'tumbling.' It wasn't going down in steps...just rolled down...just on its own impact rolled down! I *think* that's what Gideon caught – don't go and do something you can't do when you haven't got swords. Just act like it would be a great big loaf of bread rolling on their tents and they were terrified! And they went. And so you get this *fantastic* situation. Then they followed them up, and then, of course, as they did in those days – they must have had swords or something in those days because they got fighting. They destroyed their leaders and so on. We needn't go into that further detail here. But there wasn't *one* Israelite hurt...not one Israelite *involved!* As *one man!* The whole tribe as one man! "I'll smite them as one man." And one man they'll take!

So it's a remarkable story, when you look inside of it – not story, *his-tory* of the **processes of faith** which start in conditions in which God seemed out-of-sight...things are *wrong* somewhere. An individual gets concerned...'shouldn't be like this'...why isn't God working! That's when God says, "I'll do it *through you*, because you've got the power – because *I am in you to do* it, and you've got to fight and argue and so on. And then bit by bit, *somehow*, God shows you *how* to operate, and then to move in one way locally...and then something happens which sparks/startles! It becomes public knowledge! It begins to go out and other people begin to catch on. Or we say...what we want is not the running away...but coming to Christ, of course.

So it is a remarkable, simple story to teach us again – *we* don't do a thing; *God does it*! All we do is mighty little, mighty little...walking around Jericho, blowing trumpets, shouting, "The Lord's given you the city." And down went the walls...standing here blowing trumpets, showing silly, playing kids, showing torches and so on. God bless!

So I'm only saying as we know – it is a very simple life, isn't it? It's – *God* does it! He does it *by us*. He does it by things working... **no**...He does it by us, and then we walk this *carefree way*. There are no signs; he didn't know what to do! He just did the next thing, the next thing, the next thing...had no indication he had *any* idea where to get this idea – torches and so silly and trumpets. Where'd he get it from? He could have got trumpets from Jericho maybe, not torches. Where did he get it from? I think it *suddenly* occurred to him in his mind. He didn't try and do a thing...if its "Oh, let's go and fight them." He didn't. They hadn't got swords, not that we knew. Anyhow they weren't using them...just do the next thing.

Rather like Jesus. How do you feed 5000? Do the next thing; use the five loaves. Alright, use the five loaves. Use what you've got...alright. I'll expand five loaves to feed 5000! Alright, you've got no fish; you've got nets anyhow. Use the nets then; put the nets in...you'll get the fishes.

We're relaxed...just do the next thing with what we have got. Out of what we have got comes the harvest! So it must have occurred to him – at least we can do that. That soldier said, "It's the sword of Gideon and the Lord's with us"...alright, I can say that – I can say the sword of the Lord and Gideon. *We* can make a shout. *We* can trump trumpets. *We* can catch a time at night when the people are nervous, and have a new guard. There was crowd of people relaxed, and so sleeping. And they did it! Enormous risk! The whole crowd fled for their lives, and the other tribes came in and took prisoners as they did in those days. That's about it!

SAMSON

God has His *original* plans for every life! It is a dangerous habit to think that only *certain* men are special, for God has some *unique expression* and *operation of Himself*...that He is moving out from each of us. This should be the *standard* for anyone who is a member of the body of Christ...and therefore an expression of the Head. These Biblical characters are merely illustrations of how the Holy Spirit comes in His *unusual* ways to fulfill some purposes of that time. Size and location are of no importance in His ministry to people.

In the case of Samson, God's purpose was to give Israel a period of deliverance from forty years of Philistine oppression by a man who would be His agent. The history that we are looking into centers entirely around the man himself...and how God used him to deliver them, rather than upon the people or kings. This was the day of judges which preceded the kings. We are to see how God worked in bringing into being this *man* who worked by Him.

The Israelites had been under the thumb of the Philistines for forty years. This is one of these special places where, not unlike what happened at Jesus' birth, God appeared to a godly woman by His angel and told her that she was to bear a very special child. He was to have a public sign of *total* separation unto God – the Nazirite sign. Nazirites did not drink liquor and did not cut their hair. John the Baptist, Samuel, and possibly Elijah were also Nazirites. This was a *symbolic* age when God could only speak to the *inner* heart through *outer* forms. *Only* a few people could catch the inner meaning.

This woman had never had a child, and in simple faith she accepted the word and told her husband of it. He, too, was responsive to God, but with a more cautious, *rational* outlook. It *may* be that God speaks quickly and intuitively to women and then men come along... and need to have a more rational understanding. It is not that they are *not* going to believe, but often they need a more tangible basis for their faith.

Manoah was not like Zechariah, who went dumb for a time because he *did not* believe. Manoah *wanted* to believe...but he wanted to be *sure*. To meet Manoah's need, the Lord appeared a second time to the wife and she called her husband. The husband spoke to the angel and said to him that he was not *doubting* the birth, which would be miraculous because she had been barren, but he was questioning how the child should be brought up. *That* was a fair question! He wanted a better understanding of the **purpose** of the child's coming. All the angel told him was that he was to be a Nazirite from his mother's womb – meaning that he was to drink no alcohol and let his hair grow as evidence of his separation to the Lord.

Manoah had an inquiring mind and asked the angel his name, but the angel would not give it because it was secret and not to be revealed. This reflects the age they were living in. That was *why* Moses had to put a veil over his face – because he had seen right through to the ultimate of the *true tabernacle* in Christ and the glory of it shone on his face! But he could not tell the people, because they had not come to that place of understanding...and could not take the something that was glowing out of him. It was the same with Jacob. He was not given a name by the angel because, you see, God has named *us*! The Everlasting is *beyond* name. That is why we read, as we move into the *intercessory* level of fatherhood, that "You know Him which is from the beginning" (I John 2:13).

The Universal Person we call God, Father, and other helpful titles, is beyond name! We can only know the universal by one of His *particular* forms or expressions. *We* are part of the universal...expressions of

the only One in the universe. *Expressions!* The angel would not give
him His name because it is the Lord's secret...which is now revealed
to those who know Jesus, who can *see*. That is what Paul means when
he speaks of an open "mystery, which is *Christ in you*." Even so, it has
to be a **realized** mystery!

When the angel just disappeared in the flame of the offering he
had made, Manoah realized that this was a supernatural being! His
wife had moved on farther into what we would understand as *knowing*
the true relationship between ourselves and God. Manoah's reaction
to the realization of Who the angel was....was, "We shall surely die for
we have seen God." (Judges 13:22) Her reaction was: "If the Lord were
pleased to kill us He would not have received the burnt offering from
us, which went up in flame. Neither would He have shewed us all these
things" (Judges 13:24). She had moved into **knowing** that *we are the
expression* of the God of love, purpose, power and blessing!

That is all we are told about the birth of Samson. We may as-
sume that he knew about his birth, because from his early days he
was *conscious* of the Spirit of God operating by him in strangely physical strength. In those days God acted on the *physical* dimension.
Later on the Israelites were shaken up when the Philistines produced
their big champion, Goliath – because, if Goliath could be slain the
people would be subject to you, but if Goliath could slay your challenger, it was the other way around! One man like this could control
and subdue and terrify a nation. Samson was somewhat like God's
Goliath.

Somehow Samson began to *understand* that he was a man imbued
by the Spirit, symbolized by this Nazirite vow. Today our symbols are
in Christ. Symbols are *outer* forms. Within the outer form the Spirit
of God moved, and Samson began to find that *he* was different from
other men. God sometimes has very strange ways and what God used
to destroy the Philistines was Samson's partiality to women – the very
thing that we might think was a thing of the flesh! *God's* vision is much
greater than ours!

Although he was not an appointed judge for another twenty years, Samson knew full well that Israel, God's people, should *not* be under the control of the heathen Philistines. It had come about because they had given up their allegiance to God, and He wanted to show them what *happened* to them when they were apart from Him.

Samson knew that, although they were also their bosses, the Philistines were their enemies. In spite of that he suddenly began to like a Philistine woman and wished to marry her. His godly parents saw that that was against God's laws, and like Jacob, he was to find a wife from among his own people. They were to keep the line pure and not mix with the Gentiles or anyone *outside* the holy nation. Samson was going to do it anyway!

Yet, we must not judge. We must *see God operating* in His own way for His own purposes. Sometimes they are *very strange* ways. One thing we can learn from this story is not to judge, but to say: "If *God means* a person to go through that, let God take him through. If a person is doing wrong with it, let *God* take him through. Watch God turn it into a *new revelation* of His grace and liberation and blessings!"

Although Samson had a human liking, he always saw more. He understood that he was God's agent, but he was a *woman-liker*! We can see now that history can *use* that, but there was more to it than that. He was a man of the Spirit and we can see all the way through this that he was *guided* by the Spirit, because he **knew** the Spirit would release Israel from the Philistines through *him. Knowing that,* he went in to prepare for this marriage.

The custom in those days was for the families of the betrothed couple to visit, so his parents went with him to visit her. We do not know how far the Philistines recognized this unusual young man who had already performed many physical exploits. It was *probably* a shock to them that this man had chosen one of their daughters.

Samson's mind was always set on contending with – confusing and making the Philistines want to fight so that *he* could get at them. Once, on the way to visit her, he again had the manifestation of this unusual power when he met a lion and *tore* it apart! David did that once, too, though David did it more by the power of God and faith. He was not a man of muscle like Samson. Samson tore the lion apart, left the carcass there, and went on with his visit. Then on another visit, as he went along, he saw a hive of bees in the carcass and there was honey in it. Apparently he was not allergic to stings so he just got the honey, and went on his way eating. He gave his parents some of it, but did not tell them where he got it. He was *learning* to walk as God's man.

When the time came for the marriage, they went down and made the marriage feast. Their custom was to have seven days of feasts with the marriage at the beginning. After the marriage, his wife began to entice him to go in to her, but when thirty young men showed up, he began to suspect something. Undoubtedly they were *angry* about Samson coming in and taking one of the daughters of their people.

Samson had clever sayings sometimes and so he backed them into a corner with a riddle, which they could *not* get. He really angered them by telling them that if they could solve it he would give *each* of them a change of clothing, but if they could not, they would each give him a change of clothing. Because of the rivalry they did not want to give Samson thirty changes of clothing! But they could not get the riddle which was "Out of the eater came forth meat, and out of the strong came forth sweetness." Who on earth *could* solve that? He had cleverly put forth something they could *never* solve...unless they got help. But they did get help, and we see *the beginning* of Samson's weakness...which in the end God *used* for His final glorious purposes! They threatened his wife by saying that if she did not help them they would burn her, and her father's home. They would even burn their own people! So he gave in...caught up by his love for this woman! Perhaps he began to love her *more* that he should have, and *that* should have been a warning to him.

When you are not in the *union position* with God, there is always a weak spot. If it is *you* **and** *God*, then you have a weak spot. You *will* get caught up by your weakness, unless you know the life where *it is not you but He*...and then He moves *over* the weakness. At the crucial moment He will carry you through because *the real you* is He! The question we have been talking about these days is – the weakness of the ***false sense of separation*** between a redeemed person and God. When you are in the Romans 7 identity *you try* to work it out, but you cannot do it. This was the beginning sign of Samson's weakness.

He knew the Lord's Spirit was *upon* him...but he did not know that *he* was actually God's expression! He did not know the *depth* behind God's Spirit being upon him. So it was the **independent** Samson being operated by God...and he gave the secret away. Therefore, they got the riddle!

Now, again, you get these strange ways. Remember, he was there to *tear up* the Philistine nation. So, when they had the secret and he had to give them the garments, he said, "All right then, if I have to get them the garments, I'll get them from their own people." He went and killed thirty Philistines and took their garments and gave them to the men. He was so *angry* with his wife who had sold him out that, after he had given them the garments, he went home to his parents.

Later, he went back to his wife and found that she had been taken from him and given to another man. He was enraged. He rose up and said, "This time I shall be blameless in regard to the Philistines when I do this thing." I do not know how on earth he did it, but he got three hundred foxes and tied their tails together, stuck torches on their tails, and sent them flying off into the ripe corn. It burned up the Philistines' annual harvest. You never can tell what *ways* the Lord might tell a man to *use*. The *feat* was in catching the foxes! The Philistines were furious, and now the war had started. They *even* came and burned his Philistine wife and her father...their own people!

Samson retaliated by moving in and, *all alone*, slaying them in a great slaughter. The day when *one* man could do this is certainly a different day from this! Today we put a bullet to people but, of course, they did not do that in those days. Afterwards, he went and sat on top of a large rock to isolate himself.

He surely had to deal with weak people – his own people. He was *appalled* by their loss of God, their giving way to idolatry and the ways of the flesh! They gave him no aid in response to the Philistines who *now* had their armies out and had pitched camp in Judah. They were spread over into Lehi. The Israelites were appalled and frightened – men who should stand *if* they had the faith of God! Frightened! "What have you come for?" they asked the Philistines.

"We've come to bind Samson. Where is he?"

"On top of that rock." Then these palsied people came up and said to Samson, "Don't you know that these are our rulers? You'll get us into trouble instead of helping us." Where was the man of *faith* among them?

Once again the Spirit of the Lord came upon him and he said, "Bind me with cords and hand me over to them." Three thousand Israelites went up to do this. They bound him with two new cords. Then the Philistines came and shouted against him and "the Spirit of the Lord came mightily upon Him and the cords were like grass, grass that was burnt with fire and the hands were loose" (Judges 15:14). Then he moved in on them. The *strange agency* God used was the jawbone of an ass! God uses the foolish things to *confound* the flesh. The *only* buildup we need is the buildup in the Spirit! Once he used three hundred foxes; now He uses the jawbone of an ass to slay one thousand men. He was a formidable man when the Spirit of God was upon him!

Then there was a little *tender* touch…almost the *only* touch of the tenderness of God at that time. He was thirsty and apparently there was no water there. He cried to God and God in some way made a receptacle out of the jawbone of an ass, and there was water in it. It was an outstanding touch to Samson because Samson gave the place the name, "Enhakkore," which means "the well of him that called." The well that *God* supplied!

Probably, at this point he got *out* of the will of God for he visited a harlot in Gaza, one of the cities of the Philistines. On this occasion he *never* said that the Spirit of God was on him. When the Philistines saw him they surrounded the town and the house he was in. When he came out, he just walked off with the whole gate and gatepost, and took it up the hill with him. It does not say that the Lord was in that. It *may* have been that he *had* the power because he knew the *secret of power* – the Nazirite vow. It may be that he could utilize it in ways that he should not have used. Of course, in some sense morals were different from ours in those days but, still, this was different.

We come now to the famous crisis of his life when he was to *learn* once and for all – that redeemed man is no good *unless* he has found the union basis, which is what we also call sanctification. We learn that *it is not we, but God*...and that God can take us through the crisis moments because it is **He** operating. We *know* God. We have our weaknesses, but God can take us *through* them.

Samson did not know that. He loved a woman named Delilah... the famous Delilah. I do not think he was married to her, but he had a real passion for her. The five lords of the Philistines made her one of their agents by offering her eleven thousand pieces of silver to get the secret of his strength. Remember, those were external days and they did not know the secret we have *within* us today. Thank God, it is a *universal* secret today...and we are *all* Samsons in our way!

Apparently she had a great hold on him because he visited her again and again. A woman has great power when a man is grabbed by a passion for her. Time and time again she said, "Now, tell me wherein your strength lies." He pretended it was a game. He did not know there were men lying in wait to grab him when they found the secret. Three times he played his tricks with her. She got hotter and hotter, and put pressure on him. Finally she said to him, "I won't love you if you don't tell me your secret. I don't call it love when you act like this." She got him right to the bone. Thinking he might lose her, he told his secret.

He sold out his *central allegiance* to God for the love of that woman. However, that was not his *basis*. We will prove later that it was his soul, *not* his spirit! He was God's man and he never ceased to be God's man...but he *almost* sold out his very birthright. Not quite...for he was not like Esau who sold his *spirit*. The point is that flesh *cannot* exist by itself. That is why we must not judge people for going to the flesh. *Unless* God is in you, you cannot resist! It is **only** in Christ, in the power of His death and resurrection that we can walk and be delivered. We can have *confidence* in that deliverance and be *kept* in that deliverance. Samson did not have the confidence that he could be *kept* by God...so he played too far in his weakness for women. He did not have the *controlling power of God* to keep him. He did to a certain extent, for God used him. There was a *purpose* in his going too far, for he *must be broken*. If God's ultimate power was going to come through, he would have to ultimately be a broken man – a God-filled man to the death! We *all* have to go through that and this was Samson's time.

The world mocks and makes up plays about Delilah, but a *wonderful* thing was happening here. This was God! He was using the sex drive in the man for His *own* purposes. We must not say that Samson sold himself *totally* for he only sold his flesh. He got to a point where he was beyond resisting, but if he had walked with God, God would have kept him from going beyond resistance. He *would have stopped where he should have stopped* long before. God would have *held* him. What he did did not come from his center...but he sold his center out. For twenty years he had been accepted by Israel as a judge and now he had sold his commission, his nation, his reputation, himself! It is possible to go pretty far...but much less possible if you haven't moved in...because there is something in God that will not let you. God has you and He will *keep* you. There is nothing that says you will not have whatever your special tendencies or weaknesses may be, as anybody else does, but you *will not* be *held* by them. You only know that *if* you have settled into knowing you are not you but He – that He is the only One living. You are not safe *out* of union.

Samson was not safe because, although he was God's man and the Spirit of God came upon him, he did not know God in that *inner* relationship...which men like David, Elijah, Moses, and Joshua came to know. So he had to go through this and, therefore, in that sense, he could not help it. This was God's *purpose* because God was going to strike *His* final blow at the Philistines by the weakness of Samson. That very weakness problem made strength – *perfected* in that very weakness! This thing we *could call sin* was the very thing God used! The sin was *not* the sex; *the sin was selling out his faith!* In those days sex did not matter as much. Those were different days. This thing was used by the flesh in him to *cause* him to practically deny his faith – which was the real sin. Choosing to keep her love *rather than keep his faith* was his sin. It is equivalent to our setting out in a ministry, and then destroying our ministry by being involved in something of the flesh.

That is *much less likely* to happen if we have moved into this union life. We can never say it cannot happen for Paul says, "For it is a mighty force that I keep under my body, and bring it into subjection lest that by any means, when I have ministered to others I, myself should become a castaway" (I Cor. 9:27). Castaway does not mean thrown out. It means disapproved. It does *not* mean the loss of salvation. It is the same idea as the branch burned with the vine. It is men who cast you out. Samson was no good to men...to Israel. We can be cast out of our ministry, but we have not lost our salvation. We may lose our ways so that men have no use for us, but we have not lost our salvation. We have no word for them – no message. They will not come. We lose out on that level. That is the level that Samson lost out on, but he did not lose his inner relationship – his inner knowing.

This is how God moved, and so he had to go to the bottom. He had to become a helpless, weak person, put in prison, blinded, and made to sweat away at grinding corn at a mill. He became a normal, physical body, a laboring slave.

Then came this remarkable way of God! God is with his people... even these early people. There Samson was...and he knew God. He *knew* that he had lost his way. All he had really lost was *his* way; he had not lost God. His hair began to grow again and it began to dawn on him that he was getting back to being a Nazirite again. He was still in grace – God's man. He had made a mess, but the Philistines did not know that his symbol would grow again. He was conscious of coming *back* to the place where the power of *God* could come *through him!*

Not long after Samson had this growing realization, a great occasion arose. The Philistines wanted to rejoice because Samson, Israel's Goliath, had been destroyed. This Samson was a slave now and they wanted to have a great celebration. It symbolized to them that the whole nation was back under their control. They planned a great feast in a building so remarkable that they had three thousand on the roof. They certainly built in those days! In some strange way, the building was held up by two great pillars. The Lord was moving now…and they wanted to make sport of him. The pillars were centered in this building which had this great crown, including the lords of the Philistines in it. They had a little boy lead him in by the hand in between those pillars. I suppose this was a way to laugh at him best. They conveyed to him that these were the pillars that held the building up. Then Samson said to the lad, "Suffer me that I may feel the pillars whereupon the house standeth, that I may lean upon them."

Suddenly he saw it! My symbol is back with me; **God** is with me! Then he prayed. This was new. This was his *real* relationship now, because he had not thought of praying before. "Remember me, O Lord, I pray thee, strengthen me, I pray thee, only this once. I'll give my life for this." Now *he* becomes an intercessor! "My life doesn't matter; I'll give my life for my two eyes." He had been God's man and this is the way he looked at it. Obviously this was the way of the Israelites' deliverance from the Philistines…if they would take it. Then he took hold of those pillars upon which the house was borne, one with his right hand and the other with his left. That is it! *He* would die that in the end *God's work* would be glorified. He *knew* he had come back again to be *anointed* of God. He would die with the Philistines!

And it says, "He bowed himself with all his might; and the house fell upon the lords, and upon all the people that were therein. So the dead which he slew at his death were more than they which he slew in his life" (Judges 16:30). Then they took his body and buried it.

So that is the story of Samson. There are some great revelations of the way God works by people who have to come to the same way in the end. You *have to come out of the idea* of "If I'm equipped in some *separate way* I can do it." No! I have to come back into the center where the "I" has disappeared and God is the One and **all** is God. What happens to *me* is not the point. **God** will now operate *by me!* That is the history of Samson as presented to us.

HANNAH

The problem with Hannah and her husband, Elkanah, was that in their relationship to God they had not gotten to the point that they *knew* that everything is God and *whatever* happens is just *God fulfilling* His purposes. They still had the separated outlook which has the element of self-interest in it.

Although Hannah put God first, she was not happy and was always fretting because she had no children. Peninnah, Elkanah's other wife, had children, and she would taunt Hannah about it, but she was merely reacting against the fact that Elkanah had a special interest in and love for Hannah. Each year when the family went up to Jerusalem at feast time, Hannah cried to the Lord in her distress and, continually weeping, would not eat. Her heart was full of God, but she could not find the answer to *her* problem.

God has to bring us to the place where no self-interest is answered. Self-interest is the final product of the Fall and *cannot* be a part of a life in union with God. Therefore God has to take us to the place where the *totality* of our self-interest is *exposed*. Then, if we are moving into God we can move in and find the solution. Hannah was for God, yet she wanted some of her own ways in life. The clash between self-interest and God was brought to a head in a crisis for both her and her husband.

After years of Hannah's fretting, Elkanah could not take her being so miserable any longer. His household was an uncomfortable one, but because he had a heart for the Lord, he favored Hannah over

Peninnah...since Hannah was a God-fearing woman. *His* self-interest was exposed by his being continually bothered and disillusioned by her hurt. She was continually questioning...if she was God's servant, *why* did He treat her like this? We find the same idea in Job.

Elkanah decided to express himself in his own way and said, "Why weepest thou? And why eatest thou not? And why is thy heart grieved? Am I not better to thee than ten sons?" He certainly thought well of himself! Although he was God's man, he had the element of self-interest that tries to solve things by *human* wisdom. This did not work with Hannah, however, because Hannah was for God above husband or children. It turned out to be **the** *transforming crisis* in both their lives. The crisis for Hannah was that she had lost her last human anchor...her husband. Before, if she did not have children and she could not figure out why God treated her like that, at least she had a husband who loved *her* more than he loved the other wife. Now, he had turned against her, and she had reached her lowest point. Although she sensed that there would be a parting of sympathy between them now, she remained for God. She could not accept what Elkanah had to say and said, "Well, yes, I'll do the best I can. You're my husband." Instead, she went to God and cried, saying, "What am I to do?" The Scripture says that she was "in bitterness of soul" now.

It was a bitter household with Peninnah attacking and Hannah not knowing how to accept things from God – fretting, accepting the attacks and being a hurt person. *Now* there was a bitter attacker and a hurt responder, and Elkanah had no answer except what he felt he could provide in being a good husband. All three of them were mixed up in different forms of self-interest. One self-interest was basically an unsaved self-interest, which does not change *until* God changes you. The other two were saved, but were mixed in the love for God and certain elements of self-interest which were the forms of independent self – the divided self. Thank God He has His ways of bringing us to the end of it! This was the crisis for both of them. She lost her husband's support when he could not get her to be a nice little wife...satisfied with her husband. She was something more than his wife...she was God's woman, not his. So both were in the soup!

This is one of those stories where the woman is in the foreground... as with Samson's mother...as with Elizabeth...and as with Mary, the mother of Jesus. Often women are in the foreground and when it comes to *going through* with God. God pulls the husband in through the wife!

Because Hannah was God's person, she poured herself out to God. Although she was embittered, she was on the right track. "She prayed unto the Lord, and wept sore." (I Samuel 1:10) Then, suddenly, she *saw* something! She *saw* that her desire for a child was for herself. She wanted a child so that *she* could be a mother and be proud that she had children. Although God was foremost in her life, still it was God combined with *her* having what she desired. That was the answer! She said, "Look here, God...here's my answer. You give me a child and I'll never see him again. I'll lay him down. He'll be a Nazirite." Now a *change* had taken place and she had begun to be an intercessor! She had begun to find that the *true* purpose is for *God's will only* by the way He deals with you. She *never* could have seen this if she had not been barren! What she had to see is that it is *only by death that you see life.* It is *only by darkness that you see light.* If we catch it, this is the 'way' we can see!

When we have a very tough problem that is the best sign that God has some **big** thing that is not for *us*...but that, *through* it, something will come out for others...as we get ourselves in tune with Him. *That* is what is meant by saying that as death works in us, life works in others. If Hannah had not been barren it would not have *occurred* to her to hand a child over to God alone, never to be a member of the family again. She would have been satisfied with her life as it was. But *God* would not allow that for her. Now God had her in the condition in which *He* could come through her, though she still wanted to be a mother. So she struck this bargain with the Lord, "You give me the child and I'll give the child back to you." That is the *inner seeing* that puts us into the union where we begin to be somebody *for others.*

Hannah was *destined* to be the mother of Samuel – one of the great men who led God's people back to Him. This was the time when God spoke by prophets and when they prayed, God listened. Several times it says that Samuel was marked by God as a special man of prayer and faith…through whom God could really manifest Himself. He anointed the first two kings, Saul and David, and though having kings was not always satisfactory, David was one of the great ones.

All of this was to come out of the intercession she began…though she *could not see it at the time.* God confirmed her intercession in one of the little ways He has that makes things fit together for us. He did it through Eli, the old judge at that time. Eli was a godly man but he was *weak* with his children. His two sons were ungodly and misused the sacrifices by taking the best for themselves. Also, they defiled the name of the Lord by behaving promiscuously with the women who came into the temple. Eli did rebuke them, but he never *stopped* it. There is a time when you must take a stand and *stop* a thing, if it is possible to do so. He would not do that, so God had to put him aside. However, Eli knew the Lord used *his* voice to confirm Hannah. What happened was that when he saw her weeping and praying in the temple, he thought she was drunk, because although she was speaking from her heart, her eyes were moving. Now, you would not expect to see a drunk person worshipping in a temple, would you? So it looks as if Eli was only too familiar with the people who lived this dissolute life led by his own sons. Because he *was* for the Lord, he rebuked her, saying, "Put your wine away."

Then, explaining that she was not drunk, she poured her soul out and told him her problem. He immediately sensed that this was a woman of God and said to her, "Go in peace. God grant you your petition." That was her *outer* sign. Because he was not used to finding a woman who was just weeping herself out before the Lord, he remembered her very well when she returned the next year with the child.

God had called her to obey and then the high priest himself individually talked to her, heard what she had to say, and confirmed her request to God. He spoke the *word of faith* for her. *That* is the important part of the story. It is when *she* became an intercessor.

The child was conceived. Elkanah came in then and sided with her. He was altogether with her in this giving. *That* is why I see that Elkanah moved over, too. He saw that she had been right in refusing his suggestion. When the next year came, normally the son would be brought up to the sacrifice, but she said that she wanted to wait until he was weaned and then take him to the temple and give him up once and for all. That Elkanah perfectly concurred with her in this shows that *he* was in effect saying, "We are in the stream of God's will now," and he became a co-intercessor...willing...with her to give up their son to be a Nazirite, *never* to be in the official family again.

After the child was weaned they went up and made the necessary offerings and enjoins and brought the child to Eli. Such a godly woman must have been *rare* because Eli remembered her very well. It was quite a *dramatic* moment. She said:

"For this child I prayed; and the Lord hath given me my petition which I asked of Him; therefore also I have lent him to the Lord; as long as he liveth he shall be lent to the Lord. And he worshipped the Lord there."

This puts Elkanah there worshipping the Lord with his wife by giving Him his son!

Then there follows one of the marvelous songs that we get in the Bible, which magnifies the Lord through weakness, which is the way we have to go:

"My heart rejoiceth in the Lord, my horn is exalted in the Lord... There is none holy as the Lord...The bows of the mighty men are broken and they that stumbled are girded with strength. They that were full have hired out themselves for bread; and they that were hungry ceased to hunger; so that the barren hath borne seven; and she that hath many children is waxed feeble."

The Lord *filled* her soul with rejoicing...but on the *basis* that we do not come to the Lord in our fullness - *only in our weakness*. She saw that *God* brings us to the weakness of ourselves, and when we are in the weakness of ourselves, *then* we find *it is really God expressing Himself through us*! The *real* one is God when we have moved into the union relationship where I'm not I, but He. She finally went all the way. She said:

"The Lord killeth, and maketh alive; He bringeth down to the grave and bringeth up. He raiseth up the poor out of the dust, and lifteth up the beggar from the dunghill, to set them among princes, and to make them inherit the throne of glory; for the pillars of the earth are the Lord's."

She saw the Universal! It is the *only* way!

This simple woman sang this song which has come down through history. It is a song glorifying the *fullness* of the power of God when the human, in the false self-relationship, has gone to the bottom and come up again – and now it is the *Lord* through the *redeemed* self!

Each year when she came with her husband to the yearly sacrifice, she brought Samuel a little coat. The final word was that God blessed Hannah and Elkanah with three more sons and two daughters, and the child, Samuel, grew up in the Lord. She got what she asked of the Lord, and much more!

This is a very simple, but *real* story of how the Lord has *unknown* purposes. *God has a purpose for every life.* When we are on the intercessory level, God has something He does **by us** for others. There is some area of the harvest in which *we* are involved. He is Lord of the harvest!

DAVID – SAUL – JONATHAN

The history of our human history are the gradual processes by which God conditions us for the Saviour to be manifested as one of us, and then to go through His way of salvation as representing us and come up and bring *us up* on the other side. This He did by founding on earth…in the midst of nations which are the forms of the normal way of life in this world…having **one** nation, which is *His* nation…who came into being under His calling and guidance through Abraham, through Isaac, through Jacob…until it became formed as a nation under Moses and then begins to function as a complete nation when Joshua brought us into the land under David and the kings.

The foundation principles or philosophy of this earth-nation is Law and Grace. Law is necessary when we are not the Law. If you are not the Law, you are *under* the Law. You either *are* the Law or *under* the Law. If you *are* the Law in Christ, you just are the Law…and there is *no other* Law. You are just Christ in the liberty of love. When we are not that yet…which we are not until we have moved into this union relationship through faith…then we are under the Law. Under the Law says, "You shouldn't be that." The Law is – you are this. The Law in Christ – *you* **are** 'this'! *You* **are** joined to Me. *You* **are** an expression of self-giving love. *You* **are** a son.

If you are not that, as pertaining to this fact, you are under the Law…apart from it…and God appears to you (appears to us) under an assumed form which we really project on Him…as if He is a "No" God, when He is only a "Yes" God. When we don't know that He is a "Yes" God, He has to condition us – "You shouldn't be that; you should be this. You shouldn't *be* that." And so He appears to us as a "No" God – you *shouldn't* do that; you *shouldn't* do this...**Law**...which isn't God at all! It's only a kind of outer projection, a kind of character *we* impart on God...which is a projection of our own rebellion really...which comes back and says, "You shouldn't be that; you shouldn't be that...if you are, there is a curse." The curse isn't in the Law; the curse is in us! The curse is the negative part of being a self-centered person. So you get the fruit of self-centeredness which is hell on earth and hell on earth eternally...chaos we live in, if we are in that dimension.

Because self is so subtle, we are so blinded we try to make out we are all right, knowing what we should be...and knowing what the Law says we should be, we pretend to what we are. We live under pretense, to a certain amount. We hide our real basic self-centeredness, self-gratification, self-giving appearance to certain conformities...moral conformities. They have to be stripped from us. They are stripped from us in God's bringing into being this nation to whom was presented in outer form the Law, which even then they said they would fulfill, which of course they can't.

At the same time...because God isn't Law, but Love...the revelation of the Law is imbedded all the time in the revelation of Grace. So in the earthly Israel it is imbedded in the revelation of the Presence of God in the tabernacle and the sacrifices which are a presentation to a God who accepts, a God who forgives, a God whose Presence is there...not wholly there, because we are not there in Him yet. We are apart from Him, so we are a wrong kind of people...under the Law which is to expose to us that we are under it. Because the whole point of Law is that it awakens sin. Where the Law says, "Thou shalt not sin," self says, "I will." That is how we come to know what we really are. So Law becomes the strength of sin, it becomes the exposure of Sin. That's the purpose of it.

At the same time, even though we are not yet in the New Birth relationship (some of them were in that relationship before Christ came on earth in history, in the main, where they came in history as the true Israel...which is the Israel of the Spirit), there is always the Presence of God in giving grace, not total, that's why there is a veil up in the Holiest. But a constant possibility of forgiveness, acceptance, through the sacrifices, and so on with the veil up, because we can't live in the Holiest. When you live in the Holiest, you are a part of the Holiest. We are a form of God's perfection when we are in Him.

So what is the condition of this earth-nation which is having this measure of revelation – the exposure of their wrong and the presence of the right – the exposure of the wrong through the Law and the expression of the right in the grace. That would be prepared ground... background in which the True Adam can come who is Love and who could fulfill this whole process of salvation for us and take us then out of the whole Law-realm and bury it forever...and totally take us into the Grace realm, where we live! We live in the Grace realm amidst Law conditions, because we are here to be Light shining in darkness! So we have to learn how to live as grace people in Law situations...in negative situations...so that something of the positiveness of Christ can come through as a shining light in a negative situation as the negativeness comes to us.

So we have moved these days through the start of a new nation, Abraham; its development, Isaac and Jacob; and now through its establishment with a basis to it in Moses. We pass over Joshua and the coming into the Promised Land. We haven't time to do those and we are moving into a little consideration around the life of the one whom God named as the one after His own heart...the pattern of the future king – David.

The background of David's anointing and reign as king is the usual background which we see all through the history as a people having an external relationship to God...not internal, inner. You can't live by the spirit unless you are the Spirit. If you have an external relationship, He can have a certain influence hold on you, but He can't **be** you. You are never controlled by the external; you are only controlled by what you are inside. You are what you are inside in your inner consciousness. *Only when the truth has become you is it the truth to you.* Same as any profession: only a profession is your profession when it has *become* you. You can be outside a profession...knowing it, but it is not you. There comes a time when it gets inside you, and it's *you* and you operate spontaneously on the level of that profession. And this is the truth of humanity. We act like what we inwardly are.

Real national leadership is spirit leadership when the nations are spirit people. That's the present church. That's why God is busy knocking out the silly churches we make so much of, and their ridiculous ministers called reverends and all this fantastic stuff which is only nonsense stuff imposed. The church isn't Reverend So-and-So in a church called So-and-So. The church is people in the Spirit, and that's all! A vast family who are the people...and the leadership is the Spirit in and through the people. That's all there is! That's coming back...moving back into the year of the Spirit now all over the world... the breakup of this silly denominational labeled stuff and pious exercise on Sunday morning which we call worship. If you want to waste your time, you can. That's up to you!

Life is permanent worship. Life is permanently seeing and being a part of this One who is All...and that's permanent worship – when you see Him in all His forms! Life is one permanent worship because everything you see is a form of this Perfect Person. That's worship! And we are a part of this Person in these situations. This is worshipping in spirit and in truth!

So the real nation, the earth Israel, was only to be the kind of womb of the heavenly, which is we. *We* are the Israel of God, the people of the Spirit, who are united to the living Person who is not of the matter world at all – Father, Son and Spirit. And such need no leadership. They need, if you like, consultative fellowship. I have had the privilege of belonging to a mission for many years. I had not one iota of power. Because we were a consultative fellowship, all I could do was to throw out ideas and suggestions and presentations until we could gather together and say, "That's it! That's God's will in our local areas; that's God's will." So the leadership was coming from the Spirit through the cooperative fellowship in those concerned. *This* is the new Israel.

So we are not led by God. God is not our leader; He's our Friend. He's our fellow. He shares with us what He wants and gets us to agree… that's it, that's it! There's no way I am under Law. God never says, "Do this". He just says, "It would be pretty useful to do that." And you agree and do it because we function *as gods in GOD.* That old "boss" business is out. I don't believe in subjection, I believe in cooperation. I don't believe in subjection with husband and wife, if believe in co-operation. When we don't know the secrets of spirit-cooperation, we replace it by subjection.

So this was the further stage in the progress of this nation…where it could now be established in the land because of its footing in the land through Joshua…and it was divided up into tribal areas, and so forth. Now God was always pointing them to the truth…so that they could see they haven't got the truth, and be prepared (because they haven't got it) to get it. You only find the positive when you find the negative – which doesn't solve the problem. Therefore, He offered them no leadership except judges. A judge was just a judge to advise… to help them to understand the ways of God in the nation. They were not to have a king who had authority over them because that would be putting flesh in place of spirit…and the idea was that through these men who were judges, they would be interpreting the spirit to the people. Under the leadership of the Spirit…through the judges and with the people…they would be proceeding along the lines of God's will as a nation. That was too much for them to take, because only a few knew the Spirit. Some did; some didn't operate under the Spirit. The majority...oh, they must have some outer controls! That's why we have religion. That's why we have churches.

That's why our silly churches are full of people who say, "Don't do this; don't do that"...because people like that...they like the protection – a little "shouldn't do this, shouldn't do that." Because if you are just a weak self, you're glad to have somebody to give you a little control. When you find an *honest* weak self – your anointed self in Christ – and you are able to live your life, because it isn't you living, it is Christ in you and you need no controls! You are part of the controlling factor of the universe; you are in authority; you are a king with God! But until we've got that, we like to have our laws and our religious services and our don'ts and do's...we like that as a protection.

That is what came out here. They couldn't stand that. They've had some judges in the Spirit, who had strengths and weaknesses, men like Gideon, men like Samson, like Jephthah and there was a very great man of the Spirit in Samuel. They accepted the guidance of Samuel, but his sons were not following in his footsteps. Therefore, because they didn't know how to see God's handling a thing...therefore, God has somebody else. They couldn't see that because they weren't people of the Spirit who could see God handling things. They said, "Oh, goodness, what shall we *do* about it? Where can we find somebody? Give us a king. Your sons can't handle it...not the type. Give us a king."

God always conforms Himself to free will because He made free will...because free will is a free person. So He conforms Himself to free will, and then utilizes it to bring out some further operation of His grace. Therefore, *because* He conforms to free will, He conforms to the misuse of free will...so He conforms with you. That's why it says, God *determines* evil. He does not *permit* evil; He *determines* is. The Bible says that! Peter said, after Pentecost, "You are the wicked people, who by the determinate counsel and foreknowledge of God by wicked hands have crucified Jesus Christ." He says "determined"... why? *Because*

God determines freedom should be freedom, and if freedom is misused, He determines that freedom should misuse itself. It is all perfect! But what He does…He turns misuse of freedom into a new avenue of grace, to sort out the wrong with the right. That's how God *always* does it. So He determined the devil would crucify His Son…and Pilate and Judas, and so on. He determined they would be free to determine this…to fulfill their freedom. You see, out of this brought the resurrection and the end of the devil and the end of the whole system of Law and Hell and Sin, and out into the new heavenly dimension! That's how He does it!

So He does here. When the people determined to have a king, Samuel pled with Him. In his human reaction, he pled with Him about it and sought God about it. You read it here in the eighth chapter of Samuel. And God said, "Let them have it; let them have it. If that is where their condition is now, let them have a king." So He instructed Samuel to inform them that they could have a king, but with due warnings! (1 Samuel 8) He gives a detailed warning to them of the kind of domination, tyranny and demands that would be made of them by a king…how he would make them slaves and workmen and order them…and explained all that way that they would pay a sad price for having domination over them instead of Spirit.

Now with the start of a phase of the history of the earth-people…in the earth under the domination of kings…God would utilize this for many purposes that would gain of His grace and manifestation of power. So that He would come through in wonderful self-manifestation through some kings…others the opposite…because they've always got to find that they failed, because we say we can keep God's laws. *Flesh* can't keep God's laws; it isn't *meant* to! It loves itself. So we always have to revert back to failure until we find this final success when we, as I say, come out of the whole law system into the empowered system in spirit union with God.

Then He gives the calling through Samuel to the first king…Saul. God is no respecter of persons and He distinctly says that He would have confirmed the kingdom to Saul, if He could. He didn't select Saul to reject him. God never does that. He selects everybody in order to save them. He never rejects a person, because there is absolutely no rejection in God. Rejection is only self-rejection. As I said before, Paul put it right in one of his speeches when he said, "You people who rejected the Gospel judge yourselves unworthy of eternal life." You judge yourself! God doesn't judge you. So it says that He was ready to confirm the kingdom on Saul as much as He ultimately confirmed it on David, if Saul would respond to the office of Grace.

So the start is made. Samuel is told under God's guidance that he is to have one of his sacrificial feasts in his home town when they make a sacrifice, and have a feast and draw all the people together. But at that feast a tall striking young man would turn up, unknown to him, a man who belonged to a well-known family. His father was spoken about as a very outstanding man, Kish, a wealthy farmer, and he had lost his donkeys and he had sent his son on an errand to find the donkeys wandering about the countryside somewhere. This was the young man who turned up at the feast. Samuel was forewarned and so he gave him a special welcome and they had a special portion of the feast prepared for him. The next morning he took him aside up on the top of the house and said, "Now I want to say something to you. God is anointing you as king over Israel. You are to be the captain of His people. If this is surprising to you, I'll give you certain signs He's going to give you as evidence. Here they are." And then he gives him one or two signs; a person was going to meet him with some loaves and give him some loaves, and a messenger to say the donkeys have been found and that his father was more anxious about his whereabouts than he was about the donkeys. And finally, the Spirit of God was to come on him.

Now that is a reality, I suppose, for which we have no final answer, except that God is always grace. Was Saul a changed man? Was his life therefore an expression of flesh when he was really a spirit man? Was he really? Because when we are people of spirit, we know a better way; we can go very fast, especially after we know the unified life in expressions of flesh. Our basis is we are people of God...we are misusing ourselves temporarily. Was that what Saul was? It doesn't look like it. But it says twice over...that he was made another man. He became another man. In I Samuel 10, it says, God gave him another heart, in verse 8. Verse 6: He shall be turned into another man. And the spirit of God fell on him when he met this company of prophets, The Spirit of God came on him and he prophesied among them.

I suppose it is possible today that the Spirit can move on people without their becoming the persons who have become joined to Him... which is only of course, in relationship to the crucified, risen Christ, that you are joined to the Spirit. I don't know. We always hope for the best. (One of the profoundest poets who really understood the things of God was Browning. There was a great deal in Browning which can be great illumination to people who feed on things of the Spirit. Browning is not easy to read, any more than Shakespeare is easy to read...though he knew God better than Shakespeare, though Shakespeare knew a thing or two. But Browning knew very much. There is some insight in some of Browning's poetry, although he is difficult to read. He has a great poem on Saul, when he makes out that... if he longed to see Saul, God's man...he surely didn't have greater love than Christ; "See the Christ stand." It's a wonderful poem; there are some marvelous verses in it. He professes ultimately that he is God's Saul. Well, he hasn't got any biblical background for that. We must leave that.) We may hope...that's all we can say.

So Saul started as if he was God's man. There was a public selection of him confirmed in those days by lottery. In the lottery, the lot fell upon the family of Kish, and Saul started as a modest man. Doesn't seem like it was a true humility, a modest man that was hid, he knew of the anointing, he had already had it in secret. They had to find him behind the baggage and bring him out. His striking characteristic was that he was taller than any of them. Well, God likes tall men as well as small men…that's no trouble. That doesn't eliminate him because he was a tall man any more than it would eliminate him if he were a small man, like apparently David was. I don't know; he was a physically powerful, but I rather get the idea that he was a smaller type of man physically.

So there he was, anointed, accepted…with certain reservations, like you get in any presidential election. There were certain people who disapproved of him and were really opposed to him. When this public election was made, followed by a dedication at Gilgal when he gathered the people together, and again he warned them and they had a sacrifice and God gave the miracle of a thunderstorm at the time of season when you don't usually have rain and so on. He then said, "Now I'll meet you, Saul; as priest I'll make the sacrifice with you, the kind of personal dedication to you that God is with you and God will favor your reign, in seven days' time." He just put that in. He says, "In seven days I will be with you in Gilgal. Thou shalt go down before me to Gilgal; behold I will come down unto thee, to offer burnt offerings, and to sacrifice sacrifices of peace offerings; seven days shalt thou tarry, till I come to thee, and shew thee what thou shalt do."

You see, God has to eliminate *basic self-reliance* the same as He has to eliminate *basic sinfulness*. You can't be the new person and the reliable person *until* you have had eliminated at the Cross of Christ, both sinfulness and self-reliance. The ultimate of Sin is self-reliance. Sin is only products. The real ultimate is I-myself-apart-from-God; therefore, I am for myself. That is Sin! That is the evil thing; that's the satanic thing. But you don't see that. It is hidden, because we are used to operating by self-reliance…seems obvious. So there has to be this second operation of the Spirit on His servants; first of all, that they are guilty and to attain the right relationship, they found forgiveness and acceptance…and secondly, that self-reliance won't do. They haven't got the wherewithal to do it, and they are put in situations where they can't fulfill their calling. Like Moses...tremendous dedication, tremendous commitment...threw the palace affairs away to identify himself with God's purposes, and got not one iota of strength. And just moved out...all he could do was kill an Egyptian in secret and hide it. Well, that's not the way to handle Pharaoh and his hosts – to kill one of his men secretly and then be afraid Pharaoh finds out. That won't do! So that was his problem; he hadn't got what it took to be the deliverer of Israel.

Also, we have to learn, not only that you didn't do it, but that you can't do it! So God has to take us through something which tests out – are we based on self-reliance or do we transfer it to God's reliance? Now that's a very real thing because God isn't here. Where is God? He isn't here. Self-reliance says, this, this, this, like – "We must have a king." God's reliance – a judge to represent a God who isn't. Now unless you are a spirit person, you can't see that! You'll run off. You'll find your church and your laws and your organization to replace the living Spirit...because you are afraid. This is a naked walk; it is a tightrope walk in where the winds blow. There is no law to restrain you! You are yourself...you are God in your human form. And you walk a tightrope across Niagara where the wind is blowing on you and nothing to sustain you except what is in you! That's some walk! No wonder the church has gone away. No wonder they hide under church laws to avoid this and say this is crazy. It is crazy...because you are not a Christian unless you're crazy. *This* is this walk in the Spirit!

If you are in the Spirit, it is easy because you *are* that. This is our lovely spontaneous living. But if you are not in the Spirit, it looks pretty dangerous and pretty windy up there. You don't like it. That's why they couldn't take Jesus, because He just had nothing except His Father. They couldn't take this Person who went about loving people and not caring about whether you kept the Sabbath or not. Couldn't take Him! Healed lepers, oh my goodness me, we need some better religion than that! We need a good tent, and a few laws, and to get a little cash out of it too. That's it...and they crucified Him. That is the final exposure of self – it crucifies the *real* spirit walk.

This further test *has* to come. Am I really walking by the Person I can't see who says He does things and will do them, and do them through me as I go forward with His invisible resources that come through me...or do I say, "I can't take that. That's not really me, I must have a little of 'this' to help me through."

That was the seven days for Saul...the seven days' test...for Samuel was going to come down in seven days to make his public sacrifice which was a public demonstration that Saul was God's man. Because, in those days, the sacrifices were confined...because it was still the Law ordained to priests. We are all priests. We make our own sacrifices...don't need that kind of thing. You have a permanent holy communion!

I haven't taken communion for 20 years...don't care a hoot! I keep the Holy Communion inside here. As for the baptism...the baptism is inside here. Don't need a lot of water to baptize you. If you want to waste your time, you can...it's up to you. *This is the inner life!* You only settle in that by a test in which there is a dying to the outer reliances... and a resurrection to the inner reliance.

Meanwhile, Saul did well. That's why the question does arise...did he know the Lord? He first got the loyalty of Israel by a sudden challenge by one of these heathen nations around the Ammonites who seized a city on the outskirts of Israel called Jabesh-Gilead. In the ways they had in those days (and we are not much kinder these days, in our prisons and wars and so on) they encircled Jabesh-Gilead and the elders pleaded for time in the hope that somebody from Israel would rescue them. Their captors hadn't entered the city yet. "OK, we'll give you three days; when you surrender, we'll accept you as long as we put your right eyes out." Ammonites had their right eye taken out.

Well, a good negative spurs a good positive! It's the best, often. Darkness pinpoints light. Light shines *out of* darkness. So the very *horror* of the challenge, when it came back to Saul, aroused Saul, as it should! He was the king. So he sent out a communication to the nation and said, "Let's come and rescue them." And he did. He did a little clever military strategy, and he came this way and that behind the enemies...and caught them unaware, destroyed them, and released the city. So he came back in triumph. Now the interesting thing about coming back in triumph is this – now, here is a popular man; they were all going to follow him now. They were making a lot of him, but he said, "Today the Lord has brought salvation" (I Samuel 11:13). So his eyes are right, there. It isn't, I've done it. That's very good...the Lord has wrought it.

Then he added a very interesting and striking fact which is the kind of thing David did again and again. He had his enemies who wanted to displace him and kick him out. So immediately these people around only see things in the divided way of enemies and friends...which of course isn't there in Christ...they said to him, "Let's get rid of those enemies; let's put them to death." Then Saul said, "There shall not be a man put to death on this day, for today the Lord has brought salvation to Israel." That's right...not put them to death. They had a right to their viewpoint, and now they can change their viewpoint because Saul had become sealed among them as the king led by God. So there is a good deal of evidence that Saul started right.

Now there came the next issue when the seven days' test would arise. Their real enemy was always the Philistines all through those early days; the Philistines were attacking them, making invasion into Israel. Israel was very weak; they hadn't any arms. The Philistines were armed. Israel didn't have any arms. An assault had been made on them, some of them invaded which stirred up the Philistines, and they were mobilizing to attack Israel. Jonathan smote some of them and that stirred the Philistines up into action. There was a great army of Philistines...30,000 chariots, 6,000 horsemen, and people like the sand on the seashore in abundance…came pouring up to Michmash, near Gilgal (the place where they were to sacrifice). Now then, things were as bad as they could be. The people trembled it says, and began to run away because they had no weapons. They weren't used to this kind of standing up to the Philistines. The Philistines were threatening. Samuel didn't come. One, two, six, seven days, Samuel didn't come. He said he'd be there in seven days. (It is possible to read into the records, he did come on the evening of the seventh day. It doesn't quite say. But from Saul's point of view, he hadn't arrived on the seventh day.)

Now this was the test. If Saul is representing God…and this is God's nation…and God says He will preserve this nation and destroy the enemies of this nation. Now then, let's see God do it! The public evidence that it will be God doing it would be that Samuel, as the priest of God, would come and make the sacrifice…confirming to them all that God is in this thing. Now we will see God in action. Saul couldn't wait! Now, in other words, which way was Saul looking? Was he looking at the threatening Philistines, at the runaway Israelites, at his own beating heat, at the apparent failure of Samuel, or was he looking at the God of Samuel? Was he geared to Samuel, or self, or the God of Samuel? He failed. He took a drastic step which was certainly the uprising of the ego in him; he did the sacrifice himself which was blasphemy and heresy in those days. He himself made the sacrifice as if he were Samuel. Of course, making sacrifice doesn't matter really, if you are in the right spirit, but Saul wasn't in the right spirit. He did it to confirm himself in this situation.

Samuel arrived. The test on self isn't that you slip but that you stick to your slips…that you don't recognize the slip and get it through. We all slip. There's a pretty tough spot. Anybody might have done it. That was a pretty radical thing to do – to make the sacrifice. Anybody might have done it. After all, he was king. But the point was where Samuel comes in…Saul, what did you do that for? Why didn't you wait for me? And immediately he put a thousand excuses around him and wouldn't admit that he was the culprit. *That's* the thing! "What hast thou done?" And Saul says: "I saw the people scattered, and you hadn't come. It's your fault the people's fault...and the Philistines gathering themselves. It's everybody's fault except mine." *That* is the uncrucified self. That is the self that does it. Fear does it and then justifies what it does. A person really believes in himself that he can find the right way...not in God. There's the gap.

So this was the first evidence that Saul was walking as a man in the flesh. I'm not prepared to say...it looks as if he was a man in the flesh and never had been a man in the spirit, although there had been these certain evidences. So Samuel turned around and said, "You have done foolishly; the Lord would have established your kingdom." That's what he says, "He would have made you king, but now your kingdom will not continue and God will find another man." That's a blow, if it's your self...if it isn't your God's anointing, but you yourself. The important thing is you don't like that when you're told there's a successor being prepared for you.

God doesn't drop a person on one incident, if there's hope he still might be changed. Thank God He doesn't! He hadn't told Saul yet He had rejected him. He *had* said, "God would have given you the kingdom. Now He'll find another person." It is a partial rejection. He hadn't totally said, "I've rejected you." He gave Saul some indications that God can be God...if he could be trusted. The indication he got through his own son. We don't know how Jonathan knew the Lord. Jonathan was a very precious person. He is precious because he had an inner relationship with the living God. Now we don't know how he did that. We are never told, any more than we are told rebuked how Joseph came to know the Lord, but he did. And here the condition is...Saul is hurt, turned in on himself, angry, frustrated that he had been rebuked, and he sat at a certain place under a tree there with a few hundred men around him. And here was this mass of Philistines way over there.

Self is paralyzed if it is by itself. Anytime it is hurt, it is paralyzed… doesn't know how to get out of its paralysis…because the only way out, of course, is God's way out. Doesn't matter about your paralysis… God sees you through. Saul didn't know that. So he sat there. Now Jonathan caught something. Where Jonathan caught this from except that he could see what God had done through Abraham, Isaac, or Moses, or something, we don't know, but as he sat there with his father…and of course he saw that his father's disturbed, negative, resentful condition, unbelieving condition except that he was believing in things material…something came to Jonathan. God is always saying He will destroy our enemies. That's what He is here for – to preserve His people as a people through whom He can prepare them ultimately to have the Messiah. He can destroy the enemies that are trying to destroy us. Why shouldn't God do something about that now? And he said to his armour bearer, "Look here, let's put in a test. We are on one side of a valley (sort of rock place, recently archeologists have actually been looking at that valley and finding out how true this historic segment is) and the Philistines have their garrison on the other side, up on the steep rock face of the other side of the valley. Let's do something."

Only to his armor bearer, not to Saul, he said, "Will you come down to the bottom with me in the valley? Perhaps the Lord will work for us. There's no limit to God to save by many or by few." How many thousands have been inspired to save by many or by few? He can save as much by few as He can by many. He is not geared to human numbers. This is his faith – He sees God as the Lord of hosts, not the hosts – that matters. So he says, "Let's go down and put it to a little test. Like Gideon put things to a test. Now if they say to us, 'We'll come down', all right, let's wait for them down here. If they say, 'Climb up to us, and we'll do something', well, that's pretty tough to try to climb on your hands and knees and meet a garrison up there. If they say, 'Come up', we'll go because it means the Lord is going to give them to us."

Now that's putting a hard test on them. If they came down, they could meet them on their level and they could get to them as they came down, maybe. But to say...God is with us in this thing and He is going to destroy our enemies if we climb up, put our arms on our back, as it were, and climb up on our hands and feet and meet this garrison at the top...and they did that! Because when they got down there, the Philistines hailed Jonathan and his armour bearer and said, "Come up here and we'll show you a thing." They were shown a thing. "Come up and we'll show you a thing." They went up. And they stood away – faith, of course, is on top – slew a few of the Philistines!

Now we can't tell how that shook the Philistines. I suppose they thought the Hebrews were helpless anyhow. Suddenly some of their best men were being destroyed. It shook them! It put a shiver of fear through them, and such a confusion they began to fight each other, began to mistake some of their own friends for enemies, and they began to pour away.

There alone was, again...if Saul could have seen it...a sufficient indication that when God is in the foreground of operations things happen with mighty little trouble to me because God does them. They were just killed by the Philistines, that's all. The rest was done by the effects that had on the Philistine army. Saul couldn't see that. Saul was deeper and deeper in self-aggrandizement. We have to say...if he ever had any...he lost sight of being under the leadership of God. So now he proceeds on the foolish ways of self. "Oh," he says, they brought the news to him, "They are running. Let's get after them. Let's pursue them." Even there he started by consulting the priest, because he had learned the way was to find out through the priest what the will of God is. As soon as he heard the news, "Go outside and go ahead"...he wasn't going to wait for the priest. Again he wasn't going to wait to hear what God said, "Off you go." And in order to assert his ego, he added..."Let's get after these people. Let's really slay them and get the spoil, and no one is to eat until the thing is finished. I make an instruction: No one is to eat any food until the thing is finished. Just give yourself to capturing this army and getting the spoil and destroying them and so on." So off they went.

But it took longer than he thought, and the people became extremely exhausted. They hadn't got the physical stamina to go on with the pursuit. Jonathan was among them. Now he knew by now Jonathan had done this thing because he said, "Who is missing?" And they said, "Jonathan." It was Jonathan that started this thing off. It could be that he already saw the danger of Jonathan superseding him as his son. Could be that already the jealousy was there; I don't know. He knew that Jonathan was among them. Jonathan didn't know this foolish commandment...that silly commandment that Saul had given. The reason he gave for this was: "Cursed by the man that eats food until evening that *I* may be avenged on *my* enemies." (I Samuel 14:24) Do you see the self come back? It wasn't "The Lord be avenged on His enemies" – "*I* may be avenged, and you are not to eat any food until you have finished the thing...just so everybody can see what a victory *I* have."

So they went. Jonathan didn't know that. And as he passed, he passed one of these honeycombs. (I've had them in Africa, they are very lovely. You eat both the bees and the honey...very nice.) He passed by and stuck his stave in the honeycomb and dug out some honey, and had a very good feed. Of course, his eyes were enlightened, as it says...they were refreshed. They said, "Oh, you shouldn't do that! The king said we weren't to do it." Now he began to 'see' his father, which became very important in the life of Jonathan, because he said, "My father has troubled us. My father has troubled the land." He had to say, "My father shouldn't have done that."

So the pursuit continues...and in the end the people were so exhausted, that when the pursuit ceased, they couldn't even wait to kill the animals. They ate them with the blood. They were so hungry... so famished. Now that, of course, broke the Law...the Levitical Law that nobody was to eat, drink, or touch blood...because blood was the symbol of Life, of shed blood. There was this confusion going on and Saul stepped in, rebuked them, and told them to take time and prepare their food properly. Then he asked, at this time through the priest, "Should they continue with the pursuit?" No answer. Silence. That was a check on Saul. He says, "Something's wrong, why don't we have an answer? What's wrong?" So he said, "We'll find out what's wrong. Could it be somebody's broke the curse? Someone is under the curse, broke the law that I gave? So they cast lots again to find out. The lot fell on Saul and Jonathan...and Saul, still expressing his ignorance, said, "Oh, if it's Jonathan, he'll die." And it was Jonathan! So Jonathan was discovered to be the person who had infringed this foolish commandment of Saul's. Saul intended to kill him! That's how far self gone wild can go. Because to fulfill this foolish vow...not what God said, but what *he* had said...he would kill his son! The people intervened then, and the people forbade him and said, "Should Jonathan die who has brought this great salvation in Israel, for he has wrought with God today." Jonathan had wrought with God so Saul *couldn't* kill him! So again he got exposed himself. He had the confusion of humiliation; he couldn't fulfill the vow that he had even tried to fulfill.

So you get the continuing moving of Saul away from the purposes of God. The final opportunity given to Saul was with the Amalekites. Still Samuel said to Saul, "The Lord sent me to anoint you as king over Israel." He still said that! "Now if you are anointed as king, you are going to do this. God has put certain judgments long ago (we discussed that earlier on) on the Amalekites." (They would be destroyed because they were the first nation to try and destroy Israel.) "You ought to go and do it. You ought to wipe them out, the whole nation, the tribe, their property, their cattle; their everything ought to be wiped clean out." God had a special word always on the Amalekites, because they have been the special people determined to eliminate Israel right from the days of the wilderness.

Saul went again because he was in this life which is governed by its own *self*-interests – its own ideas of what's right and wrong. He destroyed the Amalekites, but he preserved the king and preserved some of the cattle. He pretended that the cattle would be just a sacrifice, but of course we can see they wouldn't all be to sacrifice, and brought them back with him...because he was governed always by what he thought was the right thing to do. So once again he had to be confronted with the verdict which was inevitable...which Samuel brought to him when he went to meet him, and he heard the bleating of the cattle...the sheep and the cattle...and asked him what it meant. "What meaneth this bleating of the sheep and the lowing of the oxen?" (I Samuel 15:14)

Then Saul tried this kind of *rationalization* that we are so used to. We try to justify ourselves. That's why God has to expose 'to justify ourselves.' So to try to justify himself, Saul said, "Well, the people kept the sheep and oxen and we can use them for sacrifices. I have fulfilled what I was told to. The rest was utterly destroyed." Then Samuel, who had been forewarned by God, said, "This is the final thing. To *obey* is better than sacrifice, to hearken than the fat of rams."

Then is when he told Saul he was rejected. "God has rejected you, because you did not obey the voice of the Lord. Rebellion is as the sin of witchcraft, and so on, God has rejected you."

Self can pray 'about'...with so-called confession of sin and forgiveness...because life isn't "I have sinned," but "I'm a sinner." Until you say, "I'm a sinner," you haven't got it. It isn't the sin that is the problem; it is the *sinner* that is the problem! Therefore, a person who doesn't know God can say, "I have sinned." We all might say that, "Oh, I've sinned." Anybody can...oh, none of us say we are all right. What we mean is we are all right underneath; it's just that we aren't on the surface. *That's the lie!* It isn't a question of what I am on the surface. It is what I am *underneath*.

The truth about humans is – we are all lost people. We are *ourselves* the sin! The sin is a person of self-centeredness. It is the sin.

Sins are products. So Saul would say, "I have sinned. Forgive me." But at the same time he was saying, "But you will honor me as king, won't you? Therefore, I pray you will pardon my sin, and return with me that I may worship the Lord." *Not* to worship the Lord as a sinner who needed forgiveness, but as someone with sins forgiven. *Now* I am all right to worship. This is this preservation of the self, subtle preservation of the self, which is prevalent in all of us till it is exposed by the Holy Spirit!

That is when Samuel said he would leave him, and Saul caught hold of his garment to hold him…got hold of his skirt, his mantle, and tore it! And Samuel said, "The Lord has rent the kingdom from you like you have torn this garment." And then, a person of the spirit is always at ease; you're not under the law. You do the next thing. The next thing of Samuel is, "All right, I've conformed so far. This isn't a matter which at the present moment disturbed the whole nation. So all right, I'll go back with you and worship publicly with you, because the time hasn't come for this to be a public issue. So this is the *freedom of the Spirit* in a person. At the same time he made a public demonstration of what God said to be done when Agag came along (the king)… and Samuel hewed him in pieces before the Lord.

That is the first phase of Saul's life as king. Samuel of course comes in again later on, but presented to us as the one God rejected and why God rejects him. Whatever else a person may be, he is just a member of the family of Israel. The leader can't be that. He's got to show in his life the true grace of God.

So we should turn on now to the call of David.

The purpose of God to have a king, who manifested Him over the nation, expressed His will, revealed Him in His grace and power and sufficiency…and would help to keep the people of God in a relationship to the living God, insofar as they could be. Again, this side of the Messiah coming, it could only be a partial relationship. But still it could be a *living* relationship! It started by the anointing of Saul as king, and He started by a touch on Saul's life in which He said that Saul became another man after he received the anointing through Samuel...who was the priest-representative in those days of the people of Israel. God had met with him by His Spirit and he had been among a group who had the spirit of prophecy on them. Twice over it said he'd be turned into another man. So there seemed to be a start in which he had some living contact with God *as the living God*...not just some external idea of a person called God...but a living contact. Because when he went out to battle in earlier occasions (and by quite a strategy he won the battle) he came and said, "This has been of the Lord. The Lord has given us the victory!"

Life is lived from within, not from without. We are outwardly... but we *are* within. The One that controls us within is the One who expresses Himself by us without. Through the Fall, we started out as a self-controlled people. That's our trouble . . . self-interest, self-gratification, self-magnification... is the driving basis of the life, no matter however much we cover it up.

God is the opposite kind of Person. He is a Person only *for others*. He has no interest in Himself. He *is* Love. He exists to complete His universe. His joy is the perfection and completion of the universe in total harmony...which is the destiny to which we move, where the whole universe is in harmony...harmonious interrelationship of love, and everyone serving one another and whatever developments come out of that.

So God is this One Person in the universe. We have missed out by being the opposite kind of person...persons motivated by self-loving love instead of self-giving love. So if God is going to manifest Himself by a life, there *has to be an inner transference* take place which we speak about in our New Testament terms as identification with Christ in death and resurrection. Death being in Christ dying to being the old kind of person we used to be under the dominion of the spirit of self-centeredness...and the Resurrection being our union with Him in the new kind of person under the Spirit of Love, the Spirit of God, the Spirit of service. Unless this change takes place in the center, our life expresses what we are. If we are self-centered, we express self-centeredness and self-interest and seeking to do things our way for our ends. If our life is basically united with the Spirit of self-giving love, we are expressing forms of service, and love, and blessing. What happens to us isn't the point; we are available to lay our lives down that others may have their needs met...just as Jesus did for us.

So a person can't be a safe representative of God until there has been an *inner transformation*...not just a first touch in which some way we have met God, and some ways He accepted us and some ways loved us or even forgave us, which is what we call the first touch of the new birth...but the *profounder change* of our center, *because* we live from our center. We are inner people, brought about because of the heart or in more technical terms, the spirit. Therefore, even after we *had* the first touch from God, we have to be brought into situations which will give us a change of settling this other matter – Am I going to do a thing my way with my resources to fulfill what I think are the right objectives... **or** am I representative of the living God with His perfect purposes, His perfect wisdom and power...expressing His character of service and love through me...so that the living God is represented by me? And those with whom I have contact are brought under some opportunity of coming into the same relationship? So there has to be some form... some crisis situations...in which we come up against those alternative choices in our heart.

Saul remained in the alternative choice of being *for himself.* He wished to protect his own honor, do it his own way, and himself be known as king so his main interest is, "I am the king." Not that God is a king through him, and God's will is done...but that he should be the king. So it became a distorted life which is centered on self-interests...and self-interests cause disturbances...selfishness, hatred, jealousy, murders and all the discords of life here that we know are the products of self-interest. So he had to be rejected as king. God rejects nobody; we reject ourselves. The Bible specifically says He would have kept Saul as king if He could...but God cannot have, as I say, the *center* of His people represent Him to His people as a person who is the opposite to the kind of person to what He is...and who are out for the fallen aims of self-interest. God's purpose of fullness and love and blessing...and leading on to the bringing of Christ into the world... where the whole world can move into finding the way to being the Sons of God.

So Saul had to be rejected, although rejection doesn't come from God. Rejection is self-rejection. Saul rejected himself because his condition made it hopeless for him to continue. Of course, we may say that is confirmed by God's saying...therefore he is rejected. Use those terms if you like. But it doesn't *come* from God; it comes from ourselves. And another, alternative king had to be found. And this was David. Here it starts specifically saying that God was satisfied by his heart attitude. Because God sent Samuel as the priest on a kind of private journey...because Saul wasn't to know, Saul was becoming a jealous, hating...hell...because jealousy is hell! *And* hate! He was becoming a person who was motivated by that kind of spirit, because he was for his own ends and anything that would defy his own ends... he was against that.

He had already been told that there would be the appointment of a successor. That's enough to put fear and jealousy and suspicion into him. So it was a private matter that Samuel went to the city of Bethlehem to the family of Jesse who had seven sons. Now we are all human and we all need chastening. Even the mighty Samuel, who was a man of the Spirit, needed a little checking...because when this family came together (by Samuel's request, of course) they highly respected Samuel. He had been the judge of the nation, because he had someone to select from amongst the family who was to be the destined king. This handsome, tall attractive Eliab came. That's all we know about him...he apparently was a prepossessing kind of person, much as Saul himself had been, and Samuel who had a human aspect same as ours was attracted to this young man, thought, "Well, this is the man." The Holy Spirit inside said, "No, the man I am after isn't the man who has the outer appearance. It is the man who has the right relationship in his heart. The heart is the center where the choice is made."

The heart is the word used as the center where we make our choice. "I must have the man who has basically made a choice between his own way and his own ends, and the privilege of being My servant and expressing Me in the world...fulfilling My purposes of blessing to the world." In other words...a man who basically changed from finding his pleasure in self-interest and self-seeking to a person who found his pleasure in being an expression of the other-loving will of God...so he would more and more joy in blessing others than in being blessed himself.

So we know this much...we know that, because a little time afterwards, a short time afterwards, when Saul was coming under a wrong spirit. This disturbing spirit is called an evil spirit, because it was taking over Saul and disturbing him. Of course, he was...because he was full of ambition which he couldn't fulfill, and self-aggrandizement which he couldn't get respect. We have already seen how again and again he lost respect because self *does lose* respect. Someone proposed him...and he got a 'quiet thing' from a young man who was a marvelous harpist and a psalmist, as well as a very efficient man. He had been first an efficient shepherd; you wouldn't think he would come out a shepherd. He was known already to be a man of some physical capacities and abilities...this young man. So we already know that actually God already knew the heart before ever they came before Samuel... already knew the kind of person David was...whose heart was set on the psalms – a psalmist..."The Lord is my Shepherd." He had already begun to write these beautiful songs – the Lord in His fullness and His power and His grace and His wisdom; God is my Exceeding Joy; God is my Rock; God is my Salvation; God is my all in all...which all comes out under the Psalms of David...and it appears certainly that the shepherd psalms were already written because he didn't go back to be a shepherd for any length of time again, only for a short time.

So Samuel was given the warning touch, the warning word, in his spirit...because most warnings come within our spirit...not to go by outer appearance that Eliab wasn't the man. So he's synthesized now. "Something I must be able to tell by which there is some difference about the man, the man who is God's man." Now I don't know how he knew it, but he passed through all the seven sons and none of them registered in Samuel's spirit...because you are a man of the spirit, you are registered in the spirit. You don't rush into things. God can give you a sort of token..."Yes, that's it, that's it"...even if you are buying a house or something. That's it or that's not it. On people..."That's it; that's the person who's got the touch I am seeking." Samuel was a man who had been in a sensitive relation to God since the days of Eli when he first had the vision of God in the temple as a child, and the word of God had been an open word to him. So he sensed somehow that these men were not the man. Was there another one? Yes, there is one other...this so-called little fellow. I don't know if he was physically little or not, ruddy of countenance...as they say, attractive in a different way, I suppose, from how Eliab was attractive..."Yes. I haven't seen him." So they sent for him. It could be...(It was even strange he wasn't there; he had already had some note about him.) even already, it was possible they were keeping him out because they didn't want that fellow to come to the fore.

It is very interesting how again and again through scriptures the younger one comes to the top – Jacob over Esau, Isaac over Ishmael, Moses over Aaron and Miriam, who were both the elder members of these families. So it comes out again and again. Now here's the one. So it somehow registered in the spirit with Samuel – this is the one! So he anointed him. Now here was a tremendous fact. This young man was anointed to be king over Israel in secret. That can touch self in a moment! King over Israel! The man was just a little shepherd boy, as we would say. A king of the nation! To replace this man who had shown himself about, all right…was well known to be an egoistic king, but he was king!

Now, if you are God's man you wait for God's timetable, and do it in God's way! You are not running under your timetable. *Very* important point – God *has* a timetable! So it comes out here now. The next event was striking and unexpected and we may say highly encouraging to little David (young David) that Saul had got this disturbed condition…an evil spirit was sent from God. God operates through free will. God doesn't send evil spirits from heaven, but he operates through free will. Where there are people who are self-centered, they are capable of expressing an evil spirit. An evil spirit is just in them probably…just comes up. Just an intimation of what we get when we see we love God…that we should be what we get freely. If we are freely that way then we get that way. Therefore, it is the will of God, because God's will is that freedom should have its freedom…not to damn us, but to save us. And when we have had enough of hell, we may find a way to heaven.

We hope Saul did. That great lover, David, to his end had a love for Saul, and even in his death honored Saul. We *hope* that behind all this chaos of hatred and jealousy and murder and finally self-destruction which was the life of Saul, he may *still have been* God's man underneath. But, in his condition, someone said to Saul, "Well, I know a man who will help you. He is a young man, noted on the harp, with songs, etc." So David was summoned to the palace (whatever the palace meant in those days) straightway to the footstool of the throne. That was very striking, when a few months before, maybe only a few weeks before, Samuel said, "You are to be king." And here he was at the footstool of the throne, ministering to a very disturbed king! He didn't see how he could slip into…from vice-president into president.

Well, *God* has to confirm us that we don't run away with things… that we don't run back to self. We have to become *fixed and confirmed* and we have to go through experiences which all life has – which are crucifying experiences where things happen which hurt the self, if you can take them, because God knows *where* we may be frustrated. All right, we accept frustration because we are on the line of what God's purpose is…coming in God's timetable.

So it came about…simple ways, searching ways…*suddenly* this radical challenge came from their great enemy, the Philistines. And the Philistines thought they'd got him this time, because in those days they did everything by challenges. Because one notable hero could be a type to do it, and could challenge the notable hero of the other (the opposing army) and they'd fight it out. The one would become the servant of the other, according to the one who won the battle. It was one of the old ways in which their battles were fought sometimes, if they had a big enough challenger. Philistines surely had it at that time, in Goliath – nine and a half feet tall; the shaft of his spear like a weaver's beam; tremendous great hulking man! Obviously must be that kind of man, if he can carry that stuff and use it. This man marched out as the champion of the Philistines and shouted his challenge out… "I defy the armies of Israel! I defy you! Bring out your man. If you can kill me, we will be your servants. If I kill him, you are my servants; you are our servants." That's the way they did in those days. There was nothing out of the ordinary in that type of challenge. What were they to do with that? The whole of the Israel army took six weeks running away; they had a regular runaway every day for six weeks. The park must have got quite dusty. When Goliath came out to make the challenge, they couldn't take that, wasn't one man to meet him.

Meanwhile, a very *little* incident took place which is a very testing incident. There was this young man, already anointed by the king, already at the footstool of the throne…linked in, favorably. Saul was like him, as his helper and servant…more than servant, as his assistant. Well, the obvious thing was he would go to battle for Saul, at least be on the battlefront and share in what was happening. So that little reverse took place. David's elder brothers, Jesse's sons, maybe again on jealousy, said, "We're going to the battle." And the first three of them enlisted, went into the army with the Israelites, and they made sure that David went back to his proper place as a shepherd, put him back. "You go back to Father's sheep." So the man who had been just on the edge of things, just going to be involved in a battle where someway maybe something might happen that would affect his future, back he went to be just a common shepherd on the old job. Now, *that* tests a person!

He was there six weeks. Now we know how he fulfilled that test by what came of it. If he had remained paralyzed with resentment, and questioning God and what this all meant, he would have been a paralytic, and paralytics don't challenge Goliaths! He wasn't. Certain things were obvious. What was this? Quite obviously he had learned, "It is God's way, I'm learning, I mustn't have *my* way. I question this... doesn't seem fair they put me back when I'm the anointed one and they come out like that. That's not the point. I'm not running this life. My God has a purpose in which He is going to reveal Himself and His power and glory and beauty and love by me, and fulfill purposes in Israel for their future in the world through me." So the start in the heart of David, as we see in a moment, quite obviously was a release from hurt, resentment, questioning. *And* an acceptance. "All right. *God* puts me back as a shepherd."

Now the purpose of God is to manifest Himself *where you are*...not where you think you ought to be! *Everything* is an opportunity when we see it! Everything is an opportunity for weak-self to prove the power of God. That's what the meaning is...self, by itself, *is* weak. But when it knows this God-relationship and God in all His wisdom and resources related to that self, then God *uses that self* to manifest Himself by the human self. *He doesn't discard the human self.* The human self becomes the agency and the human self does do acts when he goes into the action expressing the resources of God.

Now, how do we know David was like that? Because he accepted, now, his duty with the sheep. His duty wasn't by the king...so all right then, he'd better do a good job as a shepherd. One good thing about a shepherd is that he must protect the sheep from wild animals. So doubtless he had it in his mind (he may have doubted before) he had it in mind, "My job is to see that wild animals don't capture my sheep and they won't." Two incidents arose (I take it not the same day)…an attack by a bear, and an attack by a lion. In each case, David had got hold of it…"Now *God* is my resource! God has put me aside now. It is manifest to me that I am a person with His resources at my disposal. All right, I'll use them on the lion and the bear then, if not to any other way." And he went out and he grabbed the lamb out of the teeth of the lion, (I don't know if bears have teeth or not) but out of the paws of the bear, got them back. He did farther and this took some doing! One of them attacked him! That was the lion. When the lion attacked him, he went for the lion too and he took the lion by the beard (I didn't even know lions had beards although I come from Africa) and slew him. That takes some doing, you know…to slay a lion and come off unscathed.

So you see this man was a free man, freely operating under the resources of God in his situation. That's how you operate! Every situation is an opportunity. *Somewhere* in every opportunity is a lion and a bear…an *opportunity* when something happens for you to move in and say, "Now I prove the resources of God here. I see how God gives me a job, when I've lost my job. I see how God supplies money in days of inflation. I see how God puts life in this sick body. I see how God does something. I see how God touches a life that needs touching."

So we know what David's heart-spirit was…back by the shepherd because of the way he operated the power of God when *he* couldn't have done it. Now we know it is by God's power because when, a little later on, he says, "The Lord delivered me out of the paw of the lion and the bear. The Lord did that! I didn't do that just by my own know-how." So *he was operating* on the power of God.

Now something else arose. He was the anointed; he was to be the king of Israel. Now the whole point – God said, "I have delivered my people. They are My people. I am going to keep them in the place they are to be. They are to magnify Me and be witness to Me in the world. My light as far as possible until Jesus Christ comes is to shine out through My people. I promise to preserve them, I promise to defeat their enemies," and so forth.

Now he knew that! So questioning was going on in his mind… what was this news he was getting back? Israel was running away from a heathen champion who was openly saying, "I defy the armies of Israel." David didn't say it was the armies of Israel. He said, "They are the armies of the Living God." *That's* the difference. Israel is weaker than Goliath. God isn't weaker than Goliath, I don't think. That's the difference! So there was something churning up in David's heart – It isn't right that there's nobody to send out.

Now there is one interesting (and I think there's a purpose for it) why Jonathan didn't stand out, because Jonathan *had already* fulfilled exploits of faith when he'd shaken the Philistine army. He hadn't come out yet. He was one of those of all the rest, including King Saul, who ran away every day when the giant marched out and threw his insults at Israel. This is in the spirit. What is in the spirit comes out… was in the spirit of David. We are talking of Chapter 17. I'm not going into detail with this 17th chapter of First Samuel. Chapter 16 was the anointing. Chapter 17 is the Goliath chapter.

Now again, you see, when you are relaxed on God, you don't fuss around. You don't make your own timetable. God's perfectness is God. He's everything. He knows the hairs of your head if you've got any left. Even the little sparrow doesn't fall to the ground without his Father, because the Father's life is in him, so his Father knows when the light goes out, of course. Beautiful. Jesus saw this detail, every lily of the valley – God's lily. Solomon in all his glory was not arrayed like that. Isn't that beautiful? Jesus saw the beauty of God, so every tiny detail is God's, every timetable is God's. Why fuss? If you've begun the crucified, risen life, then you've begun to take the life…"I'm not going by what I think…" New Testament people say, "I've been crucified with Christ. So in Christ I am not being governed by my self activities, or self reactions. They may come up and disturb me, but I am not to be governed by them. I am governed by the Other Way."

Now what happened with this obviously disturbed spirit, (because it came out in a moment) disturbed spirit in David...well, he was shut up in the sheep. And then a quiet thing happened. Jesse said, "Here, our boys, your brothers, have been these weeks up in the battlefront. I'd like to send them a few "care" parcels...some cheeses and loaves, and so on. Go and take them with you. Go take these to your brothers." So off marched, as we would say, little David...not so little with his load of cheeses and breads and so on for his brothers. As soon as he arrived there...it was just the occasion when the Israelites were doing their 43rd runaway! After six weeks, back they were coming. David came fresh. "See that," they said, "See that! See what's happening? Do you know the king has said he would give his daughter to anybody who would put out that Goliath?" What did David say? "Who is this man who defies the armies of the living God?" *They* had said he defies the armies of *Israel*. David wouldn't take that!

The men of Israel said, "Have you seen this man that has come up? Surely to defy Israel has he come up. No, no, no, Israel is to be beaten by Goliath!" They said, "The man who kills him, Saul will give him his daughter in marriage." David said, "What shall be done to the man that kills this Philistine, for whom is this uncircumcised Philistine that he should defy the armies of the Living God?" (1 Samuel 17:26) *That's* the God man! That man sees *God* in action through everything and God has sufficient resources for things. That's the difference!

So, you see, it depends on the set of your heart all the time. What's really governing your heart-outlook...your spirit-outlook? From what angle are you seeing – the angle sight of God or the angle sight of man? There's a *vast difference* to the effects, isn't there?

Now this shook them. No one had said this, and they began to talk. Then he got his first shot. Faith means an inner conviction; faith isn't putting your belief in something. It is having put your belief in something which has become yours! This that you believe, oh, that's mine; this is a fact! Now David had this fact…that Israel had no right to be pushed about by Goliath. There should be some man, and it began to rise up in David what man, to defy and put out this man (giant). Up comes Eliab, the eldest brother who received the cheeses, and heard this conversation and there was jealousy and had been all the time. He said, "What are you doing here, you little fellow? It's the pride of your heart talking like that, making boastful remarks like that. Go back where you belong, to the sheep."

All David said is, "Is there not a cause?" In other words, you don't take attacks from man when you know what's *inside* you. If you doubt, you do. If you know what's inside you…"Oh, no. I know what I'm saying. It's God's purpose that someone should put this Goliath out. Is there not a cause that I said so?" He wasn't touched by this false attack of pride. You see, faith looks like pride. To the weak, it's human to say God should do something and do it by me, or something. That's pride. Even to say "I'm saved" is pride *because* it's human. So faith looks like pride. When faith is what it is…knowledge…when it has its evidence within you (he that believeth has the witness in himself), faith is the evidence and you *know* a fact to be so, you are not shoved about and you are not moved about by that. "Is there not a cause?" So David backed up his pride! Sure, there is a cause, someone better say it.

Now this was so startling that it got to the king. "Well, for six weeks now I've been talking like that." Apparently the king didn't recognize who this little man was, or he didn't mean to…I'm not sure which. David was brought up to him. *Now,* he had moved in…David suddenly saw there is a **man** by whom God operates, who manifests the power of God, who will meet this devil's man. A man…one man. *I'll* be that man! He was sort of cornered. "I can't go back…before Saul." I'll do it! On, ho, so he stood up before Saul and he said…pretty cheeky, "Let no man's heart fear because of him. Thy servant will go and fight with this Philistine. Be quiet, you people, be quiet. Don't be anxious. It's OK. OK, you watch." You transmit what you are. If you are quiet at heart, you transmit quietness of heart.

So he dared to say to Saul, "Don't be fussed. OK. OK. This little man! Because Saul was a big man, you know. That shook Saul, and so he immediately said back..."How can you do it? Look at you, you are a youth. This man is a man of war, and you're a youth, a teenager, a freshman at college or something. *You* defy this man?" David had already got that in focus. He said, "Sure I'm a youth, but I'll tell you something. I, as a youth, was challenged by a bear and a lion when they grabbed members of my flock, and I not only took the members of my flock back from their teeth, but, when the lion attacked me, I attacked him and put him out and killed him. And the God who delivered me from the paw of the lion and the bear can deliver me from this Philistine." So you see, you mount up from the faith you have. If you want to see something of faith happen there, let's start here. Let's be able to say, Oh, I proved it in my home. Many of us have, thank God, all of us have in our home. I have proved something. All right, I can prove it out here! I can share it with you in some bigger project now, because I have proved that God does prove things in just my little ways. Nothing is little in God's sight. Nothing! *Everything* is eternal and has value.

So that's how he answered the challenge. "Sure I am a youth, but what kind of youth am I? I am a God-equipped youth." So he transferred his attention from the youth to the One Who equipped him. Then Saul made a comment that was very helpful and very interesting. Saul was so moved. He took it. All right, he said. He accepted. Saul said, "Go and the Lord be with thee." There was something there. He accepted that, rather startling, but obviously there was always this touch with Saul which makes you think underneath, God was there. But then he did what was common sense. He said, "I'll give you my armour." I don't know what a five foot nine David looked like in a six foot seven Saul's armour. He may have rattled a bit, I think. But it was a pretty high compliment, "I'll give you my armour."

Now you see you can't operate unnaturally. Walking with God is release...you are released! You aren't messing yourself up. You are just what God tells you to be and you don't make a thing up. You are just yourself. This life has become a released self, because behind your released self is God and you are *just to be yourself!* Don't try to be someone or something else. So you don't try other people's ways of doing it. You get into trouble. Don't try to preach the sermon other people tell you to preach. Don't give the witness other people tell you to give. Give what *God* gives *you*. (I've been a missionary secretary many years and I always establish it – Don't you fiddle about and say what other people say...you *ought* to talk about that. Take no notice. If somebody says you ought to talk about the mission field and God told you to talk about your own changed life, talk about your changed life. Talk what God gives *you!* Don't be messing about with what other people think you ought to say, or their timetable. If they tell you to talk ten minutes, talk for 45 minutes and bless them. Don't say they bless you; you bless them!

So there again...but it was a common sense touch and so David tried it on...and then he saw the point! "What can *I* do in this man's armour?" Released! Freedom! Oh, what a beautiful freedom! He was so released that it occurred to him...I am myself. Well, how do *I* handle things? Oh, the one thing I am expert in is slinging a stone. All my life I have done that. I don't know if with beast or bird or what. He was evidently an expert, a bulls-eye man with slinging a stone. He was at home with it. He didn't have to work that up. He knew how to shoot a bull's eye, as we would say. That's it! I have one weapon that Goliath hasn't got – a sling of the stone and I can sure use that straight. Of course, you can't do that unless you are released, you know, because you'll be tense. Oh, I must make a right shot, or something. When you are released – Oh, I am to be myself! He wasn't himself. God was behind all this. And so he went to the brook and picked out five stones. You say, why five stones? Probably because he was used to it. Probably it was a common sense number. A man with a sling doesn't go with one stone. He normally takes five stones…probably kills five birds with them. So there's nothing to argue about why he took five stones instead of one. Off he went.

Now he faced this man. This man came up with a huge laugh. "What is this," he said, "coming up against me? What is this? Am I a dog that you come to me with staves?" And he cursed David by his gods. "Come to me, I'll give your flesh to the fowls of the air." David said, "Thou comest to me with sword, spear, and shield. I come to thee in the name of the Lord of Hosts." That means in the power! Name stands for what He is – power, the character, the operation of God. "The name of the Lord of Hosts, the God of the armies of Israel whom thou hast defied." My, he spoke out! "This day will the Lord deliver thee into my hand and I will smite thee, I will take thy head from thee, I will give the carcasses of the hosts of the Philistines this day unto the fowls of the air, and to the wild beasts of the earth." That what? That all the earth may know what a fine fellow David is? No, that all the earth may know that there is a *God* in Israel!

That was the trouble with Saul. Saul said, "That people may know what a fine Saul there is." David said, "What a fine God there is." That's why people loved David. Because they felt he wasn't a self-pro-jecting David. He was a God-projecting David. And he was cool. You see…he'd *got* it. In the *inner* sense he'd finished fast. Well, it doesn't look like it, you know. Who wouldn't be nervous? Wouldn't you be nervous? Peter was a little nervous when he drew out his sword to cut off the head of the high priest's servant at the arrest of Jesus. He missed the head and got the ear. It's a good thing he did! He was a little nervous. David wasn't nervous like Peter was. Cool. So cool he ran. I don't know if that is what slingers usually do or not. He ran where Israel had spent six weeks running from. As the Philistine drew near to meet him, David hastened and ran toward the army to meet the Philistine. He took a stone out of his sling and shot it straight.

The probability is that he hit an unarmed place. It's not likely that the man thought his temple, his forehead might be available...his neck might be, his shoulders might be, his legs might be, his head might be, but probably he never thought his helmet covering his temple, because no one would think of getting...they hadn't got those special sighted guns in those days, that you shoot accurately with. Probably as far as I can see, he struck him in the temple, and David aimed his stone directly at the spot which would stun Goliath and hit the one spot which was open, got him. Down he fell like an ox. It hadn't killed him... probably not. It stunned him, that's all that was necessary. That gave David his chance. David got there and pulled that great sword out of its sheath and with his own sword cut his head off, and took his head back as a demonstration of what *God* had done!

That's a wonderful story because you see it has the principles of what we all have in us, which is faith. It isn't a great stone slinger; it isn't anything. It's a person who in a situation has *God* as his resources and not only has God as his resources, but says, "God will operate them, you watch, and I move forward in the basis – God will supply that need; God will do that thing! The point – the faith has a substance. You understand what faith means – you've *got* something, *not* that you get it.

The faith of David was – I've *got* this thing. I *know* it is God's purpose to destroy the armies of the enemies of Israel, and this man represents them. He is a fighter, so I *know* God intends to destroy them. Therefore, *I say* he's finished! And if *I* am His agent, he will be finished *by me.* So you see, the *power* is **faith**. We all have that. We all can have our Goliath's incidents...when they issue from the way you really are, what you are within you, and must therefore issue from you.

So that was the famous first incident presented to us in this life of David. You see these stories of children......but when you think how foolish we are. These tremendous incidents have tremendous princi- ples of faith in them. We make them out as stories for Sunday school. Well, that's probably what they are. They're wonderful, but there is *far more* than stories for Sunday school in this. There are stories for adults in this...plenty! You take these stories...in our silliness we just make Daniel in the lion's den. Tremendous principles of faith, David and Goliath, behind them lay all the means by which you can function, by which God can function protectively and manifest Himself in my life or yours. You can't get a more perfect presentation that I know of in the Bible than that one, when you see the underlying principles.

So then he moved out to the next stage. Now he got to be *estab- lished* in a way of life in which God was steadily his sufficiency...not just on certain occasions, but permanently. In other words, he was established in a God union where he would know always God was his sufficiency. He hadn't got to *find* Him...because the real truth of be- ing a Son of God was your union. Your human spirit is united to the divine spirit through the death and resurrection which has cut you off from the old self you were, and put you in the resurrection of the new self...and you're in a union and you're conscious.

Faith is always conscious of what it's got! It isn't that you *theoreti- cally* say...something in you tells you *this is so*. No, I am not I any longer. The very thing Paul said...I am not I...looks like me. He says...I am a Christ in human form. That old independent self, egoistic Paul has been crucified, in Christ's Cross...that one went out. I'm *not* that one. I'm *not* that old man. I live a new man. What's a new man? A new man isn't really I, it is Christ in me. So it really is Christ in my Paul form. It *isn't* Christ **for** me; it *isn't* Christ **with** me; it *isn't* Christ **in** me; it *is* Christ **IS** me. Christ IS me. I live, no, no, it isn't I living; it is Christ living. That's *known* union. Now then, Paul says, I live by the faith of that fact. Faith is recognition of the fact.

I always use a simple illustration. For instance, you are in a faith relationship with that chair. You aren't thinking about the chair, but you sat on a chair by faith. You chose a chair, you committed your body to it; the chair comes back now and says, "Here I'm holding you." Now you forget it. But you are actually in a union relationship of faith with that chair. You are living by the faith of the fact that the chair is holding you up. You don't think about it. It's just part of you. Faith is the substance become real to you, which is you; you forget about it, but it's you. It's always there; it's doing its job. And this isn't it; it is HE.

Don't you see, it must be an engrafted experience...what James calls the "engrafted word", not the word out there; the word in here. That's the only real Word...the engrafted word become part of me. So somehow or other this is what we talk about as the Union experience – the graduation experience of a child of God. The birth experience is justification. The graduation experience is union, or whatever term you use; I just know this. When you **are** that, then you operate continually from that basis. You may have to repeat the recognition and so on as we are pressed upon by life, but you don't have to find God again. You **are** He. You recognize He really is there. Therefore, you are on a level experience, because you **are** just Who you **are**. And the real you isn't any longer 'just you.' It is *you as an expression of Christ*. Now this has to be settled in you, and you have to go through the tests in which it *becomes settled* to you. The answer is not in your reacting self, or your fearful self, your troubled self, your oppressed self. You may be all that, but you have learned that's not what I *really am*. This is really God and if I am in trouble, it's because that's the way *He's* going to come through! These troubles are the way He's going to manifest Himself.

So in all these lives there is a period, sometimes talked about as a wilderness experience, where you haven't quite settled into this yet. You have a God relationship, but it's somewhat in and out because it hasn't quite settled in you as a *final recognition that you are* **never** *you again. You* are Christ in you. David had this now for eight years or may-be ten, when Saul became his bitter pursuer. Strange thing...this man chose of God, Saul, became the bitter opponent pursuer, out to kill David because he'd got it clear that David was his successor. He wasn't going to have that. He was his own successor while he lived, and after that he'd appoint the one he wanted I suppose. He was going to run his show and no one else was going to tread on his cabbage patch. He was bitter! What a hellish thing, jealousy; bitter hatred and fear. It says, he was afraid of David, because, you see, when you are free you attract!

Now David came back and immediately all the population praised him. And praised him in terms Saul didn't like. Saul has slain his thousands; David his ten thousands. Oh, oh, oh! Saul and his thousands and David and his ten thousands! And it says he eyed David. From that time on, in the ninth verse of Chapter 18, Saul eyed David... from that day and forward. This was a man who was getting in his way, and he was afraid of him. He shifted his jobs, but every job he went to, they loved him more, because he was free from self.

He first of all started as captain of Saul's army and was immediately accepted (vs. 5). He was accepted in the sight of them all. But of course a general can be a little distant from people, and so Saul made it worse for himself. He got jealous of that so he removed David from being captain of his army and he made him just a captain of a regiment. He made him captain of a thousand; therefore, he must be with the people. And the nearer he went, it says, he went out and came in before the people. It was worse for Saul, because David became more and more popular, because he was homey, friendly, loving. He hadn't got any bit 'noise stuff' to put up, and the people loved him (I Samuel 18:13). So it got worse and worse for Saul, and several times there he was afraid.

Now God puts in beautiful little helps on the way. God comforts us. God gave Jesus His disciples, God gave Paul his companions, God gave Moses Aaron. He turned out to be a pretty good Aaron when he got through. Moses had to get through *first* with himself. And he gave David his Jonathan. Jonathan is a beautiful spirit. Jonathan is a marvelous spirit because he was heir of the throne, and he knew he had to give it up and he lovingly gave it up. Now, who gives up his inheritance? Who gives up his right? It appears to be – we know Jonathan was a godly man – we saw before how he knew God when he proved God in that battle against the Philistines, and when he reproved his own father when his father operated on self-effort levels and made trouble. It says, he reproved him, "I knew my father was wrong." I think it came out of this tremendous victory. Jonathan had a wonderful victory at Michmash where he went over and started this rout among the Philistines, just himself and his armour bearer. Smaller incident but a tremendous victory!

David, in front of the whole nation, did this thing. Now Jonathan *knew* a thing or two. He knew a man of God. He knew God. He knew a great man too, and I think that beautiful Jonathan…"this is the man"…by this time, because he knew the anointing, because Saul knew the anointing and he said later on he kept nothing from Jonathan. He always had a good relationship with his father. "My father hides nothing from me." (I Samuel 20:2) "…my father will do nothing either great or small without disclosing it to me." So they had a very confidential relationship together. Lovely, lovely. But this is a wonderful thing – that man knew God *had already* anointed David, but he was Saul's heir (Jonathan) and he then saw the greatness of David…or the greatness of God in David, and he accepted that. He demonstrated acceptance after this battle by expressing a great love for David, in which he took off his own equipment, his royal robes and put them on David. This was a kind of personal symbol that David was meant. That's a tremendous action, to put a replacement in your place…in love. It says Jonathan made this covenant with him; Jonathan loved him as his own soul. Stripped off his robe…gave it to David, his garment and sword, even to his bow and girdle. (I Samuel 18:4)

Now the beauty is this…Jonathan became the restrainer of his father, and the protector of his father against murdering David. So God put him as protector and this man gave his life to be the protection, the shadow, the guard over David to free David to take his anointing later on. So this is intercession. The man laid down his own human rights to the throne, and anything else he might do. He was a soldier, and remained with that bad spirit, Saul. He remained with Saul to restrain Saul. So it says straightaway...for instance, Saul, in verse 19, said to Jonathan, "Kill David." Saul had already used several methods, subtle methods. He had thrown a javelin at him twice (David had gone back to play for him.) thrown his spear at him twice! He used a subtle method. He had to give his daughter to David because he had promised his daughter to the one who killed Goliath. He tried on first with the elder daughter, but for some reason or other that elder girl was married to somebody else, and that left Michal. Now Michal loved David. That subtle man said to his servants, "You tell David that you're already a poor man. I'm a rich man, King Saul. You must bring more dowry for my daughter. Go and kill an hundred Philistines and bring their foreskins as evidence that you've killed them." Well, one man to kill a hundred, some going! He said, "He'll surely get killed himself in doing it." That subtle man tried to inveigle David into an action which would probably bring David's death. All that happened, of course, was that David killed a hundred Philistines...that was quite simple...and came back. Those sorts of things went on all the time. Finally, he said to Jonathan himself, "Kill him!"... (Chapter 19:1) spoke to his son that he should kill David and his servants.

Now Jonathan was David's ally, not his father's ally, although he was with his father and so he told David. He said, "Go away, David, and I'll plead with my father. I'll put some sense into my father, so you can come back where you ought to come back by his side here." Protecting David. And so he did. Verse 19 tells how he talked to his father, "Don't talk like that. This man has done nothing but good. He is wholly loyal to you. He has never sinned against you. You have no business to act like this toward him." There was a volatile spirit in Saul he would change. Twice over later on when David related to him, he said, "I have sinned against you." There was a certain element in Saul which could change back, which makes me hope that *underneath* he was really God's man – just got mixed up by the flesh. This went on. He said, "Yes, of course, it's all right, let him come back." So he came back. But again he threw a spear at David (vs. 9) and this time David felt he couldn't go on any longer. He slipped away and fled, and he was warned by Michal, who had married him by now, and was his wife and loved him. She warned him that Saul was going to send people to their house to capture him at night, so she played a little trick. She put an image in the bed and slipped out. When they found the bed they found not David but an image. He had slipped out. Even then he didn't want to give up. And he had a relationship with Jonathan and they had a little plan among themselves.

David wasn't even supposed to know that they sent and tried to capture him at Michal's home. David would absent himself and go away a day or two, and he would say he had gone to sacrifice at his father's home in Bethlehem, so he would be absent from the dinner and table where he was supposed to be. Jonathan would test the father out, and if the fatter said, "OK, it's all right," it meant that his spirit was all right and David could come back. If he poured out poison on David, he would know it was too dangerous for David to come back. This was to be the final issue. And that's what happened. He made an arrangement then with David that on the third day, David should come into a field some distance off, and Jonathan would come with bow and arrows and he would shoot a couple of arrows toward where David was standing. If he called out to his boy who went to fetch the arrows, "Go farther," it was a warning to David that it was no good, he'd better go. If he said, "Come nearer," it would mean there was still a chance for him to come back. This little plan they made.

Jonathan found that all Saul did was to pour out poison, both upon Jonathan and David. Saul's anger was kindled against Jonathan when Jonathan said, "Oh, he's just gone to make a feast in Bethlehem a couple of days." He said, "Thou son of a perverse, rebellious woman, do not I know that thou hast chosen the son of Jesse to thine own confusion and to the confusion of thy mother's nakedness? For as long as the son of Jesse liveth upon the ground, thou shalt not be established."

So you see, Saul turned on Jonathan and said, "You'll be giving up your kingdom."

That settled it with Jonathan. He didn't want it. So that showed Jonathan was no further good. So he shot the arrows, gave the signal to David, had the last meeting with David, one...but last, and he confirmed what was going to come to David and he made a covenant with him that "Out of your kindness you shouldn't cut off my house forever, that when your enemies, David, are cut off and you become king, you don't cut off the families of mine" which of course David fulfilled later on. That was where they had their final meeting...where they wept together and David exceeded Jonathan in his weeping. "As soon as the lad was gone, David arose out of a place toward the south, fell on his fact to the ground, bowed himself three times and kissed one another, and wept with one another until David exceeded." David was a tender-hearted man, that's what made him king later on. That's why he was a man after God's own heart...because he was a tender-hearted man. We will see later on how he expressed a tender heart again and again to his enemies.

So David departed. He only had one other meeting with Jonathan. Once, later on when David had begun his eight years of escape when he hid, part of them in this cave of Adullam, part of them as a guest to the Philistine king, Achish...and different places he escaped here and there from Saul who was sending people to capture him. Once Jonathan came out to meet him and this wonderful last word came to Jonathan (I Samuel 23:16), "And Jonathan, Saul's son, arose and went to David at Horesh, and encouraged him in God" (strengthened his hand). Isn't that good? This friend, strengthening his hand in his loneliness and pursuit and danger...eight years of it! And said to him, "Fear not, because the hand of Saul my father shall not find you and you shall be king over Israel and I will be next to you." He got *that* a little wrong. This precious man thought..."I'll come into the kingdom and be next to you." What a pure heart! To give up his right to the throne to work under and with his beloved David!

And so Jonathan died. He never left Saul. So I count Jonathan as a *highly honored* life. He was an intercessor for David; he gave *his* life. Instead of moving out from Saul and identifying himself with David, which would have done no particular good, he remained with Saul as a cover and protection and an advisor...and would do all he could to keep Saul from fulfilling his vengeance on David. When Saul later committed suicide before the Philistines, Jonathan fell too. And you get that famous lament of David over Saul and Jonathan which we come to later on.

So now David had this exile life...not a king's life at all...living in a cave, most of it. And his friends were with him in the cave of Adullam...very 'nice gentlemen' they were! Everyone who was in distress or that was in debt or were discontented came to David. This was David's gang. They were David's heroes...four hundred of them! It must have been a pretty big cave. He was captain over them. That man so affected them! He affected them first of all in battle. They became great warriors. At the end of 2 Samuel is a list of mighty men who did all sorts of things, battling against the Philistines, slaying a lion in the snow, a whole list of exploits, killing giants, etc. They caught from David the utilization of the forces of *God!* How do we know that? One thing we know is this – they were so devoted to David, because you see David wasn't related to his own concerns.

The selfless person wins...because if you are subject to yourself, you are attracting people's attention to the One Who *does* meet your need, Who *does* satisfy, Who *does* supply the resources. So it is introducing these wild men to God because several were receiving quiet spirits. One proof was that devotion to David was so great that on one occasion, just as a human, he expressed a human desire, "Oh, I should like a drink from my old father's home." Just a little nostalgia, a little homesickness for his home in Bethlehem. "My, wouldn't I like a drink of fresh water from that well in Bethlehem." Three men said, "We'll go and get it for you." And they'd break through by faith the host of Philistines, and drew water from the well at Bethlehem, showing how they could learn to trust the resources of God when God called them…and they felt this was a call of love, that they could comfort their beloved leader with a little touch like that. Silly little thing, but there is great truth to this human kindness isn't it, and they brought it. But look at David…wouldn't touch it! He said, "This water is the blood of my brothers; it belongs to the Lord. They are the Lord's people. They got this for the Lord. I'll pour it out before the Lord." You see how he always kept the Lord in front of him? David hadn't brought this water for 'me'; it is for the Lord. That's David!

So there's a wonderful obvious humanizing element, a quieting element, a God-believing element coming into this wild group. There are one or two touches…one is very important…which is very beautiful. These were guerillas, a rough type, the marauding type, used to living by what they could get from one or another. Look at this remark…At one time they were in contact in their wanderings with a very wealthy sheep owner, cattle owner – Nabal, a greedy, mean man, very wealthy, large harvests. At one time, he sent some men down to Nabal, when he was reaping his harvests, saying, "I've been a guard over your people for years, I've never allowed people to come in and grab your people. Instead of being grabbers, they'd protect other people. It would be helpful if you would just give us a little of your extra now with which I can feed my people." Nabal reacted violently against him. Abigail, his wife, came through. She became a wife to David later on. But look what the men said…the shepherds said this of David's wild men: "These men were very good to us. We were not hurt, neither missed we anything as long as we were conversant with them when we were in the fields." Isn't that beautiful? So instead of these men being grabbers and "we'll take off you," they protected people in their rightful establishments. Even the heathen king, Achish, who had given a city for the last year and a half (the Philistine king) for David to live in, said this… (They wouldn't let David go out to battle with them because when the Philistines went out to battle, that's the time when they killed Saul). He sent David back to the city that he had given him, the Philistine city named Ziklag. Achish called David and said:

"Surely as the Lord liveth, thou hast been upright and thy going out and thy coming in in the host has been good in my sight. For I have not found evil in thee since the day of thy coming unto me unto this day." Isn't that beautiful? That these men *around* could testify to the integrity of these men in the cave. They never went out of their way to grab and steal and destruct. That's what they got from David – the spirit of honesty and truth, love and loyalty.

Now the most startling thing about this whole eight years was David's extraordinary ability to see *God* in people...not evil. Now I should make a difference there. We Christians see God in everybody; everybody is a child of God and doesn't know it. Don't perceive people as lost people. See them as prodigal sons – as sons who have missed the way. Every single person is made in **God's** *image*...loved by God. He is misusing Himself. Haven't you been one? So don't see the misuse... see the person...and love and respect everybody. So we don't have friends and enemies, because everybody is our friend – because everybody is really a God-person. He may not know it; he may be operating as if he were a devil person. But I am not seeing the devil side of him. *That's* how you attract people. You accept them, bless them... even though they are hurting, or whatever type they appear to be, you are only looking at the *appearance* of selfishness and greed and lust and what not. *You are seeing a God-person who is temporarily misusing himself.*

Now that wasn't seen in the Old Testament. That came with Jesus, because Jesus taught us to love our enemies. In the days of the Old Testament they still had the duty which was to have a nation and protect it, and their job was to preserve that nation through which God was going to manifest Himself, and finally through which Jesus was going to come. Therefore, in their case they had enemies, but the enemies were not their brothers. Their enemies, of course, were the people around them. So they did fight and slay the people around them. They were *meant* to do so. It was, in those days, the way in which God preserved His nation.

Inside the nation, David could see nothing but God's people and his greatest enemies were toward God's people. This amazing man who was heir to the throne of Saul, whom Saul spent eight years to chase and kill by any means he could get him, still wouldn't touch Saul, who was God's anointed. "That man is God's anointed. When God wishes to be through with him, that's God's affair." That's being free from self. "I'll not work it around and push Saul out, and take his place. Oh, no! When God's timetable comes, I'll slip in. But he is God's anointed." You don't touch God's anointed!

So there are these two remarkable situations. One was, in another cave...not the cave of Adullam, another cave somewhere...it must have been a large cave. In the back of the cave Saul said to his men, "Search you around and capture David." Saul slipped into the cave to relieve himself, crouched down to relieve himself, under the very nose of David. That sly David slipped over and cut off of the cloth on the back of him and kept the cloth. Then he felt convicted; he had cut the cloth from the king's garment. Not much of a conviction, I think. He felt guilty; he had cut the cloth off the back of his cloak. When Saul left the cave, David went out and called to Saul and said, "Saul, I apologize. I want to return to you your cloth. You understand, Saul, I could have killed you, but I don't touch the Lord's anointed. Forgive me, Saul. I'm like a dead flea on a dog. Don't treat me...I'm just a flea, what are you chasing me for? You are God's man. Just accept it, leave me alone, and bless you...and don't have this animus against me."

That is one of the cases where Saul said, "I have sinned." He didn't follow through. Because I keep saying, the answer isn't to say I have sinned; the answer is to **be** a sinner. When you say you **are** a sinner, you get changed *inside*. When you just say you've done a few things, you put them off and go out and do a few more. That doesn't answer. Twice he did that. And each time the men said, "You've got him." They couldn't take it. "Well, you've got him, now kill him."

The second time was a little farther. Once again Saul was in pursuit and he was on the other side of a valley, and on this side David was concealed with his men. Nightfall came, so Saul with Abner, his chief captain and his men made bivouacs...trenches they called them... where they spent the night on the side of the cliff or whatever it was on that side of the valley. It came to David to do a naughty trick again. He said, "Will anyone volunteer to go with me?" Abishai said, "I'll go with you." Let's go among them, steal Saul's spear and his water bottle...and take them off with us and come back to where we are." From under his nose! And they *did* it. It says the Lord put the people in a deep sleep, so I don't think it was drugs. While they slept, David slipped into the army, picked up his spear, picked up his water bottle, and came back. Once again he apologized. Only this time he made some fun. He called out in the morning: "Hi, Abner. What kind of captain are you? You better have your head off. Can't you look after your king better than that? At night you allowed me to come in and steal his spear and water bottle. Come and fetch them back!" He made a joke of Abner. And then he talked to Saul. Each time he could have killed Saul, but he wouldn't touch him. Again they said, "Kill him!" No...wouldn't touch God's anointed. Isn't that something! He wouldn't touch...God will work it out, don't touch. If you've got an opponent, don't touch those opponents; let God work them out.

So that was one of the great examples of the love of God, the lover God, mind you, confined to God's people, because in those days they hadn't got the universal love which we have, which includes enemies outside of them. We have no enemies left! In those days they had. So they confined their love to their own people, but that's wonderful enough because they got enemies among their own people...*that's* obvious.

So we come to the end of David's years of trial. He had run about... he meant to. One time he had tried to be a madman, ran spittle down his beard to disguise himself because he was afraid the Philistines would get hold of him. Fear. Human. He did one other thing which is very interesting. That is what *Jesus* picked up. When you are free in the spirit, you are free of these ritualisms. All these ridiculous church business puts you under the law. Drop them clear out! Because every day of *God's* every day is the same. Sunday's precisely the same as any other day. It may be convenient to keep Sunday, maybe, for example, if you like, or because it's a rest day, or because you get a little refreshment in worshipping with other people – I hope I get more refreshment out of fellowshipping with you than you do out of the silly services...that's all. (Excuse me!)

Now David was free. *So* free that when in the early part of his flight, (he had his men with him at that time...only had 10-25 men with him...just before the 'cave company') he landed in a place where the priest was. Abimelech was his name – a priest of Israel, and he lived at a place called Nob. And in among the relics on the tent or tabernacle was Goliath's sword. David partly came because he hadn't any armor. He thought he might as well borrow back Goliath's sword, rather big to use such a thing, but still... He arrived there. Of course, this priest had no idea he had fled at that time. He thought he was Saul's honored son, and he welcomed him as such. David said, "Could you give us some food," and the priest said, "The only food we've got is the shewbread."

"That's all right...we're holy." That's right! Those special people don't touch that bread – the shew bread. Well, *everything's* holy. "That's good bread for us. Let's have it." That's the very thing Jesus took up to show that we aren't managed by the Sabbath. We manage the Sabbath! That's one of the revolutionary things He said...why they crucified Him! He said we aren't managed by the Sabbath. You are under Law; you've got to do this and this and this. You manage the Sabbath. Sabbath is for your convenience. He said, "Look at David. David had the cool cheek to use the showbread, which is sacred to the priest and sacred to the tabernacle, and give to his men to eat! We're all holy, just as holy as you – let's have it." I like that! That's the freedom which sees all men in God. Jesus picked that up to press home

His point – don't be managed by the Sabbath with all its silly laws. Be free and use the Sabbath as you please. Because when you are in God, you do what you please because what you're doing is being motivated by God all the time…by His love. Do what *you* please!

That ended in the murder of the priest. A certain man named Doeg, an Edomite, brought back to Saul this information. Of course, the priest was innocent because he thought David was his favored son. Saul, always in weakness, said, "You helped my enemy. You should be killed." He called on his servants to kill the priest. "No, I won't do it." You see, self is so weak. It can't get them to do things. David could get his men to go and fetch water from a well for him. They couldn't get them to do it. Only Doeg himself offered to do it. He was a heathen among them; he slew him. The good that came out of it was the son of the priest escaped and went to David. In those days the guidance of God came through the priests and they had what they called ephods – breastplate things through which guidance came in those days. Guidance was found through the priest who expressed the guidance of God. Now actually David got the priest with him so he could begin to get the guidance of God through the priest and became the high priest – one of the two priests. They didn't have a high priest in those days when David became king.

The finality of his wilderness days was in this final attack of the Philistines upon the Israelites. This was after Saul had committed his final sin in consulting the witch of En-dor and got a word of condemnation through that consultation. Within two days he was killed. The Philistines destroyed the armies of Israel, killed Saul…or actually he fell on his own sword…and Jonathan. At this same moment there came the *final consummation* to David of the **established life**. The established life is when you don't get hit up by things *because* you and God are one…so when things happen, you may start by a little disturbance, but no, no, no, *God's* got this thing! You don't have to call on God and find Him and get all excited. You entered the **unified life**.

Now in this last incident was the fact that they had been given this city, a Philistine city called Ziklag, on the borders of Israel, while in exile by this king. David actually went to ally himself to the king, and God preserved him in doing that – which he would have been with the Philistines fighting against Israel. The five lords of the Philistines wouldn't have David…said it was too suspicious…wouldn't have David and his men mixing with them in the battle. So Achish had to send him back to Ziklag.

Meanwhile, all those deadly enemies of the Israelites, especially the Amalekites, wiped the city out and took the wives and took the children…took everything. Now it is one thing to have burned the city. It is one thing to take the cattle. It is another thing to take the wives and children…this really hurt them. And so when they came back, even his own men turned on him when they had taken the women captive and so on…the city burned with fire. David and the people that were with him, that's his mighty men, lifted up their voices and wept, until they had no more power to weep. David's two wives were taken captive, and David was greatly distressed, for the people spoke of stoning him.

That's a crisis moment. What does it say? "David encouraged himself in the Lord his God." That's the moment in which David moved backwards – no, no, I don't go wild, I don't scream and all this. "I'm encouraged in the Lord"…his God. This is the moment when David *became solidified* in his unity. He moved, technically…from the *school of faith*, when he had to learn what it is – God's reliance…to the *life of faith* when **he** was a God-expresser. He moved now into the kingship where he expressed God through his kingship in *marvelous* ways. (I Samuel 30:6). This was the unifying moment when in the extreme moment, when all others were desperate, he encouraged himself in the Lord his God.

Then he had to find out where they had gone…to pursue them… took four hundred men…two hundred to remain behind. This again is the touch of Moses...the beautiful spirit of sympathy and under-standing that David had...two hundred men to remain behind, four hundred went. Now they found a certain person in the field who point-ed out to them which way the Amalekites had gone. They found the Amalekites all drunk, spread abroad feasting themselves...got in on them, and got all their families back...and the great spoil too! They not only took their spoil, but the spoil of the Amalekites and brought the whole lot back.

The interesting thing is we know was when they came back, the whole lot was destroyed except the four hundred who ran away on camels. The Amalekites were destroyed! Remember, God always said the Amalekites must be destroyed. They recovered all that they car-ried away and David rescued his two wives. "Nothing lacking to them, neither small nor great, neither sons nor daughters, neither spoil, nor any thing that they had taken to them: David recovered all. Took the flocks and herds and drove them back. This is David's spoil." (1 Sam 30:19, 20)

One interesting this is that he used his spoil to divide among the leaders of Judah. David wasn't for himself. That was one of the first ways in which he melted the heart of the kings of Judah. All these great things he didn't keep – what was his spoil he used to give gifts to the leaders of Judah. The interesting thing was they came to the two hundred men who had been exhausted and couldn't go through, and remained behind; those with him wanted a difference made! The wicked men said, "Because they went not with us, we will not give them ought of the spoil that we have recovered. We paid a price; they didn't, save to every man his wife and his children that they may lead them away, and depart". Then David made that great remark: "You shall not do so. As his part is that goeth down to the battle, so shall his part be that tarrieth by the stuff. They shall part alike."

That's one of those great phrases that come down through his-tory, isn't it? (I Samuel 30:24). We often use that in the mission fields, the folks who are behind are praying, some giving gifts and supporting us – they tarry by the stuff, and they share the spoil of the souls that are won, as much as those on the fields. That's a comfort to many backroom people. They may be backroom people, but God says that their part is the same as those who went down to the battle.

That was the end, because then came the news of Saul's death, and Jonathan's...followed by David's great lament for them. And then the new day dawned. That's not taking us to the end of David. In a sense there is less you can see in his time of 40 years of ruling, that stand out more, except in certain instances; there are certain characteristics which it is well to examine. That spirit of David in leadership is well worth to examine...40 years. But that would take time.

It may be an evil spirit came into Saul, although, remember...everything is inward. Isn't a God up there; God's here in us! It may be we are in union with both spirits, really, or in contact. We *were* in union with the spirit of error. We are **out** of the spirit of error; we are **in** union with the Spirit of God. But of course the spirit of error is here, and can 'reach' us...presumably...can reach us with the spirit of temptation. So it may be that if a person is sufficiently conditioned, an evil spirit can come in as a separate spirit. I don't know much about it. I *do know* that you can take the position in Christ that the thing is not there. I don't cast spirits out. I just say they have no business to be there. *I don't recognize them.* You are controlled by what you recognize. If you recognize an evil spirit in you, you've got him. You say, "I see no evil spirit in me; Christ is in me." So that's all I know.

Question: What does it mean in I Samuel 18:10 where it says "an evil spirit from God came upon Saul?"

NPG... I keep saying to you...*everything* is from God! The devil is from God. This is where you've got to enlarge your concept to **everything IS God**. The devil is a misused form of God; of course he is, because he was an angel once. Now in that sense everything is God. Therefore, if in our freedom we go ways which are evil. They are still God's ways...maybe therefore God's 'sending' them, if you like to use that expression. God has to use the expression like "sending" because outer, *external* people can't take the other. The general world cannot understand the mystical union. It wouldn't mean anything. So God has to use outer language for an outer people. Talking about sending...we really use this all the time. That's the best you can do. As I say, evil spirit isn't as if God is up here, sending an evil spirit down, because God isn't up there to start with; He's here. He's everywhere – a universal Person. Sending really means that if Saul in his freedom was in a condition in which he could be captured, moved by a spirit, invading spirit, he's free and the devil is free to operate when there is a way to operate...so it may be the devil sent the spirit in, and that's God sending him because God sends everything! God sends evil people to do evil things, because He means evil people to be evil that He may turn them to good. This is the *great secret* we've got to find.

God **means** freedom. Otherwise you can't be a person. Because He means freedom, it means you are free to do what you like. If what you do like is bad, He means you to do bad. He'll turn it to be grace, if you'll take it. God means you to be bad if you're bad, and means you to have had conditions as a consequence, because God means for you to be in freedom. Being the universal God and having provided Jesus Christ as the way out, He then utilizes that situation to face you up, with the possibility you need a change...and in Jesus Christ's case – to get Him to a death to get Him to a resurrection! He *determined* the devil would get Him, it says – He *determined* the devil would get Jesus, that out of that *determined* death will come a *determined* resurrection.

So this is the expansion of a concept we **have** to have. Everything is God, good or evil. There *is* a misuse of freedom. You can't be a person unless you're free. If you're a person, you can misuse yourself; you may be the opposite. That's how you find you *are* a person. So the moment you become a person—freedom! Freedom can take the form, which it has in the Fall, of being the wrong kind of person. So God means you to be a wrong kind of person; He *means* you to be free and have the consequences...and so He *means* the consequences.

But because He is grace, He turns those consequences into the attack on Jesus Christ which destroyed the evil, and brought about the resurrection. That's how He does it. And on us the same thing! If attacks come on us, as we go with Him, He can use that attack to bring some demonstration of His love and grace, and deliverance we can prove in a situation. We can find His love and grace and deliverance where we are hurt and turn it into a manifestation of God's love. Then evil has become an agency for good!

That's God's way because He determines evil to be evil. He determines it. Therefore, if a person is conditioned for the evil spirit, He determines he has an evil spirit. It isn't that God keeps a pack of evil spirits in a box up there and sends them down. They are part of the system – the universal system which is the spirit of error, of demons and error. We have been begotten by the spirit of error; the whole form of the world has the spirit of error in us **till** we're saved. There can remain, or enter in, evil spirits. I'm not so sure that evil spirits can enter *into* redeemed people, but certainly in the unredeemed. Therefore, God sends them because He means you to have what is your condition to have...and God means it. But He means it that you may find salvation.

Question: Wasn't Saul a saved person before?

NPG... Well, all this meeting we have talked about this. I can't answer wholly. There are indications where he didn't act like a saved man, very much not. But we have hope. David rather spoke as if he had hope when he mourned over him.

Question: Did he have any control over what the sin or the motivation was?

NPG... No, not if you're governed by an evil spirit...unless you ask to put him out. *That's* the point! So he used an outer form of David's music to quiet him. The evil spirit took the form of disturbing him, depressing him...I don't know what. The evil spirit may have been his own spirit disturbed, I don't know, because our own spirits are really evil spirits when they're disturbed as much in it. All he knew was an outer comfort through David's music. Of course, the higher comfort is to get rid of the evil spirit, because we're in God. But he didn't know that one or he wasn't willing for it. That's the nearest I can say.

The remainder of his history is his history as king, a tremendously successful king, the most successful king in the history of Israel. And one so much after God's own heart that he was called "the man after God's own heart." We can look at a few facts presented to us which are evidence to us of the way in which he was a manifestation of the love of God – of God as the love-Person and a power-Person, who was fulfilling His purposes in building the nation – could come through David. You must remember this was an earthly nation. Therefore, at that time it was to build a nation, and in the nation to build a temple in which God's Presence could be realized before all the world. That's gone out now – we aren't interested in Israel as a nation. We aren't interested in an earthly temple. We've passed right out of that now. We have found that the new nation is the *inner* nation. The real new nation is a vast number of people who are Christ's born-again people, Christ's sons. And the holy temple is people. Millions of people make the temple unto the Lord. So we've come out from these *outer* activities of making *outer* shows of Christianity. Christianity is this vast nation. That's the new one! We had not come to that in David's day.

David is seen as a man of love, because that's his chief characteristic...and he won the people by his love. He had already done that even as a young man as he moved among them. He was a free, friendly person and all the people loved David. From the time of his enthronement, there are just one or two instances which can indicate to us what we've been saying. The first was the outpouring of his love over the death of Saul. Saul was his bitter enemy. Saul had spent eight years chasing him to kill him. Saul would do anything to get him because he knew that God had anointed David to take the place of Saul. So we see the outpoured love of David, when he was beginning this new area of his life, in his lament for Saul (II Samuel 1) when he spoke of Saul and Jonathan who died together...because Jonathan was his lover. Jonathan was the one who remained with Saul to give all the protection he could to keep Saul away from fulfilling his murderous intents. In II Samuel 1:17 you find the outpouring of his heart for Saul and Jonathan. Verse 19: "The beauty of Israel is slain upon thy high places." Verse 23: "Saul and Jonathan were lovely and pleasant in their lives." *You* wouldn't say so, would you?

The man of God sees God in everybody even if they aren't showing it. If they are really a God person, they may be misusing themselves. Saul misused himself plenty, but he was God's anointed. He was God's person and right to the end of a life which had been spent for years in attempting to murder David. David turned around and said, "Saul and Jonathan were lovely and pleasant in their lives." That's how *God* sees people...that's how we are to see people. Verse 25: "How are the mighty fallen in the midst of the battle!" And then the last statement towards Jonathan, "I am distressed for thee, my brother Jonathan; very pleasant has thou been unto me. Thy love to me was wonderful, surpassing the love of women." Of course, that was true always; there was a bond of true love, because Jonathan was a self-giving servant of God just as much as David was.

Another striking incident – I am just picking out, jumping through his 40 years – there were just two or three incidents to show how David was always a lover! He couldn't see people in their contrary attitudes towards him, even if they had been murderers. He saw everybody as someone God loved and God blessed, and he would bless them. I make clear that doesn't concern enemies outside Israel. We have no enemies. The whole world is our friend today. We don't say: These people are friends; those are enemies – because every enemy is only a form of God...in one of God's sons. He doesn't know Him maybe... maybe not even know he is God's son, one of God's love persons that God' working on...so I see through the enmity to being a God's love-person. I have no enemies!

Now in these days when He was building the nation, the *earth nation*, that wasn't yet so. So they were saying other nations were enemies. In those days there wasn't the *calling* for David and his people to love the outside enemies, because they were the ones from whom God must protect and preserve the nation so it could be built and prepared for the coming of the Messiah. But inside the nation David knew no enemies, yet they were his enemies often. Here's one we see in Saul. Another was Abner. Abner was a great man. He stayed with Saul; he was a soldier, and he fermented the rebellion against David when David was welcomed to Judah...not yet the home of Israel, as king over Judah. As we said, they always loved David so it was quite easy for them to call him back when most of them knew he had been anointed long ago...to call him back to the throne of Judah when Saul died.

Abner sought to anoint the son of Saul as a rival, Ish-Bosheth, Abner took him (I Samuel 2:8) to make him king in defiance of David...took Ish-Bosheth, the son of Saul...and brought him to a certain place by name and made him king of Gilead as the beginning of taking over Israel. So here he fomented a revival in Israel to David. Now he had a row, a family row, with Ish-Bosheth after a certain time, after he had built him into power and was preparing to make him a rival kingdom inside Israel...and he changed over. He went over to say that he would prefer to join David and bring with him the people. Was he real, or wasn't he?

David had a very sharp general, Joab, and one or two brothers of Joab. They were sharp soldiers, but they were soldiers. They would kill the enemies quick sharp. They would suspect everybody until they were quite sure they were free from suspicion. So Joab couldn't take that. David had accepted Abner. Joab couldn't take that...so he secretly slipped up to Abner and slew him by a rotten trick. He met him (II Samuel 3:27) to speak quietly with him, and he smote him there under the fifth rib. He was a great man. The reason he did it was because Abner in previous wars had killed Joab's brother Asahel.

Now where would David stand? Once David stood against Joab for Abner, so formerly Abner had been his head opponent. Straightaway (vs. 32) David could weep in love. This was about one who had been his enemy up to a day or two before! They buried Abner in Hebron; and the King (David) lifted up his voice and wept at the grace of Abner, and lamented over Abner (next verse), even wouldn't eat for a day. Verse 35: "Then all the people came to cause David to eat meat while it was yet day; but David vowed, saying, 'May God do so to me, and more also, if I taste bread or anything else before the sun goes down.'" Now watch! "Now all the people took note of it and it pleased them." Love pleases! Hate turns people off. They were pleased that David could love and weep over and fast over the death which he didn't approve, which his own general had treacherously fulfilled by murdering Abner. Then he said a beautiful verse. This is the great King. His power wasn't that kind of power – Joab's. In verse 39 he says, "I am weak this day, though anointed king; and these men the sons of Zeruiah (Joab) be too hard for me." *This* is God – not some hard, bossy, strong person who beat everybody up. A man who would express all the love he could...even to those who expressed the opposite love to him.

Quite the most striking – because this was a member of his own flesh and blood – was Absalom. We are at the moment looking at the history of Absalom. What came about was really a *product* of David's own sin with Bathsheba – the fruit that came out of it. There was a family quarrel in the David family. Absalom was his beautiful son, had this wonderful hair he cut only once a year, and they had to cut it; it was so heavy. David had been a beautiful man. Absalom was a beautiful man too. He had a daughter named Tamar, and one of his brothers seduced the daughter. Of course, that was a disturbing factor in the family. Absalom determined to murder Amnon and he did. Two years later he perpetrated a trick and invited all the brothers up to a feast, and got his soldiers together and murdered Amnon. The rumor first came back that he murdered all the sons, but the rumor was checked out – he'd murdered Amnon and he knew David wouldn't take that. So for two or three years he was hidden. Joab finally got him back. But the heart of Absalom was bitter and he determined to steal the kingdom from David, and he did it. He worked up rebellion by showing kindness and niceness to the people, and finally the moment of revolution took place. He took over Jerusalem – David fled. David was outside his own city with his mighty men. Absalom took over.

Speaking of that, by certain means, Absalom was finally defeated, and had to flee. So David was back in Jerusalem, back on his throne again. Absalom was a fugitive as was David. This was the man who stole his kingdom, publicly humiliated his wives to show that he took David's wives over for himself – public humiliation of his own father – stole the kingdom, went out to announce he would kill David if he could...cut him out of the city and sent his army, and would have slain him and his men if he could.

Now the battle turned against Absalom and he was turned out and he fled. What did David say? He knew he would have to pursue after Absalom. (II Samuel 18:5) And the king charged Joab and Abishai and Ittai...three generals...saying, "Deal gently for my sake with the young man Absalom," and all the people heard when the king gave the captain's charge. They were always moved by David's love. Well, Joab wouldn't do it. He again did the same thing. He heard that as Absalom fled on his donkey with his thick head of hair, he got caught in the tree. And there was Absalom left hanging in the tree and the news was brought back to Joab..."That's Absalom over there hanging in the tree." Joab took three darts and thrust them through him – killed him!

David was a great weeper. Wonderful thing to be able to weep, isn't it? Because this was a great man; this was no weak man. This was the mighty David, slayer of Goliath and the man of total victory...as we read, victory unto victory. He was a *mighty* soldier. He was the man who trained those thirty mighty men in the cave until they could do all sorts of exploits. This was a man strong in every physical military instance. He was no weakling. But he could weep, because his *true heart* was there.

In verse 33 of chapter 18, the king was much moved when he heard that Joab had killed Absalom… went up to the chamber over the gate and wept. As he went, he thus cried, "Oh, my son Absalom, my son, my son Absalom! Would God I had died for thee, O Absalom, my son!" Yes, Absalom had done his best to kill him. That's David! He lived to love people…to be for them, to save them…within the nation, because the day hadn't yet come when *all* men were to be saved. So we don't blame him because he wasn't meant to see outside, but within the nation. He would lay down his own life for them. In fact, Joab had to pull David up for his tears. Joab's end was a tough one himself because of the ways he behaved. In fact, Joab had to turn to him (verse 7, chapter 19) and say, "Oh, steady, steady, don't weep too much. In that thou lovest thy enemies and hatest thy friends." Twasn't true, of course, but David was so absorbed in mourning for his son.

One other very interesting instance of David…if I wouldn't say love now, I would say the equivalent of love…seeing God anyhow in your opponents. Great thing to be able to do that! This is the secret we're talking about – when you're in the *universal*…in the union…God's in everything, and it is God operating through your opponents as much as it is through your friends! This is where the harmony comes – when you see *God only* in every situation, and operating along with God in the situation!

And there was this curious instance of Shimei (II Samuel 16) who was a member of the house of Saul. Saul was his uncle or something like that. So he was of the house of Saul. So when David was in exile and was fleeing from Absalom…was outside the city with his men around him, might be captured and killed any moment…Shimei came out thinking the battle was almost over…and he was for Absalom against David, because David had replaced Saul. In verse 6, it says he cast stones at David and all the servants of King David and his mighty men. He said this to David…"Come out, come out, thou bloody man, thou man of Beliel. The Lord has returned upon thee all the blood of the house of Saul in whose stead thou hast reigned; and the Lord had delivered the kingdom into the hand of thy son Absalom. And behold, thou art taken in thy mischief because thou art a bloody man." That was said under the nose of David's generals, when David was in sight…as the factions always do.

So the generals, this time Abishai the brother, turned to him and said, "Why should this dead dog curse my Lord the King? Let me go over now and cut off his head." Anyone in the natural would see that. What did David say? This is a most remarkable outlook, insight. Verse 10, the King said, "What have I to do with you, ye sons of Zeruiah? So let him curse, because the Lord has said unto him, 'Let him curse David.' Who shall then say, why have you done so?" David said to Abishai and all his servants, "Behold, my son which came forth from my bowels seeketh my life; how much more may this Benjamite do it? Let him alone; let him curse, for the Lord hath bidden him. It may be the Lord will look upon my affliction, and requite me good this day for the cursing." That's a strong one!

If a person curses me, God bids him to do so, because God has a purpose – mercy for me maybe, and for him maybe. That's the true attitude we ought to have, isn't it? If a person opposes you, **God** tells him to. This is one of the great bases to this whole understanding of life, beginning with Job. *God determines evil people should do evil things, because He's going to bring a blessing through them.* God doesn't permit it, He *determines!* You see, David didn't say, God permitted Shimei. It says, He *told* Shimei; He *bade* Shimei to curse him. That's how far you take the *sovereignty* of God!

That's a great key to poised living. When the sovereignty of God is so total that – although God gives freedom and we operate through freedom when we do our devilish works, because in our *freedom* we do them – it is God bidding us to do them. He *purposes* we should be ourselves! If our freedom has taken that form, He *bids* us to have *that form* because that form comes into being. As we are people of faith He will turn it into some blessing. If we recognize it as coming from the hand of God...God doesn't retaliate on the same level of the person who curses us. God will turn it into some form of blessing. What this had done, anyhow, is send the blessing down the centuries, because many people have been helped to take wrong things from God by this incident with Shimei.

We won't spend much time on David and his conquests. He was the victorious kind. He is the one in the Israelite history who comes nearest to have the whole land promised to Abraham, from the river of Egypt to the Euphrates. He conquered all those nations...Syria, Ammon, Moag...and he acquired vast wealth from them. Victory, after victory, after victory! The list of victories stretches through the eighth chapter. Garrison after garrison he subdued until finally, it says, "David had rest from all his enemies roundabout." In those days they had their enemies outside them...always round about.

The most significant fact was that David always learned his dependence upon God, and constantly when he went to war, he first inquired of the Lord. *That* was his secret. He would inquire what the Lord said. When he first came back to Judah, Chapter 2:1, David inquired of the Lord, saying, "Shall I go up?" And the Lord said, "Go up." Then when he went to war, again and again it lists them. "Inquire of the Lord" meant – usually in those days the voice of the Lord came through the priest and the ephod. Some word would come to him through an inner way, "Should I do this or should I do that?" In Chapter 5:19 on one occasion he cried unto the Lord, saying, "Shall I go up against the Philistines?" And the Lord said, "Go." And he defeated them. A little later, a day or two afterwards, he came up again, and again it says in verse 23, David inquired of the Lord. Then this word came back, "Don't go up; wait. And when thou shalt hear the sound of a going in the tops of the mulberry trees, then go." In other words, you'll get some indication. In that case...I suppose the wind. You'll get some indication which will tell you the right moment to go; don't go until you get some further indication.

That's all we need to say about the conquests of David which were so total, but not the area which would be of chief interest to us.

David's main interest was the tabernacle, because a tabernacle was the Presence of God in the earthly nation. *We* are the tabernacle now. Now the temple is the Presence of God **in** His redeemed people. That's the earthly temple – the world temple. In those days it was that a tabernacle...had to be exceedingly magnificent, because it was represented in the heathen nations all the devotion they had to this *living* God. So it took these outer forms which are meaningless to us today, but were very meaningful to them in those very early elementary days of revelation. At that time the ark...which is the center where the mercy seat comes, and the tabernacle that was before the temple...had been seized by the Philistines and then had been taken from the Philistines' hands and was put in the house of Obed-Edom. They had sent it back because the Presence of the Ark had troubled the Philistines, and their own idol kept falling down when they had the ark where Dagon was. So they sent it back and it lodged in this house of Obed-Edom where God blessed them.

Now it was in David's heart to get the Ark back in the center of the nation, with a view to building the great temple. And his delight was there. David's delight was in God, in His fullness and His blessing... His purpose. David lived 'around' God. He didn't live to conquer enemies. He lived to get God...manifesting God to the people...pouring his wealth out on God. That was his way of doing it in those days. *Now*, of course, we do it by the relationship and love for each other.

So he proposed to the people that they should bring back the Ark from the house of Obed-Edom and leave it in Jerusalem. So he made a great pilgrimage. I Chronicles 13 gives the best talk about it. He said unto all the congregation..."Come with us. Let us take the Ark and bring it back from Kiriath-Jearim into the city"...which they set out to do. It was very necessary then, and in another way it is necessary today, that the rightful approaches to God should be preserved. Sinners cannot approach God except through atonement. They can't just walk in to God. That's the looseness of modern philosophy which tries to make out you can walk into the Presence of God by self-effort. No, you can't. Self effort is basic sin. Basic sin cannot relate to God *unless* there has been redemption – atonement.

So the Ark was always surrounded by the sacrifices and the Levites and the priests. Now on this occasion in his excitement and his simple love, he forgot about that. They were used just to knowing the Ark had no tent; I suppose it just had a house. It had nothing around it. He quite forgot all the surroundings that the Ark had in the days of the tabernacle, the sacrifices and the priests and the holiest of all, etc. So it didn't occur to him – just get it! And bring it in. So he did. And they provided a new cart and they put the Ark on the cart – the Levites, who were the right people to do that – and two men drove the cart, named Uzza and Ahio. Simple little thing, but as they passed a certain rough spot in the road, the cattle stumbled and the Ark was a little unsteady in the cart. Uzza put out his hand and touched it! He was struck dead at once!

At this distance a little thing like that may seem ridiculous. No, no, this was a solemn way. You could not approach the Ark of God like that. He is a *living* God in His holiness. He can only be approached if you become a holy people…and you can only become a holy people through the righteousness of Jesus Christ, and the blood of Christ. You can't approach God just like that! You can only approach God if you have been a saved, redeemed…a justified sinner, made saved by grace. So it was preserving in those days in the kind of way they did in those days, because death was often the way they preserved them – this stroke which killed them. Uzza had no business to touch that Ark because that's sin…that manner.

So those things mean far more than they appear on the surface. It shook David. David felt it pretty badly between him and God. There was something which caused him to fear God. You don't fear God *unless* you're in the wrong relationship. It says in verse 11, David was displeased, was afraid of God that day (verse 12). That meant that some way he had got a wrong concept, understanding the kind of Person God is. Of course the problem wasn't in God; it was in them, because they were moving into a relationship to God they had no right to have in those days, except through the proper atoning methods. Same as we – have not been saved unless we come through Jesus Christ!

When you are afraid of *God*, it doesn't mean there is something in God that makes you afraid; it means something *in you* that needs adjusting. It's in you that you find the answer, not in God. There is something there which is causing you to miss seeing God, because *God's got no fear about Him; He's got no judgment. God's only love.*

Fear comes…"I'm doing something that I shouldn't do, and therefore it makes it appear to me that God is up against me, when really *I* am up against God." There never is a single fear in God's sight, never! If there is any barrier between God and me, it is in me, not in Him…*never* on Him! Somewhere I am not in the believing relationship. Now it can be often, I'm just not believing when I should. I can be under false condemnation and under guilt and so on…not a very acceptable shadow. There's no such thing as a shadow if you're in God…except in our unbelief! All these days we've been saying the only way life is run is by inner consciousness. You're governed by your inner attitudes. If your inner attitude towards God is a fear, it means there is something which you have as a wrong belief of God. Instead of believing that God is perfect love, you've got something which is *causing* you to look as if God was frowning on you. The frown is *inside you* – if there is one. It may be just unbelief. Maybe you just don't take it; it's a lie! "There is therefore now no condemnation to those who are in Christ Jesus." (Ro 8:1) Don't take it! We can have false guilt, false condemnation. Don't take it! You're believing a lie of the existence of some guilt or sin which is under the atonement and you should believe the atonement. And then there is *nothing* between you and God, if that's the case.

Now in this case, there *was* this matter that needed adjustment. Very much so, because this is the nation; this is the king. This is no light thing! This was the Ark they sent for the worship of God in the nation. And David found out. David had a *humble* spirit...the man after God's own heart. And after being offended for three months – God gave him a little time to cool down. The Ark remained in the house of Obed-Edom, having moved from the other man. He heard how God blessed him – blessed the Ark in that house (I Chronicles 13: 14).

Now David recalled the people for a great celebration by which he would bring...the Ark would come back in its rightful way into the city. To do that he now put things right. In I Chronicles 15:2 David said, "No one is to carry the Ark of God, but the Levites for the Lord chose them to carry the Ark of God, and to minister unto Him." (The Levites were the consecrated people to do it.) A verse or two later, he came right out with his error. He was always open this way. Verse 13: "Because you did it not at the first, the Lord our God made a breach upon us (because he didn't go the right way about it), for that we sought Him not after the due order." He involved *himself* there; he didn't say "them". "*We* sought Him not after the due order." He had to learn to find the only way in which there could be a rightful approach made to the Presence of God.

So they brought the Ark back this way to the center of the city. There is one other little lovely touch – he abandonment of a free person...freedom of a free person...when you are God's person, and you are just living your free life, you act just *spontaneously as you like!* There is this beautiful touch, well known, when David was so thrilled to bring back the Presence of his God about whom his whole life was centered – this God with His purposes of love coming out through the ages. He was thrilled! He had just a linen shirt on him and he danced all the way into Jerusalem. He was king...with bare feet and linen coat, dancing away! That was too much for his respectable wife. So it says that Michal, his wife, despised him (II Samuel 6:20). Michal the daughter of Saul came out to meet David, and said, "How glorious was the king of Israel today, who uncovered himself in the eyes of the handmaids of his servants, as one of the vain fellows shamelessly uncovereth himself!" David couldn't get over that....there's *realms* of freedom! Bless them. Bless those who use the gifts of the Spirit. Bless those who speak in tongues, and those who dance. Bless those who use tambourines. Bless them, be free! This is burnt out in the world. Be free! Let people be free...if they want to dance, let them dance, sing and praise, which may be the expression of their love to others. It may not be so, OK...

I like David's answer: This time he said to Michal (v. 21), "It was before the Lord, which chose me before thy father and before all his house, to appoint me ruler over the people of the Lord, over Israel; therefore will I play before the Lord. And I will be yet more vile than this, and will be base in mine own sight. And of the maidservants which thou hast spoken of, of them shall I be had in honor." I like that..."I'll be worse and worse, I won't let you pull me off my abandonment to God."

Building the temple was never for David. This was followed by a beautiful interview with the prophet Nathan, into which we won't go at length. Nathan told David...he first of all encouraged David to build the temple. Then God spoke again to Nathan and sent him back to David and said, "No, I love *you*. You're the one I honor. I brought you up from the sheepfolds to honor you. But you've been a man of blood in your days and that isn't the best symbol for the person who'll build this temple. And so your son can build the temple. You can begin the reparations, but I want you to know this: I will build your house. You say you will build My house: I say I will build your house." Verse 11 of chapter 7 also says, "He will build thee an house." That's where God made His covenant that there would never cease to be a son on the throne of David forever. Of course, that is Jesus Christ!

David prayed a beautiful prayer of wonder and thanksgiving. "Thy kingdom and Thy house shall be established forever before thee," said the Lord. David said, "Why am I, O Lord God? And what is my house that Thou hast brought me hitherto? And this was yet a small thing in Thy sight, O Lord God; but Thou hast spoken also of Thy servant's house for a great while to come. And is this the manner of man, O Lord God? And what can David say more unto Thee, for Thou, Lord God, knowest Thy servant..."

The completion of David's life was his amassing of treasure...vast treasure...for the purpose of building the temple. David hadn't any heart for money except for God. We would use it in different ways today, but in those days the way in which God was glorified wasn't by sending the Gospel to the world. That day hadn't come. It was to raise up this tremendous temple which was to be a building to be known throughout that known world – beyond any other building in existence in magnificence, to symbolize the magnificence of the living God. That wasn't the kind of ways which would appeal to us, but that it isn't meant to do. But we can catch the devotion and David's statement concerning that devotion is in I Chronicles 22:5.

This was moving on toward his death now. In all these years he had amassed a fortune, amassed all this treasure from Edom and Moab. He didn't expend it on himself or the aggrandizement of the people – it was given to glorify God. It was the way in those days they glorified God. (As I say, we should be sensible and give it to the mission field, but it's a different age.) So in verse 5: David prepared abundantly before his death. As he spoke of what he had prepared, v. 14, "Now behold, in my trouble I have prepared for the house of the Lord an hundred thousand talents of gold, and a thousand talents of silver; and of brass and iron without weight; for it is in abundance; timber also and stone have I prepared..." Out of his own treasure he gave this.

So that was the heart and center of David's life. His heart was *set wholly* on God. On being the instrument of God to bring deliverance to his people, protection from his enemies, destroying the enemies around so that he had rest, and prosperity (bringing in the wealth he got from all these tribes whom they had conquered) and to center everything in the raising up of this witness – this testimony to the living God in the way it was done in those days by this magnificent temple. Wealth poured into it. God said, "You are not to do it yourself." You are to prepare your son for that, but you're to make all the preparations, amass it up so he can have the resources of every type to build this temple. I suppose there has never been a building like it!

That's all we need say about the life of David...except for his two slips. One, very famous, because it was the kind of slip we know a little about, was David's adultery. Now we will constantly have this trouble. You were bound to have it in the world because the world jumps on the kind of thing it does itself – what it would like to do if it could. So the world delights in making plays and so on about David and Bath-Sheba. That's not the point. That's a *minor* matter. We are to learn to keep minor things minor and major things major, and the *major* matter was his heart of gold, after God's own heart. He loved people, gave himself for people, put all his being into glorifying God in the way in which it was done in those days, by the building of this temple.

But he made a slip. There's a difference between a *slip* and a *life of sin*. Very great difference! A life of sin means you *purposely* live like that. David didn't purposely live like that. Let's get it quite clear. David made what we call a slip. We make slips too, don't we? Now we must remember again, you're dealing with a king, with autocratic power. He could kill a person when he liked. So death from that kind of thing wasn't the same to a king in those days as it would be to a member of this nation, for instance, today. You've got to keep these in *proportion*.

Now you know what happened. He gave room for the flesh, because it was a time when he should have been occupied in the warfare. As king he should have been out around the cities they were attacking at that time with Joab. Instead, he remained at home. Then he was attracted by Bath-Sheba and seduced her. Now one deceit leads to another, of course. He'd like to have concealed it. At first it was just attraction. A seduction, an adultery, is something quite different from a rightful relationship. David had many wives - wives were allowed in those days – that wasn't wrong. But to take some other person's wife, or to seduce a person who wasn't married, that was as much a sin as it is today. *That* was his sin.

Well, he hoped he could get off with it. Then he had the news that she was pregnant. *Now* what was he to do? Well, once you start in that course, you don't necessarily keep quit......but this is a man of God's own heart. This wasn't a man whose *whole life* was going to the devil, but he was *frightened!* He was a king. He was in a bad situation and he still follows his fears. He didn't follow his lusts now; he followed his fears. How could he avoid this complication? And it struck him. Why not get the husband home – Uriah – who was in the warfare...one of David's mighty men. He was among the thirty mighty men. Deceit is a terrible thing, but fear drives a man. Mind you, a king could do those kinds of things, because he could do far worse if he didn't. Remember he was a person who was always having mercy. David was always having mercy on people you and I would have slain, if we had been king. He was continually having mercy on lives; if we had been the king, we would have slain them. He didn't do it.

But this time he was caught, caught by the devil, the flesh, fear. So he got Uriah home and Uriah was a soldier. So he wouldn't do what David wanted. David thought he would go home for a day or two, and then he'd go back into the field and then they could say "the child was conceived by Uriah." Uriah wouldn't do it. He said, "I'm not here to run home here. I'm on the battle. If you sent for me, David, I'm your servant in battle, and so I stay by you. And I'll go back to the battle again." David even descended lower to make him drunk trying to get him to go home. He wouldn't go! So he went back to the battle.

Then David had to do that terrible thing. He had to send a private message to Joab, "put Uriah in the front of the battle with those who were attacking a certain city and they're sure to kill the first attackers. Let Uriah be among them." And so he was. Joab sent back the quiet secret message that they had been attacking this wall and there had been some casualties and among the casualties was Uriah the Hittite.

On a human level, although we may say certainly rightly too, David did act honorable towards Bath-Sheba. He didn't allow her to be publicly shamed so he took her and married her. Well, of course anybody would know what that meant anyhow, by the death of Uriah. But to a certain extent he covered her. If we are to understand how the grace of God doesn't judge by flesh, it judges by spirit. The point was, it wasn't the flesh of David, it was the spirit of David that mattered. Your flesh follows your spirit. Temporarily his flesh got him…temporarily. That wasn't where David's spirit was. And because David's spirit became right with God, it became God's way or purpose that Bath-Sheba would be the mother of Solomon! So the wife who had been taken in adultery became the mother of the successor to the throne and built the temple. That's like God because God judges by spirit! And the spirit of Saul was far more of a problem to God than the spirit of David.

That is seen, as we know, by the confrontation he had with Nathan (II Samuel 12). Certainly David, whether we should say he attempted to escape the guilt and hid it even then, I don't know, but he wasn't conscious of the enormity of the sin for a whole year. There was a year after this happened that Nathan was sent to David. Meanwhile, there had been the birth of the child who died. That was the time when David spent a week, a whole night in prayer, that God might preserve the life of this child who had been born in adultery…who was now of course the son of his wife. The child died. And that was the time when David rose up quietly. They couldn't understand this man of faith, and said, "Well, it's gone now. I held onto the Lord that the child might live; he didn't live, so here I am." And he made that beautiful statement with is a marvelous statement for the Old Testament: "He won't come back to me, but I will go to him." That's a *remarkable* statement in the Old Testament; they didn't understand what we do about eternal life. "He won't return to me but I will go to him." (II Samuel 12:23) "But now he is dead, wherefore shall I fast? Shall I bring him back again? I shall go to him but he shall not return to me."

Meanwhile, there came...before that actually, it wasn't a whole year...this challenge from Nathan, in the subtle form of that illustration which stirred David's indignation, and it made it possible to pinpoint him. That was the story of a rich man who had plenty of sheep and some friend came, and he was going to prepare a dinner out of his bosom and killed it for the feast of his friend. This made David so angry he said, "Let's know who that man is, we'll have him killed." "Thou art the man!"

Of course the wonder is, you see, David at once faced it. Now this was a king! Wouldn't take two seconds to kill Nathan! But David's *heart* was right. We may presume that he was under guilt all the time within, but it only came out publicly when he was challenged. So David says (v.13) "I have sinned against the Lord." And Nathan said unto David, "The Lord has also put away thy sin; thou shalt not die." But he would get certain consequences – that ultimately came out, as we said, in the rebellion of Absalom.

The blessing to the world has been the great Psalm of repentance. Tens of thousands have been blessed by this Psalm. So David turned his sin into a demonstration to the world of how a sinner gets right with God. But not regarding it as if David was a *sinner* in that sense. He had slipped into *a* sin, and the sin was put about before God. Psalm 51, we know it, where it says, "Against Thee and Thee only have I sinned and done this iniquity that Thou mayest be justified..." because if you sin against a person, of course, he is a God-person. You're sinning against God, because *every person* is really a form of God. So if you're sinning against a person, you're sinning against God! "Against Thee, Thee only, have I sinned and done this evil in Thy sight." And he pours his heart out, seeking cleansing, "Purge me, wash me, and I shall be whiter than snow; Make me hear joy and gladness; Hide Thy face from my sins; Blot out my iniquities; Create in me a clean heart, O God, renew a right spirit within me; Take not Thy Holy Spirit from me; Restore unto me the joy of Thy salvation; Uphold me with Thy free spirit." Those are prayers!

David found the *secret* of forgiveness in the *inner* life. That's why he had to break through again and found what the people usually didn't know. They knew whatever forgiveness there was to be found in the outer sacrifices. But David got this great light. Through his great sin, he got *great light*. Forgiveness is found by a right heart adjustment to God. And so at the end of the Psalm he said, "For Thou desirest not sacrifice, else would I give it. Thou delightest not in burnt offering. The sacrifices of God are a broken spirit. A broken and contrite heart, O God, thou wilt not despise."

Where the spirit within and the heart within is broken from its guilt, and admits its guilt and brings its guilt to God, it's no longer there! Don't need any outer sacrifice because the sacrifice has *already been completed*. So David in that verse had a glimpse of the fact that the sin was blotted out, the Spirit was restored to him and he could continue in his life with God. What is essential is in the inner attitude because we live on that level.

The other sin, we needn't spend any more time on it really, was the sin of numbering the people, which was a form of pride which he shouldn't take. He insisted, toward the end, that the people should be numbered. Always God uses repentance for some further light. So out of this sin of David He brought the light of this great confession, and the way by which confession is made real by the broken heart and broken spirit based on the originally broken body of Christ. In the numbering of the people, he had certain judgments brought to him because he did this wrong thing. He chose the judgment of some temporary plague rather than being put in the hands of outside enemies. As the plague progressed, David stood in the midst before God, by the threshing floor of a person, in the middle of Jerusalem, Ornan's threshing floor. There he had a vision of this angel of wrath and he pleaded with God, "*I* am the sinner. Let this come on me and my house, not on the people." God's hand was stayed, and the plague was stayed. The slaughter was stayed...at this Ornan's threshing floor. This became the sacred place for David then. He said, "Let this be the place where we plant the ark of God." That's the center of the temple. That's the rock that is claimed to be holy by the Moslems in the center of Jerusalem. So this became the center of the temple worship. Again, what had become the sin was used to bring the provision of the place of the temple to be built.

So we end David's life with him many songs of praises, glorious outpouring of those psalms and quotes of his Psalms and praises toward the end of his life when he passed the throne on to Solomon. That may be a main lesson for us to learn from David's life – to see a thing as God sees it in His wholeness – seeing this man as God's precious, precious servant, through whom He was magnified more than by any other in the history of Israel.

ELIJAH

We'll turn our attention now to that great man of history who is
Elijah. All true history is spiritual history – God's history; the
rest is nothingness. Elijah has been picked out as a standard man, a
human manifestation of God speaking and operating in a man.

We're introduced straight to him in I Kings 17, verse 1, "Elijah,
the Tishbite, who was of the inhabitants of Gilead, said unto Ahab,
'As the Lord God of Israel liveth, before whom I stand, there shall
not be dew nor rain these years but according to my word.'" No prior
introduction. It is obvious that this was a man already in permanent
relationship with the Living God because he said, "As the Lord God
liveth before whom I stand." Not stood, or will stand, but stand – a
permanent condition. In New Testament language, we call this union
consciousness. His permanent dwelling place is standing in the presence of, and in union and communion with the Living God.

Now that's a real person. In that relationship we understand that
we are the agent, the human means through which God is working
out some of His purposes of grace and power in the world. We realize
that the conditions of our lives are God pressing us to be concerned
about certain things. So we are not caught in self concern, but in God's
concerns for the world which He has come to redeem and restore to
Himself. Our concern then is to move out to that part of the world,
which is not in this living relationship.

Now Elijah, living off on the other side of Jordan in Gilead, had a
deepening concern about the apostasy of Israel. Under the leadership

of Jezebel and Ahab Israel had turned into an idol-worshipping 'center', a Baal 'center', instead of a Living God 'center'. At that point, Elijah had linked his concern to God's concern. That's what life is – being linked to a concern. We are not really linked with other concerns while we're self-concerned. Since Elijah was standing in the relationship where it is God expressed in Elijah form, he was concerned in God's love-concern, which is redemption of all men. When we are in the relaxed, living, conscious relationship of union with God, what is concerning us is this or that situation is God's concern...for He has put us there and has caused us to be concerned. It may start only in our own family concern, though God always moves us beyond our families. We are concerned people because we are God union-people and therefore God's love concerns are our love concerns because His and our love are one. The only true life is in God-union because the only Person in the universe is God. Therefore, God's purpose is to bring all men into God-union.

God's concern was to show Israel they were off beam and His agent was Elijah. When we are off beam, God's wrath shows us. This isn't something God imposes from outside but is really God putting us in the condition in which we see that we've got it all wrong. Elijah was led to use the external form (God does this today, although He operates more on the internal forms than the external) so that this would be a means by which the people would know that there was something wrong in their national relationship. They were supposed to be God's people. He was the Lord God of Israel. Although here and there people had found the universal truths, He didn't become a universal God until after Jesus and Pentecost. In God's eyes, there is one nation, God's nation, not an American nation, or a British nation. We are gradually moving into that now, but in the days of Elijah, it wasn't that way. There was a nation of Israel because God's purposes had not yet come out in the physical manifestation of Himself and His Son.

Somewhere Elijah got the idea that God would show Israel the dried up conditions of its spiritual life through a drought in the land. God seldom uses that method today because He has inner and better ways to show us our dried up life than through outer circumstances.

We don't know much else about Elijah except what was said of him, that "he is a hairy man, with a girdle of leather about his loins." John, the Baptist was called Elijah presumably because he was the same type. Both had the same special ways of living in the desert, in the presence of God.

The final point in the introduction was that he was settled in his inner consciousness that this was what God would do. *Faith is inner knowing.* It's *inner being in relationship to inner fact.* The saving faith is, "That's it! Jesus is my Saviour." It isn't that I trusted Jesus, which might be the first human step in that direction, but the ultimate is that He whom I trusted is He who conveyed Himself to me. Faith is knowledge. Faith is a certainty – a settled thing. The only genuine faith is that it's a settled thing. Now this was a settled thing with Elijah before he went into the presence of Ahab. This lonely man was going to come up and confront an idolatrous back-slidden nation alone, so he had to know exactly what he was going to say and, why he said it and be quite certain about it. That's faith!

With this as the background, Elijah came into the presence of the king and stated as fact what was inner fact to him. He stood before Ahab and made it quite plain of Whom he was the voice. "As the Lord, God of Israel liveth." He was talking of a living Person. This self-centered life with all its operations is only death. "The Lord, God of Israel liveth, before whom I stand." What real standing means is that *our spirit stands with God.* There is no fussing about or saying, "I believe." He just simply said, "There shall not be dew nor rain but according to my word." That's pretty strong stuff...no dew or rain.

Now here's a man who knows he is identified, knows he's God, and speaks as God. **We are God in human form; we speak as God.** So I am speaking the word and it's *His* word, but I am saying it's my word. This is the union which we are talking about when we talk **as God**, because we are forms of God. So here Elijah says that this is "according to my word." This is a new quality of holy boldness which leaves behind saying, "Oh, I'm so weak, I'm so poor." I'm strong because my weakness has been joined up to God's strength and we're one! *The human is speaking as the Deity in human form.* This is a magnificent presentation to us of the full power of a mature faith, which is the faith of God spoken through the faith of man.

Self-concern had disappeared even to the limit of his own human safety because Ahab would try to get Elijah if it did or even if it didn't, come off. Faith has no more interest in itself, only God's interests, and then what happens to us is our glory...even if it is physical death. We see here a very wonderful presentation of a complete and mature operation of faith on its spiritual basis, practical enough to follow. When we take this stand we never say, "What if it doesn't happen?" Faith is, "It **has** happened," even if you don't *see* it happen. Faith is affirming the fact that the universe is Father, Son, and Spirit and we are part of Him in this great form of body. These are passing temporary expressions, not the facts, but forms of the fact.

So we begin to live in this **new dimension**...*but in our humanity, we remain ordinary, simple people leading ordinary lives as God expresses Himself by us in normal human ways.*

When Elijah confronted Ahab, he did so as the Living God expressing himself in authority. When he left the king's presence, he left as a perfectly natural human and God told him to go away and hide himself. My friend, Rees Howells, used to say, "I'm a perfectly natural man except when the Holy Ghost comes on me." By that, he meant that he was always in union with the Holy Ghost and that part was just free, fun, working and living his normal life, experiencing God's supply and provisions in a normal way. Then there were those special times, which came to all of us when God expressed Himself by him in a very special way.

When Elijah got the word to go away to the Brook Cherith and depend on it for all his needs, he knew it was guidance and he had to go. God told him that He would supply his material needs by visible and invisible means. We live by both and both are from God. The visible means was the brook; the invisible was the ravens. The invisible is what is always exciting and we say, "Oh, look what God has sent!" Or, "Look at what's turned up!" The visible is what ordinarily is coming to you, maybe your salary or your job. But you're not living on a salary or a job; you are living on God's stream. That's God's stream until it dries up. Then we begin to see that what we thought was just an ordinary way of life, ordinary securities and so on, was not the supply but the means of supply. The river is just the means of supply. God is the supply. There is a test here and when we are really free we say, "OK, this is the river-form so I'll drink it. If it dries up, it's still OK because God is going to turn up some other way." So there are both the invisible supplies which come along here and there and are such thrills to us and visible supplies.

So the word of the Lord came to Elijah that he was to go out beyond Israel to a non-Israelite woman of Zarepth in Sidon. The Old Testament has interesting little flashes showing that God is the God of the whole world family. It was a human move for human safety. He was to leave Israel – a human means to keep him out of the reach of Ahab, who in the desperation of his rage was trying to find this destructive prophet. God said, "I have commanded a widow woman there to sustain you." I've commanded it! So again, he started out saying, "OK, it's coming; God's got it. It's coming in this way." He always operated in inner certainty. It will come this way. That's a certainty. Exactly how it will work out, we'll wait and see. So it's a combination of inner certainty and outer liberty in how you operate. You operate freely but behind the freedom is the certainty that it's coming through. You don't know the exact detail, but you move and you venture step by step and behind it all is this certainty, the inner knowing.

So he went to Zeraphath. When he came to the gate of the city, a widow was there gathering sticks. A single woman out at the gate gathering sticks was probably somehow an indication for him that this was the one. This is similar to the time that Jesus told his disciples to go and prepare the feast and they would see a man carrying a pitcher of water. Elijah called to her to "fetch me some water in a vessel so that I may drink," possibly testing her to see if she would do it for him, and then added, "Bring me a bit of bread in your hand, will you?" That brought out something - now we're getting down to the facts of life.

Her response to Elijah, "As the Lord thy God liveth," was a clear indication to him that she knew who Elijah was; a affirming that there was a link of faith and she knew that there was a living God. She was a woman rather like Rehab, who also had this faith. If Elijah could say to her later, "You're to give me food until the Lord sends the rain," then we know she knew.

However, He wasn't her God yet in a deep relational sense because she replied, "Oh, I can't do that. I've just come out to gather a few sticks to make one last meal, and afterward we die."

Then Elijah added this to her, "If you will go and do what I tell you and make a little cake first and bring it to me, then afterwards there will be some for you and your son. The Lord God of Israel said for me to say to you, 'A barrel of meal will not waste, the cruse of oil will not fail until that day when the Lord sends rain upon the earth.'"

With that, her faith came. I'm sure she knew because you don't move out into faith like that unless you're prepared spiritually. The likelihood was that she had an inner sense in her that this was the prophet of God and if he said that this was God's word, then this could be relied upon. She took her step of faith and did what Elijah said. They ate many days and the amount of food and oil did not change, according to the word Elijah had given.

Now though she had a living faith, it was an external faith, which was not unified yet because she couldn't operate like Elijah could – as God doing it for her and by her. That wasn't God's purpose. God has to bring us to an end of that divided self which grabs us and prevents us from seeing a God-interpretation. It results from the fall where we began seeing good and evil. When you're in God there is only one power. Satan's power is only God's power. It's God because there is only one Power in the universe. Satan is a form of God's power. Satan goes the wrong way to show God's power. The difference is that God has a purpose in love behind Him. If He can't change Satan, He'll use him anyhow. So every time that God's love comes through, that's union.

We don't see evil, we only see one Person! One Power, One Grace, One Light and Love through everything and everybody. That's union! But we can't have the union until the last holds of self have been exposed and we've seen them where they belong, cut off in the Cross of Christ. But we have to see them before we see them cut off.

So here was God having an incidental work of grace through Elijah in his private life in getting this woman into this God-union life. It had to come about through something which would bring her to the point of seeing her desperate self-concern and the desperation hung on all that she had – her son. Suddenly, he fell sick and was apparently dying. Now that roused up in her an area in which she didn't yet know, as we would say, a total crucifixion with Christ in a union with Him. There was an undelivered area which was blocking her, hidden away...apparently some sin. Perhaps it was something in her life, which she knew had been a sin, and was like a guilt between her and God so she had a guilty faith. I'm not talking about her like we talk about a lost person, but as if she was a redeemed person in which there is some blockage in her life – something which she hasn't made totally clear and is trying to run away from. It had to come out so she said, "What have I to do with you, oh, man of God? You've come to call my sins to remembrance." She didn't accuse and it's interesting how real she was. She was on the right track. She wasn't blaming God or blaming Elijah, for she was saying, "I know I am to blame, but why must you have brought this up, this hidden thing I have tried to escape."

God has to have ways of demonstrating Himself and His faithfulness. When we are on the level of KNOWING God, we have no need of demonstrations such as miracles, public prayer, or the like. Jesus had to perform miracles because He needed to demonstrate that He was the Son of God, the Messiah, but the real miracle today is God living and expressing Himself through human forms. Because Elijah had no way in which he could show this woman that God loved her, such as we might through scripture or experiences. He moved in to get the child healed. He took him up to the loft and started with a negative. "Oh, Lord, hast thou brought evil on this woman? Surely, that's not so." Now Elijah started negatively, but that's not wrong because a positive must have a negative to push it into focus, to bring it into manifestation. You could not see light unless there was darkness to be swallowed up. It wouldn't show. It has to swallow up dark to make light. That's the only way.

So he stretched himself but on the lifeless form of the child and said, "Oh God, I pray, now let this child's soul come back." What he meant was that the child was going to come back, of course. This was again moving in from a little touch of the negative into the positive confidence that God was doing this thing. The Lord heard Elijah and he brought back the child.

This really got the woman's attention and she said, "Now, by this I know that thou art a man of God and the word of the Lord in thy mouth is truth." Now she was there, because it wasn't Elijah, it was the word she saw. The sin business was no longer there and she could say, "He's my God now. This word is true to me and I can now operate as one with the Person who is All in all. It is He and I together, and He by me."

So right in the hidden life of Elijah, the natural life, there comes out the natural source of supplies whether by the irregular or by the regular brook way. The redeeming grace of God goes out to the individual as this woman is brought into what we call the *fullness of life in union with God.*

After three years, the word of the Lord came to Elijah and said, "Go show yourself to Ahab and I will send rain upon the earth." You can see here that what lies behind our word is God's word, for Elijah had said to Ahab, "According to **my** word there will be neither rain nor dew." One thing the flesh can never take is to see us talking as if we know *everything* is God. They don't know that we live with a wink. It isn't we; it's He! So in the hidden private life God had indicated to Elijah that there wouldn't be dew nor rain and there hadn't been. Now there would be rain! And so he went to show himself to Ahab.

I like to watch the inner strength of people when they know where they are going. The word of the Lord just comes. It may not even appear to be the word of the Lord, but just be something that comes to us. Don't be afraid of yourself. If you're in union life, you are the way by which God is thinking, speaking, and acting, so don't be afraid of your thinking, speaking, and acting. If it's a big thing you can wait until you are sure, but the point is to operate from an assured situation. We can cut the maybes out of our lives when we realize that we act **as God***. Our will is God's will, for it is God working in me to will and to do of His good pleasure. Therefore, He expresses His will through my will.* So when it became clear to Elijah that this was what God said to do, he did it!

Because the country was in desperate condition, Ahab had gone to great extremes to try to find out where there was water. He sent to every nation to try to find Elijah, this man who was troubling them. Ahab had a prime minister named Obadiah who greatly feared the Lord. He sent Obadiah in one direction while he went in another in their search for water.

Elijah met Obadiah and Obadiah recognized Elijah. When Elijah told Obadiah to tell Ahab that now there would be rain, Obadiah became terrified for his own life and said, "I won't do that, for I know you are a man of the spirit and if I go tell Ahab, the Spirit of God may take you elsewhere and you may be sure that Ahab in his rage will kill me if I tell him you're here, and then you disappear." Then in defence of himself, "Haven't you heard, Elijah, that when, Jezebel was slaughtering the prophets of the Lord, I hid them by fifties in the cave and fed them bread and water?" That took some doing...fifty men in two batches, maybe one after the other, hidden in a cave and fed. So

Obadiah was not with the Jezebel party; he was with God and identified himself with God.

There are two sorts of man, redeemed and unredeemed. The redeemed person can wobble, but because he is redeemed, he'll come back to his redemption...to who he is in Christ. The unredeemed person may wobble and listen to the word, but he'll go back to his unredemption which is the devil. The redeemed person may have Christ and yet not have found his union, but because he *is* Christ's he will come back to Christ. Now that was Obadiah. Obadiah was on God's side, but because he didn't know union as Elijah did, he became frightened. Ahab, on the other hand, would listen and Elijah could talk to him, but because he belonged to the devil, he would always go back to the devil. Jezebel was a fixed devil and Elijah never spoke to Jezebel, except to tell her what was coming to her.

Elijah became frightened later and ran for his life, but there was a difference in his fear and Obadiah's. Elijah moved slightly for a time, through his flesh fears, but because he knew union, he knew when to come back to where he belonged. Obadiah didn't know union so Elijah was unable to have fellowship with him because you can't have true fellowship with those who don't know the One who **is** reality. Obadiah was caught up in self-fear and didn't know how to move over into where Elijah was. Because Elijah was doing God's will, he could walk into the very presence of Ahab and not be concerned about what happened to him. Obadiah was a godly man, but he was one of those who identify outwardly with Christ and are used of God and do his works, but never actually find Him. So we don't hear of Obadiah anymore, but we bless God for men like Obadiah. He meant something to God because God said, "I have seven thousand who have not bowed the knee to Baal."

Someone may say, "Well, I don't know whether or not I'd be like Obadiah. Maybe I would be afraid, maybe I wouldn't go all the way." Don't say that!

Say, "God, I'm yours. *You* make me go all the way. If in my humanity, my temptation level, my soul level, I don't know if I would, that's all right because I'm saying You'll get this through." Stand on the faith. Don't try and get yourself right, don't examine yourself. Say, "God, I'm yours. That's settled. You grabbed me. You moved me into your crucifixion, resurrection, and ascension. In with You there, and now it's up to You to keep me there! If I need a little widow dealing with, give me some widow dealings...that's all." So don't remain in condemnation, don't remain in question. Move into who you are. You are not you. You are joined to Him and He is in you, and you're in Him crucified, risen and ascended and He is expressed by you! Stay there and leave Him to inhabit any area in which something needs to be settled and can only improve you. It can settle you a little more in who you are, that's all. A little more recognizing it's He, not you! When we read these things such as about Obadiah, don't let us run into condemnation or conviction. The Lord is showing us things!

Now Elijah moved into what God had planned. He had had plenty of time at the Brook Cherith and at the widow's house to make plans and, of course, *his plan and God's were one and the same,* because he was in union with God. The plan was that there would be a public show, which would be a demonstration of the destruction of the self life. By self-life I mean the life we operate as though we were fighting the battle by our independent selves and don't know union. God was going to come in a destructive way, by burning fire. That was what happened at Calvary.

When he met Ahab, Ahab said what flesh always says, "You troubler." God bless you if you are a troubler! If you are not a troubler, you haven't gotten very far yet. Notice that the widow didn't say, "Elijah, you troubled me when my son was sick." Instead, she said, "I am troubled about my sin." She had come through, for unredeemed flesh doesn't see sin in itself, it says, "You are the troubler with your salvation witness and the change you've brought into our whole life because you are now God's person." This kind of thing will happen. You will be a troubler. There is no liberation without offense, and that is the offense of the Cross. That's what human Jesus wept over. There had to be those who could not take it and He longed to take them up like chickens under the mother hen's wing, but they wouldn't come. This is a good thing for us to remember. If your life is God by you, you are a troubler!

There may be someone who seems impossible. It's really the first sign of grace in them because grace has to start negatively. Through their opposition to you, their misery, wrongness, and darkness, they are being prepared for the light. So, for you to be an offense to them is to be a blessing to them, though, of course, they won't feel like it.

In this case, Elijah was straight with Ahab. He said, "I'm not the trouble, it is you who have done it." There is nothing that is trouble on the outside. It is only the way we *react* to our troubles that is the problem.

After saying that to Ahab, Elijah, said, "Let's prepare a plan. Get all the people and all eight hundred of the prophets of Baal together." There was in Elijah this sense of authority, and we do carry authority. That's how our word gets home! They said of Jesus that he talked as one having authority, not as the scribes. This type of authority made an impression on Ahab!

Again, I say, Ahab was 'appealable to'. The difference between Ahab and Jezebel was that Elijah couldn't bargain with Jezebel. She sent a message to Elijah, saying, "You'll be dead in a day." But Ahab didn't talk like that and so he could hear that voice.

All through scripture people like Felix, like Agrippa, almost said, "I'd like to be a Christian." Felix, when he said, "I would like to hear more of this another time." There were those who were appealable to, but they are on the wrong side. And so the power of darkness has a hold of them. Self-centered self has a hold; they swing back there unless, of course, they are prepared to take the steps of faith. They see right and wrong, but because they haven't moved over and received Christ and Christ received them, they can't get right. There are others who see right and wrong, but although they don't realize union they're right because they know Christ, so they move back to where they belong. Ahab was the first type and died. The Bible tells in very strong terms that Ahab was more wicked than the other kings before him. Ahab's wickedness was weak wickedness; Jezebel's wickedness was strong. Therefore, Ahab would listen to what Elijah said and could see that this was something, which had come from God.

Now we come to one of the most famous stories of Bible history - the one about the fire of God burning up the sacrifice with the water poured over it. When Ahab had gotten the people and the priests together, Elijah told them, "Don't hesitate between two opinions. If the Lord is God, follow Him. If Baal, then follow him." He proposed that they should have this test. The prophets of Baal were to make an altar, prepare a sacrifice, and Elijah would do the same. Then each would call upon their God and the one who answered by fire, he would be God. And all the people agreed to this.

That is the kind of incident which has tremendous drama. It's beyond our present experience and so to that extent, on a historical level, it doesn't touch us because we don't see that sort of thing happening today. That's because God isn't really interested in the external. He's interested in the internal. He's interested in people being for people in love...God expressing His love by us. These outer forms may help you or may not help you. There's no evidence that this interlude of fire really changed this group, although doubtless there must have been some who changed and there already were seven thousand, but Israel as a whole went on into idolatry. The kings that followed Ahab were just as evil as Ahab and there's no evidence that Israel turned back to the Living God.

The fire of Pentecost is something different. When the Holy Ghost comes at Pentecost there's an inner change, not an outer change, and the whole world knows that we are changed people. The outer doesn't do the work although it may be preparation for an inner relationship. It wasn't a preparation in Ahab for although he humbled himself for self-interest, he didn't change. Thank God, in many cases the outer is preparation and people do move into a relationship with God, like the widow did.

The interpretation that has meaning for the present day is that self-effort can't get us there. These priests cried all day, cut themselves with knives and bled, and ran and jumped around. Self can't change self and Baal was a symbol of dead self, of course, and no god. They were worshipping themselves and Baal was the expression of what they were.

Some of these newer things that we have today, as psychology and transcendental meditation are merely self trying to change self. They can't help. There is a psychology that is preached with Christ here and there that can help and there are, here and there, psychiatrists who will bring people to Christ, but on the whole all this is a mass of human self effort. We have it in politics where the government promises to do good for all, but we know it won't work. Only a remedy that brings people to Christ is a true remedy! Self only brings up further self in manifestations of hates, problems, differences, battles and so on. The lesson we get from the priests of Baal is that self can't deliver.

The fire came from God. The fire from God to us is Jesus Christ. He came as the Son of God and His death was the fire in which we are cut off from these things that lure us in the ways of the flesh. So we become dead to sin and dead in Christ to ourselves and dead to those things which drove us into all these kind of Baal things. He burns up whatever form of self there is as an offering to Him. That fire fell on the Son in our behalf in His crucifixion and therefore to us as a thing that **has** been done!

We must put this incident of the fire falling on the altar back in human terms because I don't think we get much by just seeing it historically. I want to live in the present day and I don't think it will do much good talking about something which isn't happening today. I don't think I want that kind of demonstration. It is outer and at best only babyhood. That's why Jesus said you are to do greater works. Until He had been through the process of atonement and resurrection and the Spirit came, He couldn't introduce them to the inner life. A few knew it, as the disciples, but there was no public way in which this could be, so He had to demonstrate Himself outwardly to them. But we are to do greater works. The revelation of God in Christ is not an outer revelation. It does not come just by outer miracles, outer things. It was the only way He could come at that time because the whole inner life, as Paul said, "the mystery hidden from generations now made manifest, Christ in you," wasn't available in a total universal sense until Christ had come and taken our place and been made sin, and the Spirit came to confirm. **Then** we could move into the inner way! I want to stress that outer forms - miracles, rituals – can't do a thing for us *unless* they happen to be a stepping stone to the inner. One leper out of ten found it and there are those who have found it this way, but most didn't.

In the days of the Old Covenant and on into Pentecost, which includes the days of Jesus, God could only speak, on the whole, by outer symbols The day of the inner consciousness of what we speak of as the inner union of God and us – Spirit with spirit – was not established in a universal sense until after Pentecost. It was just here and there that folks were coming into the inner relationship as Elijah himself had. All through history, there were these outer manifestations, which would demonstrate to them that God is the Living God...as Jesus did by His outer miracles and healings.

The whole emphasis is changed over today to the outgrowth of the body of Christ where the relationship is to be the inner one and the manifestation of God is by His people expressing Him and His love nature. By the outer challenge of the sacrifices, which were offered by the priests of Baal and himself in the presence of all the people, Elijah was demonstrating for all to see, the helplessness of self to deliver self. Baal was only a form of self-image made by man and because self can't demonstrate its power to overcome self, they cried in vain.

Elijah showed them that the only way in which there could be true deliverance for man was by a manifestation of the power of God, which was by the fire eating up the sacrifice.

If actual happenings of this kind occurred today, they would take the same form as Satan's temptations of Jesus. "If you would jump off the temple, everybody would worship you with awe and fear," not because they wanted to know Him as He is, and to be identified with Him, but merely as some outer symbol which self can cling to, yet remain a self. Jesus came to show us God...and what God was like. He walked this earth as a common man. He drew the nation's attention to Himself by His miracles because the only way at that time that the truth could come was in outer form. But His total aim always was that they should believe on Him as they saw the kind of Person He was, because that is the kind of Person which God is – a Person who is motivated by love.

He was always saying, "**Believe** *on Me*", but only a few could see what He meant. When He fed the five thousand they crowded around Him to make Him king because they wanted more bread. They were interested in that which fed their fallen selves, in the outer self. He said, "This is the work of God, that you believe on Me." Only a few could see that He who walked the countryside of Palestine with nothing but healing, serving love had *no other interest* than that people should understand that this is what God is — a God of saving, fulfilling love. Only those who could see something wrong with self-loving itself could see it. They could begin to catch that this Person was a different kind of Person.

Of course, that destroyed Him, because it exposed their religion as self-loving self. The temple and so on was to elevate themselves as self-sufficient selves. That was because of the fall. Except in rare cases, miracles only created interest. There must have been some interest all the way through because the first three thousand who came after Pentecost undoubtedly came because of interest in what they had seen and heard of Jesus. Masses were interested and came to hear, but only a few followed. He hadn't any interest in healings except out of compassion which was expressed as an outer means of showing that God is love.

Breaking through the rituals, which were only the self-loving forms of religion, He deliberately healed on the Sabbath. He said that man isn't made for the Sabbath, the Sabbath is made for man to be used by man, and "If I can use the Sabbath to heal a man, I'll heal him." This enraged those who had made religion into a form of self-idolatry. "This is *our* religion – our Sabbath, our rituals, our temple," they said. This is subtlety. This is the form of the subtlety of the human self.

Jesus, who is the *final purpose* of the existence of the children of Israel, came to reveal the only true meaning of being a person – which is to be a person who has found what he was created to be a person in conscious union with The Person who is the expression of love and nothing else, Who lives to fulfil and perfect His universe. Our only motivation is to be a person whose being is for others, each for the other in the outer perfection in which we now operate in the body of Christ.

That is a total revolution and it destroys the emphasis on the outer so that in II Corinthians, we find Paul went all the way saying, "I don't know any man after the flesh. I don't even know Christ after the flesh. I'm not interested in the historic Christ." That was a very strong thing for him to say! He was saying he was not interested in any Christ who had outer form. He was only interested in the Person who is **the** Person with whom he had died and is now risen. *Paul knew that he existed only that the world might find that the only true life is one in union with Christ so that all self would be an expression of His Self.* The outer doesn't matter. To some extent, I forget people to whom God has spoken through me. I'm only interested in the fact that these are people who are Christ in human form, who in interaction and love and the moving out are the reconciling vessel for other people to find what we have.

The fire was only to show that there has to be something which is death to the old adulterous self, and the way in which he presented it to them produced the same kind of awe, fear, and wonder which would have happened if Jesus had jumped from the temple. They called out, "The Lord, He is God" and they meant it! Maybe some did find something, some step of faith, some restoration to the Living God, because there turned out to be seven thousand all the time who had never given in to the apostasy. However, it didn't turn the nation because nations can't be turned.

There *can't be* a Christian nation because it is *people*, not nations, who can be expressions of Christ because Christ died and rose for people. What we have is a world nation. That's the inner nation which we recognize as a holy nation. You don't recognize it as American nation, or a British nation, or the African nation, or the Indian nation, or anything else, we're only one nation. We must get out of our whole sense of nationhood. We may have certain local loyalties, but don't make too much of them. Be thankful for mercies we get for being in countries where there is something of a Christian morality, a Christian influence in which by the law of harvest you get and you reap what you sow...and so as this nation to some extent works on Christian principals and cares for the world there is a flow back to her of blessings, but that's not what really interests us! We're not interested in what the outer condition or language, or custom or color or anything else is. The new nation, which we don't know in the flesh, of which by God's grace we are a part, is what we are interested in and that can't be in a nation on a national level. So we hope and expect that many thousands did come back in their faith, at least in the external form, to what we call saving faith in the Living God, the God of Israel.

That was symbolized by the rain because the rain was to demonstrate that God was full of love and grace and full completion...not the god of fire. The fire is something, which God burns in, and it is quenched by being burned in Jesus. James says, "Your tongue is a fire, the fire of hell," the hellish, hating, fearing, selfish self which is our self. That's why Jesus came and was made sin and quenched that fire. The slaying of the priests symbolizes the final destruction of evil in our lives. It's replaced and the rain symbolizes the replacement in our lives by the God of endless perfection, completion, fullness, and love. The replaced life comes at the second dedication, and is a life which is really God living *His* life by us. It is a purposeful life.

Elijah said to Ahab, "Get up and eat, and drink, for there is the sound of the abundance of rain." The difference between the two was that one life was motivated by what satisfies the flesh; the other was motivated by what satisfies the spirit. This is this total life! Thank God, that's what we mean when we talk about union life. We move naturally in certain human conditions just as we enjoy certain things. We enjoy a meal, we enjoy everything, but that is only a detail. It's sort of a beautiful circumference to life. There's a drive, a purpose, a set purpose. Not just to eat and drink...but the abundance of rain! *Christ* is the abundance! We can't have more. Christ is the abundance in us, Christ is the abundance which flows out of us like a river. This is our set purpose.

I don't believe a person ever understands any other life. I really don't know of a life since Jesus saved me in 1914. He came in just a simple way and saved me from hell. I've never really had any other motive in life since. This has been my one drive, whether in my army days, college days, missionary days, or these days. You see God is a **total** Person. And this is our one basic truth, our one basic interest. **That** is what Elijah knew. There's a symbolic way in which we're hairy men girt about with girdles of skins. There is something in us which underneath isn't interested in things of time and space. We *can't* go along with Ahab in substituting eating and drinking for this. We enjoy eating and drinking, but we give very little attention to it. Our purpose is that Christ may become the **true** Christ...which He is when He is in human form, and when each person becomes Christ in human form and they are part of the same love motivation! It ought to be that the whole universe is loving each other — even the animal world with the lion laying down with the lamb, and so on. It's a different type of world we are going into.

So if God's got you, there is only one purpose – people! When all you are seeing is one wonderful Person and everything we see is an expression of God, then, everything is God's beauty. There's only one way of seeing; you see everything in one thrilling, wonderful Person! The whole universe is interpreted in its infinite expression of giving love. This occupies us and then through it we are part of that. That's what we are – **love**. We are He in giving love. His motivation has got us somehow. You can't give what you haven't got; you can only give what you have got.

What happens is that you become a total person, a *satisfied* person. This isn't a life in which you go hungry. It is a different kind of hunger for it's the hunger of adventure into going on for more, such as a great scientist who, knowing about the fission of an atom, wants to know what the fusion of the atom is, and all that sort of thing. That's the excitement to know a little more about how things work, like laser beams or something. That's not hunger...it's excitement for enlargement...but you don't do that when you are hungry. You can't be hungry when **you** are the bread! So just recognize that you are the bread, for the bread is He in you. So *that* hunger we don't have. Our hunger is the excitement of seeing more happening in this world, which will bring it into one with Christ!

The totality you see here in Elijah really is symbolic for we are all Elijahs put in different forms in different ways in different generations. We all are Elijah in the spirit! That's the basis to our union and God is wonderfully faithful in getting us there. He takes us into all the different Job-ways. We aren't told how He did that with Elijah, as that was probably in his early days, although we do see it in Elisha.

We want to have a liberated self because it's God expressed in human forms and the human form is in the foreground with God in the background. *God's* always our background, so we're really human selves. I can't be my human self unless I find the misuses of myself, taste them, get messed up by them and caught up by them. I have to see the potential of human self in its messed up way, and see it messed up because you can't have a positive without a negative. It's the same self with its same faculties, but it has a new drive. We are new beings with a new drive! Father, Son and Spirit are expressed by us, so we have to go through where the Spirit of God takes us. We travail in birth until Christ is formed in us. He's not an embryo, He is a formed Christ, a mature Christ in us! Then we move out to see how He becomes a formed Christ in other people by us as agents.

So what we see in Elijah is always God's purpose - a drive which is a heavenly drive, not a drive of strain. Yet there's a great intensity in his life as well as in ours. It's a serious life, yet paradoxically it's a fun life! I always say the fun side doesn't come out in the Bible too much because we are such self-people. We get on the fun side too much and forget the seriousness. I think the Bible doesn't give us too much of the fun, the joy side, because we would run with that and forget that behind the joy is an intense seriousness in which the joy becomes a part of the seriousness.

Elijah had to say to Ahab that the thing would be completed, as God said it would happen. There is a phase in which we are walking in a thing completed but it hasn't happened, and there is a certain tension on us in that condition. God had said, "I'll send rain upon the earth." Then to prepare the people for it and to make the way clear for them to turn officially to God, he, had the fire to burn up the falseness. Now he had the word and he saw it as abundance. That's a great word..."abundance of rain"! Paul uses "abounding," as in "all grace abounds." It's a great word when you're abounding abundantly in the rain, but God hadn't said that; God had just said "rain." Elijah said, "abundance of rain." This is the crisis moment, for he had said the thing and it must happen now!

He was up on the mountain with his servant and was in this posture with his head between his knees (quite a Yoga posture, I take it) and he sent his servant seven times to see if there was any sign of a cloud...until the cloud was there and they could see the rain coming like a little cloud out of the sea, like a man's hand. Now it was coming, and he told Ahab to get out quickly or it would catch him. Then the spirit came on Elijah and he ran all the way to Jezebel.

There is that setness of God given purpose that what God says *is going to happen*. It's a great word for anyone who is in what we often call the official service of Christ, but for anybody else also. I've never accepted it when people say that it's enough for us to be faithful, not successful. When the Spirit of God puts us into some form *in which* **He** *is going to come out* **by us**, we have to be successful! "Make good success," is what was said to Joshua. Jesus said, "Pray the Lord of the harvest," not the Lord of sowing. We missionaries tend to see the dark side and think we are sowing. But Jesus said the harvest is there, get the harvest; see the harvest. Don't take less for the harvest is there!

So *there* is a man who completed his intercession. He laid his own life on the altar. God came to him in those days in the fullness of revival expressed in his outer forms and he "gained his intercession" – as my friend Rees Howells used to say. No wonder he ran into Jezebel! The thrill was on him...for the thing was gained and completed what he had come to do. What happened was a demonstration that day that God was the Living God and He cares for His people. He has claimed His people and He cares for them. We see it today in terms of Jesus having already done it - *not* will do it. We enter into the **done** thing, and Elijah entered in on the faith level and then the manifested level.

In the life of Elijah we now have the sudden influx of what appears to be a soul weakness, but in reality it had behind it a spirit purpose. There are no gaps in Gods dealing with us...for God uses what may appear to be a soul deviation for some *further* form of His purpose. We don't see evil, we *only see God's operation in us*!

It comes out very famously in Jacob's life. Out of all that Jacob went through came the twelve tribes which was the first stage in the formation of the nation through which God revealed Himself through Jesus Christ. *Even* those things which we don't like in the life of Jacob, the deviations, are God's ways! And so we get Elijah, whom James said was a man of like passions as we are, saying, "I'm no different from my fathers." It's always good to know that God is using *my humanity*!

One of the great lessons we learn in our union life search is that **God means everything**! It keeps me from being judgmental of people. I can say, "Well, God *means* that. That's God's purpose"...whether it is a negative purpose or a positive purpose. It is a wonderful thing when we begin to say, "God **meant** that." It may be that if he is an unsaved person, God meant it so that the arrows of conviction of sin and corruption would sink more deeply in. For instance, something might cause a man to become frightened, yet we can see that it was exactly what that man needed, and that God has some higher and greater purposes through that experience.

After his experience on the mountain, Elijah is grabbed by fear, for Jezebel said to him, "May the gods do to me and more also if I do not make your life as one of these slain people by tomorrow about this time." When Elijah heard her threats on his life, he had the very same fear Obadiah had and ran for his life. But there is a difference between the two and it is the difference between one who knows union with God and one who is still in the Romans 7 situation. That man doesn't know how to get out of his problems because it appears that he is a separate person, and is in the illusion of fighting his own battles and doesn't have what it takes to fight them. Supposedly, God will help him and God doesn't *because God can't help self to be a false thing.*

So Obadiah didn't know how to get out of his situation, but Elijah did! He went for his life out into the desert where he was used to contacting his God. He went into the depths of despair, as we all do, and wished he was dead. "Oh Lord, take my life." That's all right because that wasn't really Elijah because Elijah was moving into God all the time...moving into God!

He went to Horeb, the place where God gave Moses the Law and revealed to Paul the reality of the **union** life. God met Elijah here and he got a glimpse of the truth in his inner consciousness – that the inner God is a still One – that His voice is a different type of voice, not an outer, external thing at all. You have to be still to know God.

As he stood by the cave he watched the strong wind rend the mountains, and the earthquake, and the fire. But God wasn't in those things, even though he had just recently seen the fire of God. The only fire of God is to burn Himself up for us! He doesn't burn people up; it's sin that burns us up. That's the fires of hell, which is self-centeredness. The *only* fire we ever have is our own fire.

And God said, "I'm not in the fire; I'm in the still small voice." That's a strange remark, isn't it! It's a contradiction in terms. A voice is a noise. The nearest we can get in human terms to the knowing of God is that it is beyond outer knowing. There is something beyond words, which is the basis of life. It's just an inner something, an inner being. Its rest. In the Oxford Group, we used to think of it as a hunch. It just seems to you to be the next thing you do and that's it...a knowing that **this** is the word!

God then took Elijah into a very great privilege, into the inner sanctuary, which Elijah always knew really, but was now being brought into focus for him. *God* told him, "Now your intercession is completed. You've done something which is a mark in history. Your day is passing and I'm going to take you along to give you a successor."

His apparent deviation when he went through a certain period in his murmuring was a beautiful touch...for only had he been in this condition of disturbance where he said "Only I remain"...could the quiet word of God come to him that there were seven thousand left in Israel that had not bowed unto Baal. That has often been a great comfort to people!

We move from there into the life of Elisha.

ELISHA

We're ready now to look at Elijah's successor, Elisha, who was outstanding in different ways from the man he learned from and followed. In some ways, he manifested *facets* of faith which were different from Elijah. It sometimes seems that there are pioneers who pay quite a price for some *new grade of faith* to be established. Others can pick up, practice, and produce what they pioneered more easily than the pioneers themselves. This is so with Elijah and Elisha. It was so in some aspects with Joshua and Moses. I learned faith from a man who paid a great price in establishing the principles of faith and intercession. He often carried a great burden over it, but he established those principles in such a way that others could follow him. I was one of them...and having learned some of the basic principles from him, I applied them in a much easier way than he did and have seen much happen, too, as if I'm building on the foundation he laid. I refer to my friend Rees Howells, and how I took the principles of faith I learned with him to my own missionary calling – the calling of the Worldwide Evangelization Crusade

When *God* is doing something with a man of the Spirit, you don't need to push about. You just move quietly along and just do that much. So Elijah's touch on Elisha is very quiet. There was no pressure, only an indication here or there, because Elisha learned he must be – a God-commissioned man, a God-anointed man – not merely an imitator or follower of Elijah. So Elijah didn't set out to train a successor.

He just picked up a follower and took him along and God did the training. This is the way Paul picked up Timothy.

It started when God met Elijah in the cave in Horeb and gave him a commission to anoint Elisha to be a prophet in his stead. Obviously, there was some *connection* between them, though we're told nothing about that. But officially, the connection between them began with Elijah visiting Elisha...who apparently was a very prosperous farmer because he was plowing with twelve yoke of oxen, a very considerable operation...and Elijah threw his mantle on Elisha without saying a thing. Obviously, that was an indication to Elisha of a 'call.' This is proof that they must have known each other and that Elisha, was reaching in this direction because Elijah wouldn't have done that unless he'd *known* to whom he was dropping this hint...and also the alacrity with which Elisha responded. Even then, Elijah wouldn't touch it.

This was a *thrilling* moment to this young man who must have had an enormous respect and marvel for this man to whom God had come so mightily! All he asked was that he might go back and see his parents and say farewell, and then he would come along. It is very obvious it was a very simple and perhaps rough life Elisha lived. When Elisha told Elijah that he wanted to go back and say farewell to his parents, Elijah kept wide open, "Oh, do what you like." There were those Jesus referred to in His day who wanted to say farewell to their parents and bury their father, but He knew in that case that it was an *excuse*, and that they really *didn't* want to be involved in following this One Who had nowhere to lay His head. This wasn't so with Elisha. He didn't go back in order to escape; he wanted to go back in order that they could *celebrate* the privilege that he was going to have...although it meant sacrificing his farming activities and his security. So he celebrated by killing one of the oxen and having a feast with his people. Then he started his new life.

We are told no more of Elisha for a few years, except that on one occasion it is mentioned that he poured water on the hands of Elijah.

Apparently he acted as Elijah's servant for about eight years. We don't know what kind of training was going on, but it was apparently part of the result of the time Elijah had with God. At the time, it *appeared* that he was running away from his previous calling under the threat of Jezebel, when it really was *God turning him* in a new direction.

The *new* direction was the training of successors, and that's a very interesting change of direction for missionaries to see...because instead of himself being the agent through whom truth would come, he would be training others who would be God's voice and manifest God's power among the people. So these schools of prophets were started up all around the nation (in place of these false priests who had been destroyed) who would be the true people of God waiting to instruct the people. This is what we missionaries did who were bringing folks to Christ, and then began helping them to become witnesses and missionaries to their own people.

It is *here* that we are given a plain insight, one of the many in scriptures, of how the Holy Spirit has to prepare us to *consciously* be God's equipped person. We see Elisha through these intervening years coming evermore clearly to the recognitions that there is a *quality* of the power and manifestation of God in Elijah, which he hadn't got himself.

Now after eight years, instead of being a thrilled young man rushing out to join his older 'brother' in God's commission, he found himself so *inadequately* equipped for the position that he was going to hold that *unless* something happened to him, he couldn't undertake it. God used two methods of *forcing* him to come face to face with his recognition. One was that Elijah told the school of prophets that God was to take him. When the time came that God was going to take Elijah up to heaven by a whirlwind, Elijah had told these prophets this and they kept saying to Elisha, "Don't you know the Lord is going to take away your master from you?" God used this to force Elisha into a corner! These prophets knew that the man from whom they had drawn their teaching and inspiration, and preparation was going to be taken from them and they knew that Elisha was to be the successor. Presumably, they knew there would be nothing outstanding about the life of Elisha, which would seem to fit him to be a second Elijah.

Here again, in history, we are given a picture of how *God* presses a man into a situation in which he hasn't got what it takes...alien! We're people of the Spirit. There is in us an *inner constraint* or *intensity* to do what we're called to do, and *have* what it takes to do it. Isn't it so in every life where God has brought us through by whatever means into the inner understanding of this "exchanged life," as Hudson Taylor called it, *when we* ***know*** *it's not we but He?* But there's always a *background of disturbance*, not only of what we haven't got, but what we must have!

The writer of Hebrews was speaking of this when he said, "Labor earnestly to enter into this rest." Isn't that interesting...*labor to enter rest!* It means to enter into a *fixed* grade of *faith* where we become at one with something. There is an application to our appropriation, and continuance in the appropriation, until we have consciously arrived at where we are seeking to arrive...because faith is the evidence of things not seen. It's not just, "I've got it." Here is the evidence that the thing is mine. It is a *substance*. Faith is more than saying, "I believe something." Faith is the faith *of God*, which says, "Here it is!" John's statement on faith is, "He that believeth on God hath the witness in himself," – the evidence! So it isn't merely in saying, "I'm believing." It's saying, "Yes, that's it!" As we move into *that* grade and become *settled* we have this acceptability to operate on that level of faith, which **is** the substance... we can do it more spontaneously.

In Elijah's case he brought fire! Sometime after the incident on Mt. Carmel, he was able to bring fire twice over on those who were in disfavor with God. He knew how to bring the manifestation of God, which was in that day to kindle Him. So there is this quality of intensity in Elisha. He wasn't stopping until he **had** what he recognized he needed to have.

He had been going through a period of apparent conviction that he hadn't got what he needed to have...the emptiness of the self...the helplessness of the self. Then he went on to this stage where the only person who *has* God is Elijah. He didn't have a written Bible or any other means…so the only container of the thing which he must have was the man whom he was to succeed. He had come into this same settled inner condition that **he** *must have* that thing in Elijah, which was the Spirit of God! As usual, our critics or our challengers are our spurs, and so these different schools of prophets spurred Elisha on by saying, "You know, God's going to take Elijah from you today."

His answer showed he was *settled*. He said, "Yes, I know it. Hold your peace. Keep quiet." That's good!

Elijah, meanwhile, didn't touch Elisha. He wanted to be sure that he did nothing to try to persuade Elisha to follow him, that he in no way interfered with the working of the Holy Spirit in pressuring Elisha. It all must come from Elisha. So Elijah said, "You stay here." But Elisha replied, "Oh, no. I've made up my mind." If he was to be a second Elijah, he must have what Elijah had. He must be **incarnated** by God. Then he moves to Jericho and again, the prophets put pressure on him, and again he says, "Be still. I'm handling that."

Finally, Elijah exercised the principal of faith by striking the waters of the Jordan with his mantle and they divided, allowing them to cross. By this time, Elijah finally felt he could say to Elisha, "What shall I do for you before I am taken away?" Now he had sufficient evidence that Elisha was set on this same pathway.

Even so, he didn't say what. The need, the supply…whatever Elisha felt he must have must come from Elijah. Elijah did not interfere with the Holy Spirit. Elisha said, "I want a double portion of your spirit." That's a strong statement to make!

Elijah's answer was again thrown back on Elisha. He called it a hard thing he asked, but he said, "If you see me when I'm taken from you, you will have what you ask. If you don't, it will not be so." It would not be a matter of him, but of God!

It happened very naturally. There was no great prayer meeting or anything because this isn't the life of great prayer meetings. *This is the life of the next thing.* They went out and talked and as they talked, something happened. Now **that** is the inner seeing! Evidently, the school of prophets didn't see it any more than the men with Paul saw it on the way to Damascus. They heard the voice, but they saw nothing. I'm quite certain that anyone with Moses wouldn't have seen *that bush*, because normal bushes don't operate like that one – burning without going out! There is ***another seeing*** when the Eternal One is manifested in His eternal reality and we *know* that *only* the eternal can see the Eternal One.

It says he was taken up in a whirlwind. We don't know what it meant or what exactly happened, but as he went up Elisha saw something which wasn't Elijah at all. Quite apart from Elijah, he saw a chariot of fire and horses of fire, the Lord of Hosts…who has millions of angelic beings. And he rent his clothes and cried out, "My father, my father. The Chariots of Israel, the horses, I've seen! I've seen the *inner reality*! I've seen the eternal sources, the inner Person; I've seen!" That's it! Like Moses at the burning bush, there's a very clear presentation of the establishment of the inner seeing. *This* is this inner union. Union is **knowing**. It isn't anything outer at all. My inner self is my knowing. My inner self is consciousness. I live by my consciousness. "What man knows the things of a man except the spirit of man within him," is how Paul put it. The spirit is the 'knower.'

What Elisha got from Elijah was interesting and curious. It was a double portion of the ability to bring things to pass quickly. Like Joshua, and like Jesus, Elisha moved into such a faith relationship – a *seeing* relationship that any moment he could say, "It's there!" He didn't pray, didn't have agonies, he didn't have to commune for the guidance. **He operated**. In some ways this is *a perfectly natural life*. This is how Jesus operated. If He needed food, He thanked the Father, split the people up, and the five loaves became five thousand! "If you need fish, put your net in on that side of the beat and you will catch fishes." "I will; be thou healed."

Elisha is, most like Jesus in that respect, though admittedly it was in *local* matters. There does seem to be a difference because Elijah dealt with great *national* matters and Jesus of Gethsemane was dealing with *world* history. That was an agony. But at least in the normal ways of life, he was able in the *simplest way* to speak a word of faith and say, "It's there; it's there."

Elisha's first step after Elijah was taken up was to go to the God of Elijah. Now sometimes people criticize because they say you're following a man. But you've got to *start* by following man; that's all you know. Elisha followed Elijah. So he went back to the water...this is his first test. "Where is this God of Elijah?" And he smote the water with the mantle, presumably Elijah's, and it opened! That was the first step in which he was saying, "I'm going to prove that this God of Elijah is **my** God."

It is quite fair for Paul to say, "Follow me as I follow Christ, and learn my ways as being Christ's." That's how we learn! We needn't be silly and fussed because somebody says, "Oh, you follow that man or that person." That's all right...as long as what you are really following is the *God* of that person. And gradually you drop off the person and just bring out what has now become real to you...for it has now become **yours**!

On the whole, I have that principle for myself when I write. I very rarely say I'm quoting anybody because what I've got has become **mine**. They got it somewhere and I got it from them. If it is a direct quotation I would say it, of course. But all we've really got is what we've got from the Scriptures.

I'm not going into the life of Elisha much more closely except to discuss a couple of instances because what we have is a whole list of the same kind of things happening in the simplest way. What we can learn from them is that there is no reason why we shouldn't say that thing's there...*you need it, you see it, it's coming, it's here*. Use faith for other people and for ourselves. It is a continuous series of incidents where I think the main point is to have this ability at once to affirm, express the resources of God for situations and to say they are there...

to see them there and they will turn up. I think that that is something we learn from our practice.

One of the two instances I'll spend a minute on was the Dothan incident which is the plain proof of that Elisha saw when Elijah went up in the whirlwind. That was the time when he, again by some inner sight, saw the Syrian king plotting against Israel and he was able to tell the king of Israel where they were making the next ambush so the king could avoid the ambush. When the king of Syria inquired as to who was giving him away he was told it was this prophet of Israel named Elisha. So the king of Syria sent a whole army in the night to capture Elisha. The next morning when the servant of Elisha had risen early, he saw this army encompassing the city in order to capture Elisha, and the servant said to Elisha, "Alas, master, what shall we do?"

Here again is one of those quick incidents because Elisha seemed to be able to work like that, and he gave a very illuminating answer. He said, "Fear not, for greater are those that are with us than with them." And then he prayed, Lord open the young man's eyes that he may see. Then the servant saw the mountains were full of horses and chariots of fire around Elisha. It was the very thing Elisha had seen when he saw Elijah taken up. Here is a man living in the sense of the *total forces of God* in the situation. Therefore, on that basis there was no need for them to fear those who were come to seize him. *That is very strong evidence to us of how we can trust God in ways when we talk about danger. Don't see the danger. Don't walk about seeing danger.* Missionaries need to learn that.

When there had trouble on the Congo field when the changeover came from the Belgium government to the native government our missionaries were divided in half. Half left and half stayed...exactly. Those who left felt they must protect their children. Some could see – God's my suffering! Of course they have been going on wonderfully ever since. God was wholly with those who remained, so that the work doubled and tripled since then. The others went home. So these tests will catch us out. Why do people so often talk about being afraid of the danger? *If the divine hosts of God are strong in me, where's the danger?* Isn't it again our tendency to move back into soul fear instead of the Spirit recognition? So that's a very good evidence of what Elisha saw when he began his ministry.

The other incident I want to discuss is the well-known story of Naaman, the Syrian army captain held in very esteem by his king, and who had contracted leprosy. There are several important points in this story. One is the simplicity of the little slave girl, captured by the Syrians from the Israelites, who told Naaman's wife, "There is a prophet in Israel who can heal him." The child had responded to the reality of God working through Elisha.

When this was told to the King of Syria, he did just as the world does by trying to pile it up on the human resource level, and sent a big gift to the King of Israel that he should heal his esteemed captain, Naaman. The King of Israel reacted by tearing his clothes in dismay, thinking it was a trick since he knew he couldn't heal a man of leprosy or anything else. Elisha heard about it and sent word to the king of Israel, "Send him to me."

So Naaman came down to visit Elisha. When he came, there was a spirit of detachment in Elisha for there must be nothing which would magnify the flesh and nothing which would give Naaman the idea that he was an important prophet doing some important thing - saying important words which would stimulate Naaman's sense of importance – because God won't touch that self-importance. Elisha really put him to the test. He wouldn't see him at all but sent him a message, saying, "Go and wash seven times in the Jordan River."

Now a nationalistic question arose. After all, what's the Jordan compared with his own Syrian rivers? So this had the preliminary effect of testing out the reality and Naaman said, "I don't want to do that. I thought at least he would come and strike the place with his hand and I would be healed. Here this man tells me to go wash in his muddy, old river."

Well, that's a reaction, but this wasn't the real man and so the servants came to have a talk with him, and said, "If the prophet had said to you to do some great thing, you would have done it, but how much more when he just says, "Go wash and be clean." And then Naaman saw it! He wasn't really after his own dignity; he was after his own healing. That's the point!

"Well, if I'm to be healed, I'll be healed that way," and then he was healed! This time, he returned to Elisha and Elisha came out to meet him, because now the question of self had gone out of it. He tried to persuade Elisha to take a gift, but Elisha knew better. He wouldn't touch a gift.

Then Naaman made a remarkable request because the healing had moved from the man's body to his heart and had settled in him. He said, "Your God is **the** God. Henceforth I don't wish to offer burnt offerings or sacrifices to any other god but to the Lord. I know now that there is no God in the world but in Israel." He had gotten it clear. So he asked for the privilege of taking two mules' burden of earth to build in a symbolic way, an altar where he could come out to Israel to worship. Right in the heathen nation, he would worship the Living God!

ESTHER AND MORDECAI

We have been looking, in these sessions, to see how God manifests Himself in His *human* agencies…which are *God in human form*. In Old Testament days, when the time had *not yet come* for His *final revelation* of who He truly is – **love and nothing else** – He manifested Himself in holiness together with His presence in prosperity and mercy by which those who obeyed and trusted Him in a personal or national way could see the kind of Living God that He is. These men and women of the Old Testament were great because, in different ways, they were *manifestors of the Living God* in His greatness.

We now center our attention on one man, less known by name – Mordecai, the foster father of Esther. The book is given the title of *Esther*. It should have been given the title of Mordecai. Esther was wonderful, but God through Mordecai was more wonderful! However, that is only a detail.

The Jewish nation was going through one of their periods of seemingly external desertion by God. Actually it was the other way around, because they had turned their backs on Him and sought earthly alliances, even to the point of having other gods. God's power is always in operation, but if we are utilizing another power we are linking our faith and cooperation to some apparently strong, but really weak, *human* resources. Then God *leaves* us in the power of those human resources until, once again, He comes through in deliverance…when those concerned relate themselves back to Him in His love and power, which in those days were particularly centered on His own people.

God's people *today* are universal people – the whole world is His people today, and all are *conscious* sons who have consciously received Jesus. In those days He had a special nation to whom He gave His first primary revelations of law and grace, a preparation by means of which a *nation of the flesh* was to be replaced by the *nation of the Spirit*. God's holy nation today is people **with Himself within them**, the human spirit indwelt by the divine Spirit, as human manifestations of Him. That's the holy nation!

It was not so in these days, and the nation of Israel was preserved from His enemies – because it was in the temporary phase of a special *flesh revelation* to prepare the world for the *universal revelation*. Today we have no enemies, for we now know everyone to be a *form* of God; we are all gods! That is why our human longing is for completion. We *want* to be completed, fulfilled, perfected, effective. We are human expressions of the divine Person! We may be distorted, prodigal sons, but we tend to major on the prodigal instead of the *son*. We have no enemies…when we see through everyone to the real person who is a son seeking to find the answer, and thinking he will find it in self-distortion. Christ, representing the human race, took the whole *distortion* into death – that *spirit of error* which had captured humanity. Christ died *for* sin and *to* sin and we die to sins *and* to sin…in Him. We participate in what He did for us and what He is now in us, because faith always participates in that to which it attaches itself. We participate in that to which we are inwardly attached because inwardly we are universals…bound in our inner selves to Him in our fourth dimensional risen relationship. We are the human negatives expressing the Positive to whom we have become re-attached. It is the same as the branch expressing the vine; the same as the body expressing its head. We become God-expressers…and because God **is** love, we become Love-expressers.

But Israel did not know these things in these days. When they needed power they did not have it because they were inwardly attached to self-interest, self-resources, and self-sufficiencies. It is easy to relate ourselves to some ally which is visible; not realizing it is just some empty thing which will be like a spear through your hand if you lean on it. When Israel's leaders turned away to these allies, they found it was like a spear through their hand. What they relied on turned around and seized them. The Israelites who began to rely on the allies around them soon found that they became the captives of Nebuchadnezzar and then were an exiled nation. There were always some, who knew the Living God, and light shined here and there among them, but they were exiles. They were the possessions of Persia, a great world kingdom. They were exiles as a nation under this outer power until there could be a means by which God's power could be manifested in delivering them.

The king of this great nation was Ahasuerus, whose other name was Xerxes. The kingdom stretched all the way from India, through Babylon, over to Ethiopia and included the Promised Land. Though the Jews were exiles, they were not bondsmen in the same sense as the Egyptians had made them. Still, they had all the homesickness that an exile will have, especially when your home is the Promised Land and should be preserved as a free nation, delivered from her enemies as God had promised. This homesickness is expressed in Psalm 137:

"By the rivers of Babylon, there we sat down, yea, we wept, when we remembered Zion. We hanged our harps upon the willows in the midst thereof. For there they that carried us away captive required of us a song... How shall we sing the Lord's song in a strange land?"

This great kingdom, and its king, was tremendously luxurious and full of self-display in ways we do not admire today. Once the king put on a magnificent feast which lasted 180 days. He had 127 provinces and he called these leaders together to this great feast. On the last two or three days of the feast he put on a special citywide feast in the palace grounds with all kinds of hangings of fine linen, purple and green, hung on silver rings on marble pillars. This was the feast to his own people, in the capital Shushan, which is like Washington. It was attended by many of the people who had some official attachment to this city which was the center of his empire.

One night, having had too much wine, he decided to show off his beautiful queen, Vashti, so he summoned her to come before the group. Not wishing to be a sex symbol in front of half-drunken men, she refused to come. That was a little too much for the chauvinistic males of those days and it made the king angry. He was quite an autocrat. He talked it over with his little group of inner counselors and they advised him that he had better put her out, because all of the women in the kingdom would become contemptuous of their husbands if he did not. He did so and he had to select another queen.

The method of selection was to collect the most beautiful girls to be found in the whole empire, gather them together and give them a year's training. Then each was to appear before the king for one night and from that, he picked the one he wanted. The rest would remain starved concubines. What a life they lived! Christianity has certainly brought some improvements, hasn't it!

Among these peoples there was a Jew named Mordecai, a godly man of the royal line of the Jews (though it was the rejected line of King Saul...as he was a descendant of Kish, the father of Saul), who himself was an important man in the days when Saul was anointed the first king of Israel. He and his wife had adopted as their own child a daughter of his uncle whose name was Esther. Evidently it was a very happy, loving family because they created in her an *intense* loyalty and an attachment far deeper than an outer attachment. It is quite obvious that she knew and loved the God that they knew. Though she was a simple girl, her life was the God-centered life which she had picked up from the parents.

Mordecai had an official position in Shushan in the palace at the gate where the officials met. There was a large population in the palace and surroundings. They lived quietly there.

Esther was selected to be one of those prepared for the king because of her great beauty. That was the way it was done in those days so she went without giving any opposition. She had learned the beauty of just being herself, a very simple girl. It is good when we learn that our beauty is *ourselves* and not something we put on and take off at night. (I have a beautiful wife. She was beautiful when I married her at 24. She is 80 now and is still beautiful!) There is beauty in a simple face, a simple light which comes through the face. This girl was like that so she *immediately* impressed the chamberlain who had the responsibility of training these women to be sensually beautiful. When the time came for her to go in to the king, she did not put a thing on other than what the chamberlain, a eunuch, gave her to wear. He knew what would look best on her because of his wide experience in these things and so in her simplicity, she just accepted what he gave her.

Meanwhile, every day through that year, Mordecai called to see about her. Esther's heart would go back in the same feeling toward him, for it says, "Esther did the commandment of Mordecai, like as when she was brought up with him."

The time came for her to go to the king. Although he had some foolish ways, he was also a very wise man. He knew right from wrong and probably knew a thing or two about women. And he saw that this beautiful girl was the one suited to be the queen, and so he appointed her queen. He gave a great feast and publically presented her to the people.

Mordecai, being a man *in tune* with God, doubtlessly often wondered what Israel was doing as exiles? Were they not God's people? Was not *God* the God of power, blessing, and fruitfulness? Had He not *said* that He wanted to manifest His power to the world by His presence in the temple? And here was Israel destroyed, the temple stolen, and the golden goblets made a mockery for idol feasts! There was no witness to God left in the world sense...and yet *all* of history had shown that God *did* come through when there were those, even one man, who dared to believe Him! One man to say, "God, You've got the power." Moses did it. Joshua did it. David put the enemies out and started the temple. Where these men showed that *they were in union with God* in His world and purposes, they could, by faith, affirm the resources of God and God would come through for them. It is remarkable as we follow the wars of Israel how *little* they fought when they trusted in God! Gideon put just a few torches in pots, blew a trumpet, and the enemy fled!

Also, Mordecai was very sensitive about the fact that *his* ancestor, who should have been leading the nation through into prosperity, had to be rejected because he disobeyed God. God had told Saul that the Amalekites must be destroyed and their spoil untouched...because they were the first tribe to attack Israel in their weakness when they first came out of Egypt as a slave nation. They were out to *destroy* Israel, and God said Israel was not to be destroyed. Saul became overwhelmed with his own ego and decided to keep the Amalekite king, Agag, and show him off a bit. He also kept some of the wealthy Amalekites's sheep and cattle, ostensibly for sacrifice. So in a *very humiliating* scene where Samuel himself hewed Agag to pieces, Saul was told that God could *not* have a king who was out of tune with Him. He was replaced by David.

It was also a sore spot that Mordecai's trouble came *because* Saul had kept the Amalekites alive. There was a highly efficient, apparently very brilliant man whom King Ahasuerus had selected to be his prime minister, who was a descendant of Agag. The man's name was Haman. The question that Mordecai faced was: Do I judge life by the *flesh*, or by the *Spirit*? Do I judge life by the things around and follow what would be the nice, healthy, and easy way? *Or* am I a person who goes the way *God* shows me to be the right way?

Mordecai knew that it was God's purpose to destroy this relative of Agag, the Amalekites. If Mordecai represented Saul...if Mordecai was God's man...and he had faith that God could rescue His people... and that *God* was in His people...then it was still God's will that the Amalekite should be destroyed.

This was the situation because Haman was next to the king. The custom was that everyone rose to their feet when he came in on his horse. When all the people rose to give him respect, Mordecai sat still. *That* was risking his life. Faith is – Where is *your* life? Are you involved…no matter what it costs…in doing what God wants you to do? Or are you going to pay with your life to try to *preserve* it? So this was the place where Mordecai risked his life…just by sitting down!

You will find all the way through that Mordecai did practically nothing. He just sat and said things that *caused* the risk. Mordecai's refusal to bow to Haman created a sensation. All the servants were reverencing this great man, Haman, and were afraid of him because they would kill a person in a moment in those days. When they asked Mordecai about it, he told them that he was a Jew. That is interesting because he had told Esther not to say that she was a Jewess and she had obeyed him. *There is a right time for everything* and now was the time to say he was a Jew.

Now he had tied himself up in knots. Of course, they told Haman. "Did you know there is a Jew here? He won't stand because you are an Amalekite." Haman had the strength of the flesh – it looked strong. *Flesh* does some foolish things out of egoism. Egoism will take you anywhere. Haman, in his very inflated state said, "This is my chance to have all the Jews killed. I won't just be concerned with a little flea like Mordecai. I'll turn this into a slaughter of the whole Jewish race. (That is what the Amalekites originally intended.) Because I'm next to the throne, the king will let me do it."

He did *not* go straight to the king, however. To make sure of himself, he consulted Pur for a year. Pur was casting lots, consulting witchcraft. (They love to do that kind of thing in Africa, where I've lived.) Gradually he came to the conclusion through these spirits that the right thing to do was to try to have the Jews killed.

Then he went to the king and said, "It would be a good thing for the control of our provinces if we get rid of these Jews. They are under a different religion from ours and they don't obey your commands. They are disloyal. They are revolutionists. I can provide some money for the purpose."

Ahasuerus said, "Take the money and use it for that purpose."

So with a bribe and lies, he gained a favorable hearing. It was decided by the king and Haman to give a year to prepare for it. Now the information would go out that in a year's time all over his provinces that they had the right to kill Jews and steal their money.

This news, of course, came back to Mordecai. Mordecai, being human, was hit *hard.* Remember you *start out* as *human*; you don't start out always seeing God. It *tore* him to pieces! The false voice would come to him... *"You're* the one responsible for the destruction of the nation. Because of what *you* have done the whole nation is going to be blotted out!" No wonder he felt desperate!

He did what they did in those days and tore his clothes and put sackcloth and ashes on himself. He went about and cried aloud with a bitter cry. It is interesting that the *whole* city was perplexed. People do not really like cruelty and many of the people there knew another side of the Jews. They were disturbed because they had not gone along with the spirit with Haman, and here was Mordecai openly making this bitter cry.

All this time Mordecai had kept in communication with his precious Esther through the chamberlain. She had remained a simple woman...not becoming a great egoist just because she was queen. She was just in the position which had been given her. She was *greatly disturbed* when the report was brought to her of her beloved father weeping, tearing his clothes and wearing sackcloth and ashes. She had the normal loving daughter's reaction which said, "We can't have this, send him some clothes." And then she sought more information about his situation.

What was happening was that Mordecai was *not* living in his crying; he was *living in his faith!* The crying was just temporary. We *all* have those times. It spurs up faith! What he was really saying was, "Wait a minute, God. *You* said that the Amalekites are a nation to be *destroyed*...that they should not be on the face of the earth...that we're with *God's* people! And here the Amalekites are about to destroy us!

What is wrong?" Then his faith moved on to, "It must mean, God, that *You* have some means by which You are going to reverse that...some means by which they *will not* destroy the Jews...and some way or other that *they* will get destroyed or their representative Haman will." That's the *inner* faith! So Mordecai was not living in his *temporary* distress. He was living in faith!

How did it turn out? He *saw* the next step, which was something that had *never occurred* to him until *that* moment. Esther is queen! Isn't this the point? Hasn't God given my simple daughter, who loves God and wants to hear His voice, to be the *key* to the king? Can't *she* get that order reversed?

So he told the chamberlain what had happened and *all* that Haman had said. He gave him a copy of the writing that was to be sent around to all these provinces that the Jews were to be destroyed. And he said this to the chamberlain: "Declare this unto Esther, show it to her, and charge her that she should go into the king, to make supplication unto him, to make request for her people."

He either did not know or forgot one point upon which Esther's life hung. There was a custom in those days that *no one* could come into the king's presence while he was on the throne *unless* the king stretched his scepter out for them. If they appeared in the inner court in his presence and he did not stretch out his scepter, they were to be killed. Of course, Esther's humanity came out now, quite rightly. She said, "Wait a minute. Tell Mordecai, 'Don't you know that you can't walk into the king's presence and make a request unless the scepter is stretched out? As for the likelihood of his seeing me, he hasn't seen me in thirty days. It doesn't seem too likely that he would see me if I pushed myself on him.'" Common sense. Just as Mordecai had shown *his* humanity in his bitter cry, she showed *her* humanity in saying, "How can I go in?"

Then the *real* Mordecai comes out, *the real man of faith*. He sent word to her, "Esther, think not with thyself that thou shalt escape in the king's house more than all the Jews. For if thou altogether holdest they peace at this time, then shall there enlargement and deliverance arise to the Jews from another place; but thou and thy fathers house shall be destroyed." He could only speak that way *because he was free*! You only do it when *you* are free. If you are *free of* man, you speak *freely as* a man. You are not afraid of man because you are doing what God *said* for you to do. Sometimes He tells you to do some strangely strong things!

"Esther, if you fail, *God* will *surely provide* a deliverer." **That** is tremendous! There was not one in sight...nothing. "You are the one hope; you could possibly do it. If you don't, that's all right; I'm not depending on you. God's not depending on little Esther, not depending on little anybody. But He uses little bodies because they become big in *His power.* That's faith! He would not be shaken from the *certainty* that the preservation of the Jews and the destruction of his enemy, Haman, would take place.

Then he added this beautiful word, "Who knows whether thou art come to the kingdom for such a time as this?" He did not say that she was; he did not force it. That's when the *true* Esther came through, which was God *in* Esther. The *center* of Esther's life was God and His will. Her love was not on her royalty, on her queenship, but on God! How do we know this? Because she asked her people to fast with her for three days. She was *centering herself* on God...building up a readiness for the time when she went in to the king. I like it that she did not try to *get* the will of God this way. She *knew* the will of God. The fasting and praying would do something *for her,* not God. It would give *her* the encouragement she needed. Then she made her great statement: "Then I will go into the king, which is not according to the law; and if I perish, I perish."

It is a strange and interesting fact that this book *full of faith* does not *mention* the word God! It is the *only* book in the Bible that does not even mention the word God, yet it is a book full of faith! It is only a name. God is *beyond* a name. A name is a human tag to make a person a little more real to us. If you are in union with God you *know*

Him who is from the beginning. He is beyond a name. It is the Spirit coming through persons because God operates through persons; this time it was Esther.

Although Esther was very great, Mordecai was greater because he had *achieving* faith. Esther had *committed* faith. The difference is that Esther would commit herself even to death. Mordecai would say, "God *will* put it through." Achieving faith is a *done* thing – I say it **is** so and it will be so! *That* is the faith by which God comes through. It is the same as saying that when you 'take' a thing you participate in it, experience it. You take food; you experience it. Esther had not quite gotten that far but she was committed. "I'll do God's will and if I die, I die."

On the third day Esther put on her royal apparel. Here we get the beauty of *freedom* in guidance. When you are a self *you* push a thing through somehow. When it is God, you don't have to push because *God* is the pusher. You just do the next thing and *God* does it! This is the *beautiful freedom* in this life when you are in union. You are not trying to 'do something' for God. You've left *that* behind. If God's got you, you are **His** agent and *you* do the next thing…obey what *your* conscience tells you to do.

It is a very significant fact that when Esther went before the king, her *relaxed* situation is what attracted him. She did not come as a beautifully attired person. She put on her royal apparel, the right thing to wear before the king, but nothing unusual. I imagine that the beauty of her restfulness and a dedication not like the women he usually had around him, won his heart and so he held his scepter out to her. "What do you want Queen Esther, up to half of my kingdom."

What she said next was very interesting. If she had been anxious and disturbed, as if everything depended on what *she* said, she might have confronted him immediately with the situation…and at once he would have been on the defensive. When you know a person is after something you are against them. What she said was, "Come and have supper with me, will you? And bring Haman with you." This pleased the king. Then she said, "And I'll tell you then." It was a strange thing to say. It was risky, the king might not want to come, but she was at ease. She could not see clearly what to do at the moment, but she felt sure she did not yet have the word for her to make a full exposure… because that meant that the king would have to turn against Haman whom he thought everything of. If she had asked the king to turn against Haman then, she would have gotten a negative reaction. *She must wait for God's guidance.* So she asked him to have a meal with her and bring Haman.

They met that evening, and as *God* chose, all it did was inflate Haman. The king did not yet know that she was a Jewess, the people who were to be destroyed, and Haman did not either! So Haman joyfully went to the dinner with the queen, and bragged about it greatly to his friends and family when she invited him to come back the next night with the king. He was really inflated by this special honor she was giving him.

On the way from the first dinner he had seen Mordecai again and *again* Mordecai refused to stand up when he saw him! On the way home, filled with this self-inflation, he said, "I'll take care of this old man." He called the carpenters in and that very night had them build a gallows 75 feet high to hang Mordecai on. The subtlety of this was that the inflation of Haman prepared him to express himself boastfully. Now what does *God* do? God plays tricks! You can never tell when God puts His tricks in. This is *God's* timetable. They just 'happen' when you are walking with Him.

Something had happened that set the stage for the next twist of events. When Mordecai was first given the official position in the gate of Shushan, which meant that he was in the palace and in touch with government officials, he had overheard some men in the government plotting to murder the king. Mordecai was a loyal subject of the king. If you are true to God, you are true to right loyalties…so he was right to be loyal to his king. His *calling* in life was to be loyal! He was salaried and financed and appointed by the king. So he exposed the plotters by passing the word to Esther. Of course, the king had them hanged when he heard about it. The king had forgotten about it, but it had been written in the chronicles of the king.

Now a *strange* thing happened just after his first supper party when Haman was all full of himself and his own glory. The king could not sleep. In his sleeplessness, he liked to go over the history of his kingdom. In the course of going through the history that night, he was told about a strange man called Mordecai who had sent the information to him that these two chamberlains, about two years before, had meant to murder him and the information had saved his life. He realized that he had never rewarded Mordecai for this and because he was a good king, he *wanted* to do right by people. It was at that moment, I suppose about dawn, that Haman arrived. God does have his jokes! Full of this peacock inflation, he was coming to ask for the right to hang Mordecai. He let it be known that he was there, and, as he was the king's favorite, the king summoned him in.

Before Haman could state his business, the king said to him, "I want you to help me. There is a man here I want to give the highest respect to. I didn't know that he had done this for me. I want everybody to know that he had done this for me. I want everybody to know that I honor this man. How can I do it?"

This old turkey-cock Haman was so full of himself that he said, "I'll tell you what. Put the king's crown on his head, put the king's robes on him, give him the scepter, and put him on a horse and ride him through the city. Have somebody by his side calling out, 'This is how the king delights to honor a person.'" That is where I think the king began to see Haman's inflation. Maybe he said to himself, "Perhaps *he* wants to be king!"

Then God cracked his joke. The king said to Haman, "This man is Mordecai. I want *you* to walk him around and call out to the nation. *You* put that crown on him and *you* take the bridle of the horse and *you* shout...'This is the man the king honors.'" So Haman had to do that among the very people who were watching to see what happened to Mordecai. Think what that meant to *those* people! Mordecai, whom Haman would surely destroy, was on a king's horse with a king's crown and Haman is shouting his praises around. My! There are some electric shocks in God's life!

Can you imagine the deflated look on Haman's face when the king said that? Do you see the wisdom of God? Through the first supper He prepared, not the king, but Haman. He prepared Haman with inflation to deflate him like a great turkey-cock...and at the right moment to prick the bubble! You may be sure the wind came out in the king's sight and that king was pretty sharp. Do you *see* the preparation?

Now Esther knew that the moment had come. God had *caused* the king to discover Mordecai and the time had come to inform the king of Haman's scheme. At the second supper table she risked everything. She could *because* she was free. So when the king said, "What is it you want from me, my beloved Esther?" she said, "I want you to rescue me and my people from destruction." He did not understand because he did not know that Esther was a Jewess. "There is an edict gone out to destroy me and my people."

"You? Who dare say this?"

"That wicked Haman." She could not say that the evening before. The king now put two and two together...what had happened the night before and *this*. She told the story of how Haman had told lies about the Jews being traitorous and rebellious, and had gotten this edict out that the Jews were to be destroyed...and that *she* was a Jewess! He never knew that before and went out of the room in a rage, into the garden, not knowing what to do. What could he do? Could he turn *Haman* out? Could he do *that*? We have these little incidents. Haman became desperate. You see, self-inflated self *has nothing. Self in God has God and does not get inflated.* Self without God is deflated when the bubble is pricked. There is nothing left in Haman that says, "I'll stand for my convictions." He had no convictions except his lies! There is nothing in Satan; he is a bubble. So Haman has no conviction to stand for.

So what did Haman do? He threw himself on the couch of Esther to plead for mercy from her. The king came back at that moment and thought he was trying to seduce her. Isn't God clever? That finished Haman! The king threw a coat over him which meant that he was to be executed. He was hung on the same gallows which he had made for Mordecai!

The rest fits simply. Esther told the king what Mordecai was to her. When he heard that Esther had the respect for a man like this and that the *reason* that she was the kind of woman he really liked – a good, pure, decent woman – was because of the training she had through Mordecai, he was pleased. He knew that this was the kind of man he could be safe with. So he promoted Mordecai and the first thing he did was to give him the whole house of Haman.

Esther came to the king once more and *again* she was in this fatal position. But she was calm about it and the scepter was held out to her. That was when she made the plea for the reversal of the edict. But how could it be reversed? When a king makes an edict it is not easily changed...even by him. A way had to be found which could reverse the edict and save the Jews...if they wished to be saved. He did it by a political move. He sent a new edict around to all his people saying that the Jews were to defend themselves if attacked, and that the Jews could take the spoil if they liked.

Meanwhile, he appointed Mordecai to be Prime Minister, and it went all over the nation that this Jew had been promoted! It changed the whole attitude of the people toward the Jews. Many of them even received the Jewish faith and became Jews themselves! This added a great many conversions...as well as a revival to the people and control over them.

When the day came some attacks were made on the Jews and the Jews responded in self-defense, but they *never* touched the spoil. *That* is the difference! By the rights of those days they had a right to attack. But a right heart say, "We are not for money; we are here because *God* is our guard and protector". It says three times that they did not touch the spoil.

Mordecai became the great man of the land. His heart was with God so he did something similar to what Moses did when he instituted the Passover as a continued remembrance of that tremendous mercy in Egypt. He instituted the Feast of the Tabernacles. Purim was added to it, which, of course, was mockery. Pur was the witchcraft. They labeled the thing the feast of witchcraft, in other words, the defeat of witchcraft. It went down that this was the defeat of witchcraft! They always since have kept the Feast of the Tabernacles. And the Bible says that God blessed the people and Mordecai.

You see how in *any* set of circumstances in a *really ordinary person,* there is something there by which God will *manifest Himself* as the God of love and power...and *reveal Himself* in some way to people *through us.* In every life the very ordinary things become extraordinary...*not* by incidents, but because *underneath* we move in with God in God's purposes. God has a purpose for *every* life. God has a purpose for each of you! I begin with the negative first...and say, "Wait a minute! God has a *purpose* in this situation." Something of His purpose will be conveyed to you by little signs. You are going along with Him. Our prayer becomes, "Now, Lord, we are going to see *You* fulfill this thing that You have put in *our* hands. We are going to see God glorified out of weakness." So the flesh cannot go on and His strength is made perfect. That is why we are saying, these Old Testament lives are *full of vital meaning to our ordinary lives.* Because no life is ordinary! It is only ordinary in itself. It is extraordinary in this cooperation with God!

Afterword

I don't believe Norman could have ended these remarkable lives of faith in any better way than with the final paragraph of Esther's life stating that we are ordinary people becoming extraordinary in our cooperation with God in His purposes for each and every life. In these lives, as well as in ours, we have found a perfect God manifesting Himself in **His** perfect humans!

"In Him we live and move and have our being"
Acts 17:28

ABOUT THE AUTHOR

Norman Percy Grubb was born August 2, 1895 to an Anglican clergyman and his wife. He was in his teens when he came to know Jesus Christ as *his* personal Savior. After serving in World War I he went to Cambridge University and while there he joined a Bible study and prayer group called Cambridge InterCollegiate Christian Union (C.I.C.C.U.). Their passion was to present the gospel and atoning blood of Jesus Christ to their fellow students. With only one semester to go the Lord impressed upon Norman that he was to leave and join the mission work of C.T. Studd in the heart of Africa, the Belgian Congo. As he was sharing his call with his fellow CICCU-ites the Lord gave Norman the vision to begin groups like theirs in other universities and colleges. Thus was born Inter-Varsity Fellowship (I.V.F.), also known as Inter-Varsity Christian Fellowship (I.V.C.F), which today is worldwide.

Norman married Pauline Studd in 1919 and they immediately sailed for Africa to join her father, C.T. Studd, in his Heart of Africa Mission, which later became the Worldwide Evangelization Crusade (WEC). Norman and Pauline had four children Noel, Paul, Priscilla and Daniel. Their firstborn, Noel, died on his first birthday in the Congo. They returned to England to lead the mission in 1931 shortly before C.T.'s "Homegoing". Norman and Pauline remained at the

London headquarters until 1957 when he was called to head the work in the United States.

Norman's years with WEC took him all over the world where he had working relationships with countless Christian leaders, churches and organizations. A small sampling of them are – Billy Graham, T. Austin Sparks, Jesse Penn-Lewis, Rees Howells, Hannah Hunnard, Roy Hession, Corrie Ten Boom, Bill Wilson - founder of Alcoholics Anonymous, Bakht Singh of India, A.W. Tozer, Mrs. Charles (Lettie) Cowman, Irving Harris and Bruce Larson of Faith at Work and Abram Veriede founder of International Christian Leadership, hosts of the Presidential Prayer Breakfast. In addition to the books and booklets Norman wrote, he also wrote *numerous* forewords for other's books... many of which can be found on www.normangrubb.com...plus articles for publications such as *Christianity Today*, *Worldwide* and *Floodtide*.

Norman retired from W.E.C. in 1965 and spent the rest of his days – 25 years – traveling about the U.S. and England sharing his heart – the truths of Galatians 2:20. Norman was glorified on December 15, 1993. His last words with raised hands were, "Abba Father".

And from Norman's final letter shortly before his "Homecall"...

"*By faith* may you find the answers that the Lord has for you... may you always walk in faith until we meet in the glory of God."